The Apple Sliced

Big Apple . . . a nickname for New York City.

Big Apple replaced in the 1970s the earlier nickname for New York City, Fun City, much used during the 1960s. The term *Big Apple* was originally used by U.S. jazzmen in the 1930s to refer to any big city, especially a big northern city. Around 1937 the *Big Apple* became the name of the popular jazz dance. The derivation of the term is uncertain. The possible origin is suggested in *Dan Burley's Original Handbook of Harlem Jive* (1944), which defines *apple* as "the earth, the universe, this planet. Any place that's large."

Clarence L. Barnhart, Sol Steinmetz, & Robert K. Barnhart, *The Second Barnhart Dictionary of New English* (Bronxville, N.Y.: Barnhart/Harper & Row, 1980)

Boroughs of New York City
- **A** Manhattan
- **B** The Bronx
- **C** Queens
- **D** Brooklyn
- **E** Richmond

Adjacent Suburban Counties
- **W** Westchester County, New York State
- **X** Nassau County, New York State
- **Y** Bergen County, New Jersey
- **Z** Rockland County, New York State

New York Waters
- **1** Hudson River
- **2** East River
- **3** Upper New York Bay
- **4** Atlantic Ocean
- **5** Long Island Sound

Neighborhood Locations
- **1** Harlem
- **2** Yorkville
- **3** Times Square
- **4** Lower East Side
- **5** Greenwich Village
- **6** Battery Park City
- **7** Bay Ridge
- **8** Jacob Riis Park

Contributors

Sidney H. Aronson (Ph. D., Columbia University), Professor of Sociology, Brooklyn College and the Graduate Center, City University of New York

Adele Bahn (Ph. D., City University of New York), Associate Director, Community Colleges Project, City University Graduate Center; Adjunct in Sociology, Fashion Institute of Technology

Joseph Bensman (Ph.D., Columbia University), Distinguished Professor of Sociology, Late of The City College and the Graduate Center, City University of New York

Vernon Boggs (Ph. D., City University of New York), Assistant Professor of Sociology, York College and Senior Research Fellow, Graduate Center, City University of New York

Aubrey W. Bonnett (Ph.D., City University of New York), Dean, School of Social and Behavioral Sciences, California State University at San Bernardino

Peter Canavan (doctoral candidate, City University of New York), Instructor in Sociology, Adelphi University, Garden City, New York

Donald F. Delano (Ph. D., City University of New York), Police Officer, The Port Authority of New York and New Jersey Police Department

Judith DeSena (Ph.D., City University of New York), Assistant Professor, State University of New York at Farmingdale

William DiFazio (Ph.D., City University of New York), Associate Professor of Sociology, St. John's University, Jamaica, New York

Sylvia F. Fava (Ph. D., Northwestern University), Professor of Sociology, Brooklyn College and the Graduate Center, City University of New York

Fred H. Goldner (Ph. D., University of California, Berkeley), Professor of Sociology, Queens College and the Graduate Center, City University of New York

Gerald Handel (Ph. D., The University of Chicago), Professor of Sociology, The City College and the Graduate Center, City University of New York

Knight Hoover (Ph. D., City University of New York), Assistant Professor of Sociology, Augustana College, Sioux Falls, South Dakota

Angela Jaquez, doctoral student, City University of New York

Patricia Kendall (Ph. D., Columbia University), Professor of Sociology, Queens College and the Graduate Center, City University of New York

Illsoo Kim (Ph. D., City University of New York), Assistant Professor of Sociology, Drew University, Madison, New Jersey

William Kornblum (Ph. D., The University of Chicago), Professor of Sociology, Graduate Center, City University of New York

Hylan Lewis (Ph. D., The University of Chicago), Resident Professor of Sociology, Graduate Center, and Professor Emeritus, Brooklyn College, City University of New York

Eric Lichten (Ph. D., City University of New York), Assistant Professor of Sociology, C. W. Post College, Long Island University

Donal Malone, doctoral candidate, City University of New York

Rolf Meyersohn (Ph. D., Columbia University), Professor of Sociology, Lehman College and the Graduate Center, City University of New York

Maynard Robison (Ph. D., City University of New York), Director of Marketing Research, John Hancock Mutual Life Insurance Company, Boston

Charles Winick (Ph. D., New York University), Professor of Sociology, The City College and the Graduate Center, City University of New York

The Apple Sliced

Sociological Studies of New York City

Vernon Boggs/Gerald Handel/Sylvia F. Fava

and Contributors

WAVELAND
PRESS, INC.
Prospect Heights, Illinois

For information about this book, write or call:

Waveland Press, Inc.
P.O. Box 400
Prospect Heights, Illinois 60070
(312) 634-0081

Contents

Preface

The Apple Sliced presents nineteen sociological studies of New York City
—the "Big Apple"—by faculty members, graduates, and graduate students
of the Ph.D. Program in Sociology of the City University of New York. The
primary purpose of the book is to describe and illuminate some of the facets
of this complex and magnetic metropolis, known for its heterogeneity, per-
sistent vitality, expansive joys, and regions of despair. The volume presents
New York City, "warts and all." Fear, impersonality, gross inequality, bureaucracies reacting at a glacial pace, and the dark side of the bright lights
are all portrayed in these pages. Yet the volume is an affirmation of the city
in general and of New York City in particular. In several chapters, New
York is revealed as a place of opportunity—for ethnic groups, ambitious
youths struggling against heavy odds, and workers in special occupations,
to mention just a few. Suburbanites abandon the residential dreams of the
1950s and 1960s to become "real New Yorkers." Visitors come from all over
the world. Entrepreneurs find opportunities.

The book ranges widely. It touches on the life of New York's African,
Asian, Caribbean, and European immigrants. It looks at work respectable
and not so respectable. New Yorkers at play, New Yorkers striving and
achieving, New Yorkers embattled in economic and political struggles—
these diverse forms of commitment and association are discussed. But obviously no single volume can presume to be a complete portrayal of any
community, much less a metropolis such as New York. The studies presented
here are drawn from recently completed or still ongoing work by particular
faculty members and graduates. They do not arise from a comprehensive

program of research but from individual research agendas or, in some cases, from agendas of small research teams. Thus the studies do not represent any kind of collective judgment, decision, or agreed-on approach to studying New York, beyond the fact that they all use qualitative methods. Participant observation, qualitative interview methods, and qualitative analysis of documents are fundamental research methods in sociology, and one purpose of this book is to present a series of studies using these methods that will be useful to students in research methods courses, courses in urban sociology, community studies, and similar fields.

Each study is introduced by a methodological note from the author. These notes all say something about how the particular study was done. They are individual in style, reflecting the fact that all social science work, like scientific work generally, bears the unique imprint of its author, as well as being shaped by the standards and ideals of a research community. These notes, though necessarily brief, are seen as following in the tradition exemplified by William Foote Whyte's Methodological Appendix to *Streetcorner Society*[1] and the notable volume edited by Phillip E. Hammond, *Sociologists at Work: The Craft of Social Research.*[2]

The idea for the book arose in the course of a conversation between Boggs and Handel, and Fava was immediately invited to join them. The book is the product of the joint editing by all three of us. That initial conversation would not have taken place but for an administrative arrangement that brought Handel to the Graduate Center for an extra assignment and Boggs to City College to take over Handel's undergraduate Qualitative Methods course for one semester. For making that arrangement possible, our thanks go to Rolf Meyersohn, then the Acting Executive Officer of the Ph.D. Program in Sociology; Solomon Goldstein, Dean of Research at the Graduate Center; William McCord, Sociology Chairman at City College; and Arthur Tiedemann, then the Dean of Social Science at City College. The editors also wish to thank their undergraduate students at City College and at Brooklyn College for their enthusiasm and appreciation in learning the techniques of interviewing and participant observation. We hope that students throughout the country, and elsewhere, will find this book useful not only for learning about New York City but also for adapting these techniques to study their own communities.

VB, GH, SFF

NOTES

1. William Foote Whyte, *Streetcorner Society*, 3d ed. (Chicago: University of Chicago Press, 1981).
2. Phillip E. Hammond (ed.), *Sociologists at Work: The Craft of Social Research* (Garden City, N.Y.: Doubleday/Anchor, 1967).

• *Occupational Achievement and Career Cycles*
  Aronson: New York, 1880–1914: Autobiographical Accounts
  DiFazio: Hiring Hall Community on the Brooklyn Waterfront
  Kim: The Korean Fruit and Vegetable Business in New York
  Kendall: Medical Faculty Influence on Trainees
  Delano: The Bus Terminal: Cops, Mopes, and Skells on the Deuce
  Lichten: Fiscal Crisis, Power & Municipal Labor

• *Socialization, Selection, and Institutional Supports*
  Aronson: New York, 1880–1914: Autobiographical Accounts
  Handel: A Children's New York: Boys at Play in Yorkville
  Bahn and Jaquez: One Style of Dominican Bridal Shower
  Kornblum: Achieving against All Odds
  Kendall: Medical Faculty Influence on Trainees
  Fava and DeSena: The Chosen Apple: Young Suburban Migrants

• *Conflict and Power: Class, Ethnic, Racial*
  Aronson: New York, 1880–1914: Autobiographical Accounts
  DiFazio: Hiring Hall Community on the Brooklyn Waterfront
  Robison: Vacant Ninety Acres, Well Located, River View
  Lichten: Fiscal Crisis, Power & Municipal Labor
  Goldner: The Daily Apple: Medicine and Media

• *Communications Media and Urban Agendas*
  Hoover: Ethnic Press and the New York Norwegian Community
  Goldner: The Daily Apple: Medicine and Media in New York

• *Marginality and Social Networks*
  Canavan: The Gay Community at Jacob Riis Park

• *The Sex Market*
  Winick: Licit Sex Industries and Services
  Boggs and Jaquez: Popcorns, Talk-Tricks, and Half-Steppers

I said earlier that the three dominant and recurring themes in this volume are the movement of people, changing institutions and networks of support, and the struggle for control of institutions and places. In this context, there are three chapters, which, together, might serve well to keynote these urban sketches. Two of them have especially apt and intriguing titles: "The Chosen Apple: Young Suburban Migrants," by Fava and DeSena; and "The Daily Apple: Medicine and Media," by Goldner. The third is "New York, 1880–1914: Autobiographical Accounts," by Aronson. These three chapters deal with present and past movement to the city and issues of power and social control. In a gross sense they suggest much about the earlier stages and the end products of urban development and the relation of local national policy to life chances in the city.

We state two truisms when we say that New York City has been, and is, the "chosen apple" for practically all past and present residents and that nearly every group or category that ever resided here was perceived as a "new" immigrant or migrant at some time. In this context, Fava and DeSena identify another new internal migrant: a "type of urbanite now emerging as the dominant type in American society—those who are suburban-born and suburban-bred." Their research is based on interviews with young adults who have migrated from the suburbs to New York City—all upwardly mobile, upper middle class, and white. The major finding—"that suburban-reared migrants underwent 'urban conditioning' typically related to special college experience"—is a challenging idea, with many broader implications for studying urban movement and processes.

Aronson deftly and cautiously uses a sample of five autobiographies in an exploratory effort "to develop a plausible description of New York City at the turn of the century." He is able "to look at observations in situations in which the writers were at the same place at the same time, and to examine reactions to situations when the authors were in different places at the same time." The materials from the five autobiographies provide a wide-range view of an earlier city "as a museum of people" and of the full range of its institutions. Goldner's "The Daily Apple: Medicine and Media," is linked here with Fava and DeSena's research on today's young suburban migrants and Aronson's description of New York City before World War I, because it deals with power in the city and the role of the press in setting public agendas, in creating a sense of community, and as "a significant factor in managing a public bureaucracy." Goldner's treatment of the role of the press in the distribution and manipulation of power in the city includes a useful allusion to the relationship between image and policy. Goldner's chapter can be related in part to Knight Hoover's description of the role of the ethnic press in creating the Norwegian community, a discussion that also has some urban power connotations. However, Goldner's treatment of the press and urban decision making is tied most closely to Lichten's sophisticated treatment of "Fiscal Crisis, Power & Municipal Labor," and Robison's study of the struggle to control the development of Battery Park: "Vacant Ninety Acres, Well Located, River View." The crucial role of the press is emphasized in both these studies of the organization of power. Robison uses the metaphor of the mystery novel to elaborate the proposition that "In American society, issues of class and issues of race are almost always intermixed." And Lichten's study of urban powerlessness and betrayal, which indicts the municipal unions for cooperating with authority, concludes that "without control over the major disseminators of public information" the unions found themselves in a situation in which "collective bargaining masks the existence of class exploitation."

Occupational mobility and career lines for various groups at different stages of the city's and the country's history are dealt with directly in several chapters: Italian-Americans and others on the waterfront, by DiFazio; Koreans in the fruit and vegetable business, by Kim; West Indian immigrants employed in "peripheral," "irregular," underground economies, by Bonnett; demand and supply in the legal and marginally legal sex industry and services, by Winick; the world of prostitutes, pimps, hustlers, and "street people," by Boggs and Jaquez and also by Delano; the occupational culture and ecological setting of the Port Authority policemen, by Delano; and factors affecting career choices and training in the medical profession in the distinctive New York setting, by Kendall. Some of the chapters describing occupations and career choices show or suggest the manner in which various factors might encourage or hinder adaptation of persons from different communities or categories. Among the factors that might influence occupational mobility and adaptation are language facility, educational background, the transferability of skills, the structure of the local labor market, age, sex, and family characteristics. The operation of some of these factors is referred to in Kim's well-received, pioneering study of recent Korean immigrants:

> The usefulness of the greengrocery business as an economic entry point for Korean immigrants depends upon several factors. First, we must recall that Korean immigrants could transfer their old family structure to the new land because the United States Immigration Act of 1965 made it possible for them to form a three-generation extended family in America. Consequently, some immigrants with an abundance of family labor but little capital have found economic opportunities in the labor-intensive fruit and vegetable business during the initial stage of their economic adjustment. Korean immigrants possess a family-centered success ethic that causes each family member to be willing to devote himself to the family business. This, together with the intense economic motivation of Koreans, establishes a "natural" affinity toward the greengrocery business, which requires intensive labor and a willingness to exploit oneself to gain economic mobility. Korean entry into the greengrocery business has revived and sustained a classic American immigration pattern of ethnic succession in economic activity.

The changing roles of old institutions, in contributing to what Fava and DeSena call "urban conditioning" and the emergence of new institutions, are shown in Handel's portrait of childhood in an earlier Yorkville; Kornblum's exploration of a black youth's "bucking the odds" of making it; Meyersohn and Malone's discussion of the meanings and functions of second homes for city dwellers; and the sensitive depiction of the made-in-New York demystification *rite de passage* for some Dominican brides.

Canavan's description of the development of a sense of community and of "turf" among gay persons at Jacob Riis Park is about invisibility in the city—the manner in which social networks developed and transformed group lives that had heretofore been one of the many "invisible slices of the apple."

It has been said that one travels to correct the imagination. Handel's students' interviews with visitors to New York underscore the incomparable strength and attraction of both the experience and the image of the city, even for those who find it "all right to visit, but. . . !" This collection of qualitative sociological studies provides help in understanding the symbol and the reality of the Big Apple for peoples of the world, the nation, and the city who choose (or have the wish) to come to stay, to shuttle in and out, or to visit. And it gives useful clues as to why the mystique and the paradox remain, no matter how the apple is sliced.

HYLAN LEWIS

PART 1

COMMUNITIES
AND
LIFE-STYLES

New York is both a single place and an assemblage of many places. As a single place, it is one city, America's largest, located between the Atlantic Ocean and the Hudson River. From a beginning on the southern tip of Manhattan Island, it grew to encompass five boroughs—Manhattan, The Bronx, Brooklyn, Queens, Richmond. Of these, only The Bronx is on the American mainland. The rest of the city is on three major islands. Brooklyn and Queens occupy the western half of Long Island; Richmond occupies all of Staten Island. These scattered pieces of land have been a single municipality since 1898, its parts linked by bridges, tunnels, America's first subway system, and the celebrated Staten Island Ferry.

Clearly, even when considered as a single place, New York is complex. It surely qualifies as an example of what Robert Redfield called "a convincing, complex entity."[1] Necessarily, this complex entity will be perceived differently by different observers, even during a single historical period. Sidney Aronson samples the diversity of perspectives in one period by examining the autobiographies of five New Yorkers who, in various ways, were articulate about the city's complexity. Some of his autobiographers were situated so as to have a panoramic view of the city's low life. One captures the city's working-class character with its labor-management strife and its radical social movements. One is a Vanderbilt, a member of one of America's wealthy, upper-class families. And the last is a drama and music critic. The perspectives on New York of these diverse autobiographers are partially overlapping, partially conflicting, and partially mutually irrelevant. New York looks rather different from such diverse bases as the Lower East Side, Greenwich Village, swanky Fifth Avenue, and the Theater District.

If one turns attention from the city as a whole to its parts, then the distinctiveness of its many communities and life-styles becomes apparent. Communities are of various kinds but can be grouped into two main types: those based on a specific territory (spatial) and those not based on a specific territory (nonspatial).

A community is a self-conscious social unit and a focus of group identification. . . . Community also implies a certain identification of the inhabitants with the geographic area, and with each other, a feeling of sharing common interests and goals, a certain amount of mutual cooperation, and an awareness of the existence of the community in both the inhabitants and those in the surrounding area.[2]

The next three chapters deal with three different types of community. Handel's is about a spatial community in Manhattan, Yorkville, on the East River. However, both DiFazio's, which analyzes the bonds among a group of dockworkers, and Canavan's, which studies a group of gay men at a public beach, show how a particular territory enters into a community's life-style even when the territory is not the original basis for the social ties that define the community.

Yorkville gained notoriety during both World War I and World War II because of the great number of Germans living there. However, the area was also inhabited by substantial numbers of Irish, Czechs, Jews, and Hungarians. Handel's chapter is about children's use of the diverse spaces of their neighborhood, and it describes the social relationships among children and between children and adults that were constructed in daily life in this multi-ethnic community.

DiFazio's chapter deals with a group of Italian dockworkers on the Brooklyn waterfront, and particularly with their efforts to maintain a sense of community under the rather paradoxical stress of being guaranteed an annual income whether they worked or not.

From Manhattan and Brooklyn the volume moves next to the Borough of Queens and to a recreational segment of the New York waterfront. Canavan portrays the way in which the beach at Jacob Riis Park is informally segmented by ethnic and cultural groups so that each acquires a particular "turf." His chapter focuses particularly on a group of gay men and portrays their style of social interaction among themselves and the social relationships between them and other users of the beach. It documents the growing acceptance of homosexual men in cosmopolitan segments of American society.

Coincidentally, these three chapters are all about communities that, in one way or another, utilize the New York waterfront.

NOTES

1. Robert Redfield, *The Little Community: Viewpoints for the Study of a Human Whole* (Chicago: Univ. of Chicago Press, 1955), pp. 1–2.
2. George A. Theodorson and Achilles G. Theodorson, *A Modern Dictionary of Sociology* (New York: Crowell, 1969), p. 63.

1

New York 1880–1914: Autobiographical Accounts

SIDNEY H. ARONSON

METHODOLOGICAL NOTE • Historical sociology, an approach created by Max Weber, has not been popular with American sociologists. It can be defined briefly as the application of the sociological perspective to the documents and other artifacts that once living members of society leave behind. Its considerable advantage is that it can deal with sociological problems that cannot be reached by conventional research procedures.

The inattention to historical sociology can be explained partly by the fact that the once-fledgling field of sociology had to separate itself from history and one way to do so was to devise a special methodology. The result was the social survey, *the* hallmark of modern sociology. The survey in itself did not rule out history as a "site" or opportunity for sociological research. It was the insistence that the instruments of the social survey, questionnaires and interview schedules, had to be administered to living respondents that did that.

The methodological objective of this chapter is to show that history can be used by sociologists in such a way that is consistent with their traditional procedures. The specific method is a qualitative analysis of autobiographies of people who lived in New York City between 1880 and 1914. The sociological question is what, sociologically speaking, life was like in New York during that period. While the precise details of the method employed are presented below, it can be stated that the autobiography as a source of information about the city—or about many other things of sociological import—is a promising, though as yet still undervalued, source of observations, one that makes it possible to broaden the application of survey research.

The objective of this chapter is to describe what it was like to live in New York City between 1880 and 1914 by using autobiographies the same way social scientists treat the replies of respondents and informants, that is, as sources of reasonably accurate information about life in society. The assumption is that the observations of the writers of autobiographies are as valuable as those made by respondents in present-day social surveys.

Historians ordinarily use excerpts from autobiographies as one type of evidence among many to support assertions about events. They do not systematically draw a sample of autobiographies as the sole or major source of observations, to make of them a social survey done historically. To what extent is it possible to develop a plausible description of New York City at the turn of the century solely by reference to the observations made by a number of autobiographers? That is the issue posed in this chapter.

An obvious disadvantage of using autobiographers as respondents is that they are not replying directly to specific questions. That means that the reader may not find answers to certain questions. But autobiographers do direct their observations to implicit questions or topics that they believe are of interest to their readers. That the researcher may not find information about all possible concerns may be more than offset, however, by the fact that the observations that are made often have the detail usually missed in the more superficial social survey.

The opportunity to use autobiographies in this way was facilitated by the compilation by Louis Kaplan of *A Bibliography of American Autobiographies* in 1962,[1] a work that includes 6,377 works published prior to 1945. There were several reasons behind the decision to study the city between 1880 and 1914 and the method of selecting the specific autobiographies used. New York during that period was America's major city. By 1894 the population of the city had grown to just under two million residents, and, in 1898, the city was transformed into a metropolis with the consolidation of the five boroughs. That change almost doubled its population.[2]

Furthermore, New York was the entryway for multitudes of immigrants from Europe, and housed every conceivable ethnic, religious, and racial group in a social structure that was widely stratified. In 1900, 37 percent of all New Yorkers were foreign born. The largest groups were Jews (700,000), Germans (370,000), Irish (326,000), and Italians (163,000). The Black population of the city was as yet relatively small, representing about 1.5 percent of the population.[3]

It seemed necessary to try to use the autobiographies of people variously distributed along these variables. To do that, a list of autobiographies in three general categories was compiled: immigrants, social workers, and socialites. These, of course, are not completely representative of all New Yorkers at that time. But since the city was teeming with immigrants, it was felt that no picture of the city would be complete without the immigrant experience. Social workers were chosen because it was assumed that they would have been witnesses to the problems and concerns of many city residents. It was hoped that the socialites' view of the city would show what New York meant to the very rich. A tentative list was compiled of forty-eight autobiographies in those three categories of people who resided in New York during the dates desired, although far fewer autobiographies were used in this exploratory study.

Of the several autobiographies "tried," only five were analyzed. It turned out that not all authors who lived in New York noticed the city in their writings. For some the city was merely a backdrop on which they recorded the purely personal events of their lives. This was especially true for the socialites; they turned out to be part-time New Yorkers who divided their time between that city and many others here and abroad. Thus, for example, the autobiographies of Frederick Townsend Martin (*Things I Remember*, New York: John Lane, 1913) and Mrs. Gloria Vanderbilt (*Without Prejudice*, New York: E. P. Dutton, 1936) contain virtually no useful observations of the city.

Among the other two categories, there were also works by people who lived in New York but who recorded no or few relevant observations. Thus the autobiographies of Rebekah Kohut (*My Portion*, New York: Thomas Seltzer, 1925), Lillian D. Wald (*House on Henry Street*, New York: Holt, 1915), and Gregory Weinstein (*Reminiscences of an Interesting Decade: The Ardent Eighties*, New York: International Press, 1928) were concerned with people, more or less distinguished, rather than on the interactions between them and their urban surroundings.

A disproportionate number of autobiography writers were Jewish, and the study could easily have been about the Jewish experience in New York. Since that would have violated the desideratum of finding writers who were dispersed over a wide range of New York City society, only one work by a Jew was chosen.

Finally, it was assumed that the work of very famous autobiographers is already familiar, so they were excluded from this study. For example, the autobiographies of Jacob Riis (*The Making of an American*, New York: Macmillan, 1902) and Ludwig Bemelmans (*Life Classes:* New York: Viking, 1938) were thus discriminated against, although in a more comprehensive study, they would surely be included.

Obviously there are problems with the reliability and validity of the autobiographer's statements, but an attempt has been made to provide observations of the same event or social situation by more than one writer. The observations and social analyses are those of the author of the autobiography, unless otherwise indicated, and are presented from the author's point of view. In a study of a handful of autobiographies, it goes without saying that one objective is to develop new insights about the historical sociology of New York that may serve to stimulate more work, while another is to test the usefulness of the method.

During the period studied, 1880–1914, many autobiographies were written that dealt with *part* of that period, although few covered the entire period. Pre-World-War-I New York has always been regarded as particularly exciting and important from the point of view of both history and sociology. It was the end of one era and the beginning of another. The subject of dates leads naturally to a discussion of the process of *dating*. None of the writers were professional historians and they were usually casual, if not downright careless, about specifying when a particular event occurred. It was difficult, often impossible, to date an occurrence, and if the following seems to be sometimes indifferent to chronology, it reflects an attitude of the autobiographers.

Konrad Bercovici: A Jewish "Gypsy's" New York

Konrad Bercovici[4] was born in Braila, Rumania, on June 22, 1882. He grew up in prosperous circumstances, surrounded by loving Gypsy servants who taught him their language. That idyllic boyhood was shattered when his father was badly beaten in an anti-Semitic outbreak that caused his family to move to Paris. There, in September 1901, he married Naomi Lubrescu, a countrywoman, who had also sought refuge in France from anti-Jewish pogroms. Soon after their marriage, the Bercovicis migrated to New York City, where they plunged into the world of impoverished immigrants; but the fact that Konrad was self-educated, with talents as a writer and musician, led him to hope for a good life in America.

The Bercovicis, like thousands of others, were introduced to the United States by way of the Lower East Side. On his first Sunday in America, Bercovici strolled Houston, Rivington, Delancy, and Grand streets as well as East Broadway. The scene was spectacular, for the streets "were lined with pushcarts whose owners shouted the prices of their merchandise, eatables and wearables in Russian, Polish, Italian and Greek." But the most popular language on the streets was Yiddish, a language Bercovici could not yet speak, which "even the Italian peddlers spoke fluently."

On one street corner, a Salvation Army "lass" was blowing a trumpet, on another a socialist was denouncing the American bourgeoisie, in Russian, and on the next a Methodist missionary was collecting pennies to convert the heathen in Asia. In his very first hours in New York, Bercovici discovered that America was a museum of people. But it was a very dirty museum. "The filth and garbage littering the sidewalks and the gutters were being kicked by street urchins who screamed at each other in half a dozen European jargons with mangled Americanese."

Bercovici soon discovered every immigrant group "lived in the same way" as in the Old World: the Russians below Second Avenue, the Poles below Monroe Street, the Hungarians along Second Street. As for the Gypsies, those from Rumania lived close to the people of Rumanian origin in New York, those from Russia close to the Russians, and so on. Each nationality had its own cafés, papers, theaters, criminal gangs, midwives, bankers, and undertakers. And every foreign group was hectored and bossed by some organization. The Mafia, for example, "had a finger in everything. Its higher-ups made millions selling a patent medicine supposed to cure gonorrhea and syphilis. Many Italian doctors were compelled to prescribe it to clients whether they had such disease or not." The "Società's" influence extended to the church, to political organizations, cemeteries, funeral parlors, Italian midwives, even to pushcart peddlers.

"I roamed the streets every day," Bercovici wrote; "my knowledge of Greek and Turkish delighted the cafegiis on Henry Street and Cherry Street." He marveled at the Syrian quarter below Rector Street with its Arabs and Copts. In the sweatshops of Allen Street, he ogled "almond-eyed Syrian girls making lace and tall Morroccan Jewish women who helped their husbands hammer out brass trays." The Moroccan Jews published a weekly in which the Ladino they spoke was printed in Hebrew. Soon Bercovici was invited into their homes, where he ate chickpeas cooked in oil and cabbage boiled in honey. He found their weddings "barbarous affairs, neither African nor Moslem but a mixture of both."

Bercovici's favorite transplanted group was the Gypsies. An accidental encounter with an old family acquaintance led him to a cellar on Rivington Street where he "met a swarm of other Gypsies who had come from Rumania recently." As far as the Gypsies were concerned, "America had just been discovered. They wonder they hadn't heard of it until now. . . . [T]hey couldn't make money fast enough to send for all their relatives in Rumania, Russia, Hungary."

Not only did it seem that New York had attracted every ethnic and religious group, but also that it had drawn every ideological position to the left of the political spectrum. Bercovici explained that fact by the extent of human misery suffered by the immigrant population and the sure prospect of failure for most. Tenement life, arduous working conditions, and low pay in the sweatshop made the newcomers susceptible to appeals of the radicals who flocked here. Because of the human misery, Bercovici wrote, there was nothing to do except shout, "Down with the bourgeoisie!" at the nearest street corner meeting. And he further noted that "the red flag was the only flag one saw in the slums and foreign quarters of New York City."

The radical and ethnic flavor of New York City could be seen in the fact that the leaders of the socialists and anarchists, two major ideological camps, were primarily Germans and Russians. Bercovici recalled a socialist convention at which an English-speaking American delegate "demanded" that English be spoken so that he could follow the proceedings. To which the audience replied as though with a single voice, " 'Heraus! Maul halten!' ['Get out and shut up!']"

Because New York had so many immigrants susceptible to leftist leanings, it served as a lure to some of the world's most celebrated radicals. Bercovici met Johann Most, Emma Goldman, and Leon Trotsky. The meeting with Most came within a year or so of the young Rumanian's arrival in New York. He attended a meeting at which Most lectured in German about Czolgosz, the assassin of President William McKinley, whom the radical extolled as a man of courage and a martyr, and asserted that the "one way" to rid the world of kings, rulers, and oppressors was "Czolgosz's way." After Most sat down, red-bloused girls in the aisles waved little red cardboards in the air and hawked, " 'Tickets for the Czolgosz Ball. Who wants tickets for the Czolgosz Ball?' " When the speeches were over, Bercovici, who had somehow attracted the attention of those who had arranged the meeting, joined Most at a table for a few beers and discussions (for which the young immigrant was given the honor of paying the bill).

Each job Bercovici held led to new lessons about survival in New York, but meanwhile Bercovici and his family often worried about money for rent and food. His first job was for five dollars a week in a factory making artificial flowers. But Bercovici never brought home that entire amount. On the Saturday he was first paid he was informed of a union meeting that night and was told, "You got to come." If Bercovici had any idea about not joining the union, the organizers, speaking a bastardized German, soon convinced him with such epithets as " 'Ein Scab dats wass you are' ["You are a scab"] and "Ein Scab ohne Klass bewustein" ["A scab without class consciousness"]. Bercovici joined the union, paid the initiation fee of one dollar, and became obligated to pay twenty-five cents a week for dues. But union membership did not provide security, for after four weeks Bercovici was fired when "a batch of fresh immigrants, huge peasants from Lithuania arrived," willing to work for three dollars a week.

It was not unusual for Bercovici, and others like him, to start a new job, work for two, three, or four hours, and then be laid off without being paid. Once he refused to leave without his wages but was arrested when the foreman called a cop, who shouted, "Move on, you goddam greenhorn." On one job shoveling snow for twenty-five cents an hour, Bercovici found that steady work depended on giving the foreman a kickback of fifty cents a day. The foreman, too, Bercovici was told, had similar expenses. The young Rumanian was next hired to wash windows for one dollar a day, then got the idea that he could start his own business, bought a ladder, a pail, and a chamois cloth and struck out on his own. But "two toughs smashed my ladder, caved in my tin pail, and would have done the same to me had I not been the possessor of two good fists." The fight cost Bercovici two dollars for disturbing the peace.

Unwittingly, Bercovici agreed to work in a factory in Bridgeport, Connecticut, but when he got there he saw that he had been hired as a strikebreaker and so he returned to New York. He found a job in a fire-escape factory for two dollars a day in New Lots, Brooklyn, but that meant five hours of daily travel. So remote was the factory from the rest of the city that some workers slept in the factory and cooked their meals over the fire of the forge.

The tendency in the history of New York City architecture to erect a building, then tear it down to replace it with a still larger one, provided Bercovici with employment in a wrecking crew whenever he needed work desperately. That such work was frequently at night provided him the time to work on his more creative talents. Working on wrecking jobs gave Bercovici first-hand knowledge of ethnic conflict in the city. On one upper-Sixth-Avenue site where most of the workers were Hungarians and Poles, the young Rumanian noticed that "First one, and then another Hungarian was hurt by falling bricks." A crowbar "accidentally" dropped by a Pole on the tenth floor killed a Hungarian six floors below. The following night the side of a wall came down "unexpectedly" and buried two Poles underneath. During "lunch time" at midnight, Poles and Hungarians fought with hammers and crowbars.

Bercovici also had a series of jobs in which he displayed his musical skills. For five dollars down and five dollars a month, Naomi Bercovici bought a piano, and her husband was soon earning twelve dollars a week as a piano teacher, offering lessons for twenty-five cents a week until the capmakers' strike deprived him of most of his pupils. The reduced income lasted until the installment company came and removed the piano. Bercovici then played piano at a nickelodeon for fifteen dollars a week, working from 9 A.M. until midnight.

From time to time the young immigrant augmented his earnings by selling the stories that he had begun to write. His first publication was written in Yiddish, which he learned on the Lower East Side. The piece won a short-story contest sponsored by the *Jewish Daily Forward*. The twenty-five-dollar prize was timely, since the Bercovicis were two months behind in rent and had a "staggering grocer's bill." Thus encouraged, he wrote in English for other magazines, such as *Munsey's*, for modest commissions, and his career as a writer was underway.

Bercovici also worked for a time as an investigator for a private charity. But he soon became alienated from his work and particularly from his co-workers in social service, whom he came to see as being "not out to help the poor but to uncover the petty lies, contradictions, and private secrets of the applicants and to try to pry into their morals." As soon as the poor applied for assistance, he observed, they were "persecuted and deprived of all privacy" and even coerced to become scabs in factory work. Some women applicants, he asserted, were treated generously by male investigators in exchange for sexual favors. He discovered that some of the most unsanitary buildings in the city, called "lung-houses" because of the high proportion of tenants with tuberculosis, were owned by charitable, educational, or religious institutions that paid no taxes to the city. To Bercovici's dismay, the "workers" who ran the settlement houses on Rivington Street and Henry Street were interested primarily in folk dances and the local color provided by the immigrant poor, "without the slightest awareness of the filth underneath." Bercovici concluded that "The whole business of private philanthropy was nauseating, criminal and stupid." These views and others were incorporated in a book Bercovici wrote, called *Crimes of Charity*.

In 1914, Bercovici accepted still another job, this time as a writer for a Yiddish newspaper in Montreal. Although he subsequently returned to New York, the year 1914 has been reached, and so our report on the Bercovici autobiography must stop here.

Mary Kingsbury Simkhovitch: Settlement Work in Greenwich Village

Mary Kingsbury[5] was descended from a family that had settled in Massachusetts in the seventeenth century. She was born in Chestnut Hill, Massachusetts, on September 8, 1867. Her father had been a captain in the United States Army during the Civil War, and a federal and state official after that. The family was one of the pillars of the Congregational Church in Newton, Massachusetts. Mary Kingsbury studied Latin literature as an undergraduate at Boston University, from which she graduated in 1890. There followed a year of economic history and sociology at Radcliffe and a year of philosophy and political science at the University of Berlin. It was in Berlin that she met her future husband, Vladimir Simkhovitch, a Russian student. She completed her formal education at Columbia University under the tutelage of James Harvey Robinson, the historian, and Franklin Giddings, the sociologist. She was sure that under their influence "a sort of mental precipitation took place. Sociology and economics and history would surely turn out to have a reality and validity for one if one could gain a wider personal experience." That experience, she believed, would come from working among the poor and, so, in September 1897, she accepted a position at the College Settlement, one of the first settlement houses in New York, and moved into its building at 95 Rivington Street on the Lower East Side.

The young Bostonian was terrified on her very first night. A shot had been fired on Allen Street, "the heart of the red light district," followed by cries and the arrival of the police. Despite the fact that Mary Kingsbury had worked "among colored" on Phillips Street in Boston and among poor Jews in the East End of London, she was unprepared for the Lower East Side. "Rivington Street was crowded and noisy and rank with the smell of overripe fruit, hot bread and sweat-soaked clothing. The sun poured down relentlessly and welded the East Side together in one impress of fetid fertility."

The inhabitants were largely from small Jewish towns in Rumania, Galicia, Russia, and Poland. As though to confirm Bercovici's assertion that private charity workers did not really penetrate the problems of immigrants, Mary Kingsbury recalled, "Life in the East Side at that time was far more picturesque than now (1938). The Yiddish drama was good before it was 'Americanized.' There were good literary clubs. In the evening at ten o'clock, when clubs and evening events at the Settlement disbanded, many of us would meet for tea at Lorber's at Grand Street to discuss East Side matters."

Where Bercovici made failure the fate of the majority of immigrants, Mary Kingsbury saw the experience as ultimately uplifting. She organized a Sunday Evening Economics Club, and its members, "who then lived in direst poverty in crowded rooms of the old 'dumbbell' tenements, are now living on Riverside Drive. From the slavery of the tenement sweatshop . . . the old East Side was the fertile production of today's judges, teachers, actors, musicians, playwrights and leaders of New York."

That outcome, however, did not blind Mary Kingsbury to the living conditions of East Side immigrants. The Jews, succeeding old German residents who had moved north, were housed in dumbbell tenements. That type of building had once won a prize in a contest to design suitable dwellings for the poor. So profitable was it to its owners that this twenty-four-family building became the dominant type in New York City, despite the fact that "through the air shafts vermin made their way and at the bottom garbage and refuse collected." Privacy was impossible, and "soiling sights and sounds became part of children's lives."

As the Germans moved out, Mary Kingsbury observed a social process that has since become familiar: churches and ministers without parishioners. Thus the Reverend Mr. Paddock, minister of the Protestant church on Stanton Street, bid farewell to the Lower East Side at a time when he had "just begun to learn what the God south of 14th Street was like and now he had to find out all over again about the God of eastern Oregon."

Despite the obvious social disorder, Mary Kingsbury discerned an underlying stability. At the beginning of the twentieth century, she wrote, "sections of the city were more shut off from one another than now as there were no subways and few automobiles, and the whole idea of 'neighborhood' was therefore more real. People stayed within their neighborhoods, whereas today the most provincial East Sider will go to see relatives in the Bronx or in Brownsville and he will know Broadway as well as Grand Street." Furthermore, each neighborhood had its church or synagogue, school and stores and sweatshops that employed residents. For those without money or food or who were in trouble with the police, the political organization provided assistance. There was no need for "surveys," Mary Kingsbury recalled, since the politicians, priests, and settlement-house practitioners really knew the neighborhood.

The East Side and other parts of the city provided true neighborhood, but one that—because of the special circumstances of the urban environment—deprived children, and adults, too, of age-old experiences. The countryside was out of reach for most, and it was "a grim fact that thousands of dwellers on the East Side had never seen any other tree than the ailanthus that managed to survive in an occasional backyard." Children never saw any animals but cats, dogs, and the fowl packed in horse-drawn wagons.

During the summer the streets were unbearable. Residents suffered intense discomfort from heat and humidity. "Summers," Kingsbury wrote, "were unpleasant with flies, for the horses fouled the streets." The horses made the neighborhood unpleasant in other ways: during the heat wave of 1902, for example, hundreds of horses died in the streets of sunstroke. (Mary Kingsbury was no longer living on the Lower East Side in 1902, but she obviously maintained a watch over her old neighborhood.) Human residents also suffered sunstroke. "That was the summer, when, all the bathtubs being full, they played the hose on the victims of sunstroke as they were brought into the Bellevue Hospital yard."

It was as one of the founders and director of Greenwich House that Mary Simkhovitch (in January 1899, she had married Simkhovitch, who had joined the faculty at Columbia University) was to find her calling, and it was to 26 Jones Street, Greenwich Village, that she and her husband moved in May 1901. Her first act as a new resident was to call the exterminator, who promptly discovered five different types of vermin.

McKinley's assassination on September 6, 1901, brought Mary Simkhovitch an interesting insight: "what is important varies from person to person and group to group." That evening Professor Simkhovitch, on his way to buy a newspaper, found that on Greenwich Village streets "everywhere people were telling one another the news—that a favorite horse had won." When he returned home and he and his wife looked at the same newspaper that had carried the race results, they read what were to them the appalling headlines announcing that the president had been shot.

The concept of neighborhood that Mary Simkhovitch had developed on the East Side was reinforced by her residence in the 9th Ward, whose boundaries were coterminous with Greenwich Village. At that time Sixth Avenue reached only to 14th Street, and Seventh Avenue did not exist at all. Thus the whole region from 14th Street south to Canal Street and from Fifth Avenue west to the Hudson was a self-contained, self-sufficient neighborhood of small streets and paths known only to its inhabitants. The provincial character of Greenwich Village could largely be traced to the fact that few thoroughfares ran through the area. Uptowners thus did not know their way south of 14th Street through the Village, so they came down Broadway east of Sixth Avenue. Businesses were local; their owners resided in the neighborhood. Families were large, and familistic values prevailed. There was as yet no evidence of the Bohemianism that came to give Greenwich Village its twentieth-century flavor.

On the contrary, in the insular, pre-automobile life of Greenwich Village, women stayed at home in the evenings, supervising their younger children at their lessons. The older girl in the family might go out with her "steady," while the head of the household had the freedom to stay at home or go to his political club—or, as in the case of the newly arrived Italian, to the café for cards or talk. Social life centered about the churches and the political and social clubs. Balls held for the benefit of the common treasury of some organization or even on behalf of some needy resident were common and popular.

Family stability was guaranteed by convention. "Divorce," Mary Simkhovitch wrote, "was unknown. For Catholics it was out of the question, for Protestants it was not respectable; and for all it was too expensive." Infidelity occurred occasionally, but it was not condoned, and "indeed, the plain old American village standards prevailed." But life was not so severe as to prevent close intimacy among young lovers during engagement.

Although, as will be seen, Jones Street was not characteristic, the social composition of the Village when the Simkhovitches arrived was, according to Mary, predominantly middle class with a sprinkling of very rich and very poor. The latter tended to congregate along the route of the Ninth Avenue elevated, which made that area considerably less desirable. In those ramshackle houses of the poor, school children made artificial flowers for seven cents a gross; or, for similar pay, they manufactured dice, hatpin tops, feathers, or toys, and did other kinds of "homework." This part of the Village had sandy subsoil; it was swampy in spots, and water backed into the cellar of many houses. Residents of the area suffered from a yellow fever epidemic, tuberculosis, and high infant mortality.

As for the rest of the Village, its occupational structure supported a middle-class population. Contractors, judges, politicians, and public officials abounded. It seemed as though it was expected that the mayor of New York would reside there. Popular working-class jobs were longshoreman and teamster. As to finding a route to middle-class respectability, "even children knew that the family budget must be stretched to meet the $300-payment for the much-coveted position of fireman and policeman." As to work done by unmarried women, Simkhovitch noted that Irish-American girls were employed in offices and stores, whereas Italian-American girls worked in factories.

Jones Street was not so poverty-stricken as the Ninth-Avenue Section, but it lacked the comfortable middle-class character of the rest of the Village. For one thing, it was the densest block on the West Side, with fourteen hundred residents. Most of these were Irish, but there was a sprinkling of native-born Italians and Negroes and people from twenty-six different countries. The street had five saloons, nine boarding houses, dumbbell tenements, and many railroad tenements (distinguished from dumbbell tenements by their lack of interior airshafts, so that all rooms not facing the street were dark).

The most common dwelling in the Village at the turn of the century was still the single-family house with open fireplaces, front and back parlors, and sunny yards. Gradually, however, floors were rented out, tenements began to sprout on many empty lots, and a new character to Greenwich Village was foreshadowed.

Despite the comfort of the single-family house, especially when compared to the dismal tenements, the former were spartan as measured by later standards. There were no baths or toilets: the yard or cellar served as a privy. "Baltimore" heaters in the basement sometimes heated the first floor, but ordinarily it was the kitchen stove that warmed the house, and coal deliveries were a necessary and dirty nuisance. The family wash was done in round wooden washtubs frequently in need of repair, and "Washtubs to mend" was a familiar cry on the streets of the Village.

One aspect of life in Greenwich Village was a defining characteristic of neighborhood life—participation in voluntary associations. Alexis de Tocqueville had noted, in pre-Jacksonian America, the relationship between a richly textured organizational life and the development of democratic institutions. No other community could have had more organizations than the Village, many of which were organized as an extension of Greenwich House. For the observer looking for clues to the community's concerns, the voluntary association was surely such an indicator.

The first association to be organized during the tenure of Mary Simkhovitch was the Greenwich Village Improvement Society, the first neighborhood association in New York. Its objective was to secure improvements

in the community. On behalf of this neighborhood association, Mrs. Simkhovitch called the borough president, George McAneny, and "said we wanted
a public bath for Greenwich Village." The Barrow Street recreation pier,
the Carnegie Library in Hudson Park, the hall for Public School Number
3 were just a few of the improvements instigated by the association.

In 1906, the Greenwich Village Public Service Committee was formed.
Among its accomplishments was the removal of the old abandoned streetcar
tracks on 11th Street just before that thoroughfare was to be paved. Greenwich House members were represented in the local branches of the Charity
Organization Society, the Consumers' League, and the Women's Trade
Union League, whose objectives and underlying concerns are fairly evident
from their names. The School and Civic League of Teachers and Social
Workers was created to foster school social centers. The Congestion Committee organized an exhibit in March 1908 at the American Museum of
Natural History to show that many of the city's ills were caused by over-
crowding. The display contained photographs of New York's slums, as well
as models and interiors to prove that the housing law "barely touched the
living conditions of a large proportion of the population."

The Village Plan Committee was organized in 1913 to make recommendations to minimize the dislocation that "would surely take place" when the
Seventh Avenue Subway was opened. Other voluntary associations included
the Women's Civic Club, the Men's Club, the Stoic Club, the Italian-Amer-
ican Progressive League, the Society for Italian Women, the Association of
Neighborhood Workers, and the Little Players.

Of course, Greenwich House itself was a voluntary association, very much
implicated in the affairs of residents and the quality of Village life. One
illustration of its activities is especially illuminating concerning the role of
associational life in the community. In 1906, acting as director of Greenwich
House, Mary Simkhovitch petitioned the city "to wipe out the Minettas,
Street, Lane, and Court," presumably because of their unsavory character.
Discovering that it was not legal to get rid of a locality because it was
"unsanitary," Mary Simkhovitch got temporary improvements by reporting
conditions in violation of the law to the Tenement House Department, the
Board of Health, and the police. "Some of the notorious characters," she
wrote, "were 'sent up the river,' and certain houses vacated." But in 1912,
there were still three "disorderly houses," two "tough saloons," and a "cadet
club" (a voluntary association of pimps!), as well as prostitution in some of
the tenements. One of the members of Greenwich House secured an option
to buy all the property on the Minettas, only to learn that model tenements
at a rental possible for "plain people" would require higher buildings than
the width of the streets would legally allow. In 1912 the Greenwich House
leadership endorsed a project to eliminate the Minettas by continuing Sixth
Avenue through its area, but that and a proposal to turn a large part of the

region into a park were, for reasons Mary Simkhovitch does not go into, to no avail.

By 1914 and the end of our interest in Mrs. Simkhovitch's account, there were a number of assaults on the conditions necessary for Greenwich Village to maintain its neighborhood quality. The Williamsburg Bridge was opened in 1903 and the subway in 1904; both installations made the Village more accessible to outsiders, as did the extension of Sixth Avenue and the construction of Seventh Avenue a few years later. In 1908 the Hudson tubes to New Jersey were built. "The use of Ford cars," Mrs. Simkhovitch observed, "available in 1909[,] had spread rapidly by 1911." Notwithstanding the changes in the opportunities for New Yorkers and others to violate neighborhood boundaries, Mary Simkhovitch concluded, "But in spite of the rapid extension and change of these first fifteen years, the Village still had a life in and of itself."

Cornelius W. Willemse: The Policeman's New York

In 1888, Cornelius W. Willemse[6] was a young helper in the galley of the Dutch ship *Obdam* on its voyage from Amsterdam to Hoboken. The fifteen-year-old youth had been born in Rotterdam to a prosperous family that owned a "big bakery" in that town. The boy apparently was either well educated or well traveled, for he already knew how to speak English, German, French, and Flemish, as well as his native Dutch. For reasons that are not stated, Willemse jumped ship at Hoboken, eluded police, made his way from Hoboken to Manhattan, and promptly settled on the Bowery.

He learned later that New Yorkers shuddered at the mention of the Bowery—"the most wicked street" in the city, but one they found irresistible. As a boy Willemse had dreamed of someday seeing "red Indians" in America, but once on the Bowery he readily gave up that longing. Why look for red Indians, he reasoned, when one could "find white ones on any dark corner away from the bright gas lights of the saloon, white Indians who would use clubs, bottles, and brass knuckles on any half-drunken man who staggered their way."

At that time the Bowery was a blending of sailors and students, prize-fighters and prostitutes, bartenders and bouncers, dancing girls and high-society matrons out slumming, politicians and professional men, Bowery gangsters and East-Side rowdies, and, of course, the permanent residents of the Bowery, bums and derelicts.

The contrast between life in Rotterdam and what Willemse encountered on the Bowery could not have been greater. There was "corruption and traffic in women which I could not understand and which horrified me, particularly whenever I thought of the quiet life of my sisters in Holland."

After Cornelius worked for a while as a dishwasher for the "good pay" of one dollar a day, he was able to broaden his vistas of New York. The center of the best restaurants and entertainment in 1888 was 14th Street. The young immigrant became an occasional member of the audience at Tony Pastor's famous theater, and, whenever he had a spare quarter, he sat in the gallery of the Academy of Music.

An illness led to Willemse's hospitalization, first at Bellevue Hospital and then on Blackwell's Island. With his health still shaky, he returned to Manhattan, too weak to work, and for five months was an outcast, himself a "Bowery bum," sleeping in doorways and hallways, or on gratings through which the steam from buildings escaped. He was restored to his health, had a succession of jobs, and regained his self-respect. On November 7, 1899, with the help of some "Tammany men," Willemse became a probationary policeman in the 28th precinct on West 68th Street.

Cornelius's first patrol was "San Juan Hill," that is, the area from Amsterdam Avenue to West End Avenue at 62nd Street. The south side of the street was "Negro" and the north side was "Irish." "Brawls were common," Willemse wrote, "and serious fights were regular events. If nothing else happened, a brick, a stone, or bottle might land on my head from some dark roof."

His beat also included the freight yards near the Hudson River. "My first taste of what a policeman might expect," he recalled, "came in a battle with the Red Featherson gang, a band of toughs which hung around the railroad yards between 59th and 63rd Streets on West End Avenue and gave the police lots of trouble. The gang looted railroad cars in the yard, and no drunken man in the district was safe from robbery. One night a number of policemen, including myself, sneaked upon the band. It was a grand mixup and I helped in knocking out several gangsters."

As a probationary policeman, Willemse covered his beat at night and attended the police school at 300 Mulberry Street during the day. "Captain Michael Smith was our teacher and drillmaster," Willemse wrote, "and he knew his business." Willemse quoted from one of the captain's lectures. "Men, when you get your nightsticks, they're intended to be used on thieves and crooks, by no means strike a man on the head. The insane asylums are filled with men whose condition has been caused by a skull injury. Strike them over the arms or the legs, unless you're dealing with real bad crooks. Then it doesn't make any difference whether they go to the insane asylum or to jail."

In February 1900, having passed his probationary test, Willemse was sworn in as a regular member of the police force and assigned to the 17th Precinct on West 20th Street. There was a blizzard on his very first night of duty and the young patrolman was warned not to let anyone freeze to death on his post. The caution was useful, for Willemse did dig out "Peter

Broadfoot, an Indian [who] was drunk." Soon after, Willemse "received another valuable lesson." He had arrested two men who had beaten and robbed a passerby. When he brought the robbers and the victim to the stationhouse, Willemse was scolded by the sergeant, who "snapped, 'Look at the condition of this poor fellow and not a mark on these two bums.' " The sergeant sent for two policemen and ordered, " 'Take these two bums outside and show this rookie how to bring them in right.' " Willemse watched and recalled, "There wasn't any time lost as we reached the sidewalk. The nightsticks flew and within a few minutes my prisoners were laid on the walk." This time the sergeant was satisfied, and told Willemse: "Well, that's something. Now, let me tell you something. They may beat you in court, the complainant may not show up, they may jump their bail, politicians may interfere, there are several ways they can beat you, but this ('and he pointed to the marks and bruises,') they've got, and make no damned mistake about it."

The rookie policeman learned the lesson of using his nightstick and later asserted that "the colored riots in 1901 came as proof positive of the power of the club." The trouble started, according to Willemse, when a detective named Thorpe was killed by a Negro man in retaliation for the arrest of his woman friend. When the news spread, "Ugly crowds of white men formed in 36th and 37th Street, west of Eighth Avenue. A few attacks on Negroes inflamed the mobs, and then came the riots. Large crowds rushed through the streets, beating every black man they could find. These unfortunates were frequently pulled from their seats in trolley cars and manhandled terribly. Soon most of the West Side was in an uproar; Negroes fled for their lives."

Dispatched with police reserves to 25th Street to protect Blacks in that area, Willemse wrote:

> Nightsticks came into play and the war was on. The next five hours made police history. It was the fiercest mass battle I have ever known. Hundreds of maddened men fought our group. Stones, bricks, bottles and clubs fell like rain. Negroes fought whites on a dozen streets, and the police soon were battling them all.
>
> How those nightsticks worked. . . . The police drove the crowds all the way from 25th Street back to 37th, clubs swinging every foot of the way. . . . When it was all over the streets were covered with injured men. The station houses were filled with badly battered whites and colored men. Almost every cop was bruised and bleeding. All night long, ambulances and patrol wagons rushed to the hospitals. Surgeons toiled in the streets, patching up the victims. But the rioting was over. A heavy toll of lynchings and murders had been averted.

Willemse's transfer to the 19th Precinct—the area from 23rd Street to 48th Street, with Broadway and Sixth Avenues as its "nerve centers"—

known then as the "Tenderloin," opened up still another world. The area was the center of illegal gambling, prostitution, and thievery, as well as the more legal but morally dubious activities of the dance hall and barroom "resorts," which were frequently covers for illicit activities. "Any cop who knew the Tenderloin," Willemse wrote of that neighborhood in 1902, "laughs when he hears the New York of today called wicked city. One block of the Tenderloin provided more vice than exists in the whole area of the present 'White Light' district." At the turn of the century such was the reputation of the Tenderloin that "men from all parts of the world came to see, to marvel and to play."

Houses of prostitution were arrayed in an unbroken row of brownstones on 29th Street. Twenty-eighth Street specialized in gambling houses for cards and roulette, while on 27th Street almost every other door led to a poolroom where one could place a bet for any racetrack in the East. "Vice was an accepted fact in city life and there seemed little that could be done to check it," Willemse wrote.

The most famous "resort" was the Haymarket dancehall on Sixth Avenue below 30th Street, named after the famous London playhouse, where "hundreds of girls went each night to drink, dance and meet men." The parties started there would end up hours later in nearby houses of assignation. Hordes of more common prostitutes lined Broadway, Sixth Avenue, and the side streets. Prostitution was associated with robbery, and with cabbies, as "half the cabbies in the Tenderloin were drawing regular commissions from steering strangers to the houses."

Drunks were also a common sight in the Tenderloin, and Willemse developed a classification. It included the kidney ("he leans to the right or the left as he staggers down the street"), singing, crying, running ("often he'll run smack into a building or a pole"), fighting, wife beating, charitable, religious, sneaky, talking or important, amorous, mischievous, sleepy ("any place is bed"), animal loving, taxi ("likes to see the meter jump").

Girl watching was then a popular pastime in New York City, and it sometimes led to rudeness and touching, and to complaints to the police. The introduction of the large department store in the latter part of the nineteenth century made it acceptable for respectable women to go into the Tenderloin unaccompanied, although "no woman who was presentable in appearance could escape the attention of the mashers."

In the spring of 1906, Willemse was transferred to still another neighborhood, the Mercer Street Station in Greenwich Village, and was assigned to patrol the "Minettas," the same set of streets that had so troubled Mary Simkhovitch. The Minettas, he wrote, were a residential neighborhood of families but one with houses of prostitution and gambling places, and with a mixed population of Italians and Negroes. The latter had been there first, according to Willemse, but by the turn of the century, large numbers of

Italian immigrants were settling there. The result was that "The stiletto was matched against the razor in any number of street brawls." Gradually, the Black population was displaced by the Italians, not entirely to Willemse's pleasure. "Among the Italian newcomers," he wrote, "were many splendid families, but the riff-raff ruled the district and the police were locked in a bitter war." Along with prostitution and thievery, loft burglaries were the major crimes of the district.

But Willemse's tenure in the Village was short lived. Accused of taking money from gamblers and poolroom keepers, he was transferred to the 7th Precinct, "a punishment precinct" that took him back to the Lower East Side. And the policing of that neighborhood brought new challenges. The area was divided up by street gangs who attacked one another with revolvers. On one of his first nights in the precinct, Willemse was caught in a crossfire between the Cherry Hill and Monroe Street mobs. When these "thugs" were not fighting one another they roamed the waterfront preying on sailors, immigrants, and drunks.

Willemse's beat in the 7th Precinct consisted mostly of old dirty warehouses swarming with rats. "Every late tour," he wrote, "was big game hunt. I would hang a piece of ham skin on a string, and then start shooting when the rats came for the bait. I killed thousands."

Another noteworthy feature of the 7th Precinct was the Catherine Street Market, the trading place of the East Side's poorest residents, a market unknown to most New Yorkers. Sunday morning was market day when peddlers showed up with fish, vegetables, and produce they could not sell on Saturday night and which would soon spoil. As Sunday afternoon drew near, the peddlers would give away whatever they had left and there would be a "scramble" around the carts by women looking for bargains or for any kind of handout.

On February 1, 1909, having passed his examination, Willemse was promoted to the rank of sergeant and was assigned to the 69th Precinct, an area in The Bronx then known as Westchester, but including Pelham Park, Throggs Neck, Classon Point, and Pennyfield. "Westchester of those days," he recalled, "was a wilderness, and the precinct covered an enormous district [whose] posts were from two to four miles long and just as wide." As to law enforcement, "there was little to do in the way of police work. We were like a bunch of retired businessmen, drawing full pay while we loafed." The Bronx was then an area of farms, amusement parks, and unspoiled countryside. "That precinct was a vacation," Willemse lamented when he was transferred to the 21st Precinct at East 22nd Street, the heart of the Gas House District.

In 1913, Willemse received another promotion, this time to the position of homicide detective. From that time onward, his narrative loses its focus on New York City and concentrates, instead, on the solution of a number of murders, a type of felony of which there did not seem to be a shortage.

Cornelius Vanderbilt, Jr.: The Poor Little Rich Boy's New York

Cornelius Vanderbilt, Jr.,[7] great-great-grandson of Commodore Cornelius Vanderbilt, and son of General Cornelius Vanderbilt, was a member of a family that was part of the American upper class that had taken shape after the Civil War. The commodore had amassed a great fortune, primarily, though not exclusively, as a railroad baron. His legacy assured his descendants wealth and social standing. Cornelius, Jr., was born on April 30, 1898, in the family mansion on Fifth Avenue, but he spent much of his time away from New York City. The boy's father was a yachting enthusiast, and summers were for cruising on board the family's elegant vessel. Nor was there any time of the year when the residence in New York monopolized the family's attention. "Tossed among New York, Virginia and Florida in winter," he wrote, "I commuted between Newport and Europe in summer."

Thus Vanderbilt's account begins in Newport, Rhode Island, on the night of September 6, 1901, when the family was enjoying a masquerade party. The merrymaking was interrupted by the announcement that President McKinley had been shot. In contrast to Bercovici's account of the celebration of that event by radicals on the Lower East Side, and the indifference witnessed by Professor Simkhovitch in Greenwich Village, the aristocrats at the ball were terrified. The Vanderbilts and their guests worried that a "whole epoch," not just a president, had been "felled" by Czolgosz. They dreaded bidding farewell "to the golden age of railroad emperors, to the bliss of coupon-clipping, to the reign of inherited millions and to the partnership of Fifth Avenue dowagers and iron-hearted political bosses, to the spirit of certainty about tomorrow's caviar and the day-after-tomorrow's orchids." The Vanderbilts prepared to return to New York.

It is not clear how the three-year-old was able to reconstruct these events and attitudes, but he wrote, "I vaguely remember being awakened in the middle of that night, lifted out of bed by my English nurse, dressed approximately, hustled away in a caleche and tossed aboard my father's yacht. We were in a great hurry to get back to New York." That was the typical response to threats to the family's wealth. "Whenever anything sensational broke out at home or abroad, anything suggestive of war, revolution or additional taxation we jumped aboard our yacht and returned to New York." The main purpose of the trip was to consult with the advisers who supervised the family's fortunes. "No tragedy of the world was permitted to enter our conversation or change our routine until we found out what . . . [the family's bankers and lawyers] thought of it."

To a large extent New York City meant the monied classes to the young Vanderbilt. The Fifth Avenue mansion was a meeting place of multimillionaires J. P. Morgan, E. H. Harriman, George W. Baker, Andrew Carnegie, Andrew Mellon, and Henry Frick, as well as less celebrated tycoons. Much conversation among the guests at Fifth Avenue concerned how to make and keep money. Carnegie "never failed to repeat to the children that the most difficult art on earth is that of holding on to money." As for Frick, "no other guest in our house mentioned the word 'dollar' so much."

It was not just that the family spent much time away from New York that restricted the boy's experience of the city, for Cornelius was largely confined to the Fifth Avenue house when the family was in residence. He was taught at home by tutors. Leaving the house, he remembered, was carefully regulated, because "kidnappers and 'commoners' were the two major threats of my childhood." Bodyguards could, perhaps, protect the child from the threat of being held for ransom, "but it required no end of strategy to prevent my talking to the 'awful street boys' and inviting them to come and skate in back of Number Six Seventy-Seven."

It was not just that such boys were from a despised class but that, being street-wise, they could give the boy lessons the family preferred to leave untaught. For example, they might have known that "my great-great grandfather once ferried vegetables from Staten Island to Battery Place." Or they might have disabused the boy of the belief that "everybody had a house in Fifth Avenue, a villa in Newport, and a steam-driven ocean-going yacht."

Until he was seventeen Cornelius was never permitted to go out unescorted. Under the circumstances, the opportunity to venture into the city was a rare occasion. The "real fun of our childhood," he wrote, came on Sunday afternoon when, accompanied by his maternal grandfather, Richard T. Wilson, and

> tiptoeing through the "petit salons" and the reception hall, we would sneak out by the back door and rush down the Avenue toward Huyler's at Forty-third Street. Huyler's was the place which advertised "fresh candy every half hour." And Huyler's was the place in front of which we would stand, our grandfather, watch in hand, waiting impatiently for the bell of the elevator which would rise to the level of the sidewalk from nowhere, bringing its wealth of fresh candy, thirty minutes old.

Vanderbilt's release from his childhood and his freedom to move about New York City and elsewhere came with America's entrance into World War I and Vanderbilt's enlistment as a private in the United States Army at the age of nineteen.

Joseph I. C. Clarke: New York, the Critic's City

Joseph I. C. Clarke[8] was born in Kingston, Ireland, on July 31, 1846. He migrated to New York City in 1868, when he was twenty-two years old. Clarke's first job in New York was on the staff of the *Irish Republic*, a weekly devoted to Irish national affairs and to the Republican party in American politics. Clarke subsequently moved from one paper to another until, in 1870, he became a reporter for the *New York Herald* of James Gordon Bennett, then the leading daily in the United States with a circulation of seventy-thousand copies. He remained with the *Herald* for thirteen years, then spent 1883 to 1895 on the *New York Journal*. Following a series of writing jobs he returned to the Sunday edition of the *Herald* in 1903 and stayed until 1906, at which time he left the newspaper world for a career in public relations.

Clarke was deeply interested in the theater and music, and, although Bennett did not permit any reporter to remain in the role of full-time critic indefinitely, the young Irishman was frequently asked to cover the openings of plays, operas, and concerts. In the 1880s, the drama and music center for the city—as noted by Willemse—was along 14th Street, the site of the Academy of Music and the Lyceum Theatre, as well as many other houses. Clarke was "amazed" (after having lived briefly in London and Paris) at the "dramatic and musical delights" available. Homemade drama of the time, he noted, was still "crude," and thus most offerings were the classics and other European plays.

Clarke's scrapbook of first-night criticisms between 1877 and 1883 is a history of theater and drama in New York for that period. "My first clipping," he wrote, "records the New York debut of Mary Anderson in the 'Lady of Lyons.'" She later appeared in *Fazio* and *Evadne*. "Other memorable performances" included Mademoiselle Modjeska in *Camille* and *Frou-Frou;* Edwin Booth in *Richelieu, King Lear, Ruy Blas,* and *The Fool's Revenge;* Lester Wallack in *Money, London Assurance,* and *Diplomacy;* John McCullogh in *Richard III, Othello, King Lear, Ingomar, Brutus,* and the *Gladiator;* and Adelaide Neilson in *Romeo and Juliet* and *Twelfth Night.*

Clarke was also first-night critic for Joseph Jefferson in *Rip Van Winkle* ("an American Play") and *The Rivals.* Other plays he reviewed were Stuart Robson and William H. Crane, in *The Comedy of Errors, Sharps and Flats,* and *The Milligan Guards* ("the seventh volume of the famous series"). And, of course, Clarke watched the incomparable Sarah Bernhardt in *Camille.*

"In grand opera," Clarke wrote, "my reviews of 1878 included a short season of German opera at the Academy of Music; Italian opera at Booth's with Marie Rose making her debut and our American *prima donna* Clara Louise Kellogg heard in many roles." The regular opera season was held at the Academy of Music, and Clarke witnessed the debut of the "great

Etelka Gersten," whose triumph obscured even "Campanini who to my thinking alone ranks with Caruso." In 1879, there was French opera at Booth's and English opera at the Fifth Avenue with Emma Abbott. In an entry for 1880, Clarke noted that Minnie Hauk sang Carmen "for the fifth time."

These serious efforts were not all there was to New York's musical life. "In lighter vein," Clarke wrote, "we had delightful performances of opera bouffe, 'Girafle-Girofla,' 'The Little Duke,' 'Madame Favart,' and 'La Grande Duchesse.' " A Gilbert and Sullivan furor in New York and many different performances of "H.M.S. *Pinafore*" stimulated a burlesque at Tony Pastor's, in 1881, entitled "Pie Rats of Penn Yan." The review for the latter production "mentions the bird-like staccato of Lillian Russell" in her first appearance.

Two anecdotes tell something about the tastes of New York audiences and their compassion for great singers. The first concerns the New York debut of John McCullogh, an actor whose company had made a reputation in San Francisco. The young Western "old-timers," Clarke wrote, were convinced that all New York wanted was the "old heroic methods" (what today would probably be called "corn"). But New York had "outgrown" those methods and now "supported an advance in art from which it had learned to reject the backwoods appeal of those daring young declaimers." Thus, Clarke concluded—with some exaggeration because McCullogh, as Clarke's own scrapbook recorded, later succeeded in New York—"the waters closed over the roistering band and New York saw little of their kind thereafter."

The other incident involved Campanini. Clarke watched the breakdown of the great Italian opera singer and later the "tragedy" of his comeback after years of retirement. "It was 'Faust,' " Clarke wrote, "and to the horror of the house he broke on his famous high C in 'Salve Dimora!' " Clarke reported that "a sympathetic audience generously demanded an encore and this time he accomplished the note." Clarke rushed backstage where he found Campanini "with tears streaming down his face" in acknowledgment that his career was over.

Of particular interest during Clarke's tenure at the *New York Journal* was that paper's sponsorship of a series of thirty-three public concerts at Castle Garden, an island in New York Harbor that had been vacated when the Emigration Commission moved to Bedloe's Island, site of the Statue of Liberty. Castle Garden had also served as a fort during the War of 1812 and later housed a concert hall in which Jenny Lind first faced an American audience. Under Clarke's direction, a new floor was laid in the concert hall, a platform constructed, and gas lighting installed. With the placing of several thousand "cheap" wooden chairs and some decorative denim, the reconstructed hall was ready.

An orchestra whose musicians were paid seven dollars a concert was directed by Sam Franko. Free tickets were made available by "political

leaders of both parties, large employers, racial groups, individual philan-
thropists," who contributed $350 for a concert in return for two thousand
tickets. Clarke and a committee appointed for this purpose "selected a night
and music that would have a special appeal to the audience. Thus we had
German, Italian, Irish, Finnish, French, and Swiss nights, many American
nights, New York nights and so on." Clarke himself was rhapsodic. "To see
them, these men and women of so many races, well-clad, smiling, cheering,
enraptured at hearing again under the folds of our flag the music of their
native lands was delighting."

Much of Clarke's autobiography deals with encounters with notables who
either lived in New York or passed through. These recollections only rarely
deal with New York City and focus mainly on the careers and character of
the celebrated respondents. Occasionally, however, a profile of a famous
person does bring an insight about New York City of that period. That is
the case with Clarke's chapter on the inventor Thomas Alva Edison. In the
early 1880s, Clarke wrote, the brilliant Edison was asked "by the newspapers
to come to the city and stop the affrighting noise of the newly elevated
railroads." Not that New York had ever been regarded as a "City of Silence"
but "the new Third, Sixth and Ninth Avenue elevated trains drawn by sturdy
little steam engines thundering and rattling day and night actually frightened
New York."

Edison was regarded as "a wizard" and it was hoped and widely believed
that he could "cure the unbearable rumpus in the air." The pressure built
up in the press for Edison to apply his genius to the problem of the elevated
could not be resisted by local authorities. Accordingly, Edison "went with
skilled assistants and boxes of sound-measuring instruments, and diligently
applied the latter to the pillars, the tracks, the stations of the elevated system
and finally to the trains themselves."

Edison did confirm that the noises coming from the elevated trains were,
in fact, frightful. He wrote a brief report, naive in Clarke's opinion, that
said that the racket was caused by vibration. He promised to study "his
figures" and to file another report. But Edison, according to Clarke, "never
reported" again. Instead, he told the reporter (no doubt off the record),
"The human ear will train itself to stand anything that doesn't burst it."

Between 1906 and 1913, Joseph Clarke was chief of publicity for the
Standard Oil Company and his autobiography for that period deals exclusively with his work at that company.

Conclusions

This chapter has raised the possibility of using autobiographies to describe
central features of life in New York City. The method has a number of

limitations, some of which were mentioned at the outset. For example, it was seen that several autobiographers did not deal with the question of living in New York despite the fact that they resided, at least for a time, in the city. That was especially true for socialites, who, in three works examined, hardly noticed New York City. Cornelius Vanderbilt's autobiography suggests that this indifference to the city may have been the result of the upper-class way of life, which insulated its members from experiencing the city as others do. If analysis of additional autobiographies should support this view, that would be a finding in itself.

Although it was the intention to try to throw light upon the entire period between 1880 and 1914, most of the observations dealt with the period around the turn of the century. Only two autobiographies, those by Joseph Clarke and Cornelius Willemse, dealt with the earlier period. Clarke was already a reporter for the *New York Herald* by 1880, and Willemse arrived in New York in 1888; but the latter was fifteen at the time, and most of his account was about his career as a policeman, which began in November 1899. Konrad Bercovici did not come to New York until around 1902, Mary Simkhovitch began her work at the College Settlement in 1897, and Vanderbilt was not born until 1898.

Finally, autobiographies are usually written years after the events they describe. Only Clarke mentioned using a scrapbook to jog his memory. Therefore, there is always the question of how accurately people remember events that happened many years before. Certain incidents can be checked against newspaper accounts and other independent sources. For example, a check of Willemse's version of the New York City race riot revealed that his account was supported by the *New York Times;* it was started when a Negro killed a policeman, Robert Thorpe, and angry whites sought to avenge the murder by attacking Negroes. Willemse, however, wrote that the riot took place in 1901, when, in fact, it took place in August 1900.[9]

Yet the five autobiographies did present considerable detail about life in different sections of New York—or, more accurately, Manhattan, although Willemse did describe a somewhat bucolic Bronx. That the five autobiographers had different occupations and lived in various parts of the city lent a certain breadth to the accounts when taken as a whole. Although the methodological model presented here has raised the possibility of treating autobiographers like respondents in a social survey, another complementary model is also relevant. The five authors in five different places can be thought of as participant observers actively involved in the social situations they described. The use of a considerably larger sample, which Kaplan's bibliography makes possible, as well as having more than one autobiographer in the same place at the same time (and at different times) would better meet the requirements of the model and should enhance its value.

It may be useful to summarize the main observations and insights in each autobiography, to look at observations of situations in which the writers were at the same place at the same time, and to examine reactions to situations when the authors were in different places at the same time.

Konrad Bercovici stressed the ethnic variety that characterized New York City, particularly the Lower East Side. The importance of Jews in the immigrant population at the turn of the century and the widespread use of Yiddish in that locality were observed and noted by both Bercovici and Simkhovitch. There is also evidence in Bercovici's, Simkhovitch's, and Willemse's accounts of the sociological processes of invasion by one ethnic group and the displacement of another group. The sometimes deadly warfare between Hungarians and Poles on wrecking crews, fights between Italians and Blacks in Greenwich Village, the race riot of 1901—or, more accurately, 1900—are vivid examples of ethnic conflict.

The radical flavor of New York was also a central part of Bercovici's account, as well as the involvement of German and Russian immigrants in far left movements. That red flags were the "only flag one saw in the slums and foreign quarters of New York City" is poles apart from the ideological climate in present-day New York, as was the "Czolgosz Ball" to raise money for the assassin of President McKinley.

That Bercovici moved frequently from one job to another may have been a common experience for immigrants in New York; Willemse also went from one poorly paid job to another before he became a policeman.

Mary Simkhovitch's perception of life on the Lower East Side confirmed some of Bercovici's views. They were both in agreement about the filth of the neighborhood. She was especially disturbed by the wretched quality of housing for the poor, and her book has many references to dumbbell and railroad tenements in New York City. As noted earlier, Simkhovitch and Bercovici disagreed about the consequences of the immigrant experience. Bercovici asserted that most newcomers were destined to fail, and Simkhovitch wrote that many of New York's professional and official elite came from the very buildings she deplored—views, incidentally, that may both be correct.

The presence of solidary communities in New York, including a stable middle-class neighborhood in Greenwich Village was the main theme of Simkhovitch's book. She explained its presence largely by the absence of main roads running through the Village. Conversely, the "decline of community"—a central theme in twentieth-century sociology—was, in part, a result of the introduction of modern transportation facilities. Sociologists have long asserted that the decline of community resulted from the processes of urbanization and industrialization, but they have tended to reify these concepts and the detailed way that they resulted in change has not been empirically specified.[10] Simkhovitch's view was that the extension of Sixth Avenue southward, the building of Seventh Avenue, the completion of the subway and the Hudson tubes, and, above all, the popularity of the auto-mobile seriously threatened the neighborhood by making it easier for strangers to invade Greenwich Village and for residents to evade community controls.

A glimpse into the values of those associated with Greenwich House is made possible in Mrs. Simkhovitch's account of the attempt to "wipe out" the Minettas. The reasons for eliminating these streets are never explicit, but it is clear that the officers of Greenwich House, including Mary Simkh-ovitch, objected to the kinds of people who lived there, their moral stand-ards, and their style of life, for she described "notorious characters," "certain houses," "tough saloons," and a "cadet club." The rights of the leaders of the settlement house to get rid of the streets, and to build on them tenements that would be owned by a member of the board of directors, were taken for granted.

What strikes the reader of Willemse's narrative is the continuity in pat-terns of behavior that have been associated with New York City. In the Dutch boy's view, and later in the policeman's, New York was always a place where anything goes: from the traffic in women, on the Bowery and elsewhere, to the wide-open vice of the Tenderloin. Indeed, Willemse believed that illicit activities were more widespread when he was a young cop in 1900 than when he wrote his recollections in 1933. The persistence of patterns could also be seen in the interracial and interethnic conflict, in police corruption, in police brutality (although this is not how Willemse would have defined it), the existence of warring street gangs, and even the huge rat population.

Willemse, along with Mary Simkhovitch, described the Minettas as a difficult neighborhood, and he helped spread stereotypes that have also lasted—Italians with stilettos and Blacks with razors. He, too, noticed the process of succession as Blacks vacated the area of the Mercer Street Station and Italians took their place. His view that, among the Italians, "riff-raff" ran the district is probably close to Bercovici's notion of the power of the Mafia among that ethnic group.

Finally, Willemse noted the relationship between the introduction of the department store and the appearance of respectable women downtown. Prior to the coming of the large emporium, women shopped in small stores in local neighborhoods, and there was no reason for them to go elsewhere. What opened the central business district to reputable women was this shopping innovation.

Joseph Clarke's account affords a unique opportunity to reconstruct certain aspects of life that are regarded as being indispensable for a true city, that is, the presence of institutions of culture, especially the playhouse and the concert hall. That the *New York Herald* already had a drama and music critic is a measure of the importance of performances, and Clarke's reviews revealed the wide range of theater and music available as well as the names of prominent singers and actors. That New Yorkers were sophisticated judges of the performing arts was a reputation early established in the cultural history of the city. The *New York Journal's* sponsorship of free concerts for the public makes that custom an old city tradition—even the name of the conductor Franko has endured in that connection—and further supports the idea of continuity in the history of New York.

Finally, Clarke's encounter with Thomas Edison is interesting in its own right—that the genius could not solve every technical problem is almost reassuring—and it also establishes that New York City of that era was a very noisy place, thanks, at least partly, to the elevated trains.

Cornelius Vanderbilt, Jr., revealed what it was like to be a boy among New York's aristocracy of wealth. He was insulated from the city; his social world was the family's mansion on Fifth Avenue, the house in Newport, the yacht, and other places where the very rich got together. The boy's recollection of the panic that followed McKinley's assassination rounded out the autobiographical reports of this event. The retreat from Newport suggests that the Vanderbilt family was afraid of impending radical change in the United States and feared that a "whole epoch" was threatened. One of the things that would be lost in the new era was the "partnership of Fifth Avenue dowagers and iron-hearted political bosses." That intriguing statement implied that there was a political connection between the matrons of the monied classes and the city bosses, but the nature of the relationship is not discussed further.

Finally, although the boy's isolation was such that a trip to the candy store on 43rd Street was the "real fun" of childhood, nevertheless, he could not have been completely removed from "the awful boys" since he did know what they were saying about his family.

Through the examination of these five works, I have tried to show the possibilities of using autobiographies in sociological analysis and to provide a plausible description of aspects of living in New York City between 1880 and 1914. The method has limitations, and a sample of five is admittedly small. Yet many features of New York were illuminated, and it is likely that a wider sample would enrich the account. That would help fill the gaps in the present study and might answer such questions as what it was like to live in other neighborhoods in New York, particularly in the other boroughs, what the black experience was, and so on. A full-length work with a large sample could combine the advantages of quantitative and qualitative analysis.

It is common to criticize sociology by saying that the field has become too dependent on social surveys for its observations and is not imaginative enough to broaden its sources of information. The use of large numbers of autobiographies as discussed here is a promising possibility, which does not, incidentally, rule out the construction of a questionnaire to be applied to each autobiography. Having a set of specific questions in advance would guard against the dangers of post-factum analysis. Obviously, the potential scope of such studies is broad. Such surveys could be applied to many topics, from urban sociology to the sociology of the family, socialization, race and ethnicity, work and occupations, and others. Best of all, perhaps, the problem of the cooperation of respondents is solved before one starts the research. Indeed, as the Kaplan bibliography makes certain, there are at least 6,377 respondents waiting to be interviewed.

NOTES

1. Louis Kaplan, *A Bibliography of American Autobiographies* (Madison: Univ. of Wisconsin Press, 1962).
2. Edward Robb Ellis, *Epic of New York* (New York: Coward-McCann, 1966), p. 458.
3. Ibid.
4. Konrad Bercovici, *It's the Gypsy in Me* (New York: Prentice-Hall, 1941).
5. Mary Kingsbury Simkhovitch, *Neighborhood: My Story of Greenwich House* (New York: Norton, 1938).
6. Cornelius W. Willemse, *Behind the Green Lights* (New York: Knopf, 1931).
7. Cornelius Vanderbilt, *Farewell to Fifth Avenue* (New York: Simon & Schuster, 1935).
8. Joseph I. C. Clarke, *My Life and Memories* (New York: Dodd, Mead, 1925).
9. *New York Times*, 14, 18 Aug. 1900.
10. On this point see Philip Abrams, "The Sense of the Past and the Origins of Sociology," *Past and Present*, no. 55 (May 1972).

ACKNOWLEDGMENTS

I am grateful to Sylvia Fava for her encouragement, to Oscar Glantz for his considerable help in compiling the list of autobiographies, and to Mark Aronson for his helpful criticism.

2

A Children's New York: Boys at Play in Yorkville

GERALD HANDEL

METHODOLOGICAL NOTE • This study is a portrait of New York, and more specifically of Yorkville, a neighborhood on the Upper East Side of Manhattan, as it was perceived, experienced, and indeed constructed by some working-class boys who lived there in the first half of the twentieth century. Most of them still lived there as grown men, and the materials for this portrait are taken from life histories collected from them by the author between December 1973, and March 1975. These dozen men ranged in age from thirty-eight to seventy when I interviewed them. This chapter is part of a larger study that will seek to analyze their lives. The portrait presented here can be considered an instance of retrospective ethnography; it delineates a pattern of social relationships that prevailed in a particular subculture in New York City.

My effort has been to combine the perspectives of child development and urban sociology, in order to show how children form particular motivations and cognitive outlooks, shaped by the actual circumstances in which they live. The developing child becomes a particular kind of person by participating in social relationships that have a characteristic structure—a set of shared expectations, constructed through interaction that is constrained by prevailing cultural values and norms.

This chapter concerns the social relationships of the street. Age, ethnic group membership, location of residence, and school attended were the social tags that were worked and reworked into diverse patterns of support and rivalry among Yorkville youngsters. Relationships between children and adults on the street appear to have had a developmental significance for the children that is less apparent in the last quarter of the twentieth century.

Before a boy finds his path in life he must find his way around his own neighborhood. As he learns his way, he discovers that the setting in which he is located is not merely a place, but is a meaningfully organized and differentiated world. Buildings, streets, and people fuse into an organization, partly given, partly constructed from his own developing activities. He discovers that streets are not equivalent, even when parallel; some are routes to destinations, whereas some count for nothing. There are buildings to seek, and others to avoid. Lives can be partially contiguous, yet worlds apart. The same geographic locale can be a different neighborhood to its every resident, for no two people learn and know it in exactly the same way. At the same time, some aspects of the neighborhood are "given"; these, too, contribute to the neighborhood's character and to a shared experience of it by its residents.

In the two decades or so before World War II, the period when most of the men included in this study were growing up, Yorkville had a combination of urban and small-town characteristics, a quality that continues even today, though much attenuated and reduced. The portrait in this chapter is drawn entirely from the recollections of the men.

Yorkville was a separate, distinctive neighborhood, but it was not isolated from the city. Subway and trolley-car lines traversed the neighborhood, running southward to midtown and lower Manhattan, northward to Italian and Spanish East Harlem, Harlem, and The Bronx. Housing was mostly urban tenement—three to six stories high and built wall to wall, with little open space on the residential blocks. Around the perimeter were higher buildings where "the rich people" lived—along York and East End avenues on the east, along Park Avenue on the west, and along 89th Street between East End and York on the north. Yorkville was a neighborhood where poor boys could have sporadic contact with the lifeways of the well-to-do—"the rich," as they thought of them—and certain kinds of contact with "the rich" themselves. Stores and small businesses were lined up along the avenues and thus were in immediate proximity to the residential buildings. Interspersed among the tenements and stores were various service and industrial installations that stand out in the remembered cityscapes: Consolidated Edison Company gas-storage tanks; coal yards; a trolley-car barn; the breweries, Ehret's and Ruppert's; a brickyard; and various small factories: a cigar factory, a slipper factory, an ironworks. On the East River, at the edge of the neighborhood, was the ferry to Astoria and Long Island City, industrial and working-class residential areas in the Borough of Queens.

The neighborhood is remembered by these men as an ethnic meeting ground, with a more-or-less orderly dispersion of ethnic groups: Bohemians concentrated in the East 70s; Germans in the lower 80s; and Irish in the upper 80s and lower 90s, with some spillover above 96th Street. But from 96th Street north the area was partly Spanish Harlem and partly Italian

Harlem. Eighty-sixth Street is remembered for its concentration of movie houses and German restaurants and beer halls. At the edge of the river is Carl Schurz Park, the scene of some childhood and teen-age excursions, and, at the northern edge of the park, Gracie Mansion, official residence of New York mayors since the incumbency of Mayor Fiorello H. La Guardia. Some of the men remember the building before it became the mayor's residence, when it housed the Museum of the City of New York, and, in that public capacity, provided the lavatories used by boys playing in the park.

In the midst of this urban concentration—with its polyglot ethnicity, its urban railways underground and above ground, its tenement houses interspersed with coalyards, breweries, brickyards, small factories, docks and ferry boats, trolley-car barn and taxi garage, its churches specialized by ethnicity and class (Our Lady of Good Counsel for working-class Irish; St. Joseph's for German-speaking communicants; St. Ignatius on Park Avenue and 84th for well-to-do Irish and others)—some other elements might have been left over from small-town life. Young boys ran errands for elderly neighbors. Apartment doors were left unlocked. The telephone in the candy store was a neighborhood communication center, since most tenement dwellers did not have telephones; calls came to the store, and the owner would dispatch whatever boy was on hand to summon the call's recipient from a nearby apartment. Neighborhood residents turned out for locally organized street festivities. There was a sense of living in a locally organized world, with community relationships that were sustained in various ways across age and generation lines.

The business of children is play, and these men recall their play activities with greater detail and elaboration than they recall their schooling. Yorkville is remembered as a neighborhood rich with opportunities for amusement. As one man tells of his childhood in the thirties:

> *Oh, it was great home. There was no TV. We used to sit around and watch the old magic eye of the radio, if you were allowed to, if the bill was paid for the electric in them days. And when there was snow out, we went down the street—that's when you consider, snow was snow in them days. You didn't have to worry about cars, or when it snowed it was there for a month, not for a day or two, and we used to have a lot of fun: take your sled down (which, if you had one, you were pretty fortunate), and play around the neighborhood. Like I say, there was no traffic in them days. And you know, you never invited the kids up, you never heard of . . . [that] in them days. Everybody used to meet in the middle of the street, and it was a lot of fun, then. And in the summer time you were sent down to the street, you sat on the stoop, and you played games on the stoop . . . four corners maybe, when you were a kid, or something like that there, hot beans. Then again there was no traffic, so the street was wide open. It was one massive playground, New York City in them days.*

The playground that was New York was created out of the particular conjunction of land, water, people, buildings, and transportation that gave Yorkville its special urban character. Children appropriated the streets and turned them to their own uses. Sewer covers, seen with children's eyes, revealed a versatility unimaginable to their designers. They served as the ring for games of marbles; as goals for hockey played on roller skates; and as bases for stickball, a version of baseball invented in the streets of New York, played with a broom handle for a bat and a rubber ball known as a "spaldeen." The distance between sewer covers became a measure of excellence: "Like in stickball, if you could hit it three sewers, it was great."

Stickball was illegal, though nearly universal, and on some streets the police walking their beat posed a frequent threat. If they came near enough in time, they would confiscate the stick. When the cops were spotted soon enough, the sewers themselves were pressed into service, and thus was born the art of stashing a stick in a sewer in such a way that it could be retrieved and used again when the uniformed adversaries had passed. A treasured recollection for one of the men is the occasion when Mayor La Guardia wandered by on one of his walks and sat down on a stoop to watch the stickball game in progress. When the cops came by on their usual beat, they could not exercise their usual authority since it had been superseded by the mayor's interest. This was a singular occasion, which the boys in that game, using the logic of case law (or of miracles), tried to transform into a precedent. The police on the beat refused, however, to accept the mayor's observed interest on one occasion as evidence of an ongoing blessing; they reasserted their customary authority, and thus kept alive one of their own street games in the New York playground.

The streets supplied the basic organizing principle of what may be called the children's ecology of Yorkville, the specialized patterns of interrelationship between people and their environment. But the other man-made and natural features of the area were also utilized. The tenement buildings provided not only homes for the boys. Their cellars were workshops for making things and, later, during adolescence, for early heterosexual explorations and for experiments in drinking. Their roofs served as escape routes in games that required escaping detection or capture. For boys living in modest walk-up buildings, the elevators in nearby middle- and upper-income buildings became transportation for luxury joyriding, until the apartment house doorman or superintendent discovered the irregular ups and downs and expelled the intruders.

The East River provided the primary water playground for Yorkville boys. Most of them learned to swim there, sometimes against their parents' wishes, but supported in their efforts by "the big guys," older boys who provided instruction, encouragement, and, sometimes, lifesaving assistance. A man now in his mid-sixties recalls:

*When the summer used to go by, we had our big swimming things and every-
thing, and you would learn to swim. We had two basins down there, one on
80th Street and one on 81st Street, two natural basins, and they were surrounded by rocks on each side. We learned how to dog-paddle there. Then
when we were old enough and we had our first dog-paddle swim, we were
taught overhand and underhand. Then when the big guys thought we were
smart enough, they took us up on the dock. There was a manhole there, water
sewage. Now, this wasn't very healthy, but we didn't mind it. We were told,
they got out there and formed a circle and their first instruction was, "Don't
be afraid. We are here. You know what you are doing, so don't be afraid."
So we'd jump off the dock, our initiation of becoming a swimmer. Then—they
were always there—and then they brought us in to the dock landing. We'd
get up, and if you were brave enough, you did it again. Then you were one
of the fellows, you were a champ. But nobody was ever frightened, and so
one day I went off the dock and there was this here new Hungarian boy in
the neighborhood. He had just come over from Europe a little while before,
and I guess he practically didn't understand this method. There was no such
thing as pulling on a fellow's leg and pulling him under. If you wanted to
jostle around a bit, you'd splash water on a fellow's face, or you'd yell at him,
you might say, "Hey, you mick," or "You guinea" or something, but it wasn't
a feeling of badness; it was a feeling of joking around. There was no illness
of any feeling, no name calling. Oh, name calling was there, but it was a
different thing. But today when somebody calls somebody something, they
really mean it. This here was a pal sort of stuff. And this here fellow jumped
in, and, unaware, he caught my leg and brought me down, and he held me
down, and it frightened me. When I came up I was gasping for air and I lost
my sense of balance. I forgot to remember what they had told me. My brother
had seen him do it. My brother immediately jumped in and he pulled me
ashore; then about four guys went in after this guy. They went in after him
and they gave him a ducking which he never forgot about. Then they brought
him up, and they told him, "Don't ever scare a kid." And he remembered that,
I guess, for a looong, loooong time.*

The big guys set the rules and regulated life at the waterfront and, as I
shall have occasion to note in other contexts, also governed various aspects
of youthful street life.

George Flynn, now seventy, recalls a lifeguard on the dock at 91st Street
during his childhood, the years ending about 1920. Larry McGuire, now in
his mid-fifties, who learned to swim in the same general area of the river,
describes it as essentially unfit to swim in, an unlikely spot for a lifeguard:

*We used to go swimming in the East River. I was about seven years of age,
and at 93rd Street and First Avenue, by the East River, there had been a
barge loaded with lumber. It was a favorite spot for the fellows from the
neighborhood to be swimming in, especially the younger fellows. We used to
call down 93rd and 92nd Street "bare-ass beach." It was very dirty. There*

was nothing there but filth from the sewer. There was a sewer going into the river from 92nd Street right next to where the ferry slip had been, the 92nd Street ferry, and at high tide, all the garbage would come in. Whenever we went swimming we just had to push that out of the way. Many times you'd see rats floating around. On one occasion I remember a pig. He probably came from the slaughter house down around 44th Street where the UN is now . . . And around that area there was jutted rocks, there was glass, and it was unbearable to think what we went through and yet survived.

For all its filth, the East River was nonetheless also a place to go fishing, and there were evidently fish to be caught in it. For variety, a trip to the West Side to fish in the Hudson River provided a day's outing. These excursions reveal, at least on one man's recollection of the early years of this century, a kind of patronage relationship that seems less probable in today's social climate:

If the tide got too low, we could always do some fishing, and one of the best things to fish for in those days were large eels. If that didn't satisfy us, we could take a hitch through the 81st Street tunnel through Central Park and go over to the Hudson River. In the Hudson River the water was much deeper and nobody worried about low tide. You could swim all the time, and you could go fishing, too. It was quite a ways from the East River to the Hudson River, and naturally, being rather young, you got hungry. Well, we had a solution for that, too. On 77th Street on the Hudson River we had the New York Yacht Club. If we would take a walk down to the New York Yacht Club, we would always go in there and say, "Hey, mister, we are hungry," and we were always lucky in getting a sandwich. If we got chased from there, we'd go along the river, and we'd generally run across a tugboat that was tied up somewhere. The tugboats always had a nice kitchen, and we'd go up to them, and if we were very nice and had a nice smile and a nice way and we said "Please," we'd always get something to eat there, too.

Such ready patronage by strangers does not appear in the recollections of the men younger than seventy, but whether this is due to individual differences in experience or to a historical change in standards of approachability cannot be determined from the information at hand.

Other emergency aid was also forthcoming, as Frank Schmidt recalls:

We used to swim over to Welfare Island, which is Franklin D. Roosevelt Island today, and we used to swim over B.A. I don't know if you know what that means. The B.A. means—we used to say—"bare-assed," and we used to swim over there and we used to swim back. Sometimes we used to find our clothes stolen. Somebody had picked them up. Well, we had a lot of tug boats and barges along the East River, and they used to lend us clothes to get home.

There was, then, some easiness in the relationships between boys and men. When necessary for a stickball game, boys might ask a man to move his car, if it stood in the way, and it would often be done. Food could be cadged from strangers, and, in an emergency, even clothes.

This was not, however, the whole story of relationships between men and boys. At least as significant is the array of adversary relationships sustained in the neighborhood. The police as stickball adversaries have already been mentioned. More than one of the men recalls being whacked on the backside by police using their nightsticks, whether for turning on fire hydrants or simply for congregating in the policeman's path. There are recollections of "good cops" who left kids alone, but there is also a recollected wariness stemming from youthful purposes that were unacceptable to the peacekeepers of the streets.

Perhaps the most important adversaries were certain neighborhood shopkeepers, chosen either for the goods they sold, or for their ethnicity, or both. Virtually every one of the men interviewed recalls cooking "sweet mickies" in the street—potatoes cooked in a tin can. And much as the old recipe for rabbit stew begins, "Catch one rabbit," so the recipe for making sweet mickies might well begin with, "Swipe one potato." There were various strategies for accomplishing this. Terry Doherty recalls:

> . . . *[W]e had our ways of getting mickies. We would go to one of these Jewish delicatessens and would walk in and say, "Can we have a can of Spanish olives." He'd say, "Spanish olives I haven't got." We'd say, "Oh, yes, you've got them, way up on the top shelf." So he'd look for Spanish olives and in the meantime we'd dig into the pickle barrel or the potatoes or canned goods that were standing around, and then run like hell. That was the way we did in our day. As we say, we didn't mean to do it, but we figured we weren't harming anybody—he was a rich man. But we did it. Then we blessed ourselves and asked God to forgive us.*

George Flynn recalls a different strategy:

> *When we swiped potatoes we also had an art of potato swiping. We used to have a long stick, and on the end of the stick we had a nail, and you held that stick down close to the ground and you'd look inside at the fellow, and you'd be sticking the nail into a potato, and then you'd put it behind your back, and you'd turn this way and walk away and you'd have your potato. It really wasn't an art [laughs], but still and all that was part of the game, too, you know—how you stole the potato, the finesse involved [laughs heartily]. In those days it wasn't such a big crime to steal a potato because they were so cheap, you know. Apples was another story. I don't know whether I ever stole apples, because with me potatoes was my thing. I liked potatoes. In fact, I still like them.*

George Flynn's comment indicates more explicitly than most that these boys in Yorkville sought, at times at least, to live artfully, to develop finesse in carrying out their purposes, and that their arts were more various than simply those needed to be skillful in games. Each activity is a context in which notions of excellence are created or emerge, and satisfaction comes not simply from engaging in the activity but from doing it well.

The adversary relationship with shopkeepers developed, in part, from youthful efforts to obtain merchandise according to a youthful set of rules, one that differed from the set followed by the merchant. The goal was thus twofold: to obtain a desired item and to obtain it in one's own way. There was satisfaction in outsmarting the merchant. Some played rougher games, in which the goal of harassing the merchant was more important than that of obtaining merchandise. Rudy Bauer is candid about his activities:

We had Jewish store owners that we used to harass. Maybe that's why their kids didn't hang out with us. They were probably told to stay away from us, because we were the way we were, not malicious, just, you know, like we wanted to kid around with them a bit. [Q: "How did you do that?"] There was a guy, Jewish guy, had the hardware store on Second Avenue, and he used to put his wares out in the street them days in boxes, and we used to run along, and I'd pick up the toilet paper and open it up without him seeing us, and maybe take two or three rolls, and we'd throw it in the store, roll it in, and the customers . . . it would be all over the place! Or open cans of turpentine in them days, or break brooms. Of course, we needed a stick to play stickball—we'd steal one, you know, when he wasn't looking, and burn the bottom off so we'd have a new stickball bat. Put the lights out in the store, lock the door (because in them days the doors used to open into it, if you were inside you had to pull the door towards you to get out). We used to put a stick in there, that no one could get out of the store, and there was no phones in them days. Not that there was none. There was very few, and sometimes the store didn't even have a phone on the inside to call somebody on the outside to help the poor guy out. He had to wait for somebody that knew him, or looked in the store, to open the door for him. Or we might knock over a couple of displays, nothing that would break the place up, just, you know, tell the guy, "You know you're fooling with us." Then we had another guy had a vegetable store, used to put everything outside, whatever you wanted you sampled. Not to put the man out of business; just to say, "Well, I did it to him today." . . . But you know, in the neighborhoods we got along. The Jewish store owners were good. The grocery guy, he used to buy us a couple of spaldeens, because if he didn't buy us spaldeens we'd get twenty guys to sit on the stoop. . . . The candy store, an Italian guy, we used to drive the poor guy crazy. He had no children. Good thing he didn't have no children 'cause he probably would have went bankrupt with us going in with the kid. We'd go in, bother him all day, you know, sit on the floor, run machinery, people coming in, they want a pack of cigarettes and they used to end up buying us all candy or we wouldn't let the guy out of the store or, you know,

make a mockery of him and all that there. . . . Every time you did something,
he'd grab you and beat you up, punch you, not enough to hurt you, just to
let you know that he still was the boss. Give you an egg, what do they call
it, a knuckle on the head. That used to hurt for about an hour. But again,
you never—when you walked out of the store it was all forgotten about. Then
like I say, ya never stolen it from the guy, like ya maybe took a piece of candy,
he got it back in some other way, you know. Another time you walk in there,
you had a quarter and bought three cents worth of candy, he'd take a nickel
out, and you were giving him a big argument, "You only gave me twenty cents
change." He'd say, "You forgot about last week when you took the other two
pieces, didn't you?" You know, you figure, "OK, you got me now," and you
steal two more pieces of candy, then next week he gets you all over again. You
know, it was like an open account with him, you know. If he knew you couldn't
afford it, then there'd be no problem. If you wanted a piece of candy, you
know, he'd put it on the counter and turn his back toward you.

In these life histories, whenever a shopkeeper is remembered as an adversary, his ethnicity is usually also remembered, and there is no instance in which the remembered ethnicity of the shopkeeper is the same as that of the man who remembers. No Irish or German shopkeepers are remembered as adversaries, and the Italian men in the group do not mention Italian shopkeepers.

Other working establishments in the neighborhood attracted youthful attention, and they were guarded by functionaries who, though occasionally defeated in carrying out their protectiveness over their domain, were more often effective. The watchman in a brickyard at 80th Street and the river would fling broken bricks at Terry Doherty and his friends when they tried to gain entrance. One of Larry McGuire's streetmates had an even harder time:

There was this kid named Dooley, and his brother had drowned at the 90th
Street dock. Well, this kid was stealing coal from the Burns Brothers yard at
93rd Street and 94th Street between the river and First Avenue. They had
barbed wire at the top of a fence. The watchman gave chase to this kid one
day as he was going over the wire, and his face got caught in it. He landed
in a pile of small peat coal—that is the smallest anthracite coal that we seen
around this area. He had to go the the hospital. I seen him a couple of years
later, and his face still had some of the blue coloring from the coal in his head.
It must have been like shrapnel. The doctors couldn't get all of it out. Needless
to say, he was named "Blue Lips."

The closeness of working establishments to the tenements in Yorkville contributed to a varied round of activities, in the course of which boys were frequently making forays and excursions into adult-governed spaces: to obtain some of the materials that were handled there; to challenge the rules and authority that excluded them; or to observe the activities that went on. From time to time, their excursions took them out of the neighborhood. Henry Lindenholz recalls a time in the late 1930s:

> When I was a boy maybe twelve, where the United Nations buildings are today, that was the old Wilson Meat Company, and a couple of friends and myself, we used to go down and watch them unload the barges with the sheep, and we used to watch the Judas goat, you know, walk and walk the sheep come off the boat. And sometimes we used to sneak in front of them and see where they tried to slaughter them. It was nice, and you stayed until you were chased. . . . Then there used to be barges, down a little further, I believe it was on 23rd Street or 24th Street. You'd just walk on. We took our chances. You went there, and if they were there, they chased you, the barge captain, or whatever they got, the watchman that lived on these barges. That was it, you played the game, and then they came and chased you, okay, you left, and that was the end of it, no tantalizing, you left.

The preferred method of traveling out of the neighborhood was by "hitching"—riding as a nonpaying customer on the rear of a trolley car or bus or as an uninvited guest on the tailgate of a truck or the bumper of a car. All forms of public and private transportation were assessed for the footholds, handholds, and exterior seating that they afforded the unofficial traveler. On occasions when street transportation proved too limited for traveling the desired distances, the elevated railway and the subway would be used, the technique of entry being to sneak beneath the turnstile and dash onto the train just before the door would shut. Occasionally, when some cash was available, a Yorkville boy might pay his way for a ride on the open top deck of a double-decker Fifth Avenue bus. Seeing New York City was one of the amusements for Yorkville boys of those days; hitching rides for the fun of hitching, if only for three or four blocks, was another. And sometimes the two amusements were fused into one activity, for half a day's or even a day's adventures. On a rare occasion there might be a longer trip: a one-day excursion on the Hudson River Day Line, or a boat trip from 42nd Street up the Hudson to Bear Mountain near West Point and back.

The social ecology of Yorkville gave boys growing up there a certain diversity of experience. They became aware early of diverse ethnicity. They challenged adult rules in their efforts to learn about and enjoy some of the materials and the spaces that adults managed and stood guard over. They often developed boldness in learning to use those materials and spaces according to ways they devised for themselves. And from time to time they had a glimpse of the world of the well-to-do, which was to be found mainly on the perimeter of their neighborhood. In some cases, jobs as delivery boys or selling magazines brought them briefly into dwellings where people lived more substantially than they were accustomed to seeing. A few whose residences were in the side-street tenements but whose location nonetheless placed them in the St. Ignatius parish, attended the parish school of this Park Avenue church and thus were cast into more prolonged contact with children from well-to-do and even wealthy families. Richard Ryan recalls some of his impressions:

When I was about [seven years old] we moved to 84th Street between Second and Third Avenues. We lived there in a furnished apartment until I was about nine years old . . . . . my mother enrolled me in St. Ignatius, which is on 84th Street and Park Avenue, and I guess I was in the third grade when I started in there. . . . That was a very good school and I have very pleasant memories of St. Ignatius. It still is. We moved to 90th Street between First and Second Avenues and I continued. I guess we moved when I was about in the fifth grade, and I continued going to St. Ignatius even though I was out of the parish, because I had started there. . . . I remember a number of birthday parties and Christmas parties that my friend Jimmy and I went to with some of our classmates up on Park Avenue and around there, and it was always a little disappointing to have to come home to Second Avenue after being at a party up on Park Avenue with some of our classmates. But they were nice kids also, and it was all part of growing up, I guess. I still remember being in some of their houses and having my breath taken away walking in the door and finding paintings on the walls. In fact, one fellow, the Signorinis, they had statues on pedestals in the corners and everything else, and it was like walking onto a movie set. I really didn't think that people had that much money at that point.

He remembers his class as being about equally divided between children from Park and Lexington avenues, whose families had money, and those from Second and Third avenues, whose families did not. While there may have been "minicliques," he recalls that mostly everyone got along "great," with little friction. In addition to remembering the school as good, he believes that he had a good experience in going to school with a "cross-section" of children.

With one or two exceptions, the men in this study recall their childhoods as having been financially impoverished. While they sometimes remember the anger they felt when they could not have even a small coin at a particular moment, their recollections are as likely to be of the stoicism or adaptiveness with which they coped with the deprivation. Larry McGuire finds some pride in contrasting today's youngsters with himself as a child:

We used to go to 84th Street and 85th Street on Madison Avenue and eat our hearts out. That store had the best collection of toys in Yorkville. We could stand there an hour or more discussing the games, toys, and other objects we witnessed on display. About four times a year we would walk up there hoping

*to see something different. I believe the name of the store was Schoenfield's.
It is not there any more.*

This remembrance occurred in the fourth interview. A month before, early
in the first interview, he had said:

*Well, as I got older, it often brings back memories of me and my younger
friends, of what we went through as far as living conditions and the little that
we did have around the area. . . . When I read of these children today who
are going around and using all kinds of alibis for the crimes that they commit,
the luck that they've had in life, I don't feel too sorry for them. My friends
and myself, we could have taken our vengeance out and went up to Park
Avenue and such areas and robbed and tried to loot their homes, but this
would never be. It was just not the way we were brought up. We just took
everything all in stride, the way it was going to come: it had to be. And in the
long run, none of us have police records, and we stayed out of trouble, mainly
to keep activated with the little bit that we had in life and making it our duty
to accept it as nothing else but the consent we had to bear.*

"The consent we had to bear." It would be hard to imagine an expression
that captures so compactly and so vividly the ongoing work that is necessary
to accept deprivation when lavishness is so near. The ambivalence of Larry
McGuire's consent is plain enough, but so also is his pride. Perhaps there
is envy, too, of "these children today" who do not accept little and who feel
free not to consent, but along with this is pride in his ability to endure.
Larry McGuire has had many experiences in the forty or more years since
he took those walks to Madison Avenue, but his memories of Schoenfield's
continue to provide him with work for his lifetime. All his years as a construction worker and tough union fighter do not prevent him from remembering the consent he had to bear—the acceptance of deprivation he felt he
had to endure—or from comparing it with the alibis of today's children.

Deprivation and fun are interwoven as themes in the childhood remembrances of these men. Money was very short, toys and play equipment
very scarce. Yet, things to do were not scarce, nor were good places to do
them. One of the remembered aspects of Yorkville that fostered some attachment to it were various neighborhood festivities, usually organized by
the politicians of the Democratic party in the local district. "June walks" in
Central Park were enjoyed by some, as were parades on various occasions.
Most widely remembered, however, are street bonfires on election nights.
These enlisted wide participation, as boys roamed the neighborhood scav-
enging wood for the fires. This activity became an opportunity for more than
one kind of enjoyment. Rudy Bauer recalls:

*But there was never no big scrapes with the cops, never. The only time we
had our trouble with the cops was, every year—well, I wasn't too young, but
growing up, watching the older fellows, the old election fires on election eve.*

It was election night, actually, and the polls would just about be closed, and they'd always have a big bonfire. That's probably an old tradition, many, many years ago that was carried on, just out in the middle of the street. The cops used to come and say, "Were you involved in the fire?" and you'd swear up and down, "No," and you stunk of all kinds of smoke—you know, all day collecting wood, stealing wood, and everything like that. But that was the biggest hassle with the cops. They would come, the Fire Department would come and put the hose on the fire. You'd wait maybe half an hour. The truck would go to 94th or 95th to put out their fire, and by the time they made ten blocks, they'd start all over again, because everybody would start putting the fires back on again. This would go on till maybe eleven o'clock at night.

George Flynn remembers the fires as an occasion when the older boys asserted some authority over the younger:

And then, of course, there was the big election fires. Even no matter how small you was, you were told by the older boys, "You have to get your license if you want to stay there and watch the fires." So you'd go all around the neighborhood, and maybe you'd find an orange box or an apple box or a basket or something made of wood, and you'd bring it up, and that was for the big election fire. When you got something, they said, "Okay, it's all right, he's got a license, he can stay and watch the fire." Of course they couldn't chase us anyhow, but that was the story and you were young and you believed it.

Terry Doherty, some twenty years older than Rudy Bauer and a few years younger than George Flynn, recalls the bonfires in the context of antagonism between street gangs of his teenage years:

Now, on 81st Street, there was a big fellow; he worked for the Sanitation. He had one of the most ugliest faces, but one of the most beautiful hearts. His name was called Pieface. Now, this other leader, Mike Flaherty, was a fighter. They were the two natural leaders of the gangs. We were called the 81st. During election years we used to go down to rob their lumber for our election fire, which was held in the middle of the street on election nights—a tremendous bonfire with a great load of wood and what-have-you . . . old furniture. But these here were happy days as we called them, looking out for the war between the 81sts and the 75ths . . . and after the bonfire a big hole with ashes for the Fire Department, which at that time was run by teams of beautiful white horses, stallions, and the old smoke pot coming down the road was a beautiful sight to see, with these here four horses drawing the engine behind them and the firemen getting off with the hoses that you had in those days, no pressure hoses, a big hose hooked up to the pump, and away on their duty, and they were brilliant.

Not all of Yorkville's politics was local politics. As one of the areas of heaviest German concentration in New York, Yorkville received direct repercussions from international politics. George Flynn's boyhood encompassed the years of World War I, and he has one vivid recollection of that period:

> This is something I've never forgotten. On 89th Street and Second Avenue—
> that's the northeast corner—there is two houses there. They got gables on the
> roof; you know, for decorative purposes, that's all they serve. During World
> War I, one of these buildings, over the doorway going into the house was the
> name "WILHELM." That was Kaiser Wilhelm. Now, on the other building—
> that's the same building—there was in stone (this was in stone, you know),
> "BERLIN." Now I remember as a kid, when we had nothing to do we'd go
> down and watch the people parading back and forth in front of this building
> and hollering at the people that lived in the building. I never knew—I thought
> later on that it's possible that maybe they are Irish. But the people were afraid
> to come in and out.

The majority of the men in the group studied were growing up or had reached young manhood during the period preceding World War II, when again the Germanness of Yorkville resulted in a somewhat unique neighborhood involvement in international politics, and so there are more recollections from that period than from the World War I period. The activities of Nazi sympathizers in the neighborhood affected even children's evaluations of their own situations. For example, as has been previously noted, St. Joseph's parish and school were oriented to the German Catholic community, while Our Lady of Good Counsel, four blocks away, was predominantly Irish Catholic. Buster Doran, who lived midway between the two schools and churches, recalls the ways in which the ordinary teasing of children who attend rival schools took on a special cast:

> So that was a thing, too, that, "Oh, you go to the Old Ladies Gossip Club."
> You see, Our Lady of Good Counsel, O.L.G.C., was called the "Old Ladies
> Gossip Club," because we were the only family in the whole block that went
> to that school and to the church. Everybody else went to St. Joseph's. That
> was a constant thing between us as kids. We were always sticking up for Our
> Lady of Good Counsel and we were always saying to them, "Oh, you Hitler
> boys, that's all you do, you learn your German for Hitler **und die Bund**." And
> we'd always go back and forth on that.

When political events occur on a street level, they are not always understood right away by young boys with other things on their minds. Rudy Bauer, talking about the ethnic makeup of the different blocks in his neighborhood, recalls a dramatic incident:

> Eighty-sixth Street was strictly all German, you know. They used to call it the
> **Bund** and everything. The Yorkville Casino, they used to claim they had the
> Nazi rallies in there during the war and all that there, and then Hans Jaeger's

on 85th was—that was closed down during the war. The government closed that because of subversive actions they were caught doing up there.

Q: *Did you ever see any of those **Bund** activities?*

A: *I seen it once at 93rd Street when Fritz Kahn [sic] at that time was reputed big boss. They raided a house up there, 326, and they brought up more contraband, radios and short-wave sets. They were teaching the kids on Sundays how to send messages back to Germany. And they made a big raid then. They sealed off the whole street. We thought they were coming after us for playing stickball, you know, the cops.*

Q: *How old were you at that time?*

A: *Quite young, fourteen maybe. You know, before I went to the service. The war was still on. I was thirteen or fourteen at the time. And the cops came from all over. You couldn't find another spot to park another police car. And they brought all these young kids out. They were probably about fifteen or sixteen. They were teaching them to be teletype operators, to send messages back and forth to, you know, Germany about movements over here or ships going in and out.*

Episodes of this kind occurred infrequently, but they dramatized a tension in the neighborhood that was felt more pervasively. Asked how his own family felt about the *Bund*, Bauer reports:

Oh, my family was never involved. You know, they didn't care. But I knew the—my father didn't like it because of the boys being, you know, my brothers being in the service, and him being a big deal in the veterans, like we always had the stars in the window, and he used to get in many a brawl in the ginmills where he served. You know, one guy standing up there and saying that Hitler had the right thought and this and that. There'd be a big fist fight and he come in a few times with a cut on his face or a bloody nose, and say what happened—"Ah, that Nazi son-of-a-gun started knocking our country."

For Bauer, as for Buster Doran growing up a few blocks away, the Nazi regime in Germany provided ammunition for childhood antagonisms. He remembers calling neighborhood German people wearing European-style clothes "Nazis" and scrawling swastikas on the doors of their apartments. The Nazi period was defined by the interviewees who were then boys growing up in Yorkville as partly a political experience and partly just one more element in an array of adversary relationships on the street. Street life had a good deal of "us and them," and there were many categories of "them": the gang on the next block, the cops, the industrial watchmen, the kids who went to a different school, and, not least, the kids and adults of ethnic groups different from one's own. Any involvement of Yorkville people in Nazi activities—or even sympathy with them—was experienced by these boys as not fitting with what should be, as they now report.

Working-class boys growing up in Yorkville recall their neighborhood as one with a great deal of vitality. Their experience encompassed bar brawls and street festivities; street games near home and adventures in the river, in the parks, and in the neighborhood workyards; antagonisms with boys from different blocks and different ethnic groups, and alternating solidarities with them. Their street life involved them with adults both as sympathizers and as adversaries. They played with the edges of conformity to adult-established rules regarding property and its use. They lived close enough to rich people to learn early what they were doing without, and struggled to come to terms with the deprivation they felt. Almost all of them know boys they grew up with, whose life course included a period in jail for serious crime, and all of them felt that they could draw the line for themselves at petty pilfering, which they did not seem to define as crime. For all the hardship, all of these men regard Yorkville as a good neighborhood to have grown up in. They believe that there were material things that they should have had—not only toys and play equipment but better housing—but none gives evidence of having had, at any time in his life, a strong desire to leave the neighborhood. Some lived for brief periods in adulthood in other parts of New York City and later returned to Yorkville. Some had opportunities in life that would have required them to leave the neighborhood, but these opportunities were turned down. These men are atypical in that they continue to live, well into middle life and beyond, in the neighborhood in which they grew up. But they may not be so unusual in their effort to form an enduring attachment to a place, only unusual in that their effort has met with some success, and unusual in that the place is one that most of them have known from childhood. None of them seems to feel trapped in Yorkville, none has soured on it as a result of childhood experiences; however, some are beginning to withdraw their attachment as they see the boundary between Yorkville and Harlem become more blurred.

ACKNOWLEDGMENTS

This material was first presented at the Conference on Childhood in American Life, Center for American Studies, Indiana University–Purdue University at Indianapolis, 31 March–1 April 1978.

The chapter, a draft from a work in progress, is based on life histories which the author obtained from a dozen men of working-class background who have spent the greater part of their lives in Yorkville, a neighborhood on the East Side of Manhattan between 72nd and 96th streets. I am greatly indebted to Charles I. Katze, then executive director of the Stanley Isaacs Neighborhood Center, who introduced me to several of the men and also provided me with space where I could interview them in privacy in their own neighborhood.

Financial support for the project was provided by the Small Grants Branch of the National Institute of Mental Health, a City College "mini-grant," and a grant from the Institute on Pluralism and Group Identity. For their encouragement and stimulating comment as the project was getting under way, I am indebted to three members of the last-named organization, Irving M. Levine, director, and two of his then associates, Nancy Seifer and the late Judith Magid Herman.

The tape-recorded interviews were transcribed by the Oral History Research Office of Columbia University. I express my thanks to the office's associate director, Mrs. Elizabeth Mason, for her helpful comments.

3

Hiring Hall Community on the Brooklyn Waterfront

WILLIAM DIFAZIO

METHODOLOGICAL NOTE • When I began doing the ethnographic research necessary for this chapter, many of the men were suspicious of my presence in the hiring hall. Two of them threatened my life the first day, thinking that I was a cop. Over the following weeks, the men began to trust me, and eventually they allowed me to participate in their daily activities. I realized that I had passed all of their tests when they began to include me in their joking behavior. When Grippo knocked my hat off my head I knew that I was in.

My own experience in the daily lives of longshoremen preceded the initiation of this fieldwork. I have associated with longshoremen all of my life: my father, my grandfather, and three of my uncles were longshoremen in Brooklyn. My first participation in longshoremen affairs occurred in the 1954 wildcat strike. Both my father and uncle worked as longshoremen at the time. With them and my older brother and a cousin, I participated in my first strike and picketed management at the age of seven. At that age it was a great adventure, and the complications of union politics eluded me.

Now, during my regular visits to the Local 1814 union hall and the Brooklyn hiring hall I am accepted by the men as one of their own. I feel the same way, at least in terms of blood ties.

Because of my family background, I have often taken for granted the interactions of longshoremen among themselves. I am now continually involved in critically analyzing these interactions, which are so crucial to this study.

This chapter describes some of the changes that occur in the daily life of workers when they are separated from the workplace, and the issue treated herein is whether occupational community is possible for such workers. Specifically, what potentialities exist within the hiring hall for the maintenance of working-class community life for Brooklyn longshoremen on the guaranteed annual income?

The guaranteed annual income (GAI) came about as a result of the struggle of longshoremen against technological changes within the maritime industry. The GAI has been in effect since 1966. It originally guaranteed all longshoremen pay equivalent to 1,600 hours of work per year. In 1968 that was raised to 2,080 hours. Thus, as of 1980 all longshoremen working the port of New York-New Jersey have a GAI of $23,000 per year. The GAI enables longshoremen with high seniority who have been displaced from full-time work because of automation to work rarely and yet receive a full annual salary. These senior longshoremen receive income without the obligation to work.

Transformation in Hiring: From Shape-Up to Computer Hiring of Longshoremen

Dockwork in the New York-New Jersey port has been transformed from the shape-up of casual workers (part-time, periodic workers) at the various piers under the arbitrary despotism of the hiring boss to the rationalized Waterfront-Commission-governed computer hiring of a stable workforce of longshoremen.

The power of the hiring foreman under the shape-up was almost absolute. It was based on his assignment of jobs in a workforce in which workers always outnumbered jobs. The hiring foreman controlled the livelihoods of longshoremen; his power was frequently abused and was often based on nepotism, kickbacks, fear, and corruption.[1]

The men were not protected from the corruption of the shape-up by the union, which substantially benefited from the system. They have not forgotten the brutality and corruption of the shape-up.[2] Nor have they forgotten the nepotism of the foreman, who gave preference to relations, or to those who shopped at his uncle's fruit store, or to those who did him personal favors. Often, to get a job, they had to bribe him, or play his game (numbers), or patronize his "loan sharking."

Though hiring is no longer under the arbitrary control of the foreman the men's hate for the system is not dead. The following discussion between Bowley and Freddy in the hiring hall expresses their remembrances of the corruption of the shape-up:

Freddy: *Look, there's Pat. That's a bastard.*

Researcher: *Who is Pat?*

Freddy: *Pat was a hiring boss and a real bitch. If there were ten jobs, he would hire nine coloreds.*

Bowley: *He would lend money to the* **moulies** *[short for "*moulignons*"("eggplants"), the Italian longshoremen's nickname for Blacks]. And then he would be sure that they would work so he could make his money back. He had to hire the* **moulies** *if he was going to make a profit.*

Freddy: *That bastard would hire the worst workers to make sure he'd make a profit. One time he sends me a worker, he shows up late and there really is no work. I have him load twenty-five cases; he works slow but when he is finished he sits down. All the other men are working, and this nigger sits down. A big truck comes in and I tell him to unload it. He refuses. He tells me that he has worked already and now he's last on line for work. I tell him there's no fucking line, that he's the only guy that's not working and that he must do it. He refuses and I tell him to go home.*

A half hour later he comes back with Pat. He tells me that I got to put him back on, I tell him I won't. Pat tells me that if I don't he'll have trouble with the N.A.A.C.P. I tell him that "I sent him home, not you. If the N.A.A.C.P. comes to him, send them to me and I'll tell them what this guy did and they'll have to agree with me." I refused to put the guy back on, and Pat left angry.

I knew full well the N.A.A.C.P. wasn't going to come down. Pat couldn't give a fuck about the N.A.A.C.P. All he cared about was that this guy was hired for the day so that he could get his money back.

Bowley: *A lot of colored would borrow money from the hiring bosses even though they didn't need the money, because they knew that as long as they owed the hiring boss money they would always work. So they'd lose the interest on the loan, but they always knew they would work.*

As a result of rank-and-file actions and official investigations,[3] the men no longer shape-up at the piers and are no longer at the arbitrary disposal of the arrival and departure of ships.

With the implementation of the GAI, the closing of the register, and the computerization of hiring, work within the industry has been stabilized. The dog-eat-dog competition for work among the men has been transformed into relatively friendly relations within the hiring hall. Men who once fought with one another for jobs can now discuss the upcoming elections or yesterday's football game while relaxing with coffee and a buttered roll.

Where the shape-up maintained control over the men through force and corruption, the hiring hall as regulated by the Waterfront Commission maintains the workers' subordination to the shipping companies in a rational manner. With the guarantee of income independent of work, the former ferocious competition for jobs has disappeared, and there is a potential for workers' community in the hiring hall.

The Contradiction

Every workday, longshoremen who have not received orders to work a pier report to the 60th Street hiring hall to "badge-in" (the computerized registering of a worker's availability for work). Depending on the business of the New York-New Jersey port, the men will or will not find work for the day: because of the GAI, those who do not will still receive a day's wage. The men whom I studied rarely work: they have high seniority and their customary pier has been closed by automation. For thirty to forty hard-worked years, these men would work with their gang when their pier was busy; otherwise they would "shape" other piers (go from pier to pier looking for work). They worked seven days a week and averaged twenty hours in overtime a week. They started working before automation, before containerization. The work was hard and a longshoreman had to be tough and strong to do the work. They understood this and took pride in their work.

In the past, when they shaped-up at the piers or in the hiring hall, they would often fight one another for jobs. Now they worry about working and will "gamble on debits," i.e., take a chance on losing a day's pay rather than work.

Work offered them an identity and a shared occupational experience with a community of workers. This community was defined not only instrumentally—for the money—but culturally as well. The time they spent together often continued into the hours after work. They all tended to be Italian. They lived in the same neighborhood and attended the same churches, and their children attended the same schools. For the most part, they shared a similar biography.

Eventually, most of them moved out of the old neighborhood, and their sense of community came to depend almost totally on their shared work experience. For many of the men the GAI shut off this community. This sense of a loss of workers' community is lamented by Rudy:

> *My opinion on the guarantee is that I would have felt better if the pier had never closed down. It would have been better for us; we were in stride. We'd meet at the pier at six [A.M.]. We'd argue, say, "Hello, how are you"; by nine we'd be working. We were in stride.*

How long, and how many times, how many days can you wash the car? I hang out, but when I was working I had a place to go and things to do. We'd work, we'd argue, we'd play cards. I was with the boys all day. We knew what we were doing. Now there is no steadiness.

There is a crucial contradiction here between the men's claim that they miss working and their actual behavior in the hiring hall—which is tantamount to a refusal to work. The refusal to work is expressed in the following hiring-hall situation.

The situation is typical during the summer and Christmas vacation periods. At this busy port there is a lot of work during times when many men are on vacation. Thus, the senior men might have to go to work. The men are nervous in the hall; they know that they might have to work. Bill shouts, "This is a working day, men."

Earl, the manager of the hiring hall for the Waterfront Commission, begins the hiring. He starts with "A" and goes down to "G" men (from those with highest seniority to those with lowest seniority), and then begins again backwards, i.e., hiring in inverse order of seniority. If the men named refuse to take a job, they will be "debited" (penalized a day's pay), and, if they accumulate three debits in one year, they will be suspended from the GAI for one year.

Earl calls the "B" men and finally reaches the "A" men. "Last call for 'A' men."

There is a rush of men toward Earl. The men offer their computer cards to the dispatchers. The last jobs are taken, saving the rest of the men from being debited. The men left without work are happy. They begin to joke with one another, expecting to badge-out, when Earl's voice is heard again. "The badge-out will be delayed. We are awaiting orders from Port Newark."

The orders from Port Newark come in. There is a lot of work, and the war of nerves begins again with the "A" men. The inverse order of hiring begins from where Earl left off. "Third call for 'A' men."

No one moves. Earl is angry, "This is not a game. Don't give me this nip-and-tuck shit." The men are gambling that someone else will take a job and no one moves. Earl begins to count. "One. Two. Three. This is not a game. You guys seem to think this is a game. Okay, you've all got debits. That's it."

Some men rush up to take jobs. But Earl will have none of it. Earl walks away, fuming, as a crowd of men rush around him. Some of the men are arguing among themselves. Two men begin to shove each other. One hundred and fifty men have been debited.

No longer fighting for work, the longshoremen now gamble with debits for not working. This contradiction between the claim to want to work and the refusal to accept work when it is available is at the core of the culture of the hiring hall.

The Hiring Hall Today

The hiring hall is the place where a researcher can meet with the men in groups and on their own terms. The hiring hall is an important element in the working-class community life of Brooklyn longshoremen. For the men on the GAI who rarely work, it is the crucial element in their working-class community life. It is here that they meet face to face and recount their daily experiences and their understandings of the world around them.

It is in the hiring hall that the affiliations that were the result of shared work and neighborhood experience are maintained, now that work and neighborhood are no longer a part of the collective experience. The hiring hall is an enclave of working-class cultural life where the men now freely associate with a minimum of worker antagonism, which once resulted from the fierce competition for jobs.

When the weather is good, the men congregate both inside and outside of the hiring hall. Outside on the street there are longshoremen hawking merchandise out of the trunks of their cars. Guido and Bill sell hairbrushes, after-shave lotion, baby shampoo, and other toiletries. Other longshoremen offer work clothing, toys, and automotive items.

Pete and Salley are discussing union politics. Salley is very critical of Anthony Scotto. (Scotto, President of the Brooklyn local—1814 of the International Longshoremen's Association—was found guilty on Nov. 15, 1979, of racketeering, conspiracy, bribe taking, and tax evasion. He is serving time in Federal prison.) Pete counters with, "The union has been very good to us. Anthony has given us dignity."

There are men both inside and outside of the hall. They talk sports and gambling, they read and discuss the news reported in the *Daily News* and the *New York Times*. On Fridays, Tony Clean-Head, who takes numbers, comes to distribute the men's checks, a service for his customers. Gambling is an important activity, and there is much talk of numbers and horse playing throughout the hall.

Big Jim, who works steadily on 39th Street (at the time the only container operation in Brooklyn), is talking about how containerization has changed the waterfront. Salley and Charley, who work two or three days a week, are talking about problems in the Canadian maritime industry that are affecting work on their pier. The men on the GAI are concerned with the amount of shipping in the port, because it has a vital effect on the maintenance of their status. Red and Bowley are discussing their grandchildren. A thick wad of paper bounces off Bowley's head, and, as both men turn in the direction from which the paper was thrown, Jerry pokes Red in the back. Red turns toward Lippy and points a finger at him in mock threat. Whatever the topic of conversation, there is a continuous stream of fooling around, both verbal and physical. It lasts until the badge-out, when the hours of waiting are over and the men leave the hiring hall. The rest of this chapter will explore how the men sustain working-class community in the hiring hall during their daily hours of waiting, between badge-in and badge-out.

Sports Talk

It is late September. The hall is crowded with men who are concerned about the pennant race in the American League. Baltimore is 1½ games out of first place.

Tom: *Baltimore's got it in the bag [he smiles at Frankie Moustache].*

Frankie: *Nah, the Yankees are going to win. Cause if they don't win, I won't badge-in here any more. I won't be able to face the guys any more. You won't let me live that down.*

Tom: *You won't show up here any more?*

Frankie: *I'll have to badge-in in the other hall.*

Salley: *They'd better not blow it.*

Frankie: *The only way the Yankees will lose is if they beat themselves.*

Paul: *The Yanks—the Yanks will win, and they'll win the World Series.*

Tom: *Yeah, what do you know?*

Bowley: *A year ago he didn't know where first base was.*

Sports are a central topic for the men in the hiring hall. Major sports events such as the Tom Seaver trade, the Super Bowl, or tomorrow's Knick game are treated with the same importance as presidential elections and the SALT talks. Thus, it is not surprising that Frankie Moustache will be ridiculed if the Yankees lose the pennant—as if he himself had made the error that lost the game. Frankie is identified by the men as being a Yankee fan, and his identity is intertwined with the success of the team. When the Yankees eventually won the World Series, Bowley felt impelled to admit to Frankie that the Yankees were the best team: a major act of eating crow for the Met fan.

Through sports talk, the men produce and sustain a meaningful world for themselves; they define themselves in terms of the teams they root for. This vicarious participation in sports becomes real within the context of the competitive interaction that comprises sports talk in the hiring hall. Yankee fans are now at the top of the pecking order, and, since the Mets are in last place, Met fans are reduced to the status of rooting against the Yankees. In terms of the culture of the hiring hall, when Red says, "They'd better win," he is also saying, "If they win, I win."

The men are given status within the hall to the extent that they are knowledgeable in sports. If a worker can continually make predictions on the outcome of sports events or explain why an outcome occurred, his position within the work group is solidified. This is especially true in terms of gambling. Leo's picks at the race track are sought after by the other men because they have paid off in the past. Sports knowledge is seen by the men as symbolic of their competence in life in general. To ridicule one's sports sense, then, is to ridicule one's common sense.

At the same time, sporting events enable the men to participate in history as it happens. Their participation may be relatively passive, but at least they can personally observe the epic spectacle of the Super Bowl. They have no access to the major political events of the time. Present political history is impersonal and external to their daily lives. The history of sports is knowable, and allows them to participate in the exciting immediacy of the outcome of an event, because it is observable and doesn't go on behind closed doors.[4]

There is also a practical, economic aspect to sports talk; that is, gambling. "Oh fuck, I missed the number."

The men will discuss the best picks at the tracks in hope of making money. Like fishermen, they discuss the "ones that got away," the close misses and the bets not made. They talk of historic past killings and runs of bad luck. Yesterday's card games are discussed enthusiastically and in detail.

Gambling offers actual participation in the sporting life and makes spectator sports even more enjoyable. Though some of the men jog and play handball when they leave the hiring hall, for most of them gambling is their sport. Gambling, especially in card games, is an activity in which they can directly participate and display their competence.

Sports talk and gambling give the men an identity, give them vicarious participation in sports history and the sporting life. At the same time, sport serves an ideological purpose. It has been observed that sport acts as a "social balm and reinforces the passivity" of people.[5] However, there is also a less authoritarian aspect to the meaning of sports talk for longshoremen. In the hiring hall, sports talk not only reinforces competitiveness among workers and displays worker accommodation. It also displays resistance to the control of the men in the workplace by the shipping companies. It maintains lines of communication among the men, lines needed for any potential development of workers' community or class consciousness. A most important aspect of sports talk is that it is a shared activity—the shared fun of discussing yesterday's Met loss and another adventure in the life of Billy Martin. Sports talk reinforces the crucial elements of a shared outlook on the world. That is why it can act as a prerequisite to the development of class consciousness. Sports talk provides a sociable way for the men to maintain and continually reestablish contact with one another, and thus at the same time it nourishes tendencies toward resistance.

News Talk

Every morning in the hiring hall, the men read the *Daily News* and the *New York Times*. They collectively discuss the most important news items. All the men get in their opinion, whether they are discussing another rate hike by Con Edison, crime in the streets, or an editorial on the fiscal crisis.

Bill: *Those judges are too lenient. They let out killers and rapers too easy, much too easy.*

Charley: *Did you see Moynihan's letter in the New York Times?*

Bowley: *Yeah, the one on aid. The one that said we should get billions of dollars in aid more than California and don't.*

Charley: *Thirty-two billion dollars. What do our congressmen do in Washington? Everybody takes advantage of New York, everybody. We get screwed. They cut police, schools. We get screwed.*

Claims have been made, on the one hand, that workers are authoritarian,[6] and, on the other hand, that they are apathetic and basically unconcerned about politics.[7] I have found myself guilty of these biases even though all my evidence demonstrates that the men are both concerned and informed about contemporary political events. I found that I had to read both the *Daily News* and the *New York Times* on the way to the hiring hall in the morning so that I would be able to discuss political events with the men. They demonstrate their political concerns in their discussion of the Bert Lance hearings.

The hearings occurred during a tight American League pennant race, and I expected the conversation to be about the Yankee loss to Boston the night before. As I entered the hiring hall and took my place on line, the major topic of conversation was Bert Lance. Rudy, Tom, Lippy, and Charley had watched the entire hearing on WNET, the New York City public broadcasting television channel. George, Bowley, Bill, and Jerry had watched part of the hearings. The men's concern about the Bert Lance hearings suggests an ongoing concern about political events, which they had had no time for when they were working full time.

All of the men believed that Lance was guilty, but, more generally, the hearings reinforced some of their beliefs about the political system: that politicians are not only corrupt but basically incompetent, that all wealth is based on corruption.

Rudy: *They caught the bastard dead to right, and he had them shitting in their pants. He's a smart fuck, that Lance. He turned every question back on them. He made them look bad.*

Bowley: *Well, he went from a ninety-dollar-a-week teller to a millionaire: he had to be smart. But to do that you have to be a crook.*

Charley: *Sure, he was a crook. C'mon, how could you do that honestly?*

Rudy: *He really made them look bad. Javits is the only one who pinned him down. Javits was good. He's the only one who did his homework.*

Lippy: *What would the banks do to me if I was twenty-two thousand dollars overdrawn on my account? That bastard gets away with it, and I, if I'm a few dollars overdrawn, they make a big stink over it.*

Tom: *They're all crooks, the liberals, the democrats, the republicans.*

Social scientists' attribution to working-class men of authoritarianism and apathy may misrepresent the way workers understand the political system. From the point of view of the men, they are not apathetic, but they are politically powerless. They question their political relevance and ask themselves, "Why should I vote when the system is structured against me?" It is not that workers are cynical[8] but that they perceive political corruption as the inevitable governing principle of all political organizations. For these men, the difference between the Mafia and "respectable" politics—whether it's the union, big business, or government—is that the Mafia never claims to be honest.

Corruption and authoritarianism have been a daily circumstance of their life, both in the shape-up and at the workplace, and in the "old neighborhood" as well. It should not be surprising, then, if the corruption and authoritarianism of their daily lives are carried over into their perceptions of "how the world works." The men have a Mafia model of power, which transforms all forms of political action into a form of corruption, and thus into their perception that politicians are all crooks. The men believe that all attempts at social change inevitably fail. The Mafia model of power cripples social change and maintains the men's perception of their own powerlessness. The men's sense that political corruption filters into the institutions of their daily lives is expressed in the following hiring-hall exchange on the Richard Nixon-David Frost interviews:

> Lippy: *Yeah, I saw that fuckin' liar; he says he didn't do anything. He has the nerve to say, to compare himself to Truman. You know, Billy, you know I'm a republican and I never liked Truman. But Truman never did anything like Nixon and that fuck has the nerve to compare himself with Truman.*
>
> Guido: *I told you not to vote for the bum. [Guido, like most of the men, is a democrat. Lippy, as the result of his loyalty to the republican party, is a political outsider, and his views are treated with skepticism by the other men.]*
>
> Frankie: *They're all corrupt. Truman was, too. They just didn't get caught. It's the way people are. In the Knights of Columbus, when I became treasurer, they wanted me to take my percentage of the dues. I wouldn't, and they thought I was crazy. I was doing the right thing and they said I was crazy. I quit, I had to.*

All of the men on line agreed with Frankie's sense of the inevitability of political corruption, and Tom, shaking his head, summed it up, "All politicans are the same. They're all bums."

Television Talk

The talk in the hall is often about yesterday's television programs. Sports and news events, various series, and specials are regularly watched, then analyzed collectively in the hall. Accounts of the most enjoyable segments of a show are frequent. The men retell jokes that they found particularly funny, but they are also concerned with the social meaning of programs. Their views on particular issues are expressed in relation to events that they observe and experience in their daily lives. As has been stated with regard to political talk, the longshoremen are not simply either authoritarian or apathetic. In television talk they often display complexities of attitudes and values.

The showing of *The Godfather* on television is especially significant: almost all of the men on the line are Sicilian.

> Bowley: *Did ya see **The Godfather**, a great movie. I don't know what all this crap about the movie being against Italians is. It's not. They had this disclaimer before the movie, and I don't think Coppolla— after all, he's Italian—would make a movie against Italian-Americans.*
>
> Jerry: *How could you say that? Of course it discriminates against Italians.*
>
> Red: *It shows all Italians as killers and pasta benders. We're not. We're hardworking men.*

Bill.   *Sure; they should have never showed that on television. It shows Italians as murderers and thieves who are only into killing each other and they shouldn't show all that violence on T.V. It's terrible, children are watching. It's bad for them to see it and then they'll all think that Italians are violent. It's a terrible movie and shouldn't be shown on T.V.*

Tom: *How many Italians are criminal? How many?*

Augie: *Less than one percent.*

Bill: *It was in the papers.*

Augie: *Italians are hard-working people, we always worked hard. We built New York City. Do we have it easy? No.*

Bill: *Sure, they show you that Italians had it rough when they came here. But what did we do? We worked; we worked from morning till night. In the movie it shows not that we were hard workers but that we killed our way out of the slums, that we were murderers and killers.*

Augie: *It's a very good movie—good acting, exciting, and they didn't mean the movie to be discriminatory. But the people who watch it, they don't understand that, they don't know that all Italians are hard-working men. They watch the movie and they think all Italians are Mafia. You visit out of town and you try to open a business. Out of town they think you're Mafia. They think all Italians are Mafia. That's why they shouldn't have shown the movie on T.V. It makes it hard on Italians. But we Italians, we can't get together. Blacks, Jews, even homosexuals, if they think something on T.V. discriminates, they get it off T.V. But Italians, they can't organize themselves so they show* **The Godfather** *on T.V.*

The men seem to understand that the problem is not just prejudice against Italians, but, more specifically, it is also the result of a lack of solidarity among Italians. The men agreed with Augie's assertion and seemed to envy the organizational abilities of other minorities. The lesson worth learning for them is that they are helpless before the conditions of their life that they perceive as oppressive, if they are unable to organize. Some of the longshoremen have claimed that all their union benefits were really won because of efforts of the rank-and-file. The potential for solidarity exists in the men's realization that they can overcome their powerlessness through community.

The men all watched *Roots* and it was the talk of the hiring hall for the week it was on.

John: *Did you see what they did to their family?*

Rudy: *I didn't know that they abused the black women the way they did. I couldn't get over the way Chuck Connors was in the program.*

John: *What a choice, his balls or his foot. That's not a choice.*

Of all the men, only one believed that the program would have a bad effect on those who watched it. Said Jerry, "Sure, I enjoyed it, but I don't think they should have put it on T.V. It gives them a good reason to riot. It's going to cause trouble."

One of the major indicators of worker authoritarianism has been workers' purported racism. Hamilton has made an impressive argument against this claim.[9] The *Roots* discussion demonstrates that the longshoremen are not simply racist and antidemocratic.

The picture that emerges from the men's discussion of *Roots* complicates the claim of working-class prejudice. I am arguing not that workers are not racist, but that the blanket designation of them as racist is an oversimplification. In their informal talk the men demonstrate the realization that the history of Blacks is different from their own immigrant history. They realize that they are ignorant of Black history and voice a real compassion for the plight of Blacks. White working-class racism is a problem, but a complicated problem, in which the paradox of coexistent resistance to Blacks and accommodation with them is sustained. This paradox is expressed in informal conversations. It is the same longshoremen who say, "I wouldn't want the moulies in my neighborhood," who have the ability to work and joke together with Blacks both on the piers and in the hiring halls.

Another piece of evidence for the charge of authoritarianism has been the attitude of workers toward college students. This also is a complicated issue, as the men's discussion of *Washington behind Closed Doors* shows.

Guido: *Did you see* **Washington behind Closed Doors**? *I watched it every night. That Nixon, that ratfuck, he really fucked up this country. You should of seen some of the things they did. They fucked over fifteen thousand student demonstrators. They framed them. Nixon wanted to kill some of them. What fuckers!*

Guido, like many of the men, turns out to have identified not with the authorities but with the demonstrators. The men have sons the same age, who were in college during the sixties. Some of their sons even participated in demonstrations. The men have a strong sense of the structure of inequality. They understand intimately that the "system" is often structured not only against them but against their children. Another longshoremen on an adjacent line says, "It's the same old story: the rich have power and the poor don't have any."

Don: *I know. Those bastards wanted to send my kid to jail for fifteen years for one Quaalude, for one Quaalude because he wouldn't rat on his friends. But Howard Samuels's son gets arrested for heroin possession and nothing happens to him—nothing. The rich can get away with*

*anything. [Howard Samuels had been a candidate in the democratic
primary for governor of New York.]*

Joking

Joking is a critique of the formal institutional structures. This critique is
facilitated through the violation of the formal order by treating its rules and
procedures as problematic. It is thus that joking is a subversive activity.
Joking is a form of transcendence. This holds true whether the joking is
about union politics, high taxes, or prejudice against Italians. It reduces a
hard, vicious world to proportions that these men can manage. It enables
them to see through it and thus reverse the situation.[10] It transforms the
formal, impersonal, institutional world into an informal, personal world,
which they help to produce. The following anti-Italian joke is an example
of this.

Charley is telling a joke: Dominic and Luigi are learning how to fly a
helicopter. Dominic goes up and comes down and everything is all right.
Luigi goes up and everything seems all right, and then, all of a sudden, he
crashes. Dominic runs over and, seeing that Luigi is all right, asks him what
happened. Luigi says, "I wenta up one-thousand-a feet and everything was
all-a-right. I went up two-thousand-a feet and everything was all-a-right. I
went-a up three-thousand-a feet, and it started to get cold, so I turned off
the fan."

The men laugh and pat Charley on the back. Grippo keeps knocking off
everybody's hat. Red threatens to knock Grippo's head off. While Red is
facing Grippo, Guido raps Red in the head. Red yells, "A fa Napoli. Bowley,
when are you going to quit?" Bowley smiles and looks away. The men are
fooling around.

Joking behavior consists of paper throwing, hair messing, head rapping,
insults, joke telling, etc. To an outside observer, this behavior would be
interpreted as hostile and overtly aggressive behavior, not as behavior that
contributes to group solidarity.[11]

The unique aspect of hiring-hall joking behavior for men on the GAI is
that it has been removed from the workplace and the daily competition for
work. Thus, it is no longer the result of monotony in the workplace,[12] nor
is it the result of the antipathy of competitive and hostile groups,[13] nor of
the "irritation of performing arduous labor and/or working in a hazardous
place."[14] In the case of longshoremen on the GAI, the joking behavior is
closer to what Aronowitz calls "play."[15]

Joking behavior in the hiring hall can be perceived as play only because
the joking activity now occurs outside of the instrumental function of re-
lieving the tensions and hostility of the workplace. To the extent that joking

activity is play, there is the potential for the development of a community of workers in which hierarchy and the abuse of arbitrary power is suspended. Joking behavior now has the liberating potential to enable workers to freely associate with one another in terms of the meaningful experience of their collective interaction in the hiring hall, which can now be perceived by them as community.

Hiring Hall as Community

Guido: *Bill, you make me come in here to hear this crap. I'm better off sitting in my car and reading my paper than listening to this bullshit and watching these animals push each other around.*

Bill: *You've got the wrong attitude. You're better off in here. You learn things in here: what horse to play; how to fix your house, your car; you learn politics. It's better in here than in the car.*

The men agree with Bill, as Guido leaves the line to watch over his car-trunk business. The talk in the hall covers a wide range of topics—Grippo's death from cancer, a grandchild's first steps, a son flunking out of school, last night's Knick game, union politics.

The hiring hall offers an informal occasion to the men to restructure their lives in a meaningful way. In the hiring hall they can hold forum on the world that they participate in. The breakup of the "old work gang" and the closing of the "old pier" due to automation formally sabotaged the meaningful community that working together had offered them. The guarantee of income along with the dissipation of their former work community explains the men's resistance to work.

When the men hear Earl's voice—"All men who wish to work hold up their 'A' cards"—they stand back in the crowd, gambling on taking a debit and hoping that someone else will take the job. Work no longer offers community, and hence they refuse to work. The men now collectively fear for John (a "B" man) when he gets a debit. Bowley philosophical says, "He gambled and lost: he got a debit."

Lippy: *You'd think we were in front of a firing squad, the way we worry.*

Big Tom: *John took a debit. He should go to see Ed [a friendly dispatcher]. Ed will fix it for him.*

John: *I'll take an afternoon job.*

John worries that there won't be any afternoon jobs. He goes to see Ed. He gets a job on Pier 39 canceling the debit.

The "A" men are happy that they didn't have to gamble on work today. Earl's voice comes over the loudspeaker: "You may now badge-out." The men, in very orderly fashion, badge-out, and then rush out of the hall.

Work no longer has the meaning to these men that it once had. Removed from their work gang, community, for them, has moved into the hiring hall. Their resistance to work is based on this transformation of its meaning to them. To put it simply, "No work without community." For the first time, work itself lacks meaning. What has now become meaningful is avoiding it—and doing so together, as a community at the fringes of work.

NOTES

1. Malcolm Johnson, *Crime on the Labor Front* (New York: McGraw-Hill, 1950), pp. 138–39; Daniel Bell. "The Racket Ridden Longshoremen," in his *The End of Ideology* (New York: Free Press, 1960); Bud Schulberg, *On the Waterfront* (New York: Random House, 1955); Robert Travers, *A Funeral for Sabella* (New York: Harcourt-Brace, 1952).

2. Charles P. Larrowe, *Shape-Up and Hiring Hall* (Berkeley: Univ. of California Press, 1955), p. 77. Also see Vernon H. Jensen, *Strife on the Waterfront: The Port of New York since 1945* (Ithaca, N.Y.: Cornell Univ. Press, 1974) and *The Hiring of Dock Workers and Employment Practices in the Ports of New York, Liverpool, London, Rotterdam and Marseilles* (Cambridge, Mass.: Harvard Univ. Press, 1964).

3. Vernon H. Jensen, "Computer Hiring of Dock Workers in the Port of New York," *Industrial and Labor Relations Review*, 20 (1967): 416.

4. Michael R. Real, *Mass-Mediated Culture* (Englewood Cliffs, N.J.: Prentice-Hall, 1977), pp. 98–100.

5. Harry Edwards, "The Black Athletes: Twentieth Century Gladiators for White America," *Psychology Today*. 7 (Nov. 1973): 43.

6. Seymour Martin Lipset, *Political Man* (Garden City: Doubleday, 1960) and "Democracy and Working Class Authoritarianism," *American Sociological Review*, 24 (1959): 482–502.

7. E. E. Lemasters. *Blue Collar Aristocrats: Life Styles in a Working Class Tavern* (Madison: Univ. of Wisconsin Press, 1975). pp. 184–87. One manifestation of working-class apathy is in terms of the claim that they are no longer the historical subject. This argument is made by both liberal and radical social theorists. Herbert Marcuse, *One Dimensional Man* (Boston: Beacon Press, 1964), pp. 247–57; and Bell, *End of Ideology*.

8. E. E. Lemasters, *Blue Collar Aristocrats*, pp. 170–92.

9. Richard F. Hamilton. *Class and Politics in the United States* (New York: John Wiley & Sons, 1972), pp. 399–467.

10. Joseph Bensman and Robert Lilienfeld, *Between Public and Private: The Lost Boundaries of Self* (New York: Free Press, 1979), p. 12.
11. William W. Pilcher. *The Portland Longshoremen: A Dispersed Urban Community* (New York: Holt, Rinehart & Winston, 1972), pp. 112–13.
12. Donald F. Roy, "Banana Time: Job Satisfaction and Informal Interaction," *Human Organization,* 18 (Winter 1959–60): 158–68.
13. A. R. Radcliffe-Brown, *Structure and Function in Primitive Society* (New York: Free Press, 1952).
14. Pilcher, *Portland Longshoremen,* p. 113.
15. Stanley Aronowitz, *False Promises: The Shaping of American Working Class Consciousness* (New York: McGraw-Hill, 1974), p. 61.

4

The Gay Community at Jacob Riis Park

PETER CANAVAN

METHODOLOGICAL NOTE • The study began as a field exercise for a course in community studies held during the spring semester. At that time, several weekend visits were made, typically on sunny afternoons when there were the greatest number of visitors; the length of these visits averaged about two or three hours. The researcher explored the physical setting of the park and made preliminary observations about the patterns of usage. After Memorial Day, the traditional opening of the season, visits became more frequent, between three and four times a week, and lasted longer, up to six or seven hours a day. At first, the researcher concentrated his observations on the nude bathing areas of Bays 1 and 2, generally selecting peak visitation hours on warm, sunny afternoons. About half-way through the season, deliberate attempts were made to explore other bathing areas and to visit the park at different times of the day and under less favorable weather conditions, for comparison.

The quality of the interviews and the styles of the interview method varied as widely as the subjects. When I discussed patterns of nude bathing with officials of the National Park Service and the United States Park Police, I observed certain formalities. First meetings were typically arranged, through either secretaries or supervisors, and were conducted on the premises; I introduced myself formally in terms of my research position. Subsequent meetings with park personnel at the beach were more spontaneous, less focused.

In contrast, almost all interviews with bathers were spontaneous, arising from conversations related to the immediate circumstances or personal histories at the beach. These interviews rarely included reference to my formal research capacity.

This chapter is the result of a field study conducted at Jacob Riis Park during the summer of 1974, the park's first season under the federal jurisdiction of the National Park Service, as part of Gateway National Recreation Area. The study employs the methods of an ethnography: formal and informal interviews, participant-observation, field notes, and transcriptions.

Jacob Riis Park is situated in the borough of Queens, near the western tip of the Rockaway peninsula, just south of Brooklyn. Its two miles of ocean beach are divided into fourteen sections, called "bays." Each bay reflects the unique character of the different urban group that frequents it. Over a number of years, patterns of voluntary segregation have evolved among the bathers. Each of the various ethnic and cultural groups has developed its own niche, a particular area it considers its own, and the stability of the spatial arrangements indicates the general lack of confrontation between groups.

The area of Bays 1 and 2 at Jacob Riis Park has been a center of gay (i.e., homosexual) life in New York City for many years. Gay men and Lesbians have been coming to Riis Park for several decades, and they share a history at Riis Park that is both personal and political—personal, as it is experienced and shared by individual gay people, and political, as it relates to the position of gay people in society. The shared personal experiences of gay people— their choices of certain public places for congregation and entertainment, and their reactions and relationship to the larger society—are the binding and unifying features of the gay community.

The deep personal significance gay people attach to a particular location can be better understood when one considers the unique orientation of gay people to time and space.

> Space and time are the concrete boundaries of a community, in a not quite metaphorical sense. A community that is secret and stigmatized must quite literally have walls: places and times set apart from other places and times in which the community can celebrate itself.[1]

In *Identity and Community in the Gay World,* Carol Warren points to the limited environment in which gay people can interact socially and express themselves as gay people, as well as the necessity of a public but unstigmatized domain to celebrate their personal and political choice. Society has provided a range of social institutions and settings in which straight (i.e., heterosexual) people can meet, develop personal and sexual relationships, and express affection for one another, at the same time denying the expression of analogous feelings and emotions by gay people in straight settings, forcing them to remain invisible in all spheres of their lives except that which is exclusively gay.

> The gay community exists within leisure time, since the concepts of stigma and secrecy prevent its extension into worktime. The gay world, then, is a world of leisure time, structured by the concept of leisure and play, and giving

a value to leisure beyond simple relaxation. By confinement to leisure time
and through the centrality of the gay experience, sociability and play become
the most significant of life's tasks.[2]

The public places where gay people meet have greater significance in
their lives than merely as leisure or recreational facilities. As gay people are
excluded from full participation in many social institutions available to
straight people, they compensate by investing a corresponding amount of
time and energy into activities and locations that are gay. Having been
denied fully integrated identities in the straight world, gay people seek
environments in which they can complete their social identities, share their
mutual experiences, and realize more fully their identity as human beings.

The history of gay people at Riis Park has undergone many changes. At
times when homosexuals were subject to harassment and arrest (for example,
in the late fifties and early sixties), gay people acted with caution and secrecy.
A senior New York City police officer and Riis Park veteran recalls:

*I worked here twelve years ago and the gays were coming here then too, to
Bays 1 and 2. Of course, they weren't gay like they are today! [I expected
that gay people at Riis Park had always been somewhat extroverted in their
behavior, and I challenged that.] Oh, on the beach, yeah, there was horsing
around, but the gay people who came here then, did not want to be recognized,
not even on the beach.*

(Conversation, 12 July 1974)

During periods of repression, when the very existence of gay people has
been perceived as a serious threat to the standards of the larger society, gay
people have been treated severely. Meeting a neighbor I know to be gay,
I told him I was working at Riis Park.

*Riis Park! I haven't been out there in ages—it must be fourteen years—when
I first came to New York, before I met Harry. The last time I was out to Riis
Park, I was arrested.*

Q: Arrested! What for?

Wearing a bikini.

Q: You were arrested for wearing a bikini?

*I was standing in front of the bathhouse waiting for a friend, and a cop came
along. He stood there for a while, looking me over, and I pretended not to
notice. He kept staring, and it made me very uncomfortable. Then he came
over and told me I was under arrest. I said, "What for?" And he told me my
bathing suit was lewd and immodest, that you could see my pubic hair. Of
course, lewdness is in the eye of the beholder, and you couldn't see a thing,
the bathing suit was about this wide [indicating approximately six inches at
his hip—two inches wider than the bathing suits now worn by the lifeguards],
but he said it was immodest, that it was a public beach, and I was arrested.*

(Conversation, 6 June 1974)

Some changes in public attitudes toward sexual and racial minorities have occurred over the past decade, and Riis Park reflects these changes. The women's movement has challenged the appropriateness of sex-role stereotypes and the rigid role-playing behavior they imply. Blacks and other minorities have asserted themselves and the beauty of their individual cultures, and have demanded their civil and social rights. Inspired by the victories of other minorities, and instructed by their failures, gay liberation emerged as a political movement. Gay liberation is the assertion of gay people, of their pride, of the integrity of their way of life, and of their civil rights, which have been withheld on the basis of sexual preference.

It is ironic that it should be a senior officer of the New York Police Department who had to remind me of gay liberation. In fact, the officer was absolutely correct. "Of course, they weren't gay like they are today!" The gay people who come to Riis Park today *are* different!

Bays 1 and 2: The Physical Setting

Bays 1 and 2 are at once the most isolated and the most immediately visible section of Riis Park. This is a winning combination of attributes for gay people, who prefer remote locations where people will not bother them, and who depend heavily upon nonverbal indicators in their communication.

The location of Bays 1 and 2 at the eastern end of the beach offers some possibility of seclusion. Bordering the private beach of Neponsit, Bay 1 is situated directly in front of the Neponsit Home for the Aged. Access to Bay 1 is also indirect. Visitors must walk more than fifty yards from the boardwalk, and around the shrubbed property of the home, in order to reach Bay 1. The relative distance from the boardwalk separates the bathers at Bay 1 from the general bathing public, and the obstruction of the nursing home makes them less visible to passing strangers.

All visitors who bring their cars to Riis Park must approach the parking area from the east, encircling the lot before they enter. The first people the visitor encounters are the pedestrians, crossing the eastern traffic circle, going to and from their cars to Bay 2. As the driver makes the turn and faces the beach, the first area of the park to come into view is a small section of boardwalk near the softball field at Bay 2. This is the visitor's first glimpse of Riis Park, and, for gay people, its cues provide strategic information. As soon as they pass the traffic circle, and take one quick look at the scene on the boardwalk, gay people know exactly where they want to go.

Because of the secrecy and stigmatization of the gay community, its members become adept at picking up the most casual of nonverbal cues: momentary eye contact, body language, and certain articles of clothing. This is not to say that the sophisticated straight observer could not or does not pick up on these cues, but only that the gay observer is more disposed to do so. The observer might, for example, notice the number of males in a group approaching the beach, noting that they are all approximately the same age, in their mid twenties, that they wear unusual clothing—such as platform wedgies, shoulder bags, and brightly flowered shirts—and that the men in the group do not observe the same degree of separation practiced by heterosexual males, that some of the males are close and touching. As the observer becomes more experienced, it becomes possible to identify gay people on the basis of much more subtle and varied cues. Mixed groups of women and men may be identified by their spatial characteristics: for example, the gay women sit together, and the gay men do the same, or one female sits in the center of a group of males.

The limited section of boardwalk visible from the road is a hub of activity. The small brick building at the end of the softball field contains rest rooms and a small, very busy food concession. Situated at the head of the only staircase to the Bay 2 section of the beach, it is a center of traffic: people heading to and from the beach and the restrooms. There are two wooden frame booths in front of the concession where tickets are sold, which can be used to purchase food or beverages. Lines form at the two windows, and the eagle-eyed can determine the size of the crowd by the length of the lines. The particularly keen can determine its composition. The line is frequently all male, many wearing brightly colored abbreviated bathing suits. Here again, spatial characteristics, especially the lack or physical distance, may tip the observer.

The underrepresentation of females on the concession line is worthy of comment. Simplistic explanations might be that they use less food, or that they bring it from home, and this would be supported by the inferior economic position of women in our society, but the more complete explanation lies in the character of the Lesbian experience, both at Riis Park and in the larger "gay world," where, as Esther Newton has observed, they are similarly underrepresented.

> Whatever the ratio may be between those of each sex who have engaged in homesexual *acts* or even who *define themselves* as homosexuals, there can be no doubt that men far outnumber the women *in gay life*. My impression over a two-year period was that men outnumber women by a ratio of at least four to one. The males considered as a group, have a more elaborate subculture and contribute disproportionately to distinctively homosexual concepts, styles, and terminology.[3]

Whereas gay men have created and dominated an elaborate structure of social institutions, including bars and bathhouses, a structure that is external, the Lesbian, without access to the material resources of the gay male, has created an identity that is internal, that depends less on social institutions, and much more on the personal relationships she shares with other women. While the public behavior of gay males is geared to attract attention (particularly the attention of a beautiful stranger), the Lesbian's search for identity is much more private, and this privacy is reflected in her public behavior. To make a generalization, the gay man is more likely to spend his time waiting on line cruising, keeping an eye open for a new friend or an unrenewed acquaintance, while the Lesbian remains with her friends on their blanket. One of the political implications of this is that Lesbians are particularly invisible, in a society that demands that all homosexuals remain invisible in most circumstances.

Diversity among the Bathers

From the earliest visit, the people at Jacob Riis Park displayed contrasting life-styles and remarkable tolerance in their dealings with one another.

> *The wind from the ocean is strong, and, for protection, a number of people are sitting in different shrubbed entrances to the main pavilion. In one small enclosure, a gay man in a bikini lies sunning himself on a blanket. In another, an older woman in a house dress and a gray sweater sits in a beach chair reading the Sunday newspaper. There is an elderly man with her. The pattern of straight people coexisting with obvious, if not flamboyant, homosexuals, recurs. When I pass the playground, I notice some children playing near the swings. They are all warmly dressed, gray sweatshirts, navy and dark red sweaters. They are with their father. Working out on the nearby parallel bars is a blond body-builder in tight faded Levis, his shirt removed, a red bandana sticking out of his back pocket. The tan muscleman is posing and playing with his dog, a long-haired wolfhound.*
>
> (Field notes, 21 April 1974)

The predominantly gay character of the Bays 1 and 2 area, moreover, was established even at this early date.

> *The people down at this end of the boardwalk are mostly gay. There are a few bicyclists, a few single men, and several male couples. A group of four mature Lesbians are walking along. They appear to be in pairs, as they stop to pose for group photos (two of the women are carrying Instamatics on their wrists). A few men have brought their dogs for a walk, too.*
>
> (Field notes, 21 April 1974)

As the season progressed, and the weather grew warmer, more and more people headed for the beach. It would be impossible to describe the crowds who gathered regularly at Bays 1 and 2 in strictly quantitative terms—70 percent male, 90 percent gay, 20 percent nude, 80 percent white, 30 percent Latin—because the quality of the beach was so dynamic, the experience so fluid and unpredictable. Weather played a decisive role in beach attendance. The higher the temperature and humidity, and the more unbearable the heat of the city, the more people escaped to Jacob Riis Park and other summer oases. When an unusual heat wave hit New York one Friday, the crowds at Riis Park swelled. As the heat blistered through the weekend, the crowds grew; by Sunday a record-breaking 115,000 people were counted.

The attire chosen by male bathers at Bays 1 and 2 reflected the wide range of preferences and experiences within the gay community—from the most modest and conventional bathing suit to the most outrageous, from the most aggressively "masculine" to the most "feminine," from the most elaborate form of costume to no costume at all.

Because of the general "cruising" behaviors and attitudes of male homosexuals, with their dependence on nonverbal forms of communication to exchange sexual signals, particular attention is paid to the details of the gay male's dress. Generally, this takes the form of a studied appearance—items of apparel fastidiously chosen to convey a certain disposition, such as "funky," "chic," "casual," or "butch." In its extreme form, items of apparel are chosen to convey specific sexual messages. In the case of gay males who are into the "leather" or "S and M" ("sado-masochistic") scene, the keys worn either on the right or left side indicate whether the actor chooses a submissive or dominant role.

The careful observer can discern other patterns from the costumes and accessories of the bathers. After some practice, I was able to identify pairs of male lovers. These couples frequently wore similar, even identical, bathing suits, observed similar habits of grooming (beards, moustaches, and length and styling of hair), and wore similar clothes. The ability to identify gay male lovers caused me some consternation later in the season when I interpreted as a pair two men I knew to be "undercover" policemen.

> *Two handsome men are walking down the boardwalk in the direction of Bay 2. As they walk ahead of me, I observe that they are both in their early twenties and are wearing athletic undershirts, cut-off blue jeans, and sandals, and that their hair is relatively short. As I get closer, I recognize the two men as officers of the United States Park Police, and realize these are their "plainclothes." Running down the checklist of similarities in costume and grooming, I realize that these two officers match all my criteria for gay lovers.*
>
> *(Field notes, 24 July 1974)*

The caravans of these lovers are often rich in bourgeois treasure: matching beach chairs and towels (HIS and HIS), umbrellas, coolers, and refreshments of all sorts. Because of the stability of their relationship, lovers are more likely to be able to accumulate money and shared personal tastes. The stability of their relationship also makes them the frequent center of a circle of friends. These circles include unattached gay men who use their friends as a home base from which to circulate and meet people; some women, too, both gay and straight, take advantage of socializing with, and around, male lovers. Pairs of Lesbian or gay male lovers and the friendship circles that surround them are the pillars of the home-based gay community.

Many gay parents bring their children to Riis Park, and there are often large numbers of children playing at the beach.

Dick is in his late thirties, and has not been to Riis Park in many years. Dick and I were having a drink at a Chelsea bar, when he introduced me to an old friend. After the friend left, Dick explained that they had been lovers and used to visit Riis Park every week.

"He's married, and we used to bring his two little kids all the way from Jersey. They were babies then, the little boy was still in a bassinet. How old could he have been? Six months. We had to drag all the bottles and diapers. It was a real production. Sometimes his wife would come along, but she usually preferred to stay at home, get rid of the kids, and take a rest."

Q: *"Are they still married?"*

A: *"Oh, yeah, he loves his family. His daughter is starting college this fall."*
                                                              (Conversation, 15 June 1974)

Whether they are single, married, or divorced, whether they have exclusive, partial, or "weekend" custody, Lesbian mothers and gay fathers face unusual problems when they try to integrate their parenting with the activities of the stereotypically childless gay community.

Other particular groups and friendship networks within the gay community regularly visited Bays 1 and 2. Large groups of Spanish and bilingual gays frequent Bays 1 and 2 at Riis Park, but Spanish gays in New York City, especially in Queens, are so well integrated into the larger, organized gay community that they do not form an exclusively Spanish gay community, but rather represent a distinctive subgroup within the gay community.

One such subgroup of gays—whose physical impairment prevented extensive communication with the larger gay community, but whose frequent presence at Riis Park indicated a general gay identification and affinity— were the gay deaf people. Usually traveling in large groups of men and women, they often brought a corresponding amount of beach stores and accessories, such as food and beach chairs. These groups were particularly self-contained, and did little mixing with the larger crowd. They generally employed sign language for communication, and their sign language had an intriguing, unique (and difficult to describe) gay inflection, involving gay humor and campy gestures.

The gay community at Jacob Riis Park is significantly different from the gay community at large in one particular aspect: it includes a large number of straight or predominantly straight individuals, in addition to many bisexual individuals. Because of the open nature of Riis Park, as well as the voluntary character of its participants, straights who enjoy gay people and the gay scene are free to join them without hassle, and share in their life-style.

The most crowded day of the year . . . People are literally sitting on top of one another, with almost no space between individual blankets. Friendships bloom in tight spaces. Nick asks me the time once or twice, and when he and Carmen want to go down to the water, they ask if I will mind their blanket. They look young; they have been married less than a year. When Carmen says she has three children, the oldest sixteen, I am amazed.

Nick and Carmen like to have a good time. They like Riis Park. This is their third visit; the first was a little over two weeks ago. They like Bays 1 and 2 because the people are freer, and they enjoy the nude bathing. After a while, when we have all gotten a little friendly, Carmen takes off her top, and leaves it off until we leave the beach. Carmen and Nick like gay people. Carmen tells me, "When Nick and I were first married, I didn't know what scenes he was into, but when we got down together, I said, 'Fine, that's cool,' and when Nick brings me here, I like it. Now we got things down."

(Field notes, 14 July 1974)

Nude sunbathing at Bays 1 and 2 attracts large numbers of people, gay and straight, from all over the metropolitan area and beyond. It is the only beach in New York City where nude bathing is regularly practiced by a significant proportion of the visitors. It is difficult to estimate the absolute percentage of nude bathers at Riis Park, because it fluctuates widely with the time of day and year, the temperature, the size of the crowd, and the location on the beach. Carmen's hesitation and her slow decision to take off her top parallels the experience of many nude bathers, especially at a crowded urban beach like Riis Park. They judge the general climate, determine whether they find the atmosphere threatening or conducive, and make their decision accordingly. The same individuals may make several decisions during the course of the day, with the advent of strangers or a crowd, or when going to the concession stand or the boardwalk area (where bathing suits are mandatory), or when going into the ocean (where many people remove them). One particular pattern of nude bathing, practiced almost exclusively by gay men, involves removing their bathing suit either before or upon entering the ocean, and wearing it around their neck.

It is late in the afternoon, and I have been in the ocean about an hour, jumping over and diving under the waves, slightly east of the lifeguard stand at Bay 2. This is the fourth day this week that I have occupied this location at approximately the same time. Of the eight men in the general area, I recognize six of them as "regulars" from earlier visits in the week. We smile and ac-

knowledge one another. Everybody is wearing his bathing suit around his neck.

A handsome young man with black hair and a moustache approaches the water's edge. As he enters the ocean, his strapping physical appearance attracts considerable interest from the men already in the water and the greater number of gay men who stand along the shore and watch all the activity. Everyone is speculating about whether or not he will remove his bathing suit, and how far he will go into the ocean before he removes it. He seems discomfited by the attention. After a few short steps, he breaks into a run, then plunges headlong into the waves, swimming a short distance before making an abrupt stop and returning to shore. He leaves the water immediately and walks through the crowd of disappointed admirers.

Ten minutes later, a pair of lovers in their early twenties are playing in the surf. The tall blond is splashing his boyfriend, who is somewhat reluctant to get wet. A strong wave suddenly immerses them both, and they decide to go further out. When they are about waist deep, the blond takes off his bathing suit and puts it around his neck. As his lover bends over to remove his suit, it becomes tangled around his ankles, and another wave knocks him off his feet. The blond lifts him up in his arms and gives him a big kiss, and they roar with laughter.

(Field notes, 16 July 1974)

The gay male atmosphere of Bays 1 and 2 makes it relatively safer for women (straight women and Lesbians) to sunbathe in the nude, with less harassment and hostility than they would confront at most straight beaches. Women are still far more constrained than men in regard to nude bathing. There are generally between five and ten times more men than women bathing nude at Riis Park, and even fewer women, perhaps one in five, remove the bottoms of their bathing suits. The males are more open about their nudity; nude males are more likely to stand up and walk around, females more likely to remain on their blankets or walk directly into the ocean. Women are far more likely to practice nude (or partially nude) bathing when they are in the company of a friend or lover than when they are alone. It is unusual to see single women unclothed; many get dressed when their companions leave the blanket. Interestingly, the presence of so many gay men makes it very uncomfortable for some straight men to disrobe, even if they would like to. For this reason, straight males rarely remove their bathing suits when they are alone, or in all-male groups. In this environment, they need the reassuring presence of a female to preserve their heterosexual identity, and to protect their reputation.

Definitely not included in the gay community are those straight males who come to gawk and stare at the nude women. Often fully clothed, they parade through the crowd of bathers, stopping in front of nude women, and staring between the women's legs. They range in age from puberty to senility. The adolescents frequently travel in packs or "hunting parties" of four and five, rarely alone, and make catty remarks to the women and one another. The older men are more likely to wear business or street clothes and to carry large, conspicuous cameras. The clothes and the camera equipment, together with their predatory attitude, mark these individuals as "outsiders."

> *As I am lying on my blanket at Bay 2, a short, dark, middle-aged man walks by. He is wearing a white, short-sleeved shirt buttoned outside plaid Bermuda shorts, black shoes, and dark socks. Around his neck are two expensive cameras, each of them equipped with at least a foot of formidable lenses. Two bronzed Lesbians are sunbathing topless on reclining beach chairs a short distance away. The man with the cameras is circling the beach, gaping at the women from a distance, furtively avoiding eye contact with them at close range. He passes between the Lesbians and myself three times in the next forty minutes, each time pretending not to pay attention to the women. The Lesbians are seething with anger. One of them gives the man a lethal glare, the other gives him the finger. Twenty minutes later, they notice the photographer halfway down the beach, lining them up in his view finder. One of the women comments, "That little bastard! He better stay away from here. If he comes over this way again, I'm going to take that fucking camera and shove it up his ass."*
>
> *(Field notes, 12 July 1974)*

Incidents such as this occur often enough to detract considerably from the overall quality of the experience, especially for women. Needless to say, it is not the photography or the staring at beautiful people that bathers find objectionable, it is the manner in which these activities are conducted. What distinguishes this man and others like him from the bathers and photographers at Bays 1 and 2 (including the straight males) is their sense of detachment and nonparticipation. They are unwilling to share the experience of the bathers directly, refusing to sit with them or remain in their company, or even to look them in the eye. These spoilers would be the first to recognize their position as "outsiders"; they come to take a quick look around, maybe snap some nude pictures, and get the hell out as soon as they can.

Influence of Gay Culture at Jacob Riis Park

Gay people have a strong sense of identification with certain forms of popular entertainment, and this identification had many expressions at Jacob Riis Park this summer. Often in the vanguard of cultural tastes, gays are proud of their reputation as trend-setters and their ability to recognize the latest craze or the most promising new performers. On the basis of their "discovery" and their loyal support of these entertainers and these cultural genres, gays develop a possessive instinct regarding them, and claim much of the responsibility for their success.

Gays are one of several groups responsible for the revival of discotheques in the early 1970s. The pulsating beat of modern disco music derives much of its rhythmic energy from the urban experience of the young Blacks, Latinos, and gays who frequented the bars and the private clubs where the music rocked,[4] long before the success of John Travolta in *Saturday Night Fever* (1977) made "disco" acceptable to white heterosexuals. These same urban groups converge at Bays 1 and 2 at Riis Park, and their shared musical tastes are reflected in the disco music that dances in the air. The music that found its original popularity in the Black clubs and gay discos during the spring soared to national fame in the summer, and the sound of "Rock the Boat" and "Rock Your Baby" rocked the bathers at Bays 1 and 2 from portable radios, tape recorders, and phonographs.

Certain female stars have drawn the adulation of gay men. When they were Broadway fledglings, both Barbra Streisand and Bette Midler depended heavily on the loyalty of their gay audiences. Streisand began her nightclub career in two gay bars in Manhattan called "The Lion" and the "Bon Soir," and Midler dashed uptown after the last curtain of "Fiddler on the Roof" to perform at the Continental Baths to an audience of gay men wearing only towels around their waists.[5] These women and others—notably the late Judy Garland, Bette Davis, Diana Ross, Marilyn Monroe, and Marlene Dietrich—have achieved the status of cult figures for certain gay men. They occupy a special place in the gay community, and their songs are brought forth in bars and other community celebrations to evoke feelings of joy and sadness.

The gay bar is the most important institution in the gay world. Not only does it serve as a central meeting-place for gay people and a conduit for gay culture, the gay bar also has a special significance in the life of the individual gay person. When a homosexual walks into a gay bar for the first time, it is often the first setting in which s/he declares herself/himself as homosexual, and the first time the gay person meets others with similar interests and identities; it is often her/his first introduction to the gay community. Gay bars exert considerable influence on the ambiance of Jacob Riis Park. The music, the atmosphere, and many of the patrons of the gay bars are transplanted, *in toto*, at Bays 1 and 2. Gay bartenders, generally young and gorgeous, are lionized in the gay community; they know many people and have many followers. When they appear at Riis Park, their friends rush over to greet them and fill them in on the local happenings. Bathers are commonly identified by the bars they frequent.

*Late afternoon, a crowd of about fifty gathers around a nude man dancing
with a topless female. As I observe the performance, the man on the next
blanket comments, "Oh, him again! He does the same act every weekend at
Le Jardin."*

(Field notes, 8 August 1974)

Riis Park is a general meeting-place for the regular patrons of certain bars.
On sunny afternoons, plans to attend bars are confirmed, and phone numbers
exchanged. One enterprising bar in Queens attempted to organize a regular
Sunday bus ride to Riis Park, to be followed by brunch, called the "GAES-
CAPADE." It was disbanded after a few weeks because the patrons of the
bar preferred to sleep later and drive their own cars.

Drags and Showtime

All the elements of the gay community previously described (the celebration,
theatricality, liberation, lavish costumes, and humor) are epitomized in the
exaggerated appearance and behavior of the drag queens at Riis Park. "Drag
queen" (or "drag") is the slang term for a transvestite or a man who dresses
and behaves like a woman. Drags of all kinds contributed to the enjoyment
of the gay community at Bays 1 and 2.

*Even amidst the exotic costumes commonly found at Riis Park (caftans, tur-
bans, headpieces, monokinis, and peekaboo bathing suits of every description),
Leslie is a definite standout. In his mid-forties, sporting a low-back, one-piece
black bathing suit, with red roses ascending toward the bust (my friend was
sure it had been designed by RoseMarie of California), Leslie wears full drag
makeup, a short blonde wig with teased hair, and the perfect nautical accessories, seashell earrings and matching pearls, and a large, black, patent-
leather pocketbook, the plain clip variety.*

*She walks down to the water several times for a dip, and wades to her
knees. Even when a wave catches her off balance, she never lets her manner
slip. So complete are her costume and demeanor that my friend and I decide
that if she were to board a crowded city bus, no one would be able to tell the
difference.*

*Before leaving, I cannot resist an opportunity to compliment Leslie on his
bathing suit. He asks my name, and introduces himself. Someone mentions
Ridgewood, a neighborhood I know pretty well, and I ask if he lives there.
"Yes, darling, I am the Queen of Ridgewood."*

(Field notes, 19 June 1974)

Queen Leslie of Ridgewood offered an excellent opportunity to test the
attitude of the United States Park Police toward gays. Queen Leslie was
rather unusual even to New York gays, and attracted considerable attention;

but for policemen who came from less metropolitan environments, s/he could prove unbelievable.

> I am on the boardwalk talking to a young park police officer (Tom Kaylor) when Leslie breaks into a swaying rock of a dance. I point her out to Tom, and ask what he thinks of the show. He seems amused and nudges a young fellow officer, "Hey, look, the lady's dancing alone," pointing out her lack of a suitable partner. The second officer turns the tables on Tom, and says, "Well, what are you waiting for?"
>
> (Field notes, 19 June 1974)

Further tests occurred as other queens got into the act.

> As we are standing there, some new scene is developing, and I decide to go down to get a better look. Jackie, a much younger guy in his early twenties, is doing a little drag number in a turquoise chiffon gown, one shoulder holding it up, rhinestone chains holding it together on the other side. With this he carries a matching chiffon stole about ten feet long, trimmed with white ostrich feathers. He wears no makeup, his hair is cut in a medium shag, and his only props are his gown and boa, yet his demeanor is convincingly feminine. He proceeds to dance and strip for the crowd and the photographers who convene. He turns to Leslie, and remarks about her outfit, "Simply lovely, darling!"

The addition of nudity, albeit partial and teasing, in this second performance made the reaction of the police even more significant. Once again, no action was taken to curtail these activities, and the police displayed restraint and good humor.

> At a few points in Jackie's show, he concerns himself about the possibility of the police coming down and getting angry. He plays to the policemen, doing dips and turns, wearing just the boa. At one point in the show, one of the now three park police heads in the direction of the stairs. Jackie says he hopes the officer isn't coming on the beach. I don't think he will, and, as I expect, he walks over to some people on the other side of the stairs. As the crowd of spectators grows, so does the number of police. The police who have been walking along the boardwalk stop when they come to Bay 2, to see what's going on. Two police cars, one city, one park, drive down the boardwalk to Bay 2, until there are two cars and at least a dozen policemen. They don't stay long, and they make no attempt to stop the show.
>
> (Field notes, 19 June 1974)

As the number of policemen grew, their even temper seemed slightly strained; they appeared less amused. Senior officers and management agreed that twelve officers represented an overreaction, and that the best policy was to "leave them alone." Some felt that the presence of so many police might be misunderstood and might provoke some sort of "incident."

The festivity and theatricality at Jacob Riis Park frequently escalated into full-scale performances and shows of all kinds. Crowds gathered at the slightest performance, often applauding the "star" and making requests.

> *One afternoon, around 4:30, the peak time for departure, a show begins not far from the stairs at Bay 2. This time it is a guy in white shorts and a black knit halter top, lip-synch-ing to Bette Midler singing "In the Mood." All the gestures are there and much of the enthusiasm; he attracts a good crowd. Most of the people heading home stop on their way to catch his performance. The guy who is singing, unlike the others previously described, is rather masculine in appearance. He wears a moustache, and has dark hairy legs, but he likes to "camp," and he excells at lip-synch-ing, two skills prized in the gay community. After he has taken his bows as Bette Midler, someone from the crowd of about four hundred calls out "Do Barbra! Do Barbra!" His friends improvise a turban for him, and he begins Streisand's "The Way We Were." The song is a down number, and in between lines he makes jokes in his own deep voice and everyone cracks up.*
>
> *(Field notes, 22 June 1974)*

It is obvious from the variety displayed by these three individuals that "drag" takes many forms, and that performers differ in their ability and intention to pass as female and in their dependence on props. The one feature common to all three was the wit and humor of their performance, and the enthusiasm with which they were received by the gay community.

Conclusion

The gay world is very compartmentalized, comprised of homogeneous groups, who rarely come together in any public settings. Gay bars are almost invariably exclusive to members of the same sex, often segregated by race and class. The clientele of gay male bars, in particular, bear strong similarities to one another in style, ethnicity, age, occupations, and neighborhoods. There are specific bars for drag queens, leather men, young men, old men, hustlers, Latins, Blacks, Asians, chorus boys, opera singers, and every imaginable subgroup. Even at gay pride marches, gay people are separated into different factions. In addition, there are many gay people who eschew the bar scene entirely in favor of home-based socializing, who never have anything to do with "bar people," and who never attend marches. Straight people and children certainly have little prominence in the gay world. Almost nowhere in the gay world can one find the diversity and pluralism of Jacob Riis Park. The wide variety of bathers assembled in Bays 1 and 2 represent people from a broad range of social, racial, and sexual backgrounds. Their general tolerance for one another and the relative harmony among the bathers, with the significant exception of the small minority of straight male interlopers, characterized the mood at Jacob Riis Park as it began the 1974 season under the auspices of the National Park Service. The tranquil temperament here described has been broken many times over the following years, and even during the course of this first season under federal administration, by changes in official policy and fluctuating patterns of enforcement.

NOTES

1. A. B. Warren, *Identity and Community in the Gay World*, p. 17.
2. Ibid., p. 18.
3. Newton, *Mother Camp*, p. 27.
4. Edwards, "Disco Dancers Are Back."
5. Bronski, "Judy Garland and Others," p. 201.

REFERENCES

Altman, Dennis. *Homosexual: Oppression and Liberation*. New York: Avon Books, 1971.

Bronski, Michael. "Judy Garland and Others: Notes on Idolization and Derision," in *Lavender Culture*, ed. Karla Jay and Allen Young (New York: Harcourt, Brace & Jovanovich, 1974), p. 201.

Edwards, Henry. "Disco Dancers are Back, and the Kung Fu Has Got Them," *New York Times*, 27 Dec. 1974, 2:1.

Hoffman, Martin. *The Gay World*. New York: Basic Books, 1968.

Jay, Karla, and Allen Young. *Lavender Culture*. New York: Harcourt, Brace & Jovanovich, 1974.

Newton, Esther. *Mother Camp: Female Impersonators in America*. Englewood Cliffs, N.J.: Prentice-Hall, 1972.

Warren, Carol A. B. *Identity and Community in the Gay World*. New York: John Wiley & Sons, 1974.

Weinberg, Martin S., and Colin J. Williams. *Male Homosexuals: Their Problems and Adaptations*. New York: Oxford Univ. Press, 1974.

PART 2

ETHNIC ENTERPRISE AND ADAPTATION

At the base of the Statue of Liberty placed in New York Harbor in 1886 is a bronze plaque inscribed with a poem by Emma Lazarus, a nineteenth-century American poet. The most famous lines of the poem have done much to define the meaning of the statue for the United States and the rest of the world:

> Give me your tired, your poor,
> Your huddled masses yearning to breathe free,
> The wretched refuse of your teeming shore.
> Send these, the homeless, tempest-tossed to me.
> I lift my lamp beside the golden door.[1]

The statue, and this welcoming verse affixed to its base in 1903, greeted millions of immigrants, mostly from Europe. The nineteenth- and early twentieth-century groups who settled in New York in the greatest numbers were, as Aronson noted (in Chapter 1), the Jews, Germans, Irish, and Italians.

New York continues to be a major port of entry or destination for immigrants, and not only from Europe. After World War II, immigration from the Caribbean area, Latin America, and Asia increased, bringing members of many new ethnic groups, as well as some new immigrant waves from Europe. Barbadians and Jamaicans, Cubans and Colombians, Iranians, Indians, and Thais—these are but a few of the many immigrant groups who have put down new roots or strengthened older ones in New York in the second half of the twentieth century. The chapters in this section of the book dip into New York's vast experience as a destination and commingler of the world's peoples.

The first chapter in this section deals with the role of an ethnic newspaper in the Norwegian community in New York. A word should be said about ethnic newspapers, because they contribute to one of New York's traditionally distinctive attributes. In 1950, Morris Janowitz found that eighty-two community newspapers were being published within the city limits of Chicago. He found that a similar pattern of neighborhood newspapers existed in every major metropolitan district of over a million people—except New York. One of the reasons for the relatively small number of neighborhood newspapers in New York was the persistence of the ethnic and foreign-language press.[2] Even in 1982, a single newsstand near a subway station in Queens sells newspapers in the following languages: Spanish (three), Russian (two), Greek (two), and one each in French, German, Hungarian, Italian, Polish, and Yiddish. In addition, in the English language are an Irish paper (*Irish Echo*) and the *Amsterdam News*, the latter published for a Black readership. Knight Hoover's exploration of the impact and significance of a Norwegian newspaper in New York helps to clarify the enduring vitality of the ethnic press in New York. Hoover's chapter also shares some common ground with Handel's in showing the impact of Nazism on ethnic groups and neighborhoods in New York in the 1930s and 1940s.

Illsoo Kim's chapter on Koreans moving into the fruit and vegetable business in New York discusses one of the important new Asian ethnic groups in the United States. It is also a new example of a long-established phenomenon: the tendencies of particular ethnic groups to move into particular occupations when they come to the United States. Kim presents an analysis of how and why the Koreans chose and flourished in this particular occupation.

Both Kim and Hoover deal with ethnic groups that are not as residentially ghettoized as were the Yorkville immigrant groups and those described by some of Aronson's autobiographers. "Ethnic ties without turf" is an important new development.

Economic survival is a first priority for immigrants with scant means, as are many of the West Indian immigrants. Aubrey Bonnett describes an institution devised by the immigrants themselves, the rotating credit association. For the person short of funds to set up a beginning household, the rotating credit association offers a loan that makes this possible. Not yet eligible for the services of a public lender, a bank, newcomers turn to a private voluntary association organized by a fellow member of their own ethnic group. As immigrants have done since 1657, when the Scots Charitable Society was formed, people in a new country are likely to turn to members of their own ethnic group for financial aid.

Ethnic identity in a new country is maintained in various ways. Hoover showed how a public institution, a newspaper, contributed to defining and sustaining an ethnic identity among Norwegian immigrants and their descendants. Ethnic identity is also maintained through private gatherings. Adele Bahn and Angela Jaquez have studied Dominican bridal showers in New York, a type of gathering restricted to young Dominican and other Hispanic women. Their chapter is also a contribution to the sociology of sexuality. There have been relatively few studies of ethnic group approaches and attitudes to sexuality within American society, and this study invites comparison studies among other ethnic groups. This is the only chapter in this volume that deals specifically with women's experience in the city (though note Aronson's reference, in Chapter 1, to the importance of the department store in liberating women), and this scarcity of treatment regrettably reflects the status of the field. In 1975, Lyn Lofland noted that women were just "there" in urban sociology—part of the background, not the subject matter.[3] Only recently has this situation begun to change significantly.[4]

NOTES

1. Emma Lazarus, "The New Colossus," quoted in Marvin Trachtenberg, *The Statue of Liberty* (New York: Viking, 1976), p. 214.
2. Morris Janowitz, *The Community Press in an Urban Setting*, 2d ed. (Chicago: Univ. of Chicago Press, 1967), pp. 32–33.
3. Lyn Lofland, "The 'Thereness' of Women: A Selective Review of Urban Sociology," in Marcia Millman and Rosabeth Moss Kanter (eds.), *Another Voice: Feminist Perspectives on Social Life and Social Science* (New York: Anchor, 1975).
4. See, for example, Catharine R. Stimpson (ed.), "Women and the American City," *Signs: Journal of Women in Culture and Society*, 5, Supplement (Spring 1980); and Gerda R. Wekerle, Rebecca Peterson, and David Morley (eds.), *New Space for Women* (Boulder, Colo.: Westview, 1980).

5

Ethnic Press and the New York Norwegian Community

KNIGHT E. HOOVER

METHODOLOGICAL NOTE • This chapter is based on document analysis—newspapers, organizational pamphlets, magazines, and books—and participant observation carried out over more than a decade. The study began as a follow-up case study of Christen T. Jonassen's "Cultural Variables in the Ecology of an Ethnic Group."[1] A series of case studies culminating in the content analysis revealed that Norwegian ethnicity is not limited to the spatial confines of the Norwegian enclave in Brooklyn, New York.

The bulk of the field work—formal and informal interviews of ethnic organization leaders and members and enclave residents, questionnaire distribution, participant observation, and content analysis—was done in the Brooklyn, N.Y., Norwegian-American ethnic enclave. An "emigration scholarship" from the Norwegian government enabled me to do further archival research in the University Library, Oslo, Norway, in 1980.

Ethnicity among white, North-European Norwegian immigrants and their offspring has changed forms, reflecting the urban, industrial metropolis which contains the ethnic group. Ethnicity as an identity has persisted 87 among Norwegian immigrants and their descendants in the New York metropolitan region over the past one hundred years. Ethnic persistence must have structural supports, and in this instance, the Norwegian-language press has assisted in creating as well as describing a Norwegian ethnic network. Content analysis of the major Norwegian-language newspaper in New York, *Nordisk Tidende,* and sources discussing the paper, provide evidence to support the persistence of Norwegian ethnicity in New York through a network of voluntary organizations during the past century.

Definitions

There is a distinction between a person of Norwegian birth or descent living in a spatial enclave of like-ethnics and participation in voluntary organizations that promote (either consciously or not) awareness of and identity with Norway. At one point in history, approximately fifty to a hundred years ago, the enclave and community of interest were roughly coterminous. In 1980 the spatial enclave represents only a part of the "community" of Norway-interested persons who are linked together by their interest and interaction in an interdependent network of voluntary organizations. It is the nonspatial Norwegian network extant in New York that comprises the ethnic community in 1980. Thus the "community" of Norway-interested persons is not restricted to one spatial area, but consists of persons who belong to a network of interacting and interdependent organizations. The distinction between a nonspatial community of interest and an enclave represents the changing character of ethnicity among Norwegian-born and their descendants (including a small number who are not Norwegian by ancestry, but by interest and participation only) in the New York metropolitan area.

Origins of the Community and Ethnic Press

The first modern group immigration of Norwegians to New York City occurred in 1825. It was not until the 1850s, however, that a small Norwegian settlement was established in New York City. By 1847, Scandinavians were numerous enough in Manhattan to begin publication of a Scandinavian newspaper—*Skandinavia*—which included in each issue material written in Danish, Norwegian, and Swedish. A specifically Norwegian press did not emerge until 1878, with the founding of the *Nordiske Blade. Nordisk Tidende* was founded in 1891. It was, and primarily continues to be, written in Norwegian, including advertisements.

The establishment of Norwegian newspapers paralleled the emergence of Norwegian enclaves. Norwegians began to settle on Manhattan's East Side in the 1850s, from which there was large-scale migration to Brooklyn during the last quarter of the nineteenth century. Thus, a Norwegian spatial enclave has existed in Brooklyn for more than a century. Once in Brooklyn, the settlement continued to migrate from South Brooklyn until it reached Sunset Park and Bay Ridge, where it has remained since the 1940s. The Brooklyn "colony," the term applied to the settlement by the press, contained about 75 percent (35,000) of New York City's first- and second-generation Norwegian population in 1940.[2] Although Norwegians resided throughout the greater New York region as early as the 1880s, the colony dominated as the ethnic center. The period of massive enclave dispersion did not occur until after World War II. Thus it was in the colony that the largest spatial concentration of Norwegians in the metropolitan area resided, where most organizations met, and where the press was located. In 1970 the colony still represented the single largest concentration of first- and second-generation Norwegians in the New York metropolitan area. At that time 29 percent (14,300) of the metropolitan area's 49,700 Norwegians lived in Brooklyn. Brooklyn accounted for 20 percent of the metropolitan area's population that listed Norwegian (Landsmål) as their mother tongue, while 72 percent of Brooklyn's Norwegian population listed Landsmål as their mother tongue. This compares to 62 percent for the metropolitan region.[3] Although every issue of *Nordisk Tidende* chronicles the death of Norwegian language users, *Nordisk Tidende* is the only Norwegian language newspaper for the entire East Coast (and is one of three remaining in the United States). *Nordisk Tidende*'s readership, although concentrated in the New York area, is not restricted to it. In addition to Norwegian-Americans, readers include Norwegian nationals, such as business and government employees, sailors, and students. The paper continues to be a unifying factor in the ethnic community.

Nordisk Tidende has been the focal point of the Norwegian ethnic community in Brooklyn, New York, and in the greater metropolitan region since at least the first quarter of the twentieth century. *Nordisk Tidende* has followed the migrating population from Old South Brooklyn to Bay Ridge[4] and has been an integral component of the ethnic infrastructure. It has served both to create and to reflect a broader metropolitan-area Norwegian-American ethnic community. Former editor Karsten Roedder stated that the history of the paper

is considerably more than a history of a Norwegian-American paper . . . . The paper's history also becomes the ethnic group's history.

The paper reflects its environment . . . and is strongly tied to the Norwegian ethnic group in New York, which it has served through all these years.[5]

Readers familiar with the literature on the role of the ethnic press will recall Robert Park's conclusion that the foreign-language press was an assimilation agent, enabling immigrants to understand and accept American culture.[6] *Nordisk Tidende* performed this role by printing articles for the newcomer. But from its very inception, *Nordisk Tidende's* owners and editors also had the goal of maintaining ties to Norway, of preserving the Norwegian language and culture, and assisting the Norwegian-American in preserving "Norwegianness." *Nordisk Tidende's* position and its roles in the two cultural settings in which it existed—American and Norwegian—portray the dual reality of Norwegian ethnic life in metropolitan New York. The newspaper did not perceive these two roles as conflicting: one had to be a good Norwegian to be a good American. The press sought to create a sense of peoplehood and then sought to use Norwegianness as a basis for collective action.[7] In this sense *Nordisk Tidende* created and maintained a sense of Norwegianness in both a relatively dense Norwegian ethnic enclave (the colony) and in a broader nonterritorial community within the New York metropolitan region. Park also recognized, of course, ways in which the press hinders assimilation or complete loss of ethnic identification. In the long run, Park's emphasis on assimilation is most accurate with regard to Norwegians, but even cultural and structural integration into the host society does not preclude ethnic persistence. A Norwegian ethnic community survives in the New York area a half century after the last sizable migration. *Nordisk Tidende* has been instrumental in preserving Norwegian ethnic identity in the New York area.

The history of *Nordisk Tidende*, here divided into five periods, describes the existence of Norwegian-Americans in Greater New York.

Advocacy, Growth and Legitimation: 1891–1912

By 1890 there were between 8,000 and 14,000 Norwegians in New York, up from 2,000 Norwegian-born in 1880; about 1,300 lived in New Jersey.[8] Many were unmarried sailors working on ships or in sea-related occupations in New York's expanding seaport located in Manhattan and Brooklyn. The growing harbor offered employment and opportunity to Norwegian sailors and immigrants whose skills were in demand; the Norwegian population expanded.

Nordisk Tidende underwent many editorial changes in the first two decades after its founding in 1891. Perhaps this was essential for the upstart paper to gain a foothold among Norwegian-Americans already served by the established *Nordiske Blade*, founded in 1878. *Nordisk Tidende* began as an advocate of the seamen, attacking Norwegian shipowners for the poor con-

ditions aboard Norway's sailing ships, which frequented the New York harbor and whose crews came to be among the first Norwegian immigrants on
the East Coast. *Nordiske Blade* was attacked as a mouthpiece of shipowners,
a stance *Nordisk Tidende* did not view as consistent with American democracy. *Nordisk Tidende*'s editorials also attacked the colony's religious leadership as being elitist, carrying over from the old country an antagonism
toward the Norwegian State Church as authority. The young paper and its
inexperienced editors adopted an ideology of democracy and freedom in its
support for Norwegian sailors. Since most Norwegians in New York at the
time were employed in sea-related occupations, the paper acquired a readership and became successful and "lively."[9] *Nordisk Tidende* grew from four
to eight pages, from a sporadically published paper to a regular weekly as
the colony expanded by immigration.

   Nordisk Tidende became increasingly successful and in 1910, when *Nordiske Blade* folded, became the sole Norwegian paper. By 1912 *Nordisk
Tidende* had changed from a paper of yellow journalism to a more family-
oriented paper. The change reflected the increase of family units within the
Norwegian population.[10] The paper stressed the importance of membership
in ethnic organizations, including involvement in religious life, as a new,
church-going editor sought to change the paper's earlier character. *Nordisk
Tidende* continued its advocacy for sailors but in a less sensational way,
seeking to work through established sailors' organizations.

   The sailor provided one of the links between Norway and the East Coast.
Nordisk Tidende's articles continually highlighted such links to and events
in the homeland, accenting the immigrants' allegiance to Norway. For example, it regularly campaigned for a pan-Norwegian day of celebration commemorating the signing of the Norwegian constitution in 1814.[11] The paper's
advocacy initially went unheeded as Norwegian-Americans, although cele-
brating Constitution Day, continued to do so in separate organizations often
reflecting traditional allegiance to a region in Norway rather than to the
Norwegian nation or ethnic group as a whole. At this time, when Norway
itself was still joined with Sweden and thus not an independent nation, the
paper's pan-Norwegian outlook was not sufficient to create a single ethnic
identity in New York. *Nordisk Tidende*'s community-building efforts were
bolstered by the creation of an independent Norway in 1905 when Norway
and Sweden became separate countries, and by the paper's role as the sole
Norwegian newspaper in the rapidly expanding ethnic community.·

   The precedents for the future—editors active in and advocating membership in Norwegian-American organizational life, active advocacy for the
sailors' welfare, continued reportage of events in the motherland, and an
ideology of democracy and freedom—had been set in the period 1891 to
1911.

Community Building: 1912–1929

By 1910 more than thirty thousand Norwegian-Americans resided in New York. Immigration was reduced during World War I, but it resumed in the 1920s, until the first immigration restrictions in 1924. By 1920 *Nordisk Tidende* claimed that there were eighty thousand Norwegian-Americans in the New York area.[12]

The growth of the Norwegian community was related to economic conditions in America. For the United States the period after World War I was one of growth and ascension to the status of a world power. New York City continued to develop. Transportation lines were extended into the open areas of southwest Brooklyn as early as 1915.[13] The port further expanded southward along the Brooklyn waterfront. South Brooklyn was rapidly developing, as new construction provided Norwegian workers with jobs and better incomes. All these factors enhanced the development of a working-class ethnic enclave.

There was also a small but influential number of white-collar professionals—business persons, engineers, teachers, shipowners, and Norwegian government employees—who created their own ethnic organizations and comprised a small elite in the Norwegian community. These persons were not usually a part of the more numerous working-class ethnic clubs and churches, and many did not live or have their businesses in the colony enclave. Nonetheless, *Nordisk Tidende* sought out and worked with this group by devoting column space to its business, shipping, and social activities. This group also was an integral component of the Norwegian-American community network through its connections to and frequent leadership in the ethnic charity and welfare organizations. *Nordisk Tidende*'s new leadership helped build and coordinate the organizational network and, at the same time, developed a "community" image as well as a constituency for the paper.

The new editor, A. N. Rygg, and business manager, S. J. Arnesen, cast the paper into the hub of the colony's activities. They professionalized *Nordisk Tidende*, reflected the middle-class values of the Norwegian-Americans, and forged connections to the business leaders, both in the colony and in the New York area. *Nordisk Tidende*, under the leadership of Rygg and Arnesen, became a forum for local Norwegian-American and Norway-based business, religious, charitable, and cultural interests in New York. Circulation increased, apparently due to the practices of the new management, coupled with the rising national prosperity and an increase in the density of Norwegian-American events in the mid-1920s.

Three events over which the leaders had little control, but which they used to the advantage of the *Nordisk Tidende* and to build an ethnic consciousness and community, illustrate their leadership roles in this period:

World War I, the 1925 Centennial of Norwegian Immigration to the United States, and the 1926 American Sesquicentennial Celebration.

World War I

Nordisk Tidende took up the defense of Norway's position in the international scene at a time when ethnocentrism, xenophobia, and antiforeignness were closing down or changing the content of ethnic presses. Germany was a major trading partner with Norway prior to World War I. Norway declared neutrality but was nonetheless being attacked in the American press as abetting the German cause. *Nordisk Tidende* presented the American view but countered with arguments in favor of Norway. How much impact a foreign-language press had in American circles cannot be determined. The paper sought, however, to rally Norwegian-Americans to Norway's defense. The paper did this in a way that highlighted the similarity of American and Norwegian cultures, noting, for example, the high value placed by both nations on democracy and freedom. In this way the paper sought to downplay the differences and emphasize congruent national values. The paper's position turned from a defensive to a positive one a decade later, when Norwegian-Americans celebrated their immigration centennial.

Centennial of Norwegian Immigration to America

Norwegian-American ties to Norway were primarily through kinship until World War I, and the Norwegian government made little attempt to formalize its ties to Norwegian-Americans. With the celebration of the Norwegian Immigration Centennial in 1925, this position was temporarily altered. The idea for a great celebration emanated from ethnic organizations in the Midwest, and a national event was planned in Minnesota.

Nordisk Tidende endorsed the celebration idea and spent several years publicizing the event. Norwegian Parliament representatives, cabinet officials, and high-ranking persons from Norwegian economic and religious institutions traveled to America in the spring of 1925 to attend the celebration. For the first time in history, the Norwegian government officially recognized "Norwegian-America."

The celebration was given considerable legitimacy when President Calvin Coolidge agreed to be the main speaker. Norwegian-Americans were extolled for their contributions to America. The Norwegian press covered the event. Norwegian ethnics, following a period of retrenchment during World War I, were now recognized as a discrete population by the American and Norwegian governments.

New York was the port of entry for all the Norwegian guests. The Norwegian colony and *Nordisk Tidende* capitalized on the visits—both at arrival and at departure. The New York organizations arranged a special celebration in the city in October, since the first immigrant ship had arrived there in October 1825.

Norwegian-American events flourished in the 1912–1928 period. Immigrants streamed in, the colony grew, and the social climate in America, during this period of economic expansion, was favorable to the notion of ethnic pluralism. It was a period of rising optimism both for the paper and the ethnic group. But in 1929 the optimism faded as the collapsing economy eventually halted Norwegian immigration, seriously curtailed Norwegian shipping, and resulted in the unemployment of many Norwegian-Americans. *Nordisk Tidende*'s sales declined sharply. The 1926 American Sesquicentennial was the last major event in the community-building era prior to the depression.

The American Sesquicentennial

As America prepared for its sesquicentennial celebration, a committee of Norwegian-Americans, spearheaded by the organizational leaders, arranged for a parade of automobiles to Philadelphia. Encouraged by the more favorable official climate toward immigrants, Norwegian-American leaders organized Norway Day, as one of several ethnic days to be celebrated during the 1926 festivities. Although the event received less Norwegian ethnic support than the 1925 event, the Sesquicentennial provided Norwegian-Americans and *Nordisk Tidende* with further support for the idea that one could be both ethnic and American. The paper took the position that there was no conflict in the hyphenated Norwegian-American status.

The press took the opportunity to explain the great congruence of Norwegian and American values. It was even pointed out that George Washington had been a member of Philadelphia's Scandinavian Society. As economic prosperity continued, so did the mood of optimism among Norwegian-Americans and throughout America.

The 1922–1929 period, one of financial growth, was referred to as "the seven fat years." *Nordisk Tidende*'s twenty-page editions were more than half filled with ads. As 1928 drew to a close the paper reported a good year despite some unemployment among Norwegian sailors, carpenters, and bricklayers. The center of the Norwegian born population, previously in the Midwest, was said to have shifted to the East Coast. It was estimated that fifty thousand Norwegian-born lived in Greater New York alone.[14]

Yet in spite of the optimism there was concern about the immigration restrictions of 1927. *Nordisk Tidende* detailed the changes as follows: in

1924 the Norwegian quota was only 6,453 per year, about half the figure of 12,203 effective right after World War I. The new law, effective July 1, 1927, further reduced the quota, to about 2,000 annually.[15] President Coolidge, who had praised Norwegian ethnic contributions in 1925, was perceived as a traitor for signing the quota acts in 1927, but the colony was one of young families and the overall mood remained positive at least until the turn of the decade.

Depression and Recovery: 1930–1939

By 1930 there were approximately sixty-three thousand Norwegian-Americans (first and later generation) in New York City.[16] The primary locus of the colony's population and organization concentration had migrated to the Sunset Park section of Brooklyn, and the community's population was at its height. If the earlier period had been one of growth and optimism, the period beginning in 1930 was one of contraction and pessimism as the immigration and economic outlook worsened. The United States' first restrictive immigration policies, those of the mid-1920s, had resulted in sharp reductions of immigrants. But in retrospect, it was economic depression more than quota restrictions that initially resulted in reductions in membership in ethnic organizations such as the Sons of Norway and Norseman's Federation, and in Nordisk Tidende's sales and advertisements.

The 1930s were referred to as the "lean, lively years." The Depression curtailed normal organizational life, but interim forms of activity reached new highs during this time. The apparent contradiction is explained by the fact that although money to begin or maintain organizational memberships was scarce, free time was abundant. Thus, letters to the editor increased, as did participation in ad hoc social and political groups. Unlike the 1912–1929 period of activity, only one external event came to dominate life among Norwegian-Americans as reported in Nordisk Tidende—the Great Depression.

Rygg had resigned and sold his share in the Nordisk Tidende to Arnesen in 1929, just months before the stock market crash of October 1929. Arnesen assumed the editorship, which he transferred to Hans Olav in 1930. Olav and his assistant Carl Soyland, who had begun writing for Nordisk Tidende in the mid-1920s, continued the paper's advocacy for Norwegian seamen and immigrants. Soyland began a series of investigative reports in a "Hooverville" built upon a garbage dump in South Brooklyn. Soyland's articles, "From Life's Garbage Can," depicted squalor in the life of the unemployed Norwegian sailors who resided in the makeshift dwellings. Nordisk Tidende once again began to attack the Norwegian Government and Norwegian Shipowners' Association for its lack of aid to the unemployed seamen. Nordisk Tidende's response to the effects of unemployment was a major Norwegian-American self-help drive through a charitable network consisting of philanthropic, business, social, and religious organizations.

By the fall of 1930 "need" had become a common word in Nordisk Tidende. The paper called for an "emergency czar" to direct relief activities for unemployed sailors and Norwegian-Americans.[17] Winter was approaching, and the paper proposed that a committee be established to deal with emergency relief. The paper's office was to serve as the temporary center. Charles A. Larsen, a Norwegian-American owner of "one of the largest baking companies on the east coast," was recommended and elected as its chairperson.[18]

Membership in the newly formed Norwegian-American Emergency Relief Committee (NAERC) revealed the interconnected network of the Norwegian-American community, which included the paper's staff and leaders of business, charitable, religious, and social organizations, as well as Norway's consul general in New York. Whether or not Nordisk Tidende took the initiative to create NAERC, the paper promoted and implemented the ethnic relief organization. The committee represented a continuation of the efforts of the ethnic network to enable Norwegian-Americans to meet "the great needs which exist in our Norwegian society.[19]

As the colony's population suffered financially, so did Nordisk Tidende. However, at the worst of the Depression, and despite declines in Nordisk Tidende's sales and advertising, Arnesen purchased a building owned by a defunct English-language community newspaper: a measure said to be a gesture of faith in the American economy. Arnesen restructured the Norwegian News Company by establishing a subsidiary, the Arnesen Newsprint Publishing Company, which printed materials for Norwegian-American, Norwegian national, and American organizations.[20] This expansion into the printing business enabled the paper to survive the financial decline of lost readership and advertisers. Ownership of the building was short lived, however, as Nordisk Tidende moved into a rented building on Leiv Eriksson Square in Bay Ridge in February 1938.[21] The move followed the migration of Norwegian-Americans who had departed old South Brooklyn for the open area of new homes in Sunset Park and Bay Ridge.

Two major events kept the colony in contact with Norway in the 1930s. The 1932 Winter Olympics in Lake Placid, New York, hosted a Norwegian team. In 1939 occurred the first visit to the United States by Norwegian royalty, when the crown prince and his wife visited the Norway pavilion of the New York World's Fair. In both cases the Nordisk Tidende, supported by ad hoc committees of community leaders, rallied to organize, publicize, and promote the events. Nordisk Tidende's editor, Hans Olav, was designated by the Norwegian embassy to be the royal couple's guide in their extended visit to "Norwegian-America" after the World's Fair. Olav never returned to the paper; he became employed in the Norwegian government's information office in Washington, D.C.

The *Nordisk Tidende,* during Olav's editorship, had advocated for the centralization of Norway's tourist office and other Norwegian government and business organizations under one roof in Manhattan. It also recommended the creation of a Norwegian information service in New York City as an arm of the embassy, which Olav joined in 1940.[22] These recommendations were realized in the next decades. The paper continued to promote Norwegian national and Norwegian-American ethnic events. Despite a slow recovery period, by 1939 it appeared that both the paper and the colony's organizational activities were reviving.

Despite membership losses, the Norwegian-American organizational structure remained intact. The ethnic network had become linked to the larger American society because of contacts with religious and governmental agencies through NAERC. In the late 1930s the ethnic organizations rebuilt and resumed their annual ethnic calendar of events. In 1940, when the Nazis invaded Norway, the NAERC network was remobilized, enlarged, and used to express solidarity among Norwegian-Americans to a degree unprecedented since 1905, when Norway separated from Sweden. As in past decades, *Nordisk Tidende* was a crucial mediating structure in the Norwegian-American community, actively leading Norwegian-Americans to support Norwegian-American and Norwegian causes.

World War II and Heightened Ethnic Consciousness: 1940–1945

"World War II had the effect of preserving the Norwegian-American colony for decades," said editor emeritus Soyland reflecting on those years of his editorship (he took on the position before the Nazi invasion of Norway in April 1940).[23] The war had a positive impact on the maintenance and expression of Norwegian ethnicity. Not only did Norwegian migration from Brooklyn to the suburbs cease, but the enclave became the "Norwegian center of the U.S." The war temporarily halted the population dispersion of the enclave and concentrated the disparate organizational activities on one goal: the homeland's freedom and preservation.

The Nazi occupation of Norway suddenly reversed the *Nordisk Tidende's* circulation decreases of the Depression era. A 100 percent distribution increase occurred between April 1940 and the summer of 1941; circulation reached an all-time high, about twenty thousand per week.[24] In comparison with the period of World War I, the paper's task was considerably eased by the friendship between Norway and the United States. By accident of location, the New York Norwegian community and *Nordisk Tidende* were thrust into an important role in the Norwegian war effort.

Nordisk Tidende had advocated that the Norwegian government establish a central information office in New York.[25] As the Nazis advanced through Europe in 1939 and at the urging of Norway's minister to the United States, such an information office had been planned, but it had not become reality before the Nazis invaded Norway. *Nordisk Tidende* became the information office by default, as editor Soyland, then newly appointed, was besieged by the American press for information. Not only did the *Nordisk Tidende* staff become the "Norway information center," but the paper literally became a "free press" of Norway.[26] As ties were established with the Norwegian government in exile, the paper's long-held goal, to serve as a link to Norway, was realized in a way that had never been imagined.

Nordisk Tidende's position was made clear in the first days of the Nazi invasion: "All Norwegian-Americans are with you," was the message the paper sent to Norway's prime minister in London.[27] Within nine days of the invasion, *Nordisk Tidende* organized a Help Norway Committee, which moved into the paper's offices and remained there for seven years. The publisher was one of the committee's sixteen members (and its treasurer). Rygg, former owner and editor, was also included.[28] The density of events that occurred in the New York Norwegian community in the 1940–1945 period greatly added to Norwegian consciousness.

Not only had suburban migration abated, but also New York became a "home port" for the Norwegian merchant marine, whose members called Brooklyn "home" for five years. Norwegian-Americans from the entire East Coast, some previously uninvolved in ethnic events, came to Brooklyn to assist in the war effort. Every ethnic organization turned its activities to raising funds for Norway. *Nordisk Tidende* published stories of Norway, encouraged and organized joint ethnic events, including the first May 17th parade celebrated by all factions of the Norwegian community. The paper purposefully sought to utilize the occupation of Norway to arouse ethnic consciousness.

> [T]he great dramatic and unpleasant headlines in the paper shook up the [Norwegian-American] public and brought money into the Help Norway treasury. Editor Soyland as well as A. N. Rygg [a contributing columnist] were aware of this; the editor had nothing against exaggerating things [in the headlines], but he insisted upon integrity in the news reports. . . . Help Norway had a strong supporter in [*Nordisk Tidende's*] editorials.[29]

Nordisk Tidende's links to official Norway were more solidified than ever. Former editor Hans Olav was working for the embassy in Washington. Former government officials in exile traveled to the United States and either wrote for or were interviewed by *Nordisk Tidende*. In addition, Nobel-Prize-winning author Sigrid Undset lived in Brooklyn and wrote for *Nordisk Tidende*. The paper exploited the circumstances to promote Norway, ethnic consciousness, and itself. The motto of King Haakon VII of Norway, "*Alt for Norge*" ("Everything for Norway"), became the paper's goal. Reviving an interest in Norway was not difficult, since most Norwegian families in the metropolitan area had relatives there. The paper urged its readers to send in any news received from Norway. The English language was being used to a greater extent, so American-born readers could follow events in Norway. However, the paper continued to be written predominantly in Norwegian. The paper's regular "English Column" became "Our American Column." With the advent of war, "ethnicity" no longer suggested an undue interest in the past; it had unwittingly been cast into modern Norwegian history. *Nordisk Tidende* became a driving force for the Norwegian cause.

Like the centralized effort *Nordisk Tidende* had helped to spearhead in the Depression, the "Norwegian Phlanx" became the New York area committee to guide a federation of Norwegian-American organizations. The Phlanx was incorporated in the summer of 1942. Its first president was *Nordisk Tidende*'s owner.

Throughout the war the Phlanx organized annual April 9th celebrations commemorating the Nazi occupation of Norway. Proceeds from the events were divided between the Norwegian Seamen's Welfare Fund and "Little Norway," a Norwegian air-force base located in Canada. The first April 9th gathering at Carnegie Hall in Manhattan featured Norway's Crown Prince Olav as principal speaker.[30]

The war signaled the first time in the history of Norwegian settlements in the United States that Norwegian-Americans and the Norwegian state were linked at quasiofficial organizational levels. Immigrants and their organizations were explicitly recognized as valuable to Norway.

The war also advanced the consciousness of Norwegian-Americans, Norwegian and American born. At the organizational level, ethnicity was becoming more centralized, linking Norwegian ethnic organizations in the United States from coast to coast in the fund-raising effort for Norway. The bureaucratization of ethnicity was an unnoticed effect of World War II. Coupled with other phenomena of the postwar period, ethnicity among Norwegians survived the relatively rapid dispersion of the Brooklyn enclave, as the spatial base of ethnicity became increasingly replaced by an organizational base in a nonterritorial community.

Postwar Travel and Ethnicity: 1946–Present

The New York Norwegian population and *Nordisk Tidende* entered the postwar period financially sound and with a renewed consciousness of Norway. Several thousand immigrants a year entered the United States during the 1950s, many of them settling in Brooklyn and contributing to the Norwegian presence.[31] The community's location near the port of New York enabled it to continue to take advantage of the economic, political, and social exchanges there. The Norwegian state department formally recognized the efforts of the Norwegian-American press for Norway during the war, and *Nordisk Tidende*'s Soyland and twelve other Norwegian-language newspaper editors were given a one-month tour of Norway.[32]

Soyland wrote twenty-three travel articles for *Nordisk Tidende* as a result of his tour. Long an advocate of tourism to Norway, he encouraged Norwegian-Americans to visit Norway. Attitudes among Norwegian-Americans about travel to Norway were described as "ambivalent" before the war, but the war and accompanying changes in technology soon changed this. The paper's poll of one thousand readers indicated that "80 percent had dreamed of traveling 'home' to Norway" in 1947.[33] Tourism was given additional impetus in 1946, when the newly created Scandinavian Airlines System (SAS) made history with its first regularly scheduled flight to New York with editor Soyland aboard.

"Airplane introduces a new epoch in contact between Norway and U.S.A." read the headline in the 24-page special issue of *Nordisk Tidende* dated 26 September 1946 and dedicated to SAS. Five of the ten first-page articles were devoted to the airplane age. Editor Soyland was enthusiastic about the possibilities of air travel and devoted considerable space to SAS in following issues. SAS purchased several ads in the paper, and many ads praised the SAS accomplishment. SAS became a permanent advertiser and topic of reporting in 1946 and continues to remain an integral part of the Norwegian ethnic network in New York.

Throughout the 1950s *Nordisk Tidende* covered the activities of shipping and airplane companies; they in turn advertised in the paper and supported other ethnic programs. In addition to tourism, New York remained a major port for the Norwegian merchant marine. Changes in shipping technology, however, resulted in smaller crews, which were docking the ships at piers more distant from the enclave. Further, the port of New York began to decline as the major U.S. port. Thus the role of the seaport, a vital aspect of the Norwegian colony's history, began to decline. The nature of Norwegian ethnicity as intimately linked to the sea began changing. Other postwar developments also changed the nature of the Norwegian colony.

The ethnic enclave in Brooklyn declined from 16,000 Norwegian-born heads of family in 1940 to 13,347 Norwegian-born by 1950. By 1960, only 14,561 first- and second-generation persons resided in the same area, as the ethnic population suffered losses to death and suburban migration. The first- and second-generation figures were less than 10,000 in 1970. Despite the continually declining population, the organizational base—business, philanthropic, religious, and social—remained in southwest Brooklyn. American-born generations were beginning to outnumber the Norwegian-born mainstay of the ethnic organizations. The Norwegian-American population in the greater New York area in 1970 was approximately 50,000; that is, one in five Norwegian-Americans lived in the enclave. This demographic shift suggested the future demise of the enclave.

Nordisk Tidende sales reflected the declining immigrant population. By 1954 the paper was no longer a member of the Audit Bureau of Circulation, an organization which, the paper had boasted only a decade earlier, insured advertisers that their ads were being read.[34] In the same year the number of average pages per issue declined from sixteen to twelve. When Arnesen sold the paper to the staff in 1958, circulation had dropped to 9,448.[35] Attempts to appeal to American-born readers by increasing the amount of English were not successful; the paper returned to publishing almost exclusively in Norwegian.

The *Nordisk Tidende* still sought to organize local events during the 1950s by capitalizing upon anniversaries and events relevant to the ethnic community. In 1941, when *Nordisk Tidende* was fifty years old, the war necessitated postponement of the celebration. In 1951, editor Soyland decided to move the delayed celebration ahead from January to May to coincide with the May 17th celebration. The issue from 10 May 1951, a sixty-eight-page anniversary special, the largest in the paper's history to that date, traced the record of the paper. The Phlanx had been revived to plan a "People's Party." The guest of honor was the Norwegian prime minister. The *New York Times* editorialized:

> The reputation of the paper is reflected in its ability to bring Norway's popular Premier, Einar Gerhardsen, as the principal speaker at the sixtieth anniversary of the *Nordisk Tidende*. This is the first peacetime visit by a Norwegian governmental leader. President Truman has congratulated *Nordisk Tidende* for "helping those Americans who have come to us from Norway fit themselves more easily into the American scene." We join in offering our congratulations and best wishes.[36]

The Truman letter, printed on page one of the *Nordisk Tidende* anniversary issue, continued, "By helping to maintain contact with the homeland by Americans of Norwegian descent, your paper has also contributed to our excellent relations with Norway, which are based on mutual understanding and respect."[37] It was not uncommon for the paper to be praised for its role in integrating immigrants, but the paper's livelihood depended on Norwegian awareness. The latter role, recognized by Truman, was a major goal of *Nordisk Tidende*. Events during and after World War II—e.g., Norway's NATO membership—served to further legitimate relations between Norway and the United States.

Nordisk Tidende sought to consolidate gains made during the war and postwar period. For example, the paper strongly urged the resumption of a pan-Norwegian May 17 parade. Such an event had been a rallying point for Norwegians and Norwegian-Americans with its inception in 1942. In

1946 the parade ceased, but through *Nordisk Tidende's* encouragement was revived in 1952. The May 17 parade has become the principal annual Norwegian-American event. The parade is held in the colony and brings organizations and people from the entire New York area. Continuing a tradition set during the war, Norwegian speakers share the grandstand with Norwegian-Americans. *Nordisk Tidende* issues a larger special edition for each parade.

In 1962 *Nordisk Tidende* capitalized upon postwar travel technology, expanding its travel promotion with a special issue publicizing travel to Norway. The travel issue seeks to appeal to a broader audience and is printed primarily in English. The travel issue is an enlarged second section; it is mailed to all subscribers but is printed in larger quantities for separate sale. The travel section has been successful. It features articles about travel and events in Norway during the summer and contains ads from Norwegian and Norwegian-American companies. Editor Soyland, who initiated the travel issue in his last year as editor, considers the paper's focus on travel "natural," considering its role as a link to Norway.

During the postwar period, at a time when Norwegian-American ethnicity began to change, ties to Norway became closer. The links to Norway were now at two levels: personal, based on increasing travel, and organizational, based on increased trade relations reflecting realignment in foreign policy after World War II. Personal relations, which had been a mainstay of earlier links to Norway, began to decline as generations passed, but these ties were now being renewed because of modern travel. The paper was also consolidating organizational links to Norway through expanding trade and travel opportunities.

The paper's changing role reflected technological and demographic changes. As the paper's organizational network expanded in the metropolitan area and to Norway, its local influence declined. *Nordisk Tidende* had always taken advantage of events in the local New York environment by organizing programs in the ethnic enclave but now, its constituency having spread over a broader area, it strongly advocated for national and local expressions of Norwegian-American ethnicity. For example, the paper editorialized, without success, against the decision of the Norwegian-Lutheran Church in America to delete "Norwegian" from its name. Editorials notwithstanding, the Norwegian Hospital in Sunset Park became the Lutheran Medical Center. The name changes had no discernable impact on the newspaper. The local churches still advertised as before. The paper still continued to write about the hospital, first as a Norwegian organization and later as a local hospital. Nonetheless, the colony's organizational destiny was and is decreasing.[38]

In 1972 *Nordisk Tidende* introduced a new series of issues promoting Norwegian business and products in the United States. The special industrial

editions were primarily in Norwegian and initially appeared on an average
of two to three times per year, but in the late 1970s began to be produced
a half-dozen times a year. Commencement of an "oil age" in Norway has
created additional material for the industrial issue.

By 1978 *Nordisk Tidende's* circulation was about 7,600 twelve-page copies
per week. The paper began its ninetieth anniversary year in January 1981.
The paper's size has remained at twelve pages since 1954. Census figures
indicate a declining Norwegian-American population in New York in the
1980s. A small, aging ethnic enclave still remains in Bay Ridge and Sunset
Park. The last big migration to Bay Ridge, where the majority of the Norwegian population now resides, occurred in 1970. Religious and social activities, while declining, are still concentrated in southwest Brooklyn. These
events, as well as those in the larger New York area, are reported in *Nordisk
Tidende*. Based on 1970 census statistics, there are about twenty-five thousand Norwegian language users in the New York area. A large number of
subscribers are included among the retired in Florida. Norwegian citizens
residing in the United States provide another small contingent of readers.
Nordisk Tidende's future is unclear. In its ninetieth anniversary issue, a
forty-page edition published 22 October 1981, its supporters contended that
the paper was fulfilling a need and claimed that it would survive as long as
a need was being met.[39]

Norwegian ethnicity still persists in the New York metropolitan area in
the 1980s despite the decreasing size of the enclave. The decline in numbers
has resulted in the centralization of organizations; nonetheless, the organizational structures do remain. The Brooklyn Sons of Norway, for example,
has merged seven lodges into four in the last decade. The press in New
York has also centralized and has once again come to include several Scandinavian groups. Although one paper does not publish in three languages,
as was the case in New York a century ago, three of the four Scandinavian
papers in Brooklyn are published by Northway Printers, which publishes
Nordisk Tidende. Ethnic centralization reflects the centralizing tendency
that emerged in the United States after World War II, the same tendency
that was prevalent in New York in the 1850s, when Scandinavians were few
in number. There is, as of yet, no pan-Scandinavian ethnicity in the United
States, although discussions of such a possibility began in 1973 with a
Scanpresence conference in Minneapolis jointly sponsored by the Center
for Northwest European Studies at the University of Minnesota and the
Scandinavian Airlines System. A sequel followed in the fall of 1977. To date
each Scandinavian group maintains its own "community," organizations, and
press.

Nordisk Tidende's adaptations to changing circumstances have been a
matter of necessity. Its goals are similar to those of the 1920s: to stress and
maintain its links to Norway, to maintain and create ethnic awareness, and

to support the ethnic community. In 1981, however, only about one-fifth of the Norwegian-Americans in the New York metropolitan area remained in the spatial enclave. Nonetheless, *Nordisk Tidende* has remained a major—perhaps even *the* major—communications link among Norwegian-Americans in metropolitan New York and on the East Coast.

If *Nordisk Tidende* survives to 1991, it may be the first Norwegian foreign-language paper to reach the century mark. Even without the paper, Norwegian-American ethnicity may persist. To do so, new communication vehicles must continue to focus on, create, and sustain Norwegian-American ethnicity at centralized, national, and international levels.

At this time, however, it is accurate to say that *Nordisk Tidende* has not only reflected the ethnic group but has helped create and maintain Norwegian-American ethnicity in the metropolitan New York area and in the United States.

NOTES

1. Christen T. Jonassen, "Cultural Variables in the Ecology of an Ethnic Group," *American Sociological Review,* 14 (Feb. 1949): 32–41.
2. Christen T. Jonassen, "The Norwegians in Bay Ridge: A Sociological Study of an Ethnic Group." Ph.D. diss., New York University, 1947, pp. 274, 349.
3. U.S. Department of Commerce, Bureau of the Census. Statistical Package for the Social Sciences, Princeton University, 1975.
4. Jonassen, "Cultural Variables"; Jonassen, "Norwegians"; 1947; Knight E. Hoover, "Organizational Networks and Ethnic Persistence: A Case Study of Norwegian-American Ethnicity," Ph.D. diss., Graduate School and University Center, City University of New York, 1979; Karsten Roedder, *Av en utvandreravis' Saga: Nordisk Tidende i New York gjennom 75 år,* 2 vols. (Brooklyn: *Norwegian News,* Northway Printers, 1966 and 1968).
5. Roedder, 1:5.
6. Robert E. Park, *The Immigrant Press and Its Control,* Americanization Studies, vol. 7, William S. Bernard (ed.) (republished ed., Montclair, N.J.: Patterson Smith, 1971; orig. ed., New York: Harper & Bro., 1922). See especially ch. 3, "The Immigrant Press and Assimilation," pp. 49–88.
7. Martin Dann (ed.), *The Black Press, 1827–1890: The Quest for National Identity* (New York: Putnam, 1971). See Introduction for a similar function performed by the Black press.
8. Jonassen, "Norwegians," p. 349; Roedder, 1:15.
9. Roedder, 1:15–20.
10. Ibid., 1:41.
11. Ibid., 1:18.

12. Ibid., 1:79; Jonassen, "Norwegians," p. 349, indicated that there were 40,544 first- and second-generation Norwegians in New York City, based on 1920 census data.
13. Jonassen, "Norwegians," p. 259.
14. Roedder, 1:101, 159; e.g., *Nordisk Tidende*, 15 July 1926.
15. *Nordisk Tidende*, 6 Jan. and 3 June 1927. One can argue that the quotas had less impact on Norwegian immigration than the Norwegian press suggested. The depression of the 1930s and war of the 1940s would have kept Norwegian immigration low through the mid-1940s based on historical push-pull factors. Following World War II, economic improvements and rebuilding efforts in Norway apparently helped keep immigration down; e.g., the 1947 quota of about 2,500 was not filled (*Nordisk Tidende*, 4 Dec. 1947).
16. Jonassen, "Norwegians," p. 349. *Nordisk Tidende's* estimates are generally for the New York area. The paper did cite U.S. Census figures for the entire state of New York.
17. *Nordisk Tidende*, 30 Oct. 1930.
18. Ibid., 10 May 1951, 27 Nov. 1930; Roedder, 1:189–90.
19. *Nordisk Tidende*, 10 May 1951. This was a special sixtieth anniversary issue, which contained numerous historical articles.
20. Ibid., 4 Feb. 1932.
21. Ibid., 10 Feb. 1939; Roedder, 1:238.
22. *Nordisk Tidende*, 24 Nov. 1932, 9 Aug. 1934.
23. Interviews with Carl Soyland, conducted 1967–69.
24. *Nordisk Tidende*, 8 May 1941. Newsstand sales reached 5,200 copies by mid-April, 1940. This figure represented less than one-half of the paper's total distribution, based on figures for newsstand sales in 1940. The 20,000 figure is a *Nordisk Tidende* figure.
25. Ibid., 29 Aug. 1934.
26. This role was not unique to *Nordisk Tidende*, as other Norwegian-American papers did likewise; however, *Nordisk Tidende's* East Coast location provided it with advantages over other Norwegian-American presses.
27. *Nordisk Tidende*, 10 May 1951.
28. Ibid., 25 Apr. 1940.
29. Roedder, 2:25–26.
30. *Nordisk Tidende*, 16 Apr. 1942.
31. The national-origins quota system was abolished on 1 July 1968, when the full provisions of a 1965 act went into effect. The 1965 act regulated immigration partially on the basis of reuniting separated families. Since most Norwegian immigrants in the United States had their families with them, Norwegian immigration was restricted. See American Immigration and Citizenship Conference, Fact Sheet: *The Immigration Act of 1965—Public Law 89–236* (April 1967), pp. 1, 2. Even without the new law it is doubtful that Norwegians would have immigrated to the United States, because of continually improving social and economic conditions in Norway. Average annual Norwegian immigration to the United States in the 1950s was 2,293 per year, in the 1960s, 1,548 per year, and in the years 1970–74, 420 per year. U.S. Bureau of the Census, *Statistical Abstract of the United States: 1974* (95th ed.) (Washington, D.C.), p. 99.
32. Roedder, 2:170–71, 191.

33. Ibid., 2:181.
34. *Nordisk Tidende* published its Audit Bureau of Circulation on its masthead weekly. The citation ended in 1954.
35. *Nordisk Tidende*, 9 Oct. 1958.
36. *New York Times*, 17 May 1951, as quoted in Roedder, 2:230.
37. *Nordisk Tidende*, 10 May 1951.
38. Such was the case, for example, with the Norwegian Lutheran Church, founded by Norwegian immigrants in the United States. The Lutheran church has been called the major institution maintaining Norwegian identity in the U.S. But by the 1930s, the use of the Norwegian language at services was beginning to dwindle. The Norwegian Lutheran Church in America, seeking to attract a more diverse membership, wished to drop the descriptive "Norwegian" from its name. The issue had arisen in the 1930s and 1940s. During the war it was agreed within the Norwegian-American community and within the church itself to keep the name until after the war to show solidarity with Norway. *Nordisk Tidende* sided with those who argued that the church had been built by the Norwegian people on the basis of their Norwegian heritage. "The Dutch had a church (the Dutch Reformed Church), why not the Norwegians?" it argued. A name change would result in a colorless name with the church losing its identity among other Lutheran congregations in the U.S. (Roedder, 2:177–78). The name was changed. Soyland editorialized, "A Page Has Been Turned in the Saga of the Norwegian Immigrant" (*Nordisk Tidende*, 27 June 1947).
39. *Nordisk Tidende*, 22 Oct. 1981. This paper included an additional 38-page industrial issue for Fall 1981.

6

The Korean Fruit and Vegetable Business: A Case Study

ILLSOO KIM

METHODOLOGICAL NOTE • I came to New York City from Seoul, South Korea, in 1970. In 1973 I enrolled in the Ph.D. program in sociology at the Graduate Center of City University of New York. I had gotten ample opportunities to observe and intermingle with Korean immigrants not only in my Korean neighborhood in The Bronx, but also in other areas of the New York metropolis, while working for my doctoral dissertation on the Korean community, of which Korean greengrocery business is a part, during the period 1974–1979.

I embarked with the most "primitive" but the most reliable and always available methodological tools—ears and eyes. By simply taking advantage of being a Korean, I conducted long, unstructured interviews with Korean immigrants, or simply engaged in casual conversations and gossip. In the case of Korean businessmen, especially greengrocers, I could observe many of their daily activities in both homes and shops.

In many cases, my interviewees were not aware that they were being interviewed or "interrogated." In digging out and sifting data, however, I always tried to keep an outsider's point of view and discarded the materials that did not meet my own subjective criteria of objectivity. At the same time, I related their stories to the major theoretical problem of my study—how their biographies and their attempts to construct an ethnic community in new land are affected by broad social, economic, cultural, and political changes in both South Korea and the United States. This theoretical problem or framework greatly influenced the selection of particular data. 107

Korean greengrocers narrated in nontechnical, plain language their life histories as shaped by the external, impersonal forces associated with their immigration to the United States. In response, I presented their stories not in terms of established theories or concepts but in terms of an eyewitness, reporting how their biographies had been molded by exigencies in both South Korea and the United States.

Because the interviews were conducted during the entire period of the study, the questions asked reflected continuously emerging perspectives and dimensions of analysis. Since the interviewees reflected their unique social positions, experiences, and parochialism, I checked their stories against my own observations, the information provided by other informants, and other written materials, including Korean-language newspapers.

Background

When the United States Congress passed the Immigration Act of 1965, a "blessing from heaven" fell upon Asians in general and Koreans in particular. Thanks to the act, Asians have become a dominant immigrant group, constituting an annual average of 37 percent of some 450,000 immigrants accepted into the United States each year. The passage of the act resulted largely from the liberal, egalitarian, and civil-rights movements of the 1960s, and had nothing to do with Koreans either in the United States or in South Korea. The immigration of Koreans was a serendipitous by-product of these larger and basically internal political pressures.

The Korean immigrants to the New York metropolis constitute some 15 percent of about 100 Koreans who daily enter the "New Land," as the United States is called in South Korea, with an intention to settle permanently. According to the South Korean Ministry of Health and Social Welfare, in 1980 a total of 33,638 Koreans emigrated to the United States; this figure comprises 90 percent of total Korean emigrants to foreign countries. Since the enactment of the Immigration Act of 1965, some 340,000 Koreans have entered the United States on immigrant visas and another 50,000 have permanent resident status in the United States. Taking into account the unknown number of illegal aliens and immigrants' offspring born in the New Land, it is estimated that the total Korean population in the United States exceeds half a million, of which some 80,000 reside in the New York metropolitan area.

Koreans have generally immigrated in their basic social unit, the nuclear family. This is so in spite of the fact that frequently a family is temporarily separated so that a pioneer member can establish an economic base, or because of a bureaucratic delay under the United States or South Korean migration laws. The favorable conditions for either continuing the old family unit or creating a new family in the United States were laid by the humane nature of the Immigration Act of 1965, which permits reunion of immediate relatives. This is clearly responsible for the fact that 86 percent of the Korean householders in the New York metropolitan area were married in 1975; and that 40 percent of the Korean families were supported by two working family members, usually husband and wife. This family structure contrasts with that prevalent among older Asian immigrants at the turn of the century, who encountered an immigration law hostile to the creation or continuation of their own families in the New Land. It also decisively contributes to Korean success in small business enterprises in the New York metropolis.

The Emergence of Korean Greengrocers

Korean immigrants began to enter the fruit and vegetable business in New York City in 1971. The number of Korean-run fruit and vegetable stores has increased rapidly since 1974; by 1978 there were some 350 Korean stores in all, and by 1981 there were some 400 Korean stores, of which about 100 dealt in regular groceries in addition to fruits and vegetables. These stores are maintained in almost every neighborhood—White, Black, and Hispanic—of the New York metropolitan area; Korean greengrocers cater to all segments of the population. In entering the fruit and vegetable business, Koreans have revived an older immigrant pattern of striving for an ethnic takeover of certain ghetto business enterprises. A vivid illustration is provided by the *New York Times*.

> "It's like this," said a veteran produce supplier in a raspy Brooklyn accent, as he unpacked a crate of extra fancy figs at a Bronx Hunts Point Market stall. "When I first came into this business—that was before the war—to do business here you had to know Jewish phrases. Then, some years later you had to pick up a few Italian words to make it. Now I'm trying for all the Korean words I can. There are that many Korean buyers now."[1]
>
> If Ill Y. Chung were Chinese and he had immigrated here, he might well have gone into the laundry or restaurant business. If he were Greek, he might have gone into a coffee shop or delicatessen. But Mr. Chung is Korean and so he entered the newly popular Korean-American enterprise: he opened a fruit and vegetable store.
>
> "What else can I do?" asked Mr. Chung, 35 years old and the holder of two masters degrees on city planning from a school in Korea and one in mechanical engineering from the University of Hawaii. "I need money but there are no good jobs for Koreans. . . ." In fruits and vegetables, traditionally an immigrant business, first it was Jews, when it centered in the Washington market area, then Italians. And now up in the Bronx, it's the Koreans.[2]

Korean immigrants who entered the United States via Latin American nations were the first to enter the fruit and vegetable business, in 1971. These immigrants had run various businesses in Latin America after having encountered severe difficulties in progressing from the designated agricultural colonies of their original settlements to the metropolitan areas of Latin America. From there they migrated again, to the inner cities of the United States. During the years of uncertain and hostile journeys in foreign countries, they acquired a remarkable business acumen and a special sensitivity to economic opportunities. Furthermore, . . . they were heavily drawn from among the North Korean refugees in South Korea, who constitute a tough-minded, aggressive, and marginal group in South Korean society. It is no wonder that the members of this Latin American contingent first detected economic opportunity in the fruit and vegetable business when they settled in New York City. News of their success quickly spread throughout the Korean community in the area, and new immigrants from South Korea quickly followed them into the business. This economic news also spread to Koreans in Philadelphia, resulting in the emergence of Korean fruit and vegetable enterprises in that city.

The Three Causal Factors

Three structural factors can be linked with the emergence of the Korean fruit and vegetable business. First, the business can be opened with little capital and can be operated and managed without much knowledge of English. Given the small amounts of capital available, Korean immigrants with high economic motivation have entered this business.

> Mr. Huh, who immigrated five years ago, started his immigrant life as a janitor; a few months later he became a T.V. repairman. During the first year in the United States he saved about $4,000; Mr. Huh found a Korean partner and invested his savings in the opening of a fruit and vegetable store in Manhattan. In four years he has earned more than $100,000. Mr. Huh now employee eight workers. . . .[3]

Second, Korean immigrants with an abundance of family labor but little capital have either pushed out or taken over the businesses of old Jewish and Italian shopkeepers, who are too old to compete with a new generation of relatively young and economically aggressive Koreans. A Japanese journalist observed the importance of family labor for Koreans running fruit and vegetable businesses in New York.

> Mr. Kim bought his store two years ago from a Jewish American for a total payment of $15,000—$10,000 for the store price and $5,000 in key money. He and his son daily purchase vegetables: at four o'clock every morning when

the dawn is coming, they get up and drive to Hunts Point in the Bronx, where a city-run wholesale market is located. . . .

In the market they run and run in order to buy at low prices as many as one hundred and seventy different kinds of vegetables and fruits. All the transactions are made in cash. At 7 o'clock they return to the store and mobilize the rest of the family members in order to wash and trim vegetables. Here we can find the Koreans' secret of economic success in the business. In American supermarkets they do not wash and trim. . . .[4]

Shopkeepers who do not have sufficient family labor employ new Korean immigrants who otherwise could not find jobs. They exploit these non-unionized immigrants. The president of the Korean Produce Retailers Association of New York wrote some revealing advice on this matter.

Recently, officials from the Food Employee Union have frequently visited the Korean fruit and vegetable stores, asking for a collective mutual contract with the union. If we continue to turn down their offers, it may be possible for them to picket in front of our stores or to attach a protest statement to our store windows. Thus a ready-made answer should be prepared in advance to stave off their demands. We can make an excuse as follows: "This store is run by family members," or, "We, partners, run this store." It should be noted that American law allows three partners at a maximum. We should be especially cautious in employing Americans, because union officials may encourage them to become union members. Once they belong to the union, extra expenses such as overtime payments, the hourly minimum wage, and social security taxes follow. Small Korean fruit and vegetable stores cannot afford to pay all these extra costs. . . .[5]

Since new Korean immigrant workers are, as a whole, well educated, individualistic, and ambitious enough to start their own business or to find other, better economic opportunities, shopkeepers who cannot mobilize sufficient family labor face the problem of continually securing new laborers from among the latest arriving immigrants. Ethnic newspapers carry daily advertisements of jobs offered by owners of fruit and vegetable stores. One of the advertisements runs, "Urgently seek healthy young man who wants to work in a vegetable store." Nevertheless, there is a quick turnover of workers. One greengrocer complained, "To employ Koreans is really a headache. They work only two or three days and quit without giving notice. One guy started to work in the morning and disappeared in the evening without giving a word." Sophisticated and well-educated Korean immigrants are reluctant to work long hours at low wages; six Korean workers employed at a Korean fruit and vegetable store on Fourteenth Street in Manhattan petitioned the United States Labor Department because they felt that they were being exploited by being paid less than the minimum wage.[6] Mainly because of this difficulty in securing easily exploitable workers from among the Korean population, a Korean greengrocer suggested to a newcomer that "if you do not have sufficient family members willing to help you, you might be better not to start this business."

Third, Korean greengrocers who can employ sufficient family members are able to compete with supermarket chains because they can work the long hours it takes to do daily wholesale shopping at the Hunts Point Market. This shopping is necessary to provide a steady supply of fresh fruit and vegetables to customers. In addition, family members are effectively employed in the clipping, sorting, and washing necessary to reduce spoilage and waste. Thus the existence of family workers gives Korean greengrocers a marginal advantage over their competitors, supermarkets and non-Korean fruit and vegetable storeowners, most of whom subscribe to a delivery service for their retail products.

Intraethnic Conflict

Partly because of these structural factors, many Korean immigrants have set up new fruit and vegetable stores without buying established businesses. Once a Korean immigrant opens a new store, nearby non-Korean stores face serious competition. Many of the older Jewish or Italian stores have been forced out of business, and this leads to a new form of competition among Korean shopkeepers themselves. Here is an example of how interethnic competition transforms itself into intraethnic competition:

> In 1975, Mr. Lee, his two brothers, and one sister set up a new fruit and vegetable store near the South Bronx. They invested their total savings, which they had earned through menial work. At the opening of their store, they were uncertain about their economic future partly because they had to compete with an established Italian shop located a few blocks away. But, Mr. Lee once boasted, "When we started our business, they (the Italian shop) operated with four cashiers. Six months later, the number of cashiers was reduced to two. About nine months later, the owner came to our shop and asked whether we were interested in buying his shop." Mr. Lee's family could not take over the shop, because of its lack of capital. The shop eventually went to another Korean, named Mr. Oh, who owned two fruit and vegetable stores when he purchased the shop. Since Mr. Oh's taking over the shop, a fierce intraethnic competition has taken place between the two Korean stores. Mr. Oh could purchase retail items from wholesalers at much lower prices than Mr. Lee because Mr. Oh, an owner of three retail stores, buys large amounts of retail items. Thus Mr. Oh's retail prices were generally lower than Mr. Lee's. Mr. Lee once grumbled that Mr. Oh's store was practicing "dumping." [Field notes.]

Intraethnic competition also takes place when Korean immigrants buy stores from native Americans. The "key money" necessary for buying fruit and vegetable stores in New York City has increased substantially because Korean immigrants have competed among themselves in purchasing stores from non-Koreans. In 1974 the amount of "key money" needed to purchase a fruit and vegetable store was approximately five or six times that of the total weekly sales of the store. By 1977, the ratio of "key money" to total weekly sales had increased to seven or eight to one. In face of this increased capital requirement, Korean immigrants have opened new stores by leasing stores that became vacant after their owners were forced out of business. These newly opened Korean stores have encroached upon the sales territory of nearby stores regardless of whether the latter are run by Americans or Koreans. If the new Korean greengrocers compete with small American-run stores, they can easily overcome the competition because of their lower costs. But, if they encounter other Korean greengrocers, chances are that "they will ruin each other." Korean ethnic newspapers frequently offer some standard advice to potential greengrocers: "Competition among our *gyopo* [fellow countrymen] should be avoided."

Thus, one of the major functions of the Korean Produce Retailers Association, which was established in 1974, is to defend the interests of established Korean stores against newer Korean greengrocers. The association has systematically discouraged new arrivals from opening fruit and vegetable stores in areas near established Korean stores. An example can be found in the following episode.

A Korean named Mr. Lee was in the process of setting up a new fruit and vegetable store in the vicinity of an established Korean store located in the South Bronx. The established Korean greengrocer, named Mr. Kim, reported this event to the association, saying that if Mr. Lee opened his business both of them would lose business because of the limited number of customers.

The association's officials came to Mr. Lee and tried to persuade him not to open the business, by promising to grant him all the expenses that he had spent in setting up his business out of the association's fund. But Mr. Lee turned down their offer. Thus, in order to set an example designed to curb new openings by other Koreans, as well as to rescue Mr. Kim's store, the association decided to open a new store in the same block where Mr. Lee was opening his store, and it planned to dump vegetables at wholesale prices. [Field notes.]

Taking advantage of the widespread aspiration among Koreans for economic success, Korean business "hawks" emerged at the initial Korean entry into the greengrocery business. The hawks set up new stores and, after running them for a while, sold them to Korean newcomers, reaping smart profits in the form of "key money." Or they purchased stores from older ethnic owners and resold them to recent arrivals at inflated prices. A gimmick frequently involved in this kind of resale was the fraudulent inflation of sales volume. A Korean ethnic newspaper reported one example.

> A (Korean) couple in Flushing worked sixteen hours a day for two years and accumulated some savings: the husband had labored in menial jobs and the wife had toiled at a garment factory. Their dream was simple: they wanted to have their own business rather than work for someone else.
>
> One day, a church member [in their Korean church] approached and asked them whether they wanted to buy a fruit and vegetable store, saying that the owner of the store was a conscientious Christian. He added that the business of the store was very good but that the store owner had to sell the store because of a lack of hands.
>
> When the couple heard this offer, they were very excited. The couple loitered around the store for two weeks and watched the customers patronizing the store in order to determine the volume of transactions. Then they decided to buy the store for the payment of $20,000 in "key money" because the store had always been crowded with so many customers.
>
> They finally took over the store. But two or three weeks later they realized that they had been swindled. The once-teeming block customers suddenly disappeared. The former owner had cut his retail prices in half while they watched his store.[7]

Interethnic Conflict

In entering the fruit and vegetable business, Koreans have encountered some discrimination from Jewish and Italian wholesalers at the Hunts Point Market. In response, Korean greengrocers, for the first time in the history of New York's Korean community, staged a mass demonstration in the spring of 1977 "to protest what they say is discrimination against them in pricing practices and even in the allocation of parking services."[8] A Korean ethnic newspaper covered this event as a front-page story with the headline: "The Demonstration Showed Our Solidarity for a Common Interest." About a hundred greengrocers participated in the demonstration, which was formally touched off by a "racist slur" by a Jewish salesman in the market. The salesman was interviewed by an *Eastside & Westside* reporter, and the reporter's interview, after being translated into Korean, attributed remarks to the salesman to the effect that all Koreans are "stupid" and that they are all controlled by Sun Myung Moon's Unification Church.[9] Confronted by the Korean greengrocers, the salesman apologized and insisted that the newspaper report was quite different from what he had actually said. The Korean Produce Retailers Association used this episode as an excuse to flex its muscles, but basic structural conditions had led Koreans to undertake the demonstration.

American wholesalers have frquently taken advantage of the Korean retailers' inadequacy in English and their lack of business experience. Wholesalers have sometimes sold them rotten fruit or vegetables, and they have
sold their products to Korean greengrocers at higher than market prices;
some Koreans were beaten up when they tried to complain about such unfair
business transactions. Koreans have been robbed at the market's parking
lot in the South Bronx, and Korean retailers have frequently fought with
white retailers over parking space. When fights broke out, Koreans became
the victims because of their small size. In some cases, however, several
Koreans ganged up and knocked out white Americans when they saw fellow
Koreans fighting the Americans over parking space and other minor matters.
However, all these attacks against Koreans have taken place on an individual
basis. And there has been no systematic, conspiratorial discrimination by
wholesalers against Korean greengrocers. But the Korean Produce Retailers
Association, with an increasing membership, felt that the newspaper interview provided an appropriate opportunity for them to demonstrate Korean
"clout" and thus to put psychological pressure on the Hᵣ ınts Point establishment.

Most wholesalers at the Hunts Point Market welcome the entry of Koreans
into the business. This is so because, as one wholesaler (whose family started
their business three generations ago with a pushcart in lower Manhattan)
said, "They're good businessmen, they buy good produce and they pay their
bills in cash. . . . That's something we could use around here from everybody."[10] To show their good will, wholesalers contributed some three thousand dollars in 1977 to the Korean Produce Retailers Association. The
association used part of this contribution to pay the cost of its 1977 (annual)
picnic for its members and their families.

The Greengrocery Business as a Means of Capital Accumulation

For the majority of Korean greengrocers, the fruit and vegetable business
is just a means to accumulate capital with which they can start "clean" and
"comfortable" small businesses. Several Korean greengrocers own more
than one store and have set up a "chain store" management to run them;
but the majority do not enter this business permanently. Frequent changes
in ownership characterize most of the Korean stores. Partly because of this,
Korean greengrocers have not formed cooperatives through which (as some
advocate) they could purchase as a group from the producers in California
and Florida, at much lower prices. One of the basic reasons for the frequent
turnover of Korean fruit and vegetable stores is that to run such a business
requires painstaking work. Some Korean greengrocers said that, "no matter
how much energy, health, and stamina one may have, one cannot stand

more than two years of this daily toil." They use expressions such as "bloody urine," "drastic loss of weight," and "benumbed fingers like a leper's" when they describe the daily struggle of operating their businesses.

Many Korean greengrocers have "made it" by getting out of that business and reinvesting the capital they acquired from it in small businesses requiring less exploitation of themselves and their families. In doing so they have converted this self-exploited labor into capital and thus decreased the amount of primitive exploitation necessary for capital accumulation. Some of them, however, have sold their stores but have returned to the green-grocery business, saying that "no small businesses in America can beat the fruit and vegetable business." Some of them have become absentee owners by renting their stores to new Korean immigrants under agreements stipulating that a percentage of business profits be paid to them. Most of these absentee storeowners own and run other small businesses.

To sum up, the usefulness of the greengrocery business as an economic entry point for Korean immigrants depends upon several factors. First, we must recall that Korean immigrants could transfer their old family structure to the new land because the United States Immigration Act of 1965 made it possible for them to form a three-generation extended family in America. Consequently, some immigrants with an abundance of family labor but little capital have found economic opportunities in the labor-intensive fruit and vegetable business during the initial stage of their economic adjustment. Korean immigrants possess a family-centered success ethic that causes each family member to be willing to devote himself to the family business. This, together with the intense economic motivation of Koreans, establishes a "natural" affinity toward the greengrocery business, which requires intensive labor and a willingness to exploit oneself to gain economic mobility. Korean entry into the greengrocery business has revived and sustained a classic American immigration pattern of ethnic succession in economic activity. . . .

NOTES

1. *New York Times*, 18 Feb. 1976.
2. Ibid., 25 June 1977.
3. *Hankook Ilbo*, 28 Dec. 1976.
4. *Jugan Hankook*, 16 Jan. 1977.
5. *Hankook Ilbo*, 26 Feb. 1976.
6. *Joong Ang Ilbo*, 1 Aug. 1977.

7. Ibid., 4 Aug. 1977.
8. *New York Times*, 25 June 1977.
9. "Moonies," or followers of Reverend Sun Myung Moon, run fruit and vegetable stores in New York City; but Korean greengrocers have nothing to do with Rev. Moon's Unification Church.
10. *New York Times*, 18 Feb. 1976.

ACKNOWLEDGMENT

Most of this chapter first appeared in Illsoo Kim, *New Urban Immigrants: The Korean Community in New York*, copyright © 1981 by Princeton University Press, in "The Korean Fresh Fruit and Vegetable Business: A Case Study," pp. 112–21, and is reprinted here by permission of Princeton University Press.

7

Voluntarism among West Indian Immigrants

AUBREY W. BONNETT

METHODOLOGICAL NOTE • The methodology employed involved a number of techniques—published material, a mailed survey, and finally some unstructured, in-depth interviews.

Brooklyn has the highest number of first- and second-generation Black West-Indian immigrants, and this weighed heavily in the choice of Brooklyn as the area for study. Rotating credit associations are informal voluntary associations. They are not formally listed or registered anywhere, nor are they advertised publicly, but are known on the basis of primary group contact. In short, there is no way of gauging how many associations there are in a given area or of determining the total membership.

West Indian beauty parlors, some social clubs with West Indian clientele, barber shops owned by West Indians, and food markets catering to West Indians were contacted in order to try to ascertain who were some of the organizers of these associations. Of the ten organizers named, all were contacted in order to ascertain past and current members. From these organizers a list of a hundred names was compiled; each person was contacted. Of these, fifty-five either responded to a mailed questionnaire or answered questions from an interview schedule.

In order to have some basis for comparison, we also drew a random sample from West Indian social clubs in the area. Of the ninety persons in this control group who were contacted, forty-eight responded. Data were recorded on occupation, 118 education, socioeconomic status, sex, membership in ethnic associations, use or nonuse of rotating credit associations, life styles, and feeling of awareness of discrimination. In-depth interviews were also done with the ten organizers of rotating credit associations. Some of the information obtained on them and their organizations related to membership, organization, contributions, transferability of funds, order of rotation, form of interest paid (if any) and manner of determination, sanctions, and extent of diffusion to other ethnic groups.

In conclusion, some of the data are quantitative in nature and some qualitative. In total, it is felt that this several-pronged approach yielded substantial information that met the specified purposes of the study.

Introduction

This chapter focuses on a specific type of voluntary association found in the West Indian community and attempts to analyze the functional importance of these associations. Known in academia as a rotating credit association, this type of association is not unique to this ethnic community and has many vernacular names in both the West Indian and other ethnic communities: *susu* among the Trinidadians; *pardner* among Jamaicans; *sociedad* among Puerto Ricans; *san* among Dominicans; *gae* among Koreans. Indeed, there are as many names as there are communities.

Our study is restricted to West Indians and was done in 1974–75 in Brooklyn, which has one of the largest concentrations of West Indian immigrants in the United States. Both quantitative (survey design) and qualitative techniques (in-depth interviews with organizers, informants, and participant observation) were used. This multi-pronged approach was extremely useful in tapping insider sources that would not have been available otherwise.

Rotating Credit Associations: Origins and Transference

The rotating credit association is here defined as "an association formed by a core of participants who agree to make regular contributions to a fund which is given in whole or in part, to each contributor in rotation."[1] Rotation and regularity are therefore two essential criteria used to differentiate these associations from similar ones like lodges and mutual benefit clubs.

Thought to have originated in South China, Japan, or West Africa, these associations differ with regard to membership, size and criteria of membership, types of funds, sanctions imposed on members, etc. Despite this element of variability, they are regarded as a specific type of cooperative financial institution. In many parts of the non-Western world, this type of association has served the function of Western banks and, more importantly, has assisted in small-scale capital formation among immigrants.[2] Immigrants to the United States from Southern China and Japan have traditionally employed rotating-credit associations as their principal device for capitalizing small business. Black West Indian immigrants have brought the West African version of the association, which has survived in their native lands, to the United States, England, and Canada.

Rotating Credit Associations in Brooklyn

These associations have existed for at least fifty years. Among West Indian Blacks their use is surrounded with a certain ambivalence. Some scholars have commented on the manner in which they have been used to help some immigrants validate their middle-class aspirations through initial down payments on homes or purchases of businesses.[3] However, others have seen them as a "relic of the past, an anachronistic institution that would surely disappear with true passage of time, especially in a highly urbanized impersonal environment.[4]"

We hypothesized that these associations are used by immigrants as a general adaptive mechanism to cope with the complexities of New York. Consequently, we believed that their use would be important among first-generation immigrants and less so among second-generation immigrants.

What follows is based on in-depth interviews with ten organizers of credit associations and numerous informants, who volunteered the information on the condition of anonymity. We also attempted to increase our comprehension of this type of association by mailing questionnaires to one hundred immigrants reported to have been members and ninety persons reported to be nonmembers. Fifty-one members and forty-eight nonmembers responded, and there were striking similarities of responses on a number of items concerning the workings of the associations.

The Rotating Credit Association: An Example

Phyllis, a recent immigrant to the United States, resided in Brooklyn and was employed as a nurse's aide at a Brooklyn hospital. With her small salary she found it very difficult to support her two children and herself, and her financial position would have been greatly meliorated by a loan of at least $400. Repeated loan applications at both Black- and White-controlled commercial banks in the area had proved futile: she was considered a poor credit risk, and could not provide any collateral.

One day at lunch in her hospital cafeteria, Phyllis mentioned her plight to an old schoolmate of hers who was employed at the same hospital as the assistant director of nursing. Her friend referred Phyllis to a close friend of hers from Guyana, who was organizing a "box" (fund). Mrs. H., the organizer, saw Phyllis later that evening and, largely on the basis of the mutual friend's recommendation, Phyllis was accepted into the box.

Phyllis was told that the size of the fund was $450. She was expected to pay $15 a week to the organizer, who also had fourteen other members. The box was to last for approximately five months, and Phyllis was told when she could expect to receive her $450 fund. Phyllis got her money in four weeks even though she was a relative newcomer. She was told that she was expected to have her $15 sent or taken to Mrs. H.'s home every Sunday and that she could not, under any circumstances, be late or stop her schedule of payments. Of course, Mrs. H. had already checked Phyllis's reliability with their mutual friend and had received a superlative report.

Phyllis was elated. This was an answer to her prayers, for now she could pay for her child's parochial school and collect the furniture she had on "layaway" at the local furniture store. She would remain forever indebted to her friend, and was glad she had cultivated that childhood friendship. Also, over the years she came to be a friend of Mrs. H. to the extent that she offered her services at a low rate as a caterer for the wedding of Mrs. H.'s niece.

Organization and Membership

No elaborate lists of rules and regulations and no written constitution, contract, or other paraphernalia characterize the associations. There are no advertisements in the media. The only advertisement is by word of mouth, and it emanates from and is confined to the immigrants' social network.

The organizers, mostly women, are persons of social stature in their community: they are highly reliable persons to whom one's money can be safely entrusted. One informant aptly describes them as "people who, given a chance, can make a buck work." If an organizer decides that she needs $900 to furnish her basement and that the association is the best way of reaching this goal, she will then canvass various friends to see who has similar needs. She will choose only those who are considered to be reliable and trustworthy and who have steady incomes.

Membership is not limited to Black immigrants, either first generation or their second-generation offspring. Native Black and white Americans have participated in these associations. In some instances primary relationships on the job, the "informal aspects of bureaucracy," were often the compelling factor when an outsider such as a white American or native Black American sought membership. In Brooklyn, members' occupations vary, although in a number of associations nurses seem to predominate.

The total number of members varies from approximately ten to fifty in the larger associations, depending on the size of the fund. For example, if the organizer decides that the group needs $500, she might spread the sum over twenty weeks and get twenty members to "throw" (contribute) $25 a week. One organizer stated that she tried to get enough members so that the amount would not prove too difficult for anyone, hence lessening the possibility of default. Friends of the organizer can also recommend persons for membership, thus using their friendship as collateral for others. It was through this method that Phyllis became a member in Mrs. H.'s box, for she was not personally known to the organizer and had to be vouched for.

Contributions

All contributions are made in cash, and the amount of money a member contributes remains constant, with members paying the same contribution after receiving their fund as before.

The organizers normally stipulate when payment of the "throw" or "hand" is to be made, and then pass this information to members. The throw is normally paid weekly on Sunday, although in some instances allowances are made for monthly employees to pay at the end of the month. No receipts are given when payments are made, as a large amount of trust among the participants is involved. However, records are kept indicating when and to whom money is paid.

The associations have no branches; however, we were told about one interesting case in which members were organized into subgroups. This particular box had a total of twenty members at $40 a week. One member, however, was unable to meet his throw and subdivided it with three other persons, each person contributing $10 to him and thus sharing in the final fund that he received.

The organizer normally determines the amount of the contribution but may take into account the ability of the members to make large or small contributions. Some form of consensus, however, is necessary, for otherwise there will be difficulty in attracting members and in meeting deadlines for payments. Doubling (where one member throws two hands) and tripling (where one member throws three hands) occur. In case of doubling or tripling, the member does not get the total fund simultaneously or even consecutively; rather, an attempt is made to space the receipt of the funds. In the case of doubling, a member may receive an early fund and a late fund.

Payment is normally made at the organizer's home or place of work, but it may be collected at a member's home or place of work. The norm, however, is for the member to take the money to the organizer. Only after some delay in receiving the money does the organizer initiate attempts to collect the money.

Size of the Fund

A fund typically yields between $500 and $600 to each member. Funds have been reported in amounts as great as $2,000 to $4,000. Depending upon the size of membership, this could necessitate a weekly contribution of $60 and the association would run for a whole year. In funds of $500, the time needed to complete the fund is approximately twenty weeks. Lower- and working-class members often predominate in the smaller funds.

Order of Rotation and Usage of Fund

Ideally, the order of rotation is determined by general agreement among the members. In fact, the members make their requests known to the organizer, who then determines the order of rotation. If, for instance, the organizer is dubious about the reliability of a new member, then invariably that member gets his or her fund very near the end of the association. (Phyllis was able to get her fund relatively early because of the extremely close relationship between Mrs. H. and Phyllis's friend.) Further, some organizers have devised an equitable way of ordering the rotation so that over a period of time each member has an equal chance of drawing an early fund in the rotation schedule. We have called this the "normalizing process."

There are no restrictions on the use of the money by a member. Some individuals use it for an initial down payment on a home, while others apply it to the purchase of clothing for their children or to meet other basic necessities. Some use the money to open fixed-deposit accounts in savings banks, where they accumulate interest at a high rate. One informant described the practice in this way:

> My son, when you are really hard up and you need money, it is best to be able to say, Here it is [rather] than where it is [i.e., where is it], you know."

Some participants deposit their funds in their checking accounts. The resulting large balances on their bank statements are then used to indicate their financial status to U.S. immigration officials. The purpose is to assist immediate family and other relatives to immigrate.

Once every member has received his or her fund the association is disbanded, until another felt need is manifested, either by former members to the organizer, or vice versa. A few associations ran continuously for over a year as one member's need kept being replaced by another's.

Interest

In most instances no interest is paid to the organizer. One informant responded to the question of interest payments in this way:

> My son, I think it is mean to take out interest. God! it's poor people using this box, you know. I have seen members take that money—all of it—and go right to purchase something they really need. Look, as far as I'm concerned, I'm doing this to help these people and I'm not looking out for nothing.

The organizer in this case saw herself as altruistically performing a necessary service for members of her ethnic community. However, in several instances the organizer expected—in lieu of interest—small tokens from the members, most of whom complied. The responses of an organizer and a member are illustrative. The organizer:

> Well, you know, it is up to them and their conscience. They know you keep their money safe and that you are helping them save money they would otherwise throw away on cigarettes or women. It's up to their conscience to give you a small piece.

The member:

> Well, I usually give the organizer $10–$15, depending on the hand. After all, she is performing a service.

Thus, we see in effect that though no interest is paid, most members do give a small portion of their fund to the organizer as a form of appreciation for their service. Among some native Black Americans who now organize these associations, members are required to give the organizer a part of their hand. This is stipulated at the beginning of the association. Phyllis gave her organizer, Mrs. H., $15 as a token of appreciation.

Sanctions

Organizers reported few instances of default by members. So rare was default that, when queried, most organizers did not know how they would deal with such a situation. Most organizers tend to take preventive measures against default. First, if a member is suspect, the organizer makes certain that that person gets his or her money very near the end of the association. This minimizes the possibility that a member will get the money early and then stop contributing. Also, some organizers try to limit membership to people whom they know very well; mainly, members of their own social network. The strong sense of cohesiveness and solidarity within the group militates against default. Finally, some organizers keep a hand from each member as security in the event of any late payment.

Intense importance is placed upon meeting one's payment. Some associations are based on kin, and default is prevented partly by the acknowledged social obligations among relatives. Other associations are based on home ties in the island of origin; defaulting members in these associations are traceable, unless they leave New York. A further and major implicit sanction lies in the fact that the news of such a misdemeanor would quickly be communicated among Black immigrants in New York, London, and the home island. This would undoubtedly give the offenders a bad name and probably would adversely affect their future relations in the community. Reputation and respectability are important elements in the Black community, and at times a defaulting member can find both severely tested. The only instance of default reported concerned a nurse at a local hospital in Brooklyn. After several attempts to get her to pay proved unsuccessful, the organizer passed the word around that she was financially irresponsible. It is believed in the community that this caused her to be passed over for promotion to the post of nursing supervisor.

Some organizers stated that, should they be confronted with a defaulting member, they would visit the individual's home. Once there they would proceed to announce to all and sundry in the vicinity what the defaulting member had done. This "cussing out," as it is colloquially called in the West Indies, can keep a member in check. Indeed the defaulting member may suffer tremendous embarrassment and loss of face, for the cussing out is often very rambunctious and at times is done on the public thoroughfare in the vicinity of the home.

It should be stated that this most severe form of reprimand is only done to correct a situation of determined default and then only as a last resort. In instances of simple lateness the organizers rely on gentle persuasion and repeated hints of exclusion from future membership, and may finally draw from the hand that is kept in reserve for such a contingency.

Rotating Credit Associations—Savings or Credit?

Because of their name, rotating credit associations are considered credit associations, i.e., groups consisting of borrowers and lenders. The "borrowers" receive their money (fund) in the first half of the round, and the "lenders" receive theirs in the second. In effect, the lenders do not charge interest, and are in effect transferring their potential interest earnings to other members. Economically speaking, had the lenders drawn their fund early in the round, their money would have been worth more. Furthermore, they have forgone the opportunity to use their money in alternative ways. In the words of one economist:

> Alternative or opportunity costs represent the cost of an opportunity which is forgone because limited resources are used in the chosen alternative and, therefore, cannot be disposed of or used for other possible income-producing or expense-reducing alternatives. Opportunity costs are not recorded in the books of accounts.[5]

More important, however, is the interest that lenders forgo. Members are aware of the concept of interest, but their definition of the situation with regard to rotating credit associations is that they are actually savings associations.[6] Rotating credit associations are regarded as the poor person's bank. They act as a form of compulsory savings by providing a repository for small amounts of money that would otherwise be spent.[7]

Some Black immigrants do not have the initiative to systematically put aside or deposit some money and leave it untouched until their goal has been reached. By linking regular saving with meaningful sanctions, the rotating credit associations help to overcome this impediment to saving. Furthermore, the associations have other advantages over banks. There are no forms to fill out, no lines on which to wait. The organizer is in close proximity to the members and thus no one has to go long distances to deposit money. Thus, one important feature of rotating credit associations is their ability to exert social pressure and thus encourage saving. As Levin states:

> Susu exerts influence through social pressure. If one quits before receiving the fund, he will inconvenience his fellow members and will gain a reputation of being unable to live up to his financial obligations. If a member quits after he received the fund, it would be the same as defaulting on a loan.[8]

Despite the strong feeling that these associations are more savings than credit associations, some members regarded them as credit institutions. One individual summed up the sentiment of the latter group as follows:

> *Look, a box is like a loan, interest is free to meet short-term commitments. Getting small sums from a bank is a hassle. All dem damn questions they ask you.*

Thus, the rotating credit associations are an uncomplicated way to obtain credit for some immigrants, especially the recently arrived first generation, whose credit references in the United States would not be extensive.

Associations Distinguished from Bank Savings Plans

Rotating credit associations are similar in some regard to Christmas Club savings plans of the various banks. For example, in each a predetermined amount of money is set as a goal, a specific amount is deposited at regular intervals, there is the encouragement of the propensity for saving, and ultimately the assurance of receiving back all that one has contributed. However, there are some differences. The rotating credit associations are informal structures with no interest payments or officially binding fixed rules, only those decided upon by the members, who are normally friends, relatives or fellow workers. Further, in a Christmas Club which pays interest, one must wait until just before Christmas before money accumulated is received. In rotating credit associations the money can be received at any time between the beginning and end of the association. Finally, while in both membership is voluntary, with the Christmas club the obligation to save is more personal than social, and some members as a result do miss payments. In the rotating credit association the perception of mutual assistance is quite strong and so the group pressure exerted to continue your contributions is often of an obligatory nature. In short, if you stop paying into your Christmas Club, you're the only one hurt; however, missed payments or default in the rotating credit association would adversely affect others who are depending on your regularity.

Also, some banks will regularly deduct sums from a member's checking account for deposit in his or her savings account. However, this form of "compulsory" savings only works for those immigrants who have checking accounts and who can afford to maintain the balances necessary for such an arrangement.

Conclusions

A transplanted ethnic association formally known as a rotating credit association exists in a viable form in Brooklyn among Black West Indian immigrants. Use of these associations seems unrelated to their status as a symbol of ethnic pride; rather, they serve as a "structural shield" to these immigrants in the metropolitan milieu.[9] This shield allows adaptive and facilitative functions to be manifested in various ways.

One adaptive function is that these associations encourage savings or small-capital formation. Many first-generation members had accounts at local savings institutions but, despite this, continued to be involved in many of these associations each year. They reportedly saw them as providing short-term savings to help purchase clothing or meet other necessities of life in New York. Once the commitment to an association is made, the saving is almost compulsory, for, unlike deposits in savings and loan institutions, contributions to the rotating credit association must be made regularly. Some organizers felt that by socializing members in the process of compulsory savings they were helping the members to avoid unnecessary and even harmful spending, e.g., on liquor and cigarettes.

There is some overlap in usage between rotating credit associations and the larger banking and credit systems. This pattern is more pronounced among the first generation, who, despite their proclivity for the informal associations, also involve themselves to the extent they can in savings and loan associations. By the second generation, however, the overlap disappears, as members' children tend increasingly to use the credit institutions of the larger society rather than the rotating credit associations. Also, although there are some similarities with Christmas Clubs, a major difference is the mutual dependency aspect of the rotating credit associations, which adds obligation to others to the members' motivation for regular contribution.

Further, the associations provide credit for small sums of money—as low as one hundred dollars—in which banks are not normally interested. Moreover, the rates of interest are extremely high at banks and finance companies, whereas in the associations no interest is charged. The easy availability of interest-free credit goes a long way toward helping the immigrant cope.

Another adaptive function of these agencies is the service they provide for the newly arrived, first-generation Black immigrant, especially the illegal alien. Illegal aliens cannot legally work in the United States, yet most of them do so. These aliens are often afraid to open savings accounts at banks; besides, at banks they must provide social security numbers, and these are becoming increasingly difficult for illegal aliens to obtain. Moreover, some illegal aliens need large and ready sums of money to pay their attorneys for American brides to help them "get straight." Through the rotating credit associations, they can both save their money and receive credit without fear of discovery. One organizer of associations even reported that on a few occasions she had helped to arrange marriages between members and Southern Black Americans whom she knew as friends.

The associations are used differently depending on the member's generation. First-generation immigrants use the funds to cope with the perceived necessities of urban life: furniture, other consumer goods, a vacation. Second-generation users—to the extent that they do participate—tend to use the funds for investment purposes, to "top off" payment on a home, or to assist in setting up a small business.

Another major function is the adaptive role of these associations as they provide varied services for first-generation immigrants, illegal aliens and permanent residents alike. Some illegal aliens use the fund to pay their attorney's fees in their endeavor to become permanent residents. Others use the money to gradually accumulate sufficient funds to eventually initiate a business partnership with some entrepreneur in New York. This is another way an illegal alien is allowed to remain, for if it can be proved that one has substantial investment in a commercial concern, then one's chance of becoming a permanent resident alien are considerably stronger.

Further, illegal aliens cannot obtain social security payments and in most instances are afraid to apply for unemployment insurance. The money from these associations is then used as insurance against unanticipated disaster. Still others use the money to assist relatives to immigrate, at times illegally, to the United States. This, it is felt, helps mitigate the profound feelings of nostalgia and loss which they experience on coming to New York.

NOTES

1. S. Ardener, "The Comparative Study of Rating Credit Associations," *Journal of the Royal Anthropological Institute*, 94 (July 1964): 201–9.
2. R. Firth (ed.), *Capital, Savings and Credit in Peasant Societies* (Chicago: Aldine, 1964).
3. Ivan H. Light, *Ethnic Enterprise in America* (Berkeley: Univ. of California Press, 1972); and Hyndman Albert, "The West Indian in London," in S. K. Ruck (ed.), *The West Indian Comes to England* (London: Routledge & Kegan Paul, 1960), 65–151.
4. R. B. Davison, *West Indian Migrants* (London: Oxford Univ. Press, 1962); and S. Patterson, *Dark Strangers: A Study of West Indians in London* (London: Pelican, 1965).
5. N. Barish, *Economic Analysis for Engineering and Managerial Decision-Making* (New York: McGraw Hill, 1962).
6. D. Levin, "Susu," *Caribbean Review*, 7 (Jan. 1975).
7. Ibid.
8. Ibid.
9. I am indebted to Frank F. Lee for the use of the concept "structural shielding," which refers to the extent West Indians in London are protected from discrimination by depending upon their families and other kin for many of their needs.

The RCA can thus be seen as a sort of structural shield. For a fuller treatment, see Frank F. Lee, "British West Indian Race Relations in Bristol, England: A Study of the Changing Racial Picture in Britain," unpublished paper, February 1974.

8

One Style of Dominican Bridal Shower

ADELE BAHN
& ANGELA JAQUEZ

METHODOLOGICAL NOTE • The research reported here was done through observation of bridal showers and interviews with guests, former guests, and women who had given showers.

Seven showers were attended in New York City; the brides were in the age range 19–22. Information was obtained on thirty-two additional showers through open-ended interviews in Spanish with fifty women who described showers they had given or attended in New York City or in the Dominican Republic. The interviews took place, in groups of up to eight women at a time, over coffee or tea in the junior author's apartment. The women were primarily of Dominican background, but some were of Puerto Rican, Cuban, San Salvadoran, or Colombian origin. Invitations to the showers and introductions to the women interviewed were obtained through a "snowball sample".

Our research process illustrates some special approaches needed to study ethnic phenomena in the city to which access is limited by language, sex, and age. The senior author had studied earlier the changes and continuities in the status of American brides, through a content analysis of United States bridal magazines from 1967 to 1977, the decade of the women's movement; British, French, and Italian bridal magazines were also examined. The analysis covered family patterns, marriage customs, sex roles, sexual behavior, birth control and family planning, consumption patterns, images of the wedding, prescriptions for wifehood, concepts of beauty, and symbols and images of the wedding. This provided a framework for the study of 131

Dominican bridal showers in New York City. The senior author participated in some of the interviews when sufficient conversation was in English.

The junior author, a graduate student in sociology, is Dominican in background, bilingual, and in her 20s, characteristics that enabled her to attend the showers and conduct the interviews. She was able to establish rapport and believes that the events and conversations were not significantly affected by her presence. Rarely was she treated as an "outsider," although on one occasion the participants deliberately did not share with the researcher their pornographic pictures and written jokes. In most instances events at the showers were tape-recorded and photographed. The interviews were also recorded, transcribed, and later translated into English.

Unlike American bridal showers, which are used as a means of helping the couple furnish their home, or to give personal gifts to the bride, the Hispanic shower, particularly the Dominican shower, is often the means of socialization for the bride in her future status as wife. Gifts are also presented at the Dominican shower, but gifts are not the primary purpose of the shower. While seemingly frivolous and festive, the customs and activities at showers reveal serious content when analyzed for their underlying meaning—content that reflects the norms and values of society and societal expectations about the young woman about to make the transition from fiancée and bride to wife.

One important factor in Dominican culture is the Roman Catholic church, but just as important are the historical ties with Spain (and thence with Arab culture); these underlie Dominican culture and translate into two basic values that are paramount in the coming nuptials: virginity for the woman and *machismo* (a culturally specific type of virility or manliness) for the man. These values are interrelated and in fact are the reason for the socialization at the shower.

The young woman is expected to be a virgin when she marries. Although some norms are changing, this remains an important one. She is expected to be innocent, virginal, and inexperienced. Although more freedom is allowed her here in this country, and although it varies from one Hispanic culture to another, virginity remains the ideal. Therefore, the shower functions as an introduction and socialization for the bride to a number of her future roles, particularly the sexual role.

> One is therefore led to think that most of these rites whose sexual nature is not to be denied and which [are] said to make the individual a man or woman or fit to be one—fall into the same category as certain rites of cutting the umbilical cord, of childhood, and of adolescence. These are rites of separation from the sexual world, and they are followed by rites of incorporation into the world of sexuality, and in all societies and all social groups, into a group

confined to persons of one sex or the other. This statement holds true especially for girls, since the social activity of a woman is much simpler than that of a man.[1]

Social Functions of the Shower

The primary functions of the shower had to do with socialization, socialization to at least four roles that are components of the wifely status in traditional Dominican family life. These are (1) the role of a woman among women, (2) the sexual role, (3) the homemaker role, and (4) the subservient role of the female in the marital relationship. The socialization is both implicit and explicit.

A Woman among Women

The shower itself is attended only by women (although often men are invited to come in at the end of the shower, at which time it becomes a party with music, drinking, and dancing). However, what has happened before the men arrive is kept secret from them, and all sexual decorations and related materials will have been removed.

The women are dressed in their best. Decorations, food, entertainment, and the order of festivities have been planned by women, usually close friends or relatives of the bride. There are limitations on who is invited. No one who is either too young or too old—or too staid—is invited. Often the mother and older aunts of the bride are not invited because it is felt that such guests would put a damper on the activities; the shower would have to be "too respectable." A number of middle-aged women even denied that this type of shower takes place at all! It seems out of consonance with the continuing norms for women of respectability and sexual innocence and indifference. Only women from about sixteen to thirty-five or forty are present at the showers, with the ages of most guests, as might be expected, clustering around the age of the bride.

Some of the women who plan the shower have a consciousness of tradition and duty to the bride: to inform her of what she needs to know and what is likely to happen to her.

Not all the guests are friends of the bride. Sometimes a woman who is particularly adept at being mistress of ceremonies at the shower, or who is known to have had experience at running showers, is invited even though she may not be a particular friend of the bride or even well known to the organizer of the shower, except by reputation. These women take pride in their ability to invent and create activities and decor and to set the order and sequence of the shower.

There may be a handwritten "book," a collection of dirty jokes, sayings, and tricks that is borrowed and lent for showers. New material that is particularly successful is added to the book and it even travels from New York to the Dominican Republic in the luggage of guests invited to showers there. The essence of the book is that it is shared lore passed from women to women. Some of the respondents referred to the "dirty papers" that are part of the collection (for example, the "Memorandum" set forth a little later in this chapter). However, some of the women who are particularly adept at organizing showers took pride in *not* using such materials. They felt they were experienced and creative enough not to need it.

Learning the Sexual Role

The Dominican-Spanish term for "bridal shower" is *"despedida de soltera,"* which is literally translated, "Good-bye to singlehood." It is a ceremony that rarely takes place earlier than two weeks prior to the marriage ceremony and is planned by the closest friends of the bride-to-be or her relatives but not by her parents.

Formal invitations are rarely used since the planners prefer to invite the bride-to-be's friends by word of mouth. This gives them the opportunity to make suggestions about bringing something that is sexually explicit, which will embarrass the bride.

The planners make arrangements to decorate the living room of the apartment where the shower will take place either on a Friday or Saturday evening. An umbrella is affixed to a decorated chair, which is usually placed in the corner of the room. Often pornographic pictures taken from magazines are taped on the walls around the chair. The scenes they depict are both conventional and unconventional, and a number of postures are shown. The balloons that may decorate the room turn out, on closer inspection, to be condoms, blown up and tied to hang satirically from the ceiling and walls.

For the New York shower, special items may have been bought in Times Square sex shops: a plastic banana that, when opened, reveals a pink plastic penis in a constant and impossible state of erection; or a "baby pacifier" that turns out to be a tiny penis.

The refreshments may consist—besides the cakes and sandwiches prepared by friends and relatives of the guest of honor—of sausage and hot dogs arranged to look like the male sex organs and served to the guest of honor. Sometimes a root vegetable, *yautia*, which resembles a long potato, is arranged and decorated with corn silk and two small potatoes to resemble male genitalia. The vegetables are hairy and exaggerated and may also be smeared with condensed milk and ketchup or tomato paste to symbolize the semen and blood that are expected to flow on the bride's wedding night.

The guests arrive at least thirty minutes before the bride-to-be is brought in. While waiting for her, the guests engage in a lively discussion about their first night's experience. When they suspect that she is at the door, they get together in the center of the room and turn off the lights. When she enters, she is surprised. Sometimes one of the guests throws a glass of water on her, which is supposed to give her good luck. From the doorway she is led to the decorated chair, where she remains for the rest of the ceremony. As the shower continues, the bride-to-be is prepared and informed about her future roles as a wife. This includes the giving of gifts that underline her role as a housewife. She is expected to be a virgin and sexually unknowledgeable, and these expectations color the rest of the ceremony. It is also expected that she will blush and show embarrassment, horror, and astonishment at the "dirty jokes," "red tales," and "fresh tricks" that follow.

A "corsage" made of stockings in the shape of male genitalia is pinned to the bride's bosom. A dildo, sausage, or plastic hot dog may also be used. She may be forced to eat the sausage or to keep the plastic effigy in her mouth. She may be undressed to her underwear and told to put on a "baby doll" nightgown.[2] A vibrator may be used on her breast and intimate parts but no penetration occurs. The bride is shown pictures of a variety of sexual scenes and told that this is what she may expect—that this could happen to her, that she must be ready and supply "anything he wants." Typically, one of the participants is dressed like a man and imitates the groom's actions on the wedding night. If no one dresses as a man, a dildo is tied around the waist of one of the guests and this "male impersonator" "attacks" the bride. The dildo is rubbed on her face and all over her body. Aside from these overt "sexual" acts, there are guests who give her "tips" about how to please a man sexually, such as how to perform fellatio successfully.

One respondent tells of a women dressed as a man with a dildo attached, who jumped out of the closet and enacted a rape scene. The respondent, at whose bridal shower this had occurred, claimed that it had been a valuable experience in that it had "prepared" her for her wedding night, which had been "rough." But because of these scenes, some of the guests protest that they "don't *ever* want a shower."

At any time during the shower, any of the participants can draw the bride-to-be's attention and tell her a "red joke" or read a litany to her. Litanies are anonymously written poems that use pseudonyms for the saints and contain a great deal of vulgarity. A popular litany that is used at showers both here and in the Dominican Republic is called "A Virgin's Bedside Prayer." The main character of this litany, who is supposed to be the bride-to-be, asks the saints for a man who will be sexually satisfied by her.

Double-entendres are popular at the showers. The following example was obtained from a respondent and had been translated from the Spanish.

MEMORANDUM

For the ultimate goal of maintaining the high standard of social hygiene in our city, the Honorable City Mayor along with the City Council have decreed the following:

TO ALL LOVERS AND COUPLES

As of the 16th September 1980, the Mayor and City Council in a unanimous decision have declared that all lovers and couples caught in a theater, movie, park, beach, street or avenue, empty building or even in an alleyway, committing such acts as mentioned below, will be punished to the fullest extent of the law and fined accordingly:

1. With the hand on the thigh .... $ 5.00

2. With the hand on the thing $10.00

3. With the thing in the hand $15.00

4. With the thing in the mouth $20.00

5. With the mouth on the thing $25.00

6. With the thing in the thing $30.00

7. With the thing inside the thing $35.00

8. With the thing on the thing $40.00

9. With the thing in the front of the thing $45.00

10. With the thing behind the thing $50.00

For those who are curious about what "the thing" means:

a. It is not a bat, but it lives most of the time hanging down.

b. It is not an accordion; however, it shrinks and stretches.

c. It is not a soldier, but it attacks in the front and in the back.

d. It does not think, but it has a head.

e. It is not attractive, however, occasionally it's called "beautiful."

f. It is not analgesic, but it can be used as a tranquilizer.

g. It is not a palm tree, but it has nuts.

h. It does not belong to any club or organization, however, it's known as a member.

i. It does not produce music, but is called an organ.

j. It is not a gentleman, but it will stand up for ladies.

Any comments made by the bride-to-be during the shower are recorded or written down by one of the participants. At the end of the shower they are either read aloud or played back for the couple in a private room. The comments that she makes during the ceremony are interpreted sexually. For example, she may be forced to place her finger in a glass of ice cubes for a long time, and she may cry out, "Please take it out!" By this comment, it is understood that she will be saying the same thing to the groom on her wedding night.

Typically, home-made snacks and refreshments are served while the ceremony goes on. As the climax of the shower, the bride is told to open the gifts that she has received. The gifts consist of kitchen utensils, linen, porcelain figurines, and personal items such as nightgowns. When she opens them, she is expected to thank each donor individually and to exhibit the gifts so that the others can see what she has received. Afterward, her best friend helps her to change into her street clothes.

The role of the bride-to-be at the shower is very clear, underscoring the appropriateness of her reaction to the sexual aspects of the proceedings. She is expected to scream and show horror and surprise. The response of the girl is scripted and socially prescribed. She is expected to cry and scream to be let go, and to beg for her mother to rescue her. She is expected to be modest and maidenly. Should the bride not show the proper surprise and horror, the order of festivities changes. The tricks stop and the shower becomes more conventional.[3] Such a bride is believed by many to be perhaps "experienced" and not a virgin.

If a girl is pregnant or is known to have had sexual experience, the shower takes on a more conventional form. There are gifts and some joking, but it is mild. Interestingly, some of the respondents admit that the original purpose of the shower, to socialize and educate for sex and for the anticipated first night, may not be as necessary as before.[4] Still, they feel that it should be done "for the fun of it"—for the sociability.

Homemaker Role

The women at the older edge of the age range who are attending the shower may have a different socializing purpose. Although Dominican girls are taught from an early age to cook and perform domestic tasks at home, it was the duty of the older women at the showers, especially in the Dominican Republic, to give advice on the care of house and husband, particularly the presentation of food and the treatment of the husband in terms of comfort. They may propose the ironing of sheets, for example. Their gifts are more likely to have some relationship with cleaning and housekeeping.

At the showers observed, there was very little discussion of the housekeeper role, but participants at showers in the Dominican Republic mention that it is still a component there. In the Dominican Republic the future bride is advised to talk with her future mother-in-law in order to find out what the future husband likes or dislikes, especially with regard to food. Along similar lines, she is advised to clean the house well, particularly the bedroom and bathroom since these are the two rooms that men use the most. She is advised to serve his meals properly and make sure that he has everything he needs at the table, including toothpicks, napkin, and cold water. She is also told that she should keep herself well groomed in order to hold his interest in her as a woman. She should be tolerant, kind, understanding, show him compassion, and be sweet all the time. This type of premarital conversation with the future mother-in-law does not seem to take place in this country.

The Subservient Status of Women

The marriage is said to be in the bride's hands. She is said to be solely responsible for its success and for the happiness and comfort of her husband. Traditionally, she was dependent upon him for financial and emotional support. It will be her fault if the marriage breaks up. The woman internalizes these norms and is expected to conform. If the man leaves, it is believed that she was responsible. If he strays, that is to be expected: it is "natural" for a man to have others. And as for nagging, or even mentioning the man's misbehavior, that is worse than anything he may do. The proper role is for a wife to act even more loving and understanding.

The internalization of these values is associated with the concept of machismo,[5] the superiority of the male over the female in every area. A frequent theme is the wife's inadequacy as a sexual partner. If the husband is unfaithful and needs an excuse, or is impotent, or feels some dissatisfaction, it is her fault. Her vagina is too big rather than that he is an inept lover. The size of the woman's vagina is believed to be critical to the sexual satisfaction of both. She may be told to use ointments that will shrink her vagina temporarily before having sex. The size of the vagina is a subject of conversation among the girls and women and a good deal of anxiety is reflected in the conversation and jokes. There is little acknowledgment that the clitoris is the primary area of female pleasure and that more expert manipulation or adjustment might make sexual satisfaction a reality for both. Blaming the size of the vagina allows the man to say that it is the woman's fault for being "so big"—and she, internalizing his perspective, agrees.

Some respondents speak of the old days in the Dominican Republic when, in the event proof of virginity was lacking, the wife could be sent back to her parents. One respondent, whose husband trained as a physician in the Dominican Republic, notes that even recently operations have been performed, primarily on upper-middle-class women who might have had sexual experience, to restore their hymen or to at least make penetration seem difficult. Another respondent, who was a virgin at the time of her marriage ten years ago but did not bleed, notes that her husband (who is not a Dominican) still mentions it and that it is the last word in any argument they have.

The concept of *machismo* is broader than explicit sexual relations. It also covers the wife's contact with men and women in general. Under the rules of *machismo*:

1. No males are allowed to visit a woman when her husband is not at home.
2. She is not allowed to "hang out" with a group of friends.
3. She is to restrict her friendship to females.
4. She should not be too friendly with others of either sex.

Many jokes told at the shower are forms of reactions to *machismo*. Most jokes are antimale and tend to fall into two categories. The first has to do with sexual inadequacy on the part of the husband. The second has to do with his cuckoldry. In both cases, the women may be expressing the laughter of the oppressed. The jokes are a way to say that which is unsayable, that there is an unequal distribution of power. The jokes constitute an ideological attack on a system, and make manifest another ideology: that the weaker one may also have a weapon; that "he" is not so powerful after all and "she" may have a weapon at her disposal. The antimale joke that follows has been translated from the Spanish:

Apartment for Rent

A prosperous businessman propositioned a prostitute, and she agreed to spend the night with him for the sum of five hundred dollars. When he departed the following morning, he told her that he didn't carry money with him, but he would tell his secretary to send a check with the indication that the check was for renting an "apartment." On the way to his office, he felt that the "program" did not warrant the fee and was not worth the amount agreed upon, and for that reason he ordered his secretary to send a check for two hundred dollars with the following note:

Dear Mrs.:
I am sending you a check for the renting of your apartment. I am not sending the amount agreed upon because when I rented your apartment, I was under the impression
  (1) That it had never been used;
  (2) That it had heat; and
  (3) That it was small.
But last night, I noticed that it had been used, that it did not have heat, and that it was excessively big.

The prostitute had hardly received the note before she sent back the check with the following note:

Dear Sir:
I am sending back your check of two hundred dollars, since I do not understand
how you can have imagined that such a pretty apartment would not have been
previously occupied. In reference to the heat, I want to tell you that you didn't
know how to turn it on, and as for the size, I am not at fault that you did not
have sufficient household goods to fill it.

Ethnic Adaptation in the Bridal Shower

In New York City, the Dominican bridal shower appears in two forms, the
"pure" Dominican shower and the American-Dominican shower. A "pure"
shower is characterized by Dominican hospitality and warmth shown to
people in general. The Dominican tendency to share, to talk, to open themselves up makes everyone feel at home. Fewer commercially purchased
items are used. For decorations, pictures taken from pornographic magazines are usually used. The dildoes are all homemade rather than bought
in sex-item stores. The snacks and refreshments are personally served and
the souvenirs are individually pinned on the guests. This is not always true
at American-Dominican showers.

The language spoken at the "pure" Dominican showers is Spanish,
whereas at the American-Dominican one, bilingualism is quite prevalent.
Here the guests are found forming little social groups who chatter among
themselves. They also help themselves to the snacks and refreshments. The
difference, it appears, is that the "pure" shower is more strongly characterized by collectivism, while the American adaptation reflects more indi-
vidualism.

The Americanized bride-to-be seems to show less shock and astonishment
at the goings-on than does the "pure" Dominican bride, whose reaction is
very strong, spontaneous, and full of tears. The sexually explicit material
that is shown her often brings about refusals to look at or to participate in
the acts. However, the American-Dominican bride-to-be responds less dramatically and seems to enjoy it all. This "take-it-on-the-chin" attitude of the
Americanized bride seems to be the result of having been exposed to much
more sexual information, either in school, at work, on television, or at the
movies.

Another important distinction between American-Dominican showers and
their "pure" counterparts is the integration of different ethnic features in
the ceremony. There is a considerable influence of Puerto-Rican and Cuban
culture in some showers held in New York City, whether they are "pure"
or American-Dominican. This is illustrated by the types of litanies and dirty
poems read at the showers. Most of the vulgar words used to describe sexual
organs and acts are slang from Puerto Rico or Cuba. For example, the word
"pinga" is Cuban slang for "penis," and *"chocha"* is a Puerto Rican slang

word for "vagina." The Dominican immigrants have learned the words through social interaction with other Hispanic groups domiciled in the city. In fact, many Dominican males were nicknamed "*Chicho*" at home, but are not called that here, since for Puerto Ricans it is the slang word for "sexual intercourse." As has already been noted, vulgarity is not commonly used by Dominican women, but is quite acceptable and indeed pertinent at the showers in both countries.

The showers are rapidly being affected by the technology of modern society. The tape recorder is taking the place of written notes; the film projector is beginning to replace the sex education "classes" held at most ceremonies; and cameras are being used to record these events. This is happening not only here, but also in the Dominican Republic, probably introduced there by Dominican immigrants who travel constantly between the two places.[6]

Conclusion

Exploration of the showers suggests that they might be a good indicator of the degree of assimilation to American values of marital egalitarianism, even allowing for class differences within the Dominican family structure, particularly in New York but also perhaps in the Dominican Republic.[7] It used to be that "*New Yorkinas*"—girls who grew up in or came to New York— were seen to be on the track of a loose life: corrupted somehow, nonvirginal, or at least on the way to being that way. But the true "corruption" may be nonacceptance of the traditional subservient role, a major change that immigration has brought. There is a continuous exchange between the Dominican Republic and Dominicans in New York. People go back and forth. When they first came here, the old norms remained strong at first. But changes in the family structure having to do with economic and social life here in New York have changed some of the norms and have at least made others the focus of conflict.

Both men and women work here in New York. In fact, the employment opportunities for women in factories and the garment district may be better than for men. More women go to school than men. Many young women serve as the brokers for their families, dealing with city officials and social agencies and thus gaining experience and autonomy. The broker role, traditional for men in the Dominican Republic, serves here to give women power in their families; but it may also cause conflicts. For example, a woman's fiancé may retain the traditional values of Dominican family life, even though he may be earning no more than she and may be less educated. The shower, whether reflecting old or new norms, prescribes and reinforces some of the traditional roles for the bride. But she, while enjoying the attention her friends are paying her, may be making an adjustment that will not necessarily be helpful to her in her new status as a married woman in a family structure that is in flux. Changes in the social context in which the marriage will be embedded, as well as the urban environment in which she lives, require education, independence, and aggressiveness on the part of both men and women.

A Case Study: Maria's Shower

José and Maria, who met at a party in Upper Manhattan, have now been going out for eight months. Their relationship had to be approved by Maria's parents, who ultimately agreed that José could visit her regularly at her home. Since they decided to have a steady relationship, it was expected that a formal engagement would follow. José bought Maria an engagement ring and presented it to her in front of her parents. Their next step was to set up a wedding date. Maria decided to get married in spring. Maria's friends and relatives were anxious to learn the exact date of the wedding. Her best friend and her future sister-in-law wanted to give her a shower. They felt that it would be good for her to participate in one, since it would be a time for her to have fun with all her friends before she got married.

Two weeks prior to the wedding, the word was spread, at her job, at the church, at the local bodega, and throughout the neighborhood that she was going to have a shower. Nobody was supposed to reveal to Maria that such an event was being planned for her. It could not take place at her home because the preparations might make her suspicious. It would no longer be a surprise, as it is supposed to be. Her best friend offered her apartment in Washington Heights (Manhattan), which she and two other friends cleaned and decorated, particularly the living room. On a Saturday evening in March, one week before the wedding, the shower was held. When the planners invited other friends, they suggested that they bring dirty jokes, "fresh" gifts, and anything else that would amuse and embarrass the bride-to-be. They divided up the work, and two women made kipper and pastelitos; these were the snacks that would be served at the shower along with Pepsi-Cola and orange soda.[8]

One hour before the shower everything was ready. During this time, the guests, all females, arrived and awaited the bride-to-be's entrance at seven o'clock. Thirty-four well-dressed women of all ages, most of them in their twenties, were present at the ceremony. However, one young girl fifteen years of age was in attendance. The living room contained a decorated chair with an umbrella placed above it, a wishing well, and a table with an elaborately decorated pink cake on it. Under the chair was a tape recorder. On the wall were pornographic pictures of nude white men and women with abnormally large genitalia and of couples engaged in various stages of sexual intercourse. In the center of these pictures, a large home-made penis had been placed. It was made by one of the participants out of a nylon stocking and paper. (The woman who made it is Cuban; she stated that she loved to go to bridal showers.) Next to the cake was a doll dressed in pink with a hot dog on its head.

All of the participants were from Latin America. They began discussing their own experiences on their wedding nights. A Dominican said that she almost died of a heart attack when she saw her husband naked for the first time: "He had a big member." Another participant replied, "It's quality not quantity that counts." Some of the women admitted that they were afraid on their wedding night, and others said that they were anxious to find out what it really was like to have sex for the first time. All of the participants engaged in this type of conversation.

At the moment of the bride-to-be's arrival, one of the women said, "She's coming. Silent! Quiet!" There was a lot of tension in the air, as people tried to decide where to place themselves so as to completely surprise the bride. The light was turned off. One of the women was standing in the middle of the room with a glass of water in her hands. When the bride appeared in the doorway, the water was thrown in her face and everyone shouted, "Surprise!" The bride covered her face and began to cry. She said, "José and I have an appointment with the priest right now, but I guess that we will have to go another day."

Everyone was speaking Spanish, telling jokes, and generally having fun. The only words spoken in English were "Okay" and "Nice." A young woman took the penis from the wall and pinned it on the bride as a corsage. The bride-to-be begged, "No, please. It's ugly!" The woman replied, "You have to wear it because from now on, you're always going to have one chasing you and following you around." Another woman asked the bride to put it into her mouth. She refused to do so. Another woman took it and forced it into Maria's mouth. "There's nothing to be afraid of! Just be a good girl. This is harmless in comparison to what you're marrying." Another person asked, "Do you like it the way it is—hard like a rock?" Whenever the bride touched it, other women would say, "Oh, look how she caresses it. I knew you were going to like it."

One woman took a glass filled with ice and forced the bride's finger into it. She had to keep her finger in it until it hurt so that she could beg and scream for them to stop, saying things like, "Please stop doing this to me. I hate you. Are you crazy or something? I didn't know you were going to do this to me." Meanwhile, everything she was saying was being recorded. This was later played back for the groom at the shower's end. The women then said to him, "Listen to all the things she's going to say to you on your wedding night."

A woman picked up a penis that she had made from the protective rubber of her sewing machine and dropped it in Maria's lap, saying, "This thing loves to be between legs. You have to get accustomed to it." Another woman said, "Do you know which number is going to be your favorite? You mark my words, it will be sixty-nine." Another participant showed Maria a red baby-doll nightgown and told her, "Come on and put it on! Take off your panty-hose." Maria seemed surprised and said, "I am okay in my dress." A woman told her, "No, you have to wear the gown, now." Two women helped her to undress and to put on the nightgown while others applauded and commented, "She is going to look good. Not bad! You're going to drive him crazy. Sexy. That's the way he wants you." A woman picked up the home-made dildo and quickly rubbed it on the bride-to-be's vulva. Another young woman who was standing up said to her, "I am going to show you the woodpecker style, but you have to be drunk to do it." She stuck her tongue in and out and said, "Pick, pick, with the tip of your tongue. Touch his ass simultaneously right in the hole." Everyone laughed, and the bride-to-be, although laughing with them, was amazed. A woman in her late thirties approached Maria, who said to the woman, "Look, auntie, what these women are doing to me." Her aunt smiled at her and another woman stood up and said, "Listen to Maria's prayer. She used to say this prayer every night before she met José." A litany was read aloud and everyone laughed at each sentence. The name of the litany was "A Virgin's Bedside Prayer." After the litany had been read, the reader asked the bride-to-be, "Is this true? No, don't answer because we know it's true." Maria told them that they were "a bunch of fresh women." She was beginning to feel more comfortable. Meanwhile a copy of *Playgirl* magazine was being passed around and the women made jokes about the naked men, the size of their penises, etc. Suddenly, someone cried out, "José is coming!" Immediately, a young woman impersonating a man walked in. Everyone began to laugh. She had a home-made penis hanging from the zipper of her pants. She came up to the bride and wiped the penis across her face. Then she took Maria's hand and made her squeeze the penis. "This is yours, my love." Laughing, the bride pushed her away. Then the young girl with the "penis" began chasing all the women in the room. Everyone was having fun.

A native of Colombia had brought a film projector along to show some X-rated films. Everyone sat on the floor and the first film was shown. It was about two women engaged in a homosexual relationship. Most of the women protested and one of them said, "We don't want to see homosexuals. We want to see the real thing." Finally, the woman changed the film. Another woman said to Maria, "Pay attention, Maria!" The film showed two women engaged in various sexual acts with a man who was in a bathtub. Someone said to Maria, "You have to be ready to do it anywhere at anytime, Maria." The film showed the man ejaculating, and someone said to the bride, "Look at all that milk. You have to get accustomed to it. And look at how vulnerable a man can be when he comes!" The film ended and the kipper and pastelitos were served to the guests by two of the women in attendance.

At the time that this was happening, a thirty-five-year-old Dominican woman was giving Maria advice and telling her to wear something blue, something old, and something new on her wedding day for good luck. (It is part of the Dominican folklore to do this.) Two young women suggested that she should start opening her gifts. The first gift that she opened was a table set. Then she opened a box containing kitchen utensils and other boxes containing bathroom towels, an automatic broom, a nightgown, etc. On the whole, the gifts were household gifts, mainly items for use in the kitchen or bathroom. (There seemed to be a great deal of curiosity about who brought which gift.) The bride thanked everyone for their gifts and at 10 P.M. she was helped into her street clothes and prepared for the arrival of José. Then someone said to her, "Maria, guess who's here?" José shook hands with all the women and some of the male relatives, who came in when it was clear that the shower had ended. No one discussed what had gone on during the shower and at 11 P.M. everyone went home, including the bridal couple.

NOTES

1. Arnold van Gennep, *The Rites of Passage* (Chicago: Univ. of Chicago Press, 1960), p. 67.
2. Of the seven showers observed, there was nudity or near-nudity of the bride-to-be in six cases. There was some discrepancy in the reports of the respondents about its occurrence at showers. Some respondents said that it was not typical and, in fact, violated strong norms of personal modesty.
3. The word "conventional" represents what the respondents say is more like an "*American* shower" (emphasis ours).
4. The respondents noted that some girls had attended sex education classes in school in New York City. Some said they had gotten information from friends and had attended other showers. Many made a point of saying that their mothers had told them nothing.
5. For a general discussion, see Manuel de Js. Guerrero, *El Machismo en Republica Dominica* (Santo Domingo, R.D.: Amigo del Hogar, 1975).
6. See Glenn Hendricks, *The Dominican Diaspora* (New York: Teachers College Press, 1974).
7. Comparative family structure, including Latin America, is described in Betty

Yorburg, *Sexual Identity: Sex Roles and Social Change* (New York: John Wiley & Sons, 1974). See also Vivian Mota, "Politics and Feminism in the Dominican Republic: 1931–45 and 1966–74," in June Nash and Helen Icken Safa (eds.), *Sex and Class in Latin America* (Brooklyn: J. F. Bergin, 1980).
8. At the showers, alcoholic beverages are typically served only to the bride-to-be.

ACKNOWLEDGMENTS

The authors would like to thank Carmen Salcedo and Altagracia Mejia for the initial invitations and Vernon Boggs for his encouragement of the study.

PART 3

WORK OF ANOTHER KIND: THE SUBCULTURE OF SEX

The chapters by Winick and Boggs and Jaquez deal with activities that are just as much a part of urban living as are all the other issues discussed in this book. Granted that pornography and prostitution may be seen as immoral or only semilegal businesses, they nevertheless flourish side by side with legitimate businesses and are very often frequented by patrons whose daily lives are considered to be morally upright. The issue raised by the chapters in this section is the following: is commercial sex in New York City a unique barometer of moral decay or is this phenomenon, which is also found in other urban centers, part and parcel of human society?

To a certain extent, the question can be answered by comparing the Times Square commercial sex industry with that of two urban centers in Scandinavia, namely, Copenhagen, Denmark, and Malmö, Sweden. Both countries enjoy a reputation for sexual permissiveness, but the commercial sex industry in Copenhagen and Malmö is strikingly similar to and located near the entertainment districts in those cities, just as the Times Square "stroll" is. Broadly speaking, commercial sex must indicate social order and human needs, rather than their absence. Its prevalence in the heart of the city clearly demonstrates that it is tolerated, even though, in the case of New York, it may be illegal.

In the case of sexually permissive societies, like those of Scandinavia, the emergence of a flourishing commercial sex industry means that immorality is a necessary part of human society, to use a Durkheimian concept. Furthermore, this immoral industry, upon close observation, is far from disorganized; it is structured in an orderly fashion with a normative system closely resembling that of the larger society. Therefore, it should not seem surprising that such an industry persists throughout time.

One of the key issues in this type of human behavior is the question of legality. Intense battles have been fought in American courtrooms over the question of commercial sex's legality. This question has been raised not only in this country but in Scandinavia as well. However, the real issue is not so much legality as it is the degree of a community's toleration. For example, in Sweden prostitution per se is not illegal, but there are laws against disorderly conduct, loitering, and, more importantly, asocial behavior, that is, behavior that wounds the public morals. All of these laws could theoretically be enforced and used against prostitutes and others involved in the industry. But a subtle spirit of toleration holds sway both there and in Times Square, where prostitution is de jure prohibited. This spirit of toleration is an indication of social support for the proliferation and existence of commercial sex. Thus, the central issue is not one of legality or illegality, but the degree of public toleration.

Both in Scandinavia and in Times Square, prostitution and pornography were tolerated until some incident occurred that provoked a public outpouring of outrage against their existence. In the latter case, a number of foreign tourists who patronized prostitutes were assaulted, robbed, and killed by street prostitutes in New York City in the 1960s and 1970s. In addition, it was thought that the bicentennial celebration and Democratic national convention of 1976 would be marred by the convergence on the city of hundreds of prostitutes. Thus, the New York City Police vigorously enforced the laws against all facets of the commercial sex industry and throughout the vice district. In Denmark, Finland, Norway, and Sweden, where prostitution per se is not prohibited, the emergence of foreign pimps into the subculture—as well as drug abuse, the killing of prostitutes by pimps, and the rapid acceleration of the "underground economy" in Denmark and Sweden—created a favorable atmosphere for police intervention and the suppression of the commercial sex industry in those countries:

> In 1975, a group of officials in Malmo—the social welfare department, the police, the district attorney, local tax authorities and county administration officials—decided to undertake an investigation of the social structure and significance of certain clubs and commercial industries. What lay behind their decision was a worry over some nagging problems around a number of restaurants, bars, and similar premises. Bootlegging of whiskey, gambling, narcotics trafficking, pimping, fencing of stolen goods and other criminal activities seemed to be occurring more frequently and to a greater degree than before in connection with the business activities of a number of bars and restaurants.[1]

As the excerpt above clearly demonstrates, the question of legality or illegality of commercial sex seems to take a backseat to public morality. It appears that public toleration is the "thrust and drag" of the legal machinery which regulates the ebb and flow of prostitution and pornography on a world-wide basis. When the American public has reached its threshold of tolerance, that is when mass arrests and crackdowns occur. Even so, the courts are seen as revolving-door justice for most of the prostitutes: in jail one day and out the next. Those involved in pornography are frequently required to fight long and contested battles in courtrooms, which involve tremendous legal fees, but after the public outrage subsides, the issue of pornography frequently returns to a posture of business as usual.

Although Scandinavian prostitutes fare better in their countries than do their American counterparts, they too are subjected to pressure when an untoward incident comes to the attention of the public, especially prostitutes with children. When the "heat" comes, it usually takes the form of social authorities questioning the fitness of the female concerned as a parent. In any event, the main issue at stake is not legality but public toleration. Thus, one can say that pornography and prostitution are an integral part of the urban environment and, more importantly, a constant reminder of the way in which people perceive their needs, respond to them and instill normative patterns in their daily behavior; behavior found both here and abroad.

NOTES

1. Sven-Alex Månsson *Könshandelns Främjare Och Profitörer* (Promoters and Profiteers of Commercial Sex), trans. Vernon W. Boggs (Karlshamn, Sweden: Doxa, 1981).

9

Licit Sex Industries and Services

CHARLES WINICK

METHODOLOGICAL NOTE • The basic approach to data collection in the study of licit sex industries and services must involve systematic observations of the characteristics and flow of clients and interviews with clients after they have made a purchase.

The lack of a trade association to supply industry-wide information and the caution of proprietors of these establishments in discussing their business with outsiders combine to make for a relatively difficult atmosphere for data collection.

It was necessary to visit the establishments discussed at different hours of the day and night, on different days of the week, over a period of several months, in order to develop a reasonable impression of the clients and the degree of use of the facilities. Systematic observations were made on costume, appearance, gender, individual versus group attendance, age, and related characteristics. Data on behavior and motivations of clients were derived from clients who were interviewed after they had made a purchase at one of the establishments. Once such clients recovered from their surprise at being accosted and asked about their recent purchase, a substantial proportion were willing to speak to an interviewer.

New York City has a number of industries and services related to licit sex activities. These industries include "adult" bookstores, peep shows, and movies; burlesque; live sex shows; swing clubs; gay baths; topless and/or 151 bottomless bars; massage parlors and spas; and establishments that combine several of these services or products under one roof and are often called emporiums. Every one of the five boroughs has some combination of these products and services, although their greatest concentration is in Manhattan. Staten Island has the least availability of such materials.

Most large cities in America offer comparable materials. New York City does not have the most daring or unusual sex materials and services, but its size, port status, access to other practitioners of the popular arts, and huge proportion of transients and tourists, all contribute to its special status as a resource for such materials and services. There is also reason to believe that a number of the major distributors of sex-oriented materials are head-quartered in New York City; whether for this or some other reason, there is a wide choice of sex materials, especially with recent or new content. The area around Times Square, and especially 42nd Street between Sixth and Eighth avenues, has a particularly heavy concentration of sex-oriented businesses.

The following discussion is based on interviews with consumers and proprietors, which were conducted under the auspices of the "Bright Lights" project of the City University of New York in 1978 and 1980. There will be a brief description of each type of establishment and a discussion of trends and consumers.

"Adult" Bookstores, Peep Shows, and Movies

It is unfortunate that the term "adult" has assumed connotations of sex-related materials, implying that such content represents adulthood, to the exclusion of other social dimensions. The term has developed wide-spread acceptance to describe content that is largely sexual. "Adult" bookstores sell magazines, books, 8-millimeter movies, and "marital aids," such as vibrators. Some stores also sell videotapes, and many also have peep shows: one- or two-minute movies presented to the consumer by way of a small machine into which he looks after depositing an appropriate amount in coins. The peep-show machines are in small booths that can usually be closed by a door or curtain.

Printed materials are usually organized into interest areas, such as homosexuality and sadomasochism. The stores are very quiet and customers seldom talk to one another. The manager or cashier is in an area, sometimes raised, from which he can observe the customers. There are approximately 120 such stores in New York City.

Theaters indicate that they show "hard-core" movies—usually defined as presenting an erect penis, sexual intercourse, and other types of organ interaction—by conspicuous use of the word "adult" on the marquee, by the use of "X," "XX," or "XXX" on the marquee or sign, or by specific warnings near the theater entrance or box office.

They usually charge about one dollar more than ordinary theatrical movies, although the production of hard-core movies costs only a fraction of the production costs of ordinary films. Even the stars, such as Johnny Wadd or Desirée Cousteau, do not get the enormous fees of Hollywood actors.

Forty theaters in New York are primarily devoted to hard-core movies. Most other theaters routinely show "soft-core" sex material, which does not include erection or interaction of sexual organs, and most of the movies that are rated "X" by the motion-picture-industry's ratings administration, like *Last Tango in Paris* (1973), are soft core. Very few hard-core movies get a rating from the ratings administration, but most give themselves an "X"; any producer may give his film a self-designated "X" rating.

Burlesque

In a burlesque theater, women disrobe provocatively to a musical accompaniment. The seven Manhattan burlesque theaters range in decor from relatively luxurious to fairly sleazy. Several theaters have runways that extend into the audience and along which strippers walk. New York used to be the country's burlesque capital until the theaters were shut down by Mayor LaGuardia. New York's role was particularly significant because no country has ever had so much interest in burlesque as America, the world leader in what may be called optical lubricity.

Live Sex Shows

Live sex shows present two or more people engaging in simulated or real sex in a theater or theaterlike setting. Manhattan has five theaters that feature heterosexual sex, several of which also present Lesbian coupling. Most theaters show hard-core movies between the live performances. Four theaters present live sadomasochistic or bondage-domination performances.

Swing Clubs

New York City has thirteen swing clubs providing facilities for on-premise or off-premise social activity, nudity, and sex, conducted privately or in groups, and is thus the country's leader in this type of entertainment. Initial admission involves a fee for membership, which may last for up to a year.

Nonalcoholic beverages and food are usually available, along with dancing and a pool and/or whirlpool bath. Most clubs permit couples and/or women, but not unescorted men.

The city's first and most famous club is Plato's Retreat, which is an "on-premise" facility, where sexual encounters are permitted on the premises. Other clubs are "off-premise" facilities, where dancing and socializing but no sexual encounters are permitted.

Gay Baths

There are thirteen gay baths in the city. The baths provide steam rooms, showers, and lounge areas. A major reason for attendance at the baths is the opportunity for a sexual encounter. Some baths provide musical entertainment; singer Bette Midler first became famous by performing at a gay bath in New York.

Topless/Bottomless Bars

Over a hundred bars in New York offer topless or bottomless waitresses and/or dancers. Most of the bars have a raised runway around which the customers can sit. Typically, one or more go-go dancers dance along the runway to the accompaniment of recorded rock music. They may stop in front of each customer and do a dance directly in front of him, for which he is expected to give a direct tip of a few dollars.

Men who do not wish such personal contact sit at one of the tables on the periphery of the room, drinking for as long as they wish. Very few bars require their customers to have more than one drink or to leave after each set or performance. A dance or performance may last for about an hour, with perhaps a half hour before the next one begins.

Physical contact between customers and waitresses or dancers is prohibited by the State Liquor Authority, which licenses the bars. In June 1981, the U.S. Supreme Court ruled that bars that serve alcoholic beverages do not enjoy First Amendment protection for their performances. Since this decision, a number of establishments have become "juice bars," which sell only fruit juices and other nonalcoholic drinks, and it appears likely that most of the bars will do so.

Massage Parlors and Spas

There are sixteen massage parlors and seven spas in New York City. Both types of facilities offer a model who provides a massage to a customer in a private booth or room, for a session that may run from fifteen minutes to an hour. Various tanning parlors and studios for nude photography offer analogous services.

Spas are larger and more lavish than massage parlors. Spas also have showers, lockers, valet service, and free drinks, and most have whirlpool baths. The private rooms in spas have mirrors and carpeting.

Emporiums

The city has four emporiums, or establishments that offer several sex services under one roof. A typical emporium might sell books, magazines, films, and marital aids, and offer a variety of peep shows. It may also have fantasy booths, where a customer can talk about his fantasies to a woman, and a live peep show, in which the customer in a booth can observe a woman engaging in an erotic dance. Live sex shows are also likely to be found. Admission to the emporiums is free, but customers pay for each service or activity. Proprietors of emporiums and other sex establishments make every effort to keep prostitutes and minors out, in order to minimize trouble with police and other law enforcement agencies.

Law Enforcement, Public Opinion, and the Sex Industries

Although all of the activities reviewed above are legal, a number of them have been the subject of special attention from city authorities. It is probable that some of these businesses have received an unusual amount of surveillance from health and fire inspections, at least through 1978. The city's massage parlors have been subjected to considerable pressure in terms of such violations, and this pressure is probably at least partially responsible for the decline in the number of massage parlors from more than sixty in 1974 to sixteen at the time of this study. Live sex shows of all kinds seem to be subject to substantial harassment by the police.

In recent years, there have been relatively few obscenity prosecutions in New York City. Prosecutors do not seem very disposed to pursue such cases and juries are relatively unlikely to convict. Because of concern over other crimes against the person, obscenity is not a priority offense. As a result, there has been a steady expansion in terms of permissible sexual content in the various industries.

Public acceptance of these industries has probably also increased because of larger social forces making for tolerance of previously deviant sexual activity.[1] New York has several special features that have helped to domesticate the sex industries, notably cable television sex-oriented programs and the availability, since 1969, of *Screw,* a weekly consumer guide to a number of the sex industries' products.

The cable television channels regularly present "Midnight Blue," a magazine-format program with excerpts from movies, interviews with sex celebrities or entrepreneurs, and feature stories. Another popular weekly program, "Ugly George," features a television cameraman who picks up women on the street, takes them to his studio, and photographs them nude. Each episode deals with a different woman. Other programs involve people playing phonograph records while they discuss sex fantasies. Such cable programs contribute to a relatively casual public attitude toward other sex businesses.

Screw, a weekly tabloid newspaper with a circulation in six figures, contains reviews, interviews, features, photographs, editorials, and advertisements for sex-oriented businesses and services. A substantial part of the paper is devoted to critical evaluations of the various sex activities available to the consumer. New hard-core X-rated movies are reviewed in depth, and capsule reviews of other movies are included. Theaters are described in terms of cleanliness and quality of their movies; details are given of live sex shows, burlesque, swing clubs, gay baths, massage parlors, and spas. In every case, the newspaper gives information on price, any special conditions of access or availability, and relevant comments ("claims a capacity of 350. . .couples tend to be professional people. . .the crowd is youngish. . .the staff is friendly and efficient. . . a small, narrow, but clean theater. . ."). *Screw's* reputation for integrity has made it a significant factor in the city's sex industries.

The Consumers of Sex-Oriented Businesses

Customers for sex services and businesses have various needs. To attend an X-rated movie in a theater is a different kind of experience from seeing a peep show in a small booth, attending a swing club, or being alone with a model in a small room in a spa. The costs involved range from twenty-five cents for a peep, to two dollars for a movie admission, to twenty-five dollars for a live sadomasochistic show, to sixty dollars for an hour at a spa.

These services and facilities also differ in the number of persons who can be accommodated. A movie theater or emporium can handle thousands of people in a day, whereas a massage parlor can service a limited number of clients in a day. A bookstore may have material of interest to a broad spectrum of people, but a gay bath house presents a very specialized appeal.

Salience of the activity also varies. Some fans devote large portions of their income and time to sex-oriented activities, whereas others visit a movie or bookstore out of curiosity, and still others go occasionally to a specific kind of activity. Some customers make a special trip, but others are patrons only if they happen to be in a particular area with some extra time.

Some data on consumers were obtained by the West 42nd Street Study Team of the City University of New York,[2] which surveyed customers of sex establishments in Manhattan, Brooklyn, and Queens. The consumers were interviewed after leaving a sex establishment, over a six-month period, with interviews taking place seven days a week from 10 A.M. to 4 A.M. For purposes of comparison, Table 9.1 gives comparable data on customers of adult movies and bookstores who were surveyed in 1970 on behalf of the President's Commission on Obscenity and Pornography.[3]

The 1980 consumers are substantially younger than those in 1970. There are also slightly more women and more Blacks and Hispanics, who have come to represent a larger proportion of the general New York City population.

Of the consumers interviewed in 1980, 25 percent lived in Manhattan, 23 percent in Brooklyn, 13 percent in Queens, 8 percent in The Bronx, and 2 percent in Staten Island. Table 9.2 gives the occupation, education, and annual income of the respondents, who appear to include all socioeconomic groups, with the higher income and educated groups more likely to be present than they are in the general population.

Fourteen percent of the patrons live outside the metropolitan area or in a foreign country. Twenty-nine percent of the patrons visited an adult establishment more than once a month, 16 percent did so from five to twelve times a year, 38 percent did so from one to four times a year, and 17 percent had not visited another such establishment during the year. Only 15 percent came to the area specifically for the purpose of patronizing sex-related establishments; the others had another primary reason for being in the area. More than a third of the patrons visit more than one establishment in an area in one day.

Another approach to the characteristics of regular customers of the sex businesses is provided by data from a study of readers of *Screw*.[4] This study, conducted independently of and not sponsored by the newspaper, involved interviewing persons who had bought the publication at a New York City newsstand. Five newsstands, at different locations in Manhattan, cooperated in the study. Anyone purchasing a copy of *Screw*, it was reasoned, was likely to be a serious patron of some sex establishment. The study was conducted over a period of four months; there were 432 respondents.

Ninety-eight percent of the purchasers were male, 2 percent were female. The age range was from nineteen to fifty-seven, with a mean of thirty-five. Forty-six percent had at least some college education and 39 percent had some high school. Forty-four percent earned $20,000 a year or more, and 39 percent had $10,000 to $20,000 income. Only 4 percent earned less than

Table 9.1   Changing Characteristics of Patrons of Sex-Oriented Businesses

	In Percentages	
Characteristic	1980 (N = 546)	1970 (N = 1700)
Sex		
Male	97	99
Female	3	1
Ethnicity		
Asian	3	4
Black	19	12
Hispanic	17	13
Other White	58	71
Other	3	
Age		
18–25	25	17
25–34	41	28
35–44	20	23
45–54	8	21
55 +	6	11

Table 9.2 Characteristics of Patrons of Sex-Oriented Businesses (1980)

Characteristic	Number	Percentage
Occupation		
Professional	115	27.2
Manager	45	10.6
Clerical	49	11.6
Sales	40	9.5
Craftman/Foreman	32	7.6
Operative	23	5.4
Service	43	10.2
Laborer	21	5.0
Retired	3	0.7
Student	31	7.3
Unemployed	8	1.9
Housewife	3	0.7
Military	1	0.2
Education		
Elementary	28	5.4
Some High School	57	11.0
High-School Graduate	115	22.2
Some College	144	27.7
College Graduate	112	21.6
Graduate School	63	12.1
Annual Income		
Under $5,000	51	10.5
$ 5,000–$ 9,999	65	13.4
$10,000–$14,999	98	20.2
$15,000–$19,999	100	20.6
$20,000–$24,999	59	12.1
$25,000–$29,999	46	9.5
$30,000–$34,999	21	4.3
$35,000 +	46	9.5

$10,000. A wide range of occupations was represented among the readers, 70 percent of whom were married.

These several sources of data on consumers, developed for a variety of purposes and over a period of some years, suggest that the socioeconomic characteristics of consumers of the products and services of sex-oriented businesses are not very dissimilar from those of the general population. The stereotype of the anomic old man, carrying his raincoat, is not confirmed by any of these studies.

The Future of Sex-Oriented Businesses in New York

The largest concentration of sex-related businesses in New York is around Times Square. Municipal authorities have complained that the visibility of such materials in the area is likely to give visitors an unfortunate impression of life in the city. Proprietors of the area's establishments argue that their premises are clean, free of crime, and visually inoffensive, and that they provide employment for many exconvicts and others who are not easily employable, pay taxes, and, most importantly, satisfy significant needs.

Feminists denounce Times Square's availability of sex-related materials because they believe that such materials dehumanize women. Women Against Pornography, a feminist group, has a storefront in Times Square from which it conducts tours of the sex establishments in order to promote its slogan, "Pornography is the theory, rape is the practice," a slogan that has been elaborated in various publications.[5]

The consumers are not vocal, but their steady patronage documents their continued interest in the availability of the services and materials, in the face of repeated efforts by successive mayors to "clean up" the city by shutting down the sex establishments. There are many reasons for consumers' interest in these establishments.[6]

None of the many previous efforts to drive the sex businesses out of Times Square, and especially off 42nd Street, has succeeded. It is possible that some new legal or civic initiative could do so. As if in anticipation of such an eventuality, several other Manhattan locations have become centers for movies, spas, bookstores, and swing clubs; they could expand. Times Square offers a patron the unique asset of being able to go from one place to another and make choices, much like the so-called Combat Zone in Boston, also for sex services, or the Strip in Las Vegas, for gamblers. If there were a dispersal, whether formally through zoning changes as in Detroit or informally through space availability in particular neighborhoods, consumers would find it more difficult to obtain what they want.

About 30 percent of the customers are fans who patronize sex-oriented establishments at least once a month. These regular customers would presumably be willing to experience inconvenience to get access to what they want. Many of the occasional customers would surely be discouraged if they had to travel out of their way to find sex materials or experience.

Decentralization of the sex industries would certainly change their appeal. It is not likely that the sex industries in the outlying boroughs would expand much, with the exception of movies, because customers seem to prefer to patronize places not located near their homes. If decentralization occurs, there will probably be a decline in the number of customers. If things continue as they are today, with Times Square as a focal point of commercial sex, the business is likely to keep expanding. The informal designation of the area as a kind of "open city," which serves a safety-valve function for New York and exercises its own form of social control, is likely to continue, unless some combination of civic and economic pressure is successfully applied.

Considerations of Social Policy

Some significant discussions about sex industries and services in New York are likely to be conducted in the near future. These discussions will involve theoretical and policy dimensions—e.g., the extent to which cultural pluralism, as it relates to recreational sex, should be accepted in New York; the ability of civic and business leaders to achieve their goal of dispersing or eliminating sex-oriented business; and the application of cost-benefit considerations to complex cultural and social matters. Another question is the ability of the most powerful borough, Manhattan, to impose its wishes on the four outlying boroughs. Since the sex-oriented businesses will surely resist efforts for relocation or elimination, the dispute will probably be solved in the courts, and relevant social research may play a role in the ultimate decision.

NOTES

1. Charles Winick, "From Deviant to Social Change: Changes in the Acceptability of Sexually Explicit Material," in E. Sagarin (ed.), *Deviance and Social Change* (Beverly Hills, Cal.: Sage, 1977), pp. 219–46.
2. West 42d Street Study Team, *Sex Industries in New York City* (New York: City Univ. of New York, 1980).

3. Charles Winick, "Some Observations on Characteristics of Patrons of Adult The-
   atres and Bookstores," in *Technical Report of the Commission on Obscenity and
   Pornography*, vol. 4 (Washington, D.C.: U.S. Government Printing Office, 1971),
   pp. 225–44.
4. Charles Winick, report of a study of readers of a sex tabloid. Available from the
   author.
5. Andrea Dworkin, *Pornography: Men Possessing Women* (New York: Perigee/
   Putnam, 1981).
6. Winick, "Deviant to Social Change."

10

Popcorns, Talk-Tricks, and Half-Steppers

VERNON W. BOGGS
& ANGELA JAQUEZ

METHODOLOGICAL NOTE • The research reported herein was principally carried out through participant observation and was subsequently supplemented by interviews with pimps, prostitutes, tricks, patrons, and owners of sex-related establishments in the Times Square district of New York City during 1978–1979.

The senior author, who spent more than ten years abroad studying the subculture of prostitution in several Western European urban locales, spent considerable time as a participant observer at several meeting places for those in "the life" in midtown Manhattan. While doing so, the senior author lived at a residence that served as a rehabilitative residence ("halfway house") for men returning to New York City from confinement in upstate penal institutions. Some of the people with whom he resided played a peripheral but significant role in the subculture that was then prominent in Times Square. He became known as a possible player and gained entry into the world of pimps and prostitutes. Simultaneously, he interviewed members of the New York City Police Department's "pimp squad" and "pussy posse." Thus, his prior knowledge and experience, as well as his—in the words of one of his senior colleagues—"protective coloration," allowed him to penetrate this world with relative ease.

The junior author, a graduate student in sociology, participated in two different research efforts in midtown Manhattan: (1) interviewing passersby and strollers on 42nd Street, and (2) standing outside commercial sex establishments in the Times Square district and interviewing patrons as they left these establishments. Through writing field notes on a daily basis and assisting in the analysis of the data gathered, the junior author was able to provide good insights into the world of "tricks." 163

This chapter is based on an ethnographic study of the subculture of prostitution in New York's Times Square district. Books, papers, and journal articles on the subject of prostitution, which purportedly present in-depth analyses, might easily lead one to conclude that this subculture is homogeneous, encompassing many "actors" and "actresses", and that it can "easily" be explained in the following fashion: the female (prostitute) sells heterosexual services to a male customer (trick) for a set sum of money. She, in turn, hands her earnings over to another male (pimp), who fritters it away on drugs, flashy clothes, cars, gambling, etc. Thus, the "actress" in this scenario usually ends up as a "broken" woman.

This is a simplistic view of the subculture of prostitution. Pimps and prostitutes are not a monolithic mass. The subculture is far from monolithic; it is rather quite dynamic and diverse. The misconception is primarily caused by scholars' unwillingness to penetrate the walls that separate them from the commercial sex industry, resorting to generalization based on superficial and front-stage impressions rather than gaining data from in-depth studies. This chapter will deal with certain aspects of pimp-prostitute relationships.

Selecting a Pimp

The manner in which a prostitute selects a pimp is called "choosing." "Choosing," in New York, means that the woman has to offer the pimp a sum of money to insure that she isn't "playing on" him; that is, that she is serious about asking him to be her "man." The giving of gifts is a ritual that signals that both parties are seriously interested in each other. Once chosen, the prostitute will "give up choosing cake"—that is, give a lump sum of money as a "dowry" to her chosen pimp.

Offerings of drinks, sex, or money are the crucial elements in the choosing process, although not the only elements. The choosing act is a task that is left primarily up to the woman.

Dress

In choosing her pimp, a prostitute will be influenced by the manner in which the men are dressed. The general view of pimps is that they dress in a uniformly unconventional manner, like flashily dressed peacocks who do nothing but strut about town, lavishly and foolishly spending money. Admittedly, there is some truth in this view, but our research tends to warn against making broad and sweeping generalizations about all pimps. The fact is that, not infrequently, men who dress as just described are labeled by other "players" (pimps) as "popcorn pimps," a term of derision used for those who occupy the very lowest rank in pimping. Furthermore, pimps who dress in this fashion may have a shorter playing period in the life than do those who dress in a more conventional fashion. Pimps who dress flashily are more likely than other players to "draw heat" (come to the attention of law enforcement agencies). In addition to this, prostitutes who choose this type of man are frequently shunned by other women in their profession. In any case, choosing a well-dressed man is a sine qua non in the world of prostitution; pimps and prostitutes place a great deal of emphasis on being well dressed ("pimped down" or "pieced down").

Clothing plays an important role in this subculture in that it gives the individuals concerned status among their peers. Prostitutes who choose the flashy "Superfly" types are more likely to be streetwalkers than call girls. It is highly unusual to see a prostitute and her pimp dressing in fashions antithetical to each other. However, it must be remembered that there is no commonly agreed upon dress code; dressing in the life is an outgrowth of individual style and taste. These styles and tastes vary as widely in the subculture of prostitution as they do among conventional couples. Nevertheless, prostitutes both expect and encourage their men to dress well.

Money

Aside from being expected to dress well, many prostitutes expect their men to be able to handle money well ("control the cake"). The pimp is expected to pay bills, raise bail money, pay fines, and cover any expenses that the two may incur. Budgeting, fiscal planning, and allocating monies is his responsibility, he is the "man of the house" and his fulfillment or nonfulfillment of this role expectation is a significant variable in determining the duration of their relationship.

The role of money may take on greater or lesser importance for individual couples. Prostitutes who have experienced financial instability because of a pimp's compulsive gambling habits, alcohol-prone behavior, drug addiction, or conspicuous consumption very often become reluctant to entrust their man with their earnings. They may resort to asking friends or relatives to safekeep part of their earnings ("holding out"), show considerable apathy while working ("coming up short"), or run away from a pimp.

Pimps active in New York City have been known to demand a set sum of money to be brought home each day ("a trap") by their women. If the woman comes up short, holds out, or runs away—and this is discovered—she may be punished. The pimp's responses to these transgressions range from apologies to murder, but usually consists of a "charge" being placed on her for being "out of pocket."

Types of Pimps: Popcorns (Simps) and Boss Players (Macks)

Among pimps there is a status hierarchy, often based on the type of woman who has done the choosing. The "class" of prostitute "copped" by a player lends status to his position in the hierarchy of pimpdom. For some of the "simps," also called "popcorn pimps," the Port Authority bus terminal is seen as a lucrative place for "copping" (recruiting). In contrast, a player who's "on his job" will attempt to recruit elsewhere. In the eyes of players, there is considerable danger of running afoul of "the man" (police) in a place that is known to attract social deviants and runaways. Thus, the bus terminal is frowned upon. The thinking employed by players in not actively seeking recruits at the bus terminal represents a fundamental ideological cleavage between "popcorns" and players; a cleavage that strengthens the notion of social stratification in their subculture: popcorns and simps vs players.

There is a consensus of opinion among the pimps that there are two main types of pimps: the popcorn pimp or simp and the "boss player" or "mack." The popcorn pimp usually comes to the attention of law enforcement agencies, mass media, and the public through his bizarre actions and dress. He is often depicted—and often quite accurately—as a violence-prone and brutal sadist. His arrogance toward the larger society is clearly demonstrated in the manner in which he drives a gaudy car in public ("gangster leaning") while loudly proclaiming that he is "a pimp and proud." He has few if any real friends and his favorite motto is, "All rules are made to be broken." When things go bad for him, he may resort to snatching pocketbooks, jumping subway turnstiles, jostling, begging, or any type of petty crime to survive. In his view, every woman whom he meets is a potential "ho" to be "turned out" as soon as possible. The popcorn pimp, who may make headlines in the daily press, is ranked lowest in the hierarchy of pimpdom.

The contrast between the popcorn pimp and the boss player[1] is revealed in this evaluation by one of the boss players:

You see the motherfuckers you got here are "simps" not pimps because they be simple motherfuckers. You see, a simp will tell a ho [mimicking]: "You got to choose me." You dig that shit. Choose him. You know what I say? Choose shit! You don't tell no ho to choose. I tell a ho she got to **earn** *me! You dig the diff? The bitch I get know I got a bad mama ho who has earned, you dig,* **earned** *the right to me. So no new ho ain't gonna come in here and* **choose** *me. The bitch got to* **earn** *me. These simps they be saying to the bitches, "I charge you" [again mimicking]. I say charge what? What I look like charging some ho? Fuck that simple-ass shit. Make the bitch* **earn** *you. These motherfuckers are simps, you know. The first thing they do is put a "trap" on a ho. You see a mother-fucking simp put a trap on the ho and fucks up. You see the best game is a mack game. A mack man will sweet-talk a working girl. No kidnapping. When a motherfucker kidnaps a bitch his game, if you can*

*say he has a game, is quite shaky. The mack will talk that working girl out
of her money. He's sweet to her. She wants to give him that bread.*

A set of field notes from Times Square reveals the variety of stratagems
to which popcorn pimps resort:

*Left Sloane House Y.M.C.A. and walked north on east side of 9th Avenue,
up through arcade to 42nd St. & 8th Ave. Went on the stroll. Maybe (five)
20+ white females [five women over twenty years old] on the stroll. Went
into the bar. Talked with owner and barmaid and bought them a drink. Four
"player types" in the bar. Had given barmaid a $20 bill and received $16
change which laid on bar counter alongside my bottle of Heineken and pack
of Salems. Player type eased over to me and asked for a cigarette. We rapped
about "nothing here on the ho-side." He hadn't "checked any traps in the last
three days." He was "ho-less." Discussed "catching" and futility of having a
"stable" as opposed to a "git-down stepper." We discussed "half-steppers," his
poverty, etc. He asked me for $2 so he could buy something to eat and he
ordered a hamburger. We talked about pimping in Germany and how he
"caught" a German ho at an Army base in Colorado and had her "stepping"
on 8th Avenue. He said that "She ran away after three or four days." Then
we talked about "charging" and how a prostitute "cracked on me while on the
stroll":*

Researcher: *So I cracked back, "You choosing?" So . . .*

Popcorn Pimp: *No, you should've tricked the bitch up to your room and told
her that you're a pimp and she's charged cause she's in a
pimping position. You didn't come to get laid, you came to
git paid. So what can her man do? He's a player and un-
derstands the game. The bitch was out of pocket and got
charged.*

*Meanwhile two other popcorn pimps moved close to us and one cracked, "I
ain't got no ho, but I got some paper!" and flashed his money. After a while,
I left the bar and walked home.*

The boss player or mack is ranked, even by the popcorns, as the essence
of pimpdom. For the most part, he lives not so much by "the book"—the
informal rules that govern pimping—but by a fairly clear conception of what
it takes to become successful in a dog-eat-dog world. One of the most
important concerns for him is "not drawing heat." Running afoul of the law
and having public attention focused upon him is both unnecessary and costly.
In his mind, drawing heat is a self-defeating act, whereby nothing but
notoriety and trouble are gained. The popcorn, in contrast, thrives upon
this troublesome state of affairs despite the fact that he realizes that his
actions are self-defeating and that they cause others in the life to suffer
("pollutes the game").

By juxtaposing the behavior of a popcorn pimp with that of a mack, one can see that their respective actions are basically polarized. The popcorn pimp subscribes to myopia, disdains long-range planning, uses raw violence to control a person or situation, and constantly asserts his "manhood" in the company of others. These are just some of the major characteristics that differentiate him from the boss player. While the two may frequently share the same frontstage, they have little else in common. Rivalry is always present when the two types are in close proximity, and they therefore try to avoid each other as much as possible. In the now-defunct Manhattan Sea Gardens in Times Square, those who considered themselves boss players would either come in alone and buy drinks for the "losers"—as popcorns were sometimes referred to—or come in with their "ladies" and treat them regally while the losers would argue or spin around on the bar stools. Clearly, hierarchical arrangement was at work.

There is one common point upon which pimps agree: who controls the cake. In their world it is unquestioned that it is the man's prime responsibility to handle the money gained from prostitution. If a prostitute's male companion does not receive the proceeds of her earnings, yet has established an intimate relationship with her, he is "less than a man"—a trick, a man who is being "played out of pocket." Although most researchers attribute this feeling to pimps' greed, it is seen by men in the life as the ultimate sign of a prostitute's recognition that he is a *man*. And being paid is the signal that he is a "sho-nuff flat-footed player."

This concept of manhood is tremendously important in the world of prostitution, and especially in a man's dealing with any woman. The concept of manhood is tremendously important in the world of prostitution and is inextricably bound up with the management of money. Greed plays an important role; but few pimps will admit to it or avarice or will attribute their quest for money to misogyny.

To reiterate, money plays the same role for boss players as for popcorns, and the rules governing the use of money are also the same. To allow a prostitute to pay the bill at a restaurant or bar or to buy the couple tickets to the theater is virtually unheard of, and "going dutch" rarely occurs. If these acts do occur, it means that the male companion is either not a player or not the prostitute's "man."

Tricks and Talk-Tricks

Research on prostitutes has postulated two views that male customers— "tricks"—have about female prostitutes. Some scholars assert that the trick views the prostitute with disgust and disdain, which would account for the physical and verbal abuse that prostitutes often encounter while at work.

Others suggest that the trick may be sympathetic to the prostitute's plight, as he may leave her a tip before departing, may say that he would like to "rescue" her, and may make bedside confessions of love and admiration. But despite these kind gestures, both the prostitute and the trick expect little from each other besides mutual protection of their intimacy and satisfaction of each other's needs. The protection of their intimacy is a key factor in their relationship. Although there are no written rules, the two should not "recognize" each other in public. Perhaps a slight nod of the head, but nothing more.

Anonymity is only a small example of the role expectations held by men and women in commercial sex when one considers the following "Dos and Don'ts" of the relationship between trick and prostitute:

1. The trick cannot kiss her while having sex.
2. The trick cannot touch without her explicit approval.
3. The trick cannot assume any position he wishes during intercourse.
4. The trick must pay ahead of time.
5. The trick must leave the premises within a specified time regardless of reaching or not reaching ejaculation.
6. The trick never receives a refund.
7. The trick must pay for extra services; nothing is free.

It must be pointed out that these are rules made to be broken in accordance with the prostitute's desires. Selectively enforcing, ignoring, or strictly adhering to these rules is a matter of individual choice. Role expectations, norms, and values are as dynamic in the life as they are in the straight world. The following excerpted fieldnote from research in Times Square shows how "casual" prostitution functions and how it underlines the heterogeneity found in commercial sex:

Went to usual bar for a beer. Spoke with Rosa the barmaid for awhile. L., the former barmaid, came in and sat between me and a 30+ P.R./male "regular." L. ordered a bottle of ale and "a shot of White Label with ice water on the side." L. started talking to me about how she had to do something tonight because she had to pay her rent. She didn't want to but she had to. We talked awhile and then a 20+ white male seated behind me asked her if she wanted to go to a party with him. She said sure if he had $140. He said that he didn't "want to get laid." L. said she understood that because that would cost extra. She looked at me and started laughing. She told me that's the way to get the guy to shut up. Researcher asked her why an odd sum like $140. L. said that's the two weeks rent she owes. We continued talking and she took out her address book, asked the barmaid for change (dimes), asked researcher to watch her pocketbook and left for a while. She returned and began telling researcher about her education in a Catholic school; how the *nuns made her sit on her left hand in order to write with her right; when she lived on W. 82nd St. she disliked the bars because up there they were full of "social workers and teachers" with whom she didn't get along because the women treated the men like babies; she wants a real man with a hard dick because she likes to fuck; she was a "fish" when she came to this bar six years ago; she knew nothing about pimps and hos but learned quickly in order to survive; she never liked working at the front end of the bar because she felt it was dangerous despite the other barmaids telling her that's where the tips were; she is 29 yrs. old (white) and says that she's never been a junkie although she "smokes" and snorts a little cocaine; spoke with her about being "high" tonight, how she used to have an afro but likes her hair (dark brown) short and intends to get it "frosted" which will cost $50–$60 . . . L. looks out the window and beckons to a 50+ black male who she evidently knows. Researcher moves his drink two seats away allowing L. and the b/m to talk. L. tells b/m to get a pint of Scotch and they laugh and joke awhile. Finally b/m gets up and goes around the corner to the liquor store . . . B/m returns and hands L. a brown-paper bag with a bottle in it. L. smiles and b/m leaves. L., obviously under the influence of both liquor and drugs, announces that she's going out for cheese. She tells barmaid to watch her pocketbook. She stumbles outside and goes to the store and returns with crackers and cheese. L. sits down and asks for her pocketbook. Then she asks out loud, "Where's my honey? Did my honey come back yet? He said he was going to punch out (He works in the Post Office) and come back. Boy, I'm going to do some good fucking tonight!" L. gets up and gives one b/m some cheese and crackers, then leans her whole body on the researcher's back and gives him some cheese and crackers via putting her arms around the researcher's shoulders. Finally, she sits down and continues eating. . . .*

It seems that the ex-barmaid had a list of customers, as do some call girls, whom she intended to call. However, the arrival of a black male with whom she was acquainted made it possible for her to consider the possibility of combining "fun and business" by engaging in sex with him. It is probable that the two engaged in sexual intercourse and then L. explained that she was in dire need and hoped that he could help her out with a "loan," which she would not be expected to repay. Since L. will approach the man in this fashion, he will not be made to feel like a trick. Their mutual needs will be met and they will not interpret what they've done as comprising an unemotional exchange of sex and money.

Talk-Tricks

Commercial sex behavior consists not only of oral, anal, and genital heterosexual contacts, but of "rap sessions," sessions in which male customers, "talk-tricks," solicit the verbal services of prostitutes who act as paraprofessional "counselors" or quasi-psychiatrists rather than solely as sexual objects. Verbal interaction is an integral part of the encounters between men and women in the commercial sex industry, just as it is for human beings in general.

The ability for a female to articulate demands and show compassion through the use of words while involved in the commercial sex industry is not only desirable but necessary. Servicing males with verbal skills and agility denotes a kind of role-playing that argues against the view of prostitutes as merely "flat-backers," women who provide only sex. Contrary to popular belief, talk, in the commercial sex industry, is *not* cheap.

Hos, Prostitutes, and Half-Steppers

Prostitutes rank one another as to place of work—street ("half-steppers"), club, or call girl—and the ethnic background of their male companion. Other significant variables in their hierarchical ranking are (1) the section of the country they come from, (2) their socioeconomic status, (3) the length of time in the life, and (4) any outside interests they hold in common. Status is also conferred by other means; e.g., by frequenting certain establishments in and around "the stroll." One place served as an "information speed-up point and dead-end center" for those in the life. The owner of this establishment offered credit to the men and women who frequented the premises, loaned them money, took calls for them, and protected the women's valuables while they worked. By doing so the owner lent support to the idea that there were at least two main groups who came into the bar: insiders and outsiders. This notion is an integral part of the ranking system that one finds in human society. At the now-defunct Manhattan Sea Gardens and PlayPen bars, ranking was apparent in the patronization of these places almost exclusively by streetwalkers. Prostitutes, known to work in the nearby commercial sex establishments, such as the massage parlors, and those working at upper East Side brothels, did not frequent these particular bars. Thus, it can be argued that a de facto social segregation was in effect and lent itself to the ranking process utilized by those in the life.

Summary

In this chapter, we have hypothesized and tried to demonstrate that the subculture of prostitution has norms, values, role expectations, and social ranking, analogous to those in traditional societies. Furthermore, prostitution and pimping are neither unstructured nor monolithic.

Our view is that the subculture of prostitution demands a more precise examination in order both to understand it and to formulate meaningful policies for the control of its spread. Commercial sex is an important aspect of human behavior that has been glossed over and neglected by scholars who, fearful for their own safety, and morally in opposition to it, make broad and sweeping generalizations about commercial sex that will not stand up to critical analysis.

NOTE

1. Terry Williams and Vernon Boggs, "Street Drug Markets and Hustling in the Bright Light Zone," in William Kornblum (ed.), *West 42nd Street Study: The Bright Light Zone* (New York: Graduate School & University Center of the City Univ. of New York, 1978), pp. 135–136.

PART **4**

Power Struggles in the City

Part IV examines power and decision making in New York City in three recent case studies. Maynard Robison details the fifteen-year odyssey of the attempts to build Battery Park City in downtown Manhattan, which, as his epilogue notes, finally obtained funding in 1980 and is only now scheduled for construction. Eric Lichten contends that there was a relative loss of power by the city's public service unions during the fiscal crisis of the mid-1970s. Fred Goldner, from an unusual participant-observer vantage point as a high appointed official of the New York City Health and Hospitals Corporation, provides a fascinating insider's glimpse of the interplay between the HHC and the media.

These case studies differ from one another but are consistent in displaying the complexity of the public decision-making process in New York City. Each set of power brokers controls only part of the action and is interdependent with other power bases. Consequently, conscious direct change is difficult to achieve and the public interest may not be well served. Battery Park City, partially underwritten by public monies, is being built as luxury housing; unionized city employees may be bearing a disproportionate share of the cutbacks necessitated by the fiscal crisis; the HHC finds it difficult to present and maintain a coherent health policy.

Another theme runs through the three case studies: the importance of the mass media in the decision-making process. Print and other mass means of communication—specifically, radio and televison—are necessary adjuncts to the decision-making process in democratic societies, especially in very large cities. However, the media are not merely neutral transmitters of information, but have become players in the decision making. This is most clearly illustrated in Goldner's account of the intricate adjustment and counteradjustment of the HHC administration and the media, as each attempted to use the other. The result is another level of reality in the print and electronic media, bearing little resemblance to the actual conditions and larger issues of health care in New York City. Robison makes clear that the full explanation of the (non)building of Battery Park City could not be obtained from published reports. Lichten notes that, during the fiscal crisis, attacks on civil servants and their unions were routine in the city's newspapers and that "without control over the major disseminators of public information it was indeed extremely difficult for the city's working class to mobilize effective and informed mass opposition to austerity."

One especially interesting aspect of these chapters is the mesh between their analyses of power in the city and the power bases described in the only comprehensive study of power and decision-making in New York City (a study cited by none of the authors in Part IV). This original study, undertaken by Wallace Sayre, a professor of public administration, and Herbert Kaufman, a professor of political science, was reported under the title *Governing New York City: Politics in the Metropolis.*[1] Published in 1960, it detailed five major groups involved in the New York City power structure: "The party leaders, the public officials, the bureaucracies, the nongovernmental groups (including the press and the other mass media of communication) and the officials and bureaucracies of the state and federal government involved in city affairs."[2] A decade later Sayre enlarged briefly on these power groups, modifying them to encompass recent changes.[3] Significantly, Sayre assigned the communication media a power category of its own, withdrawing it from the nongovernmental interest groups—organizations representing various business, labor, geographic, ethnic, and religious blocs—a shift which parallels the importance of the media as reflected in the case studies presented in this part. Sayre also makes a prescient statement about the interplay between the media and the other power bases, which Goldner's description of the HHC and the media documents.

> The communication media . . . are . . . also prominent agenda setters for the leaders of the other constituencies—particularly for the mayor, the other elected officials, the major appointed administrators and commissioners, and quite often also for the interest group leaders or those of the organized bureaucracies. What the media emphasize as "the news" serves to anticipate, identify, or even create what the constituency leaders will perceive as the "crises" requiring their attention.[4]

What is the fundamental nature of power distribution in New York City? Community power studies in the United States have been divided between the findings of those who contend there is a monolithic power structure and those who see a pluralist power structure.[5] Sayre and Kaufman are unequivocal in concluding that there is no power elite in New York City, but a "loose-knit and multi-centered network in which decisions are reached by ceaseless bargaining and fluctuating alliances among the major categories of participants in each center, and in which the centers are partially but strikingly isolated from one another."[6]

Has the power alignment shifted in the recent past? By 1970 Sayre had already noted that the state and federal governments played larger roles in the city power structure than he had described earlier,[7] although Sayre did not view this as altering the pluralist nature of the decision making. The fiscal crisis of 1974–76 further enlarged the state's role with the creation of the Emergency Financial Control Board (later called the Financial Control Board), a state-dominated panel charged with overseeing the city's budget, but analysis indicates that the EFCB became an additional player in the fragmented power structure, not the main actor even in budget decisions.[8] The analyses of Robison and Lichten, however, suggest that New York City's power structure is dominated by business interests and large corporations, that these players are "more equal than others" among the many power bases.

Part IV provides us, then, with a measure of change in the power structure of New York City, using the Sayre and Kaufman study as a benchmark: the increasing importance of the mass media; the expanding interdependencies with state and federal bodies; possible erosion of the public service unions' position; and coalescing of power around big business. These findings represent also an agenda for research, especially in this period of continued urban fiscal crisis, when a new range of demands is being made on cities by national policies that shift costs and responsibilities to states and cities.

NOTES

1. Wallace S. Sayre and Herbert Kaufman, *Governing New York City: Politics in the Metropolis* (New York: Norton, 1965; original ed., Russell Sage Foundation, 1960).

2. Ibid., p. 67.
3. Wallace Sayre, "The Mayor," in Lyle C. Fitch and Annmarie Hauck Walsh (eds.), *Agenda for a City: Issues Confronting New York* (Beverly Hills, Cal.: Sage, 1970).
4. Ibid., p. 582.
5. See, for example, Robert S. Lynd and Helen M. Lynd, *Middletown* (New York: Harcourt-Brace, 1929); Robert S. Lynd and Helen M. Lynd, *Middletown in Transition* (New York: Harcourt Brace, 1937); Floyd Hunter, *Community Power Structure* (Chapel Hill: Univ. of North Carolina Press, 1953); Arthur Vidich and Joseph Bensman, *Small Town in Mass Society* (Princeton, N.J.: Princeton Univ. Press, 1958); Robert A Dahl, *Who Governs* (New Haven, Conn.: Yale Univ. Press, 1961).
6. Sayre and Kaufman, *Governing New York City*, p. 716.
7. Sayre, "Mayor."
8. Herbert J. Ranschburg, "New York City's Emergency Financial Control Board," *City Almanac*, 11 (August 1976), no. 2.

11

Vacant Ninety Acres, Well Located, River View

MAYNARD T. ROBISON

METHODOLOGICAL NOTE • This article describes the history of Battery Park City, a huge housing and commercial development on landfill along the Hudson River in lower Manhattan, from the project's inception in 1966 until 1980, when construction had still not begun. To reconstruct the project's history, data were gathered from four sources: (1) newspaper and other more-or-less disinterested accounts of events; (2) planning documents; (3) official records, such as transcripts of hearings; and (4) interviews with actors in the project's history. Each of these sources provided incomplete and frequently inaccurate, even purposely distorted, information. Nonetheless, data from all the sources could be fitted together like a jigsaw puzzle to produce an essentially complete, accurate picture of what occurred. Consistency provided the standard against which parts of the picture could be tested. When looked at in sufficient detail, the events were simply too complex for any explanation to fit besides the correct one.

Any useful case study suggests generalizations beyond itself; Battery Park City's history suggests several generalizations regarding the organization of power in American cities.

For the observer of the city, as for the mystery-novel sleuth, the missing— something that should be there but isn't—can be as revealing as what is there. Throughout the 1970s, one found just such an absence in New York 179

City's lower Manhattan, along the Hudson, just across West Street from the World Trade Center. This was not a minor void, but ninety vacant acres, undeveloped in an area where land costs two hundred dollars or more per square foot, where real-estate developers find it worthwhile to build sixty-story or higher buildings. More, this land, which is still almost entirely vacant, was created, landfill in the Hudson essentially completed almost a decade ago and vacant since.

As understanding why the absent object isn't there may lead the sleuth to solve the whole crime, understanding these ninety vacant acres may tell us something about New York City, perhaps even something about our cities generally and how to understand them.

Let's begin with the bare facts of the case, for the sake of argument defining those bare facts as the history of these acres as it would be known by a New Yorker who read all of the *New York Times* but who had no other source of knowledge about the project.

The Bare Facts

The ninety acres, our New Yorker knows, are the site for a project called Battery Park City; they were filled by the Battery Park City Authority, a quasi-public corporation created by the State of New York.[1] Battery Park City was proposed by then-Governor Nelson Rockefeller, in the spring of 1966.[2] His proposal called for a project of quite pedestrian design, including fourteen thousand apartments and two office towers. Sixty-six hundred of the apartments were to be conventionally financed "luxury" units aimed at "high-income" households. Six thousand were to be "middle-income" apartments, financed from the proceeds of tax-exempt bond sales and therefore less expensive than the conventionally financed housing; and fourteen hundred were to be "low-income" apartments sufficiently subsidized to bring them within reach of families eligible for public housing. (Over time, as will be discussed below, inflation in construction costs and interest rate increases would increase the cost of housing so that conventionally financed housing in Manhattan would be affordable only by quite high-income households; "middle-income" housing would be appropriate for households most people would see as having high incomes; and "low-income" housing would be appropriate for many families most people would see as "middle-income." In addition, a federal program for "moderate-income" households would be aimed at those between the "middle-" and "low-income" groups.)

Nelson Rockefeller was not the only one interested in the Battery Park City site. Just as he was making his proposal, the new city administration of Mayor John V. Lindsay was completing work on a plan for all of lower Manhattan,[3] including proposals for the Hudson River shore. Lindsay advocated exceptionally innovative architecture for the site, and also wanted the project's residential buildings to house only high-income residents.

Behind these two stood a third major actor, David Rockefeller, Nelson's brother and chairman of the Chase Manhattan Bank. Since 1955, David Rockefeller had been pressing the redevelopment of lower Manhattan. He had led Chase Manhattan to a decision to build a new, $120 million head-quarters downtown, rather than moving to midtown. He chaired the Down-town-Lower Manhattan Association (DLMA), a group made up of heads of the area's largest businesses and dedicated to reconstructing lower Man-hattan. Rockefeller and his DLMA had enjoyed great successes, most ob-viously construction of the World Trade Center, which they had proposed.

David Rockefeller had obvious interests in the Battery Park City site. His overall plans for lower Manhattan included a greatly expanded office-build-ing core, surrounded by high-income housing along the Hudson and East River shores, and including entertainment and shopping facilities like those of the upper East Side. This layout would make downtown a fashionable residential and office area, alive twenty-four hours a day, attractive to the elite of major corporations as a place to both live and work. He wanted no office space on the Battery Park City site, because such space might compete with development in the office core, including Chase Manhattan Plaza. David Rockefeller's advocacy of only high-income housing for the site was closer to Lindsay's position than to Nelson Rockefeller's; curiously, the two brothers did not work together particularly closely as the project developed.

Our *New York Times* reader would pick up a good idea of David Rock-efeller's position on Battery Park City, but could not help notice that Rock-efeller kept out of the subsequent frays, pressing always for an early start of construction but taking no public positions on most of the controversies that developed.

After Nelson Rockefeller's proposal came a period of intense conflicts over the project, lasting until the middle of 1969. First was a conflict between Lindsay and Nelson Rockefeller over the design. This conflict was finally resolved in 1968, when the two agreed that the project should be designed by a team of three architectural firms, one associated with Rockefeller; one close to Lindsay; and a third associated with neither.

The three firms completed their overall design for the project in the spring of 1969. The plan was extraordinary. At the site's southern end, three office towers of forty, fifty, and sixty stories would be built. To add visual interest to the project, they would be hexagonal in plan and connected to one another by bridges. Stretching north the length of the site, apartment towers and lower residential buildings would be built beside and above a gallery. Shopping and public facilities, even a marina, would be interspersed with the housing, and a monorail would run the length of the gallery, connecting the project to subway stations. The architectural renderings showed a wonderland city, combining the bustle of New York with the majesty of the Hudson shore. If anything could, this chic development would attract the elite to lower Manhattan.

The second and more important conflict concerned the income groups who would inhabit Battery Park City. Lindsay maintained until April 1969 his position that all Battery Park City residences should be high-income. Then, the design question resolved, he and Nelson Rockefeller compromised. Now, the project would include ten thousand high-income, four thousand middle-income, and one thousand low-income apartments.

Now, however, a new factor entered the battle over Battery Park City's income mix. New York City's liberal Democrats, near the high point of the influence they had won through the anti-Viet-Nam-war movement, organized to demand more low-income housing for the project. A wide variety of liberal groups attacked the income mix Lindsay and Nelson Rockefeller had agreed on. At a hearing on the project, for example, the Women's City Club representative said of the plan: "It is the kind of tokenism which is an affront to the needy . . ."[4]

In June 1969, political events gave the liberals extraordinary leverage. Lindsay (then a Republican although he would later become a Democrat) lost the Republican mayoral primary to John Marchi, a conservative. In the same day's Democratic primary, conservative Democrat Mario Procaccino, the city comptroller, defeated six liberals. In Procaccino's victory, Lindsay saw a chance of winning reelection despite his primary loss. As an Independent, he might win enough votes from liberal Democrats to defeat the two major-party conservatives.

In November, Lindsay did win reelection, but in the summer of 1969 he desperately needed liberal support. The liberals demanded, among other things, that Battery Park City's housing be one-third low-income, one-third middle-income, and one-third high-income, and that the income groups be mixed together in the project.

Lindsay agreed and, offered no other choice, so did the state-created Battery Park City Authority. The design and income-mix issues thus resolved, the city leased the project area land (which it owned) to the Battery Park City Authority, and work on the landfill was begun. The project's development was to be controlled by the master lease agreement between the city and the authority. Work on the landfill proceeded smoothly; in fact, the fill was completed at considerably lower cost than originally estimated.

But almost immediately, new difficulties arose in getting the project's construction off the ground. In 1970, the demand for office space in lower Manhattan started to shrink, primarily because of difficulties among stock brokerage firms; this shrinkage delayed construction of the project's office buildings indefinitely.

The authority sought developers for the first housing. Despite its commitment to build economically integrated housing, the authority planned to proceed first with conventionally financed high-income housing. A team of developers was selected, but negotiations with them proceeded slowly. Continuing inflation made housing construction more and more expensive, reducing the number of households who could afford conventionally financed housing. This made the developers reluctant to proceed without public financing that would lower their own investment, and increased the difficulty of obtaining financing not guaranteed by the government.

In June 1972, the authority requested an amendment to the master lease designed to deal with these problems. The proportion of publicly financed "middle-income" housing would be increased to 56 percent; in financing this housing, the public would absorb the risks developers and private financers were unwilling to take. By this time, the cost of "middle-income" housing was such that its residents would be quite well off. In addition, the amendment reduced the proportion of low-income housing and increased somewhat the proportion of conventionally financed housing. With some reluctance on the part of liberal members, New York City's governing Board of Estimate approved the changes.

But these changes failed to solve the problems that were keeping Battery Park City construction from beginning. Year after year the project dragged on. The authority carried site planning work as far as it could without final agreement with the developers, and even carried out some foundation construction allowed under its site-development mandate. Increasingly, it sought any sort of development to get construction started. In 1975–77, when proposals for a new convention center for the city were under consideration, the Battery Park City and Port authorities and the DLMA pressed unsuccessfully for location of the new center on the Battery Park City site. Then, in 1979 and 1980, the authority worked out a deal for location of a new American Stock Exchange building there, but this too collapsed in the face of rising costs and insecurity about the project's future.

The authority and the housing developers it had selected sought federal mortgage insurance for the project's first phase; if the project failed, this insurance would require the federal government to make good its mortgage. Not surprisingly, given the fact that many other financers apparently expected the project to fail, the federal government proved reluctant to insure the mortgage. However, mortgage insurance for the first six buildings was finally obtained, and construction began in 1980. But these buildings, which might well end up owned by the federal government after a default, would take up only a small portion of the site. Thus, fifteen years after the project was planned, the future of the project as a whole remained unclear.

During the second half of the 1970s, the Battery Park City Authority's administration also underwent various legislative investigations, replacement of its original head, and absorption into another state-created development agency.

Thus Battery Park City remains a curious white elephant for New York: ninety largely vacant acres ready to be built on, within walking distance of 400,000 jobs, with spectacular views of the Hudson and New York Harbor, in a city where housing is in chronically short supply and apartments elsewhere can command astronomical rents.

Ready Explanations

Our New Yorker, should she or he have an interest in understanding why this vacancy exists, would be left in a quandary. Several general explanations suggest themselves.

First, the plans for the project might have been impossibly ambitious and complex from the start. A good deal of evidence supports this explanation. The original physical plans for the project did prove overly complex. Setting aside possible engineering difficulties, they required financing housing, commercial, and public spaces at the same time and probably with the same mortgages. This would create legal difficulties and might prove disastrous financially, because demand for the commercial space would develop only after much of the housing had been occupied. But these complex physical plans were all but abandoned by 1972, and the authority planned to proceed with much simpler development, building one part of the project at a time. Thus, complexity does not explain the delays.

Our New Yorker, were he or she of a conservative bent, might understand the project's dismal history as reflecting a truly spectacular ineptitude of government. But this explanation, too, doesn't fit the facts very well. After all, the Battery Park City Authority had proven remarkably efficient at creating the landfill. Moreover, it was a quasi-governmental agency, purposely insulated from government precisely to make it more like a private corporation.

Still in a quandary, one might look to the economic and fiscal turmoil that beset New York starting early in 1975. The fiscal problems of the city, state, and state-created agencies like the authority certainly reduced their ability to borrow money with which to finance projects like Battery Park City's housing. But earlier, the project could have been begun with tax-exempt bond financing. Thus, reference to the fiscal problems may explain why Battery Park City remained stuck in a hole, but cannot explain why it got into the hole in the first place.

Having exhausted his knowledge of the project's history, thus, our New Yorker is left with no adequate explanation of why the city is stuck with this white elephant. Unless one assumes that those making decisions were entirely inept, one must conclude that something other than what was apparent was going on in the history of the project, that the story available to the public was only part of the reality, perhaps not the most important part.[5]

Seeking an Adequate Explanation

To obtain an adequate explanation of what happened in Battery Park City, the author reconstructed the project's history in detail, as part of a broader study of lower Manhattan's redevelopment.[6]

Data with which to reconstruct the project's history were available from sources of four sorts: (1) newspaper and other more-or-less disinterested accounts of events—the sources readily available to the public; (2) planning documents issued (for various purposes and by various agencies) at various points in the project's history; (3) official records, such as records of legislative and planning hearings, minutes of meetings of official bodies, bond prospectuses, and, where they could be obtained, correspondence and memoranda files; and (4) interviews with actors in the project's history.

Each of these sources provided seriously incomplete data. Newspaper accounts were frequently found to be wildly inaccurate when checked against other sources, and many newspaper stories were simple public relations releases "planted" by various agencies. Planning documents were almost always dedicated to pressing particular viewpoints. Official records frequently only dealt with final actions, giving few clues as to why they were taken. The most important actors could not be interviewed at all. (David Rockefeller has not submitted to any but the most assuredly friendly interviews in years; Nelson Rockefeller was vice president of the United States at the time of the research, and not giving interviews to graduate students; and John Lindsay simply refused to be interviewed.) Their close associates knew the events, but they and other respondents could hardly be trusted to give unbiased views.

Nonetheless, data from all the sources could be fit together like a jigsaw puzzle, to produce an essentially complete, accurate picture of what occurred. As important, this picture could be tested, detail by detail. Consistency was the standard against which parts of the picture were judged. Statements or understandings from one source were checked against those from other sources, and accounts of events drawn from particular sources were checked for internal consistency. Thus, reconstructing the history of the project proceeded like the work of the mystery-story detective. The detective—in stories if not in reality—proceeds on the assumption that the world makes sense, not only in a general way, but quite precisely. The Battery Park City picture was put together in precisely the same way.

Extremely detailed chronologies of events proved to be most useful in testing consistency. When looked at in sufficient detail, events are simply too complex for any explanations to fit besides the correct one.

Obtaining interview evidence presented at least two problems somewhat unusual in social-scientific research. First, social-scientific interviews usually seek information that is of interest, not for what it says about the particular respondent, but as a representation of the opinions, lives, situations, etc., of the respondent's group; therefore, the respondent is likely to believe statements that her or his responses will remain anonymous. Here, particular events and the respondents' roles in them were of interest. Although respondents were guaranteed anonymity, those guarantees were not terribly credible, because only a few individuals would be in positions to know of particular events, and others involved in the events could readily deduce who had said what to the interviewer.

Second, social scientists typically interview individuals with whom they are, at least, social equals, and respondents cooperate partly because they believe in the overall value of scientific efforts. In this case, in contrast, the interviewer was almost invariably subordinate to the respondents in age, wealth, and power. Unlike usual respondents, moreover, these respondents were used to being interviewed, and therefore not flattered by being chosen for the study.

In these circumstances, it proved essential to establish empathy with respondents: to introduce both the interview as a whole and particular topics in ways that portrayed the interviewer as appreciating the circumstances in which the respondent worked and the perhaps difficult choices he faced. Establishing such empathy required the interviewer to play the role of a junior colleague, interested in the respondent's work and accepting of the respondent's viewpoint. In the last analysis, to obtain data in such circumstances one had to rely on and reinforce respondents' belief that their actions were morally justified. Flattering respondents also proved very useful.

The methods just sketched made it possible to obtain a full picture of what happened in Battery Park City. The most important aspects of that explanation are presented next.

The Real Planning of Battery Park City

The decade of delays in Battery Park City's construction resulted, primarily, from a single cause: the desire of virtually all those deeply involved in the project to build it as a high-income enclave. To many citizens, using public powers and funds and a publicly owned site to create a luxurious housing development only the wealthiest residents of the city could afford would seem presumptuous at best. In Battery Park City, public resources were turned to this end, but the situation had another crucial aspect. *There was no real demand for expensive housing in the area.*

Lower Manhattan had, and has, substantial, even overwhelming, disadvantages as a site for expensive housing. It has almost none of the movie theaters, shops, galleries, and department stores available on the upper East Side, the area with which it must compete for wealthy residents. Lower Manhattan has no park comparable in attractiveness to that part of Central Park adjacent to the upper East Side. Most of the periphery around the lower Manhattan commercial core is, simply, ugly—decaying industrial buildings, parking lots, views of elevated highways. In fact, the only apparent advantage Battery Park City would have in competition with other luxury housing is its view of the harbor.

The Battery Park City Authority, the Lindsay administration, the Beame administration that replaced it at the start of 1974, and the DLMA all knew how weak was the demand for expensive housing in lower Manhattan. In fact, in 1967 and 1971 the DLMA sponsored surveys of demand for housing in the area.[7] These studies found demand for middle-income housing strong, demand for low-cost housing essentially unlimited, and demand for high-income housing quite limited, consisting almost entirely of a few people who would be interested in moving to the area from other parts of Manhattan. These findings were not surprising, given the other choices available to each of the income groups and the fact that lower Manhattan's workforce includes relatively few high-income workers but hundreds of thousands of clerks and other white-collar workers of modest incomes.

In 1974, moreover, a comparable housing development was completed just to the east of the northern part of the Battery Park City site. This project, Independence Plaza North, was a "middle-income" project, financed from tax-exempt bond revenues, but because of inflation and high interest rates its rents ranged from $240 for the least desirable studio to $671 for the best three-bedroom unit; according to regulations of the program, tenants could have maximum incomes from $17,000 to $56,000. After a year of intensive rental effort, only 270 of the project's 1329 apartments were rented. Then, to avoid disastrous consequences for the financing agency, the project was further subsidized with funds from the federal Section 236 program, designed to produce rental housing for "moderate-income" families. At the new rents the project was rented very rapidly to households with incomes from $13,100 to $18,000, who paid 25 percent of their incomes in rent.[8]

Battery Park City could have been developed as a "middle-income" housing development. Had financing arrangements been made in 1969 or 1970, the project would have been rentable at the resulting rates. Through 1974, construction of the project could have begun if federal Section 236 subsidies had been utilized, either alone or in combination with tax-exempt bond financing. One can argue, of course, that piling one subsidy on another is wasteful and results in devoting immense public resources to serving a very small number of people. But such tandem subsidizing of projects was done quite regularly at the time, and it could have gotten Battery Park City built.

These steps were not taken, not because of any reluctance to devote subsidy funds to the project, but because its planners did not want lower- or even middle-income people living there. The purpose of the project was to draw high-income people to lower Manhattan, and those involved in the project believed that the presence of others would make it less attractive to the wealthy. Thus, in the words of the 1971 housing market study done for the DLMA:

> If a housing mix by rent levels is established, the low and to a lesser degree the middle income construction will act as a brake on demand for luxury units. Occupants of luxury housing prefer to cluster together and the inclusion of lower income families will reduce demand.[9]

After agreeing in 1969 to a thorough mixing of income groups in the project, the Lindsay administration and the Battery Park City Authority made no visible efforts to develop low-income housing, and sought "middle-income" financing only when conventional financing proved unworkable. Although the DLMA's role in this stage of Battery Park City was nearly invisible, it too appears to have done everything possible to avoid development of housing for other than wealthy households. As Independence Plaza North's difficulties grew in 1974, the DLMA tried to get lower Manhattan corporations to rent the projects' apartments for their personnel, rather than have the project rented to moderate-income families through the Section 236 program.

The city and the authority and their architects also made extraordinary efforts to ensure that the project's high-income housing would be insulated both from any lower-income housing built in the project and from members of the public who wanted to use Battery Park City's public esplanade and park facilities. One of the architects involved talked about design techniques used to maintain exclusivity in the public project:

> Well, on our plans . . . we think we've done it . . . We do it by making it sort of naturally difficult to go someplace. In other words, you'd have a big rise or change in land levels but you wouldn't do it with a wall, which says stay away, you'd do it with terraces and planting. Or, you wouldn't have the main entrance to a compound just at the axis of a street. It would be working itself around the corner. If you wanted to find it you could find it, but it wasn't there waving a flag with a fence and saying, you're not wanted here. We would have inner courts. We'd have outer courts for everybody to go and outer spaces, which would have some policing. Then there'd be others where if you

*found your way in or you knew your way in, you see, you'd have to know
your way in . . . and if you were somebody there that looked very strange,
there'd be somebody there to say, "Excuse me, can I help you?" or something
like that.*[10]

In American society, issues of class and issues of race are almost always
intermixed. Battery Park City's planners talked about economic exclusivity,
because proposing economic segregation is far more acceptable than proposing racial segregation, but there is a good deal of evidence that what they
were really after was racial segregation, an all-white project. Virtually everyone involved conceived of the low- and, to a lesser extent, moderate- and
middle-income housing they didn't want in lower Manhattan as housing
exclusively for Blacks and Spanish-speaking people, "luxury" housing as
housing for whites (although only a very small proportion of the city's non-
Spanish-speaking white population could afford the luxury rents). The most
striking evidence of their attitude was offered by the statement of one of
the major actors, "No one would mind if Ralph Bunche lived there."[11]
Unfortunately, Bunche, the former deputy secretary general of the United
Nations and possibly the one Black perfectly acceptable to whites, had died
some time before this statement was made.

Thus, the alternatives of making Battery Park City a middle-income or
mixed-income area were rejected, until inflation and the deteriorating fiscal
position of New York made it almost impossible to build anything on the
site. To understand why these alternatives were rejected, one must understand, first, the visions of the area held by the Lindsay administration and
David Rockefeller, and second, how profits were to be made in redeveloping
the area.

Throughout his eight years as mayor, John Lindsay sought to reinforce
the role of New York City as a "national center," to use his administration's
phrase.[12] The unique importance of New York as a center of corporate
headquarters, communications, advertising, and the arts gave the city the
foundation on which to build permanent prosperity. Making both lower and
midtown Manhattan more and more attractive to a professional and managerial elite would attract more and more "national center" functions to the
city. In turn, the office buildings these activities required would pay more
and more property taxes and provide more and more white-collar jobs,
giving the city the fiscal and economic wherewithal to overcome its fiscal
problems and pull its poor citizens out of poverty.

In planning for areas of New York outside the Manhattan south of 96th
Street and in administering the police, health programs, and scores of other
city functions, Lindsay acted as a liberal. But he saw preservation and
enhancement of the central areas for the elite as crucial to the whole future
of the city.

Lindsay's plans for the city failed. Particularly after 1970, when an office-space glut brought office development to a halt, revenues failed to grow nearly rapidly enough to keep up with expenditures. The new development that did go on attracted few new jobs. (Analysis of employment changes in lower Manhattan shows that job gains and losses resulted from changes in particular industries, rather than from physical development.) And the city continued to lose corporate headquarters, both to other metropolitan areas and to suburban sites in Connecticut and New Jersey. (Given the very dominant position New York enjoyed until 1970 and the general movement of economic power to the "sunbelt" and energy-producing states thereafter, it appears that these losses were inevitable.)

Lindsay's national center strategy was one version of a set of arguments used very frequently in urban planning, particularly to justify projects in the central business district. In brief, these arguments are that (1) real estate development will contribute jobs and taxes to the city; (2) real estate development will not occur without public subsidies, or other public actions under consideration in the particular case; and (3) therefore, the public should provide the subsidies, tax breaks, or other measures necessary to encourage the real estate development in question. Like Lindsay's strategy, these arguments can be questioned both as general propositions and in specific applications. They are based on the frequently questionable assumption that public actions can have a major effect on the location of economic activities even in the face of far more powerful economic forces.

As an ideological formulation, Lindsay's national center strategy justified public steps to encourage development of lower Manhattan for an elite by identifying such development with the broader public interest. Lindsay's strategy may also have had another, more psychological, ideological function. All the evidence suggests that Lindsay and those around him sincerely wanted to contribute to improvement of the position of the poor, particularly the minority poor. On the other hand, they likely did not wish to sacrifice their own comfortable positions, including insulation from the problems of the city. The national center argument reconciled these conflicting moral pressures quite neatly. If an insulated national center had to be reinforced to guarantee the future of the city, and particularly to provide the wherewithal to fight poverty, the elite to which Lindsay and his associates belonged could hardly be blamed for participating in and identifying with that center and its delights.

David Rockefeller held a slightly different vision of lower Manhattan. For him, the future of the city lay not with the upper-middle-class professional and managerial elite favored by Lindsay, but with the city's major corporations, particularly its banks. In the words of Warren Lindquist, who has worked with David Rockefeller throughout his urban development efforts in New York and other cities, lower Manhattan had to be rebuilt to develop and sustain the kind of physical environment which would support the continued kind and amount of growth that the dominant Downtown business institutions . . . would have to enjoy if they were going to continue to enjoy their share, a reasonable share of the expanding commerce of . . . the country and of the world. [13]

In turn, the city's economy rose and fell with the fates of these businesses. To guarantee that future, lower Manhattan had to be rebuilt into an area suitable to the needs and the dignity of major corporations and men like Rockefeller and his peers.

Like Lindsay's vision of lower Manhattan, Rockefeller's served ideological as well as practical functions. Because they are located at the very heart of the city's economy, the major commercial banks are in a position to benefit from almost any business activity that takes place in the city. For example, they benefit from redevelopment by taking part in construction financing for office buildings; participating in the ownership of their own buildings and other real estate; handling public bond issues; and seeing their commercial banking activity expand as the city economy expands. From this position, séparating public from private interests is virtually impossible. In Rockefeller's view, business leaders must create and maintain settings in which business, including their own businesses, can profit and the public can be served by the same actions. This is what Rockefeller saw himself as accomplishing in lower Manhattan's redevelopment.

Lindsay's and Rockefeller's visions of the future lower Manhattan justified public creation of opportunities for private profit in the area's redevelopment. The public role in central business district redevelopment is twofold. On the one hand, government must utilize its regulatory powers to create situations in which orderly development is possible. On the other, government must absorb necessary risks private investors cannot or will not take. In lower Manhattan, government's roles were different in the office core, the peripheral area around it, and the shore areas including Battery Park City. In the core, the governmental role was minimal—enforcing orderly development through administration of the zoning ordinance and using zoning to encourage good design. Redevelopment around the core enhanced the value of properties there, simply by putting them at the center of larger areas with more activity. In addition, opportunities arose for intensifying land use by replacing old, small office buildings with new, larger ones. Thus, David Rockefeller could ensure that his Chase Manhattan Plaza gamble would work out, primarily by ensuring reconstruction of the whole area around the core.

The greatest opportunities for profits in central business district redevelopment occur in underutilized areas just outside the core, like the old, half-empty industrial slums that made up the lower Manhattan periphery in the mid-1950s. These properties can be bought cheaply; in the mid-1950s, for example, properties two blocks east of the Chase Manhattan Plaza site could be had for as little as ten dollars per square foot. If these properties can be converted into core uses, mainly first-class office buildings, the conversion will prove exceedingly profitable. These most lucrative profits of urban redevelopment are won, mainly, by real estate developers rather than by the largest corporations. However, banks and sometimes insurance companies can benefit through participation in ownership, construction, and other financing, and sometimes by occupying space at inexpensive rents, offered to them because major corporate tenants—like department stores in shopping malls—attract other tenants.

For Lindsay, Rockefeller, and the others deeply involved in planning Battery Park City, high-income housing was the only proper use of the shore area. Such housing would make it possible to attract chic restaurants and retailing and entertainment establishments to lower Manhattan. Less directly, by creating an image of lower Manhattan as an elite residential area, it would attract corporate headquarters to the area. Finally, high-income housing in insulated high-income developments would offer its developers the greatest potential profits. However, until lower Manhattan could establish a reputation as an elite residential area, and until the sorts of facilities available in the upper East Side were available downtown, developing expensive housing there would be extremely risky. Since private investors could not or would not take these risks, government had to do so.

Thus, for those planning Battery Park City, it was entirely proper that government encourage and absorb the risks of creating elite housing for lower Manhattan. The problem was how to do so in the face of pressure to use public resources and the site to benefit groups other than the elite.

Implications

Having solved the case, one variety of mystery-novel detective (represented best, perhaps, by Agatha Christie's Hercule Poirot) sits back and wisely appreciates the ways important aspects of the human condition resonate in the details of the just-solved case. In the same manner, we might ponder what Battery Park City suggests about New York and other cities and how to understand them.

The Battery Park City case certainly reinforces an impression many have had, that in planning and development matters, at least, the American city is a "growth machine," dominated by business groups and acting principally to order development to ensure private profits and to absorb risks private investors will not take.

Harvey Molotch explored "the city as a growth machine" in an article of that name.[14] The history of Battery Park City suggests one addition to his formulation. The business groups influential in public development efforts include not only real estate developers and others whose profits come primarily from real estate, but also major corporations, which stand to profit by increased development and can play the role of reconciling various business interests with one another, because their own interests are so widespread. This was the role David Rockefeller played in lower Manhattan.

The Battery Park City case and the whole history of lower Manhattan's redevelopment also suggest an addition to Floyd Hunter's classic formulation in *Community Power Structure*.[15] Hunter portrayed a business elite coordinating its actions through informal ties, and thus maintaining overall control over the city. The Battery Park City case suggests that political leaders wield power independent of business interests, and that very real, often public, conflicts occur among those wielding great power, but that business power is maintained through layer after layer of institutional arrangements that direct public power toward service of private ends.

The principal methodological implication of the Battery Park City case is very simple: events like those in this case, partly hidden from the public, can be discovered and understood. This implication should be understood with one qualification in mind. Those involved in the Battery Park City case were proud of what they did, although they frequently felt that the public at large could not understand why they did it. Their actions, they felt, were morally justified. Where this is not the case, as in situations where corruption is involved, events may be much more difficult to uncover and understand.

Epilogue

Finally, in 1980, the obstacles barring construction of the first stage of Battery Park City were overcome. The Federal Department of Housing and Urban Development finally granted the mortgage insurance sought since 1976. With this guarantee that the government would absorb any losses, the bonds from which the first stage housing was to be financed were sold readily.

Residents of this first part of Battery Park City would pay high rents indeed. Financed under programs originally intended to produce "middle-income" housing, Battery Park City apartments would cost as follows:

Studio with sleeping alcove	— $686–750
One bedroom	— $775–835
Two bedroom	— $1000–1250
Three bedroom	— $1355–1510

(Price variations within sizes of apartments reflect different floor locations and different views.)

In 1981, Olympia and York, a Canadian development firm, was selected to build the six million square feet of office space planned for the part of the site directly across West Street from the World Trade Center. Olympia and York presented a design that received rave reviews and promised to begin construction quickly. [As we go to press, construction has begun on one phase of Battery Park City.]

NOTES

1. This section is drawn entirely from *New York Times* reports, indexed in the *Times* index under "Battery Park City" and "Battery Park City Authority."
2. New York State, Governor's Office, "Battery Park City, New Living Space for New York," released May, 1966, message from Governor Nelson A. Rockefeller dated 1 Feb. 1966.
3. Wallace, McHarg, Roberts and Todd; Whittlesey, Conklin and Rossant; Alan M. Voorhees and Associates, Inc., *The Lower Manhattan Plan*, for New York City, City Planning Commission, June 1, 1966.
4. Quoted in *New York Times*, 17 July 1969, p. 4.
5. Thirty years ago, Floyd Hunter faced similar questions. He was active in Atlanta social welfare circles and concerned with problems like improvement of the city's race relations and raising the incomes of the poorest people in the city. But he found efforts in those directions continually frustrated by decisions that seemed to come from nowhere. To understand the predicament in which he found his city, Hunter explored the distribution of power in the city, how decisions were really made, and who made them. In the Battery Park City case, we face questions similar to Hunter's. How, where, why, and by whom were the decisions outside the public view made? See Floyd Hunter, *Community Power Structure* (Chapel Hill: Univ. of North Carolina Press, 1953).
6. Maynard T. Robison, *Rebuilding Lower Manhattan, 1955–1975*, Ph.D. diss., City Univ. of New York, 1976.
7. James Felt & Co., Inc., for DLMA, *Housing Potential, 1967–1982* (Nov. 1982), and *Housing Potential, Lower Manhattan* (December 1971).
8. Data drawn from files of financing agency, the New York City Housing Development Corporation.
9. Felt, *Housing Potential*.
10. Interview with principal in one of the architectural firms most active in New York City development programs. The interviewee was guaranteed anonymity.
11. The interview respondent was guaranteed anonymity.

12. This strategy was discussed most thoroughly in New York City, City Planning Commission, *A Plan for New York*, 6 vols., 1969, particularly *Critical Issues* and *Manhattan* volumes.
13. Warren Lindquist interview.
14. Harvey Molotch, "The City as a Growth Machine," *American Journal of Sociology*, 82 (1976):309–32.
15. Hunter, *Community Power Structure*.

12

Fiscal Crisis, Power, and Municipal Labor

ERIC LICHTEN

METHODOLOGICAL NOTE • The study of urban fiscal crisis is a study of power. The location of the crisis in the public sector, the participation by and conflicts among organizations representing fractions of different classes, and the attempts to deal with the crisis, all point to the power, or lack thereof, of conflicting class-based social formations.

Due to the controversial nature of the subject matter, one might expect some difficulty in researching it; power, after all, might resist exposure. On the other hand, crisis itself, it might be held, reveals rather than obscures its basis. This is why the study of crisis is crucial for understanding power structures.

This research used the following materials:

1. Government documentation: the federal government and its agencies, as well as those of New York State, have published a useful set of documents detailing the history of the fiscal crisis, including the causal roles of the city government, the investment community, and the municipal labor unions. The most important documents include: (a) The Securities and Exchange Commission Staff Report on Transactions in Securities of the City of New York (August 1977); (b) Hearings before the Committee on Banking, Housing and Urban Affairs of the U.S. Senate on "The New York City Fiscal Crisis" (October 1975); (c) Joint Economic Committee of the Congress of the U.S., "New York City's Financial Crisis: An Evaluation of Its Economic Impact and or Proposed Policy Solutions" (November 1975); (d) Reports by the Temporary Commission on City Finances; (e) Reports by the Municipal Assistance Corporation (MAC).

2. Memoranda and miscellaneous material: District Council 37 of the American Federation of State, County and Municipal Employees provided access to their extensive library on the fiscal crisis. This library includes relevant newspaper, journal, and magazine articles; reports by the Citizen's Budget Commission; and the *Fiscal Observer* and the *City Almanac*, all of which contain detailed analyses of the crisis. In addition, the library contains letters and memoranda passed among the city, unions, and banks, detailing positions and concerns over important issues, and reports by Program Planners Inc., the research firm hired as consultant to the municipal labor unions.
3. Minutes: minutes of both the Municipal Assistance Corporation and the Emergency Financial Control Board were reviewed. These provided clues to the process whereby major decisions were made.
4. Interviews: the foregoing sources were supplemented by detailed interviews with key informants from the unions, banks, Municipal Assistance Corporation, and Temporary Commission on City Finances. Much of the information concerning the setting of union strategy was obtained from these twelve interviews, as well as from the minutes of the Municipal Labor Coalition. The informants cited in this chapter were all key actors in the fiscal crisis. Their information was verified by other informants, some of whom wished not to be publicly quoted.

Together, the interviews, minutes, public records, news articles, and reports and studies by interested and involved groups (some of which had identifiable class interests) provided me with a detailed historical account of the fiscal crisis.

In late 1974 the City of New York found itself in an ever-deepening fiscal crisis. This fiscal crisis began with an increasing erosion of confidence in the city's ability to meet its debt obligations and pay back its investors. By the middle of 1975 the investment community plunged the city into crisis when the city found it could no longer market its bonds and notes. Without this source of revenue, the city could not meet either its everyday operating expenses or its long-term capital needs.

As the fiscal crisis deepened, the financial community (represented by the Financial Community Liaison Group) pressed for a prolonged and strict program of austerity budgeting.[1] As this was effected and made the city's budgetary policy, municipal workers found themselves threatened with layoffs and decreasing real wages and benefits.

This chapter details the strategies adopted by the municipal labor unions in the face of increasing pressure from the financial community, the federal and state governments, and the press for worker and union sacrifices. In particular, we focus on the early stage of the fiscal crisis from late 1974 through 1975, when alternative policies to austerity were still possible but were set aside. We shall see how union cooperation with austerity was made within a context of union powerlessness.

Fiscal Crisis and the City's Unions

From its inception, the unions responded to the ever-deepening fiscal crisis by cooperating with the emerging public policy apparently defined by the sacrifices of the city's workers and unions. These sacrifices became economically and politically "necessary" as the city found increasing resistance among investors, both institutional and individual, to its note and bond offerings. In November 1974, with Harrison J. Goldin, the city's comptroller, admitting a budget deficit of $650 million, interest rates on the city's debt obligations climbed to 9.5 percent as doubt grew about the solvency of both the city and its notes. To highlight the erosion of confidence in the city's fiscal health, one must recall that just one month earlier the city had marketed $420.4 million in Bond Anticipation Notes at a 7.79 percent interest rate. This rate was the highest interest rate ever paid by the city up to that time on this type of note offering. Further investor anxiety was caused by the decision of Fitch Investor's Service, Inc., to reduce its rating of New York City bonds from an "A" to a "BBB" rating for maturities before 1 January 1980, and to reduce those maturing subsequent to that date to "BB." In so doing, Fitch reported that the city might soon have "difficulty in meeting all its financial obligations, debt service, as well as operating expenses."[2] In order to attract investors, the city was obliged to offer from 8.6 percent to 9.5 percent interest, and even under those conditions the city could not attract adequate investor interest to meet its needs. The crisis atmosphere was further exacerbated by the city's urgent need to borrow $2.3 billion to meet operating and payroll obligations due within a few months. By the end of 1974 the city had accumulated more than $13 billion in outstanding debt and was threatened by a real possibility of bankruptcy.

In November 1974 the controversy over the city's solvency was fueled by the actions of the city administration. Despite growing concern by the city's major financial powers and authorities, the mayor's and comptroller's offices could not stop bickering in public over the actual size of the budget deficit. The mayor argued that the deficit was $430 million: $220 million less than the comptroller's estimate. Investors, already wary of the city's leadership, saw confirmation of their doubts in the confusion over the size of the deficit. Could the city be so poorly administered that its mayor and comptroller did not know the size of its debt?

While Mayor Beame and Comptroller Goldin argued, the major institutional investors began to pressure the city to produce a financing plan capable of closing the budget gap, whatever the actual size. In November 1974 the mayor announced a three-phase economy program designed to relieve the crisis. At first Mayor Beame ordered $100 million in economies; then, later in the same month, he announced the layoff of 1510 civil servants and provisional employees in order to save an additional $44 million. Comptroller Goldin, however, suggested harsher economies with additional personnel cuts. In December Mayor Beame announced over 3700 additional layoffs, including, for the first time, police, fire, and sanitation workers, as well as teachers. In addition, 2700 city workers were faced with forced retirement. The total savings produced by the two-phase cutback was announced by the mayor's office to have reduced the budget deficit from the originally estimated $430 million to $135.4 million: a reduction of $294.6 million in expenses.

In January 1975, with the crisis atmosphere growing, Comptroller Goldin reduced a planned bond and note offering to respond to "the market problem of oversupply." This action had been made in response to a memorandum by Frank Smeal, executive vice-president of Morgan Guarantee Trust, and after a meeting with Wallace Sellers of Merrill Lynch. Mr. Sellers had communicated the concern of the financial community with the growing crisis and informed city officials that the most recent note and bond offerings were a "total disaster." Therefore, he added, the January offerings would most likely not receive a bid from the financial underwriters.[3] In response to this lack of investor interest, Comptroller Goldin arrived at a plan that included issuing $650 million in notes with a one-year maturity, as well as an investment of $450 million in bonds by the city's union pension funds. For the first time during this crisis, the union's pension funds would finance a plan requiring worker layoffs. (We will discuss the implications of this strategy for the unions later on in this chapter.) Phase three of the mayor's plan, announced shortly thereafter, projected the laying off of 4,050 uniformed and nonuniformed personnel. These dismissals were projected to save $15 million. The total layoffs and dismissals up to this point, including forced retirements, supposedly numbered 12,700. *These numbers, however, were estimates at best. The confusion concerning actual totals of city workers employed, laid off, forced to retire, and/or dismissed underscored the failure of the city's administrations and management to effectively rationalize city services and, indeed, the administering of city government.* We can state with reasonable assurance that this failure to effectively rationalize city government underlay much of the investor anxiety, as represented by the concerns of finance capital (banks, investment brokers). This lack of rationality, of control and predictability, was deemed financially dangerous by those whose investments provided the city with operating funds. What could be more threatening to capital than a managerial system that does not manage the productivity and discontent of its workers and clients, one that cannot even determine the number of its employees?

In the face of these layoffs, the municipal unions began to talk about possible job actions and strikes. At first there was an attempt to unite the various unions through the Municipal Labor Committee (MLC). This committee, which had been formed in 1967, represented most of the municipal unions with the city's Office of Collective Bargaining (OCB). However, the omission of unions representing workers in nonmayoral agencies, such as the United Federation of Teachers and the Transit Workers Union, weakened the potential power of the MLC. Indeed, it may be hypothesized that one reason for the militancy of the UFT and the TWU during the late 1960s was their omission from the MLC. Being left to their own independent action may have encouraged militancy. The MLC, however, was not an organization functioning to promote militancy among union members. The function of the MLC prior to the fiscal crisis was to be the "vehicle through which the unions negotiate policy in the OCB, select their representatives in mediation and arbitration procedures, and assume the unions' share of the costs to maintain the OCB."[4] In other words, the function of the MLC was to promote the collective bargaining process and to inhibit the necessity of militant action. One might say that in that sense the MLC functioned as a tool for the management of class conflict encouraging negotiation rather than confrontation. Because District Council 37 of the American Federation of State, County and Municipal Workers, representing nearly a hundred thousand city workers, was its largest member union, Victor Gotbaum, its executive director, served as the chairman of the MLC.[5]

In late 1974, amidst growing calls from the financial community for the mass layoff of city workers, the city's unions attempted to alter the function of the MLC. For the first time in their history, the unions in the MLC were faced with "an issue which all its members could recognize as being in their self-interest."[6] Unity among these unions, however, was not easy to achieve. When I interviewed him in December 1978, Edward Handman, spokesman for D.C. 37, remembered the problem this way:

> In fact, there were hostilities within the MLC—police, firemen, sanitation all had flashpoints with each other. The uniform people were generally not too receptive to our union. There was kind of grudging participation within the MLC. However, with this first crisis, Victor Gotbaum really got the notion that the MLC had to start working as . . . the bargaining unit for all the city's employees.

The MLC, representing approximately two hundred thousand city workers, then met with Mayor Beame to discuss, negotiate, and relay their concerns with the early layoffs. The strategy that was arrived at within the MLC

> was twofold: One—to prevent layoffs of civil servants, which is opposed to provisional employees. **This is really a defense posture knowing that somebody had to get laid off.** And the second was to retain collective bargaining. Victor Gotbaum didn't want to be in a position where the city could make decisions which were uncontestable [Handman interview, December 1978].

With this defensively minded strategy, and with no long-term alternatives to austerity to offer, the unions met with the mayor. The result arrived at in December 1974 seemed to portend continuing union success in avoiding massive numbers of layoffs. The announced layoffs of late 1974 were avoided, or at least temporarily postponed, by a union plan to

> substitute cash savings for jobs. Each union accounted for its share of money [saved] in its own way. District Council 37, for example, waived a $6 million payment long due its health and security fund and saved the jobs of about 650 men and women it represents.[7]

Some city workers were able to keep working, their pay coming from union dues and funds. Nevertheless, this was a one-time, temporary, stopgap plan and, as such, could never be seen as an alternative to austerity or as a solution to the budget crisis. Some city workers kept their jobs—but for a very short time.

The 9 December 1974 minutes of the Municipal Labor Committee reveal the process by which the unions attempted to influence the city's proposed policy of worker dismissals. The sections of the minutes pertaining to the layoffs highlight the lack of concrete long-range planning by the unions either individually or collectively within the MLC. Furthermore, these minutes suggest the lack of unity that characterized union efforts throughout the first and most significant moments of the fiscal crisis. The sections of the minutes pertaining to the mayor's actions vis-à-vis employee layoffs follow.

> The Chairman then introduced discussion on the recent layoffs of civil service employees. It was agreed that the following proposal would be presented for approval to the General Membership as the MLC position on layoffs . . . "The member unions of the Municipal Labor Committee oppose any attempt by the City of New York to effectuate budgetary savings by dismissing permanent civil service employees while, at the same time, wasting funds by contracting out services which could be performed more economically by City employees and retaining provisional, exempt, temporary and other personnel doing non-essential work."
>
> In his report, Mr. Gotbaum stated that the MLC policy on layoffs would be presented to the press and to the Mayor. He recommended that since a budgetary crisis does, in fact, exist, labor leaders should look at the situation in any attempt to solve the problem before the situation becomes more severe.[8]

Regardless of this statement's implied unity, underlying the statement was an "on-your-own" attitude. The member unions of the MLC were being told to individually negotiate plans with the city to avert layoffs. In other words, these negotiations and solutions were to be arrived at independent of any long-term common strategy and position. The solution arrived at, allowing the unions to buy back the jobs of some of those laid off, was a temporary one at best. It was a Band-Aid for a cancer. More significantly, the unions clearly accepted the crucial argument that the crisis necessitated layoffs and that provisional employees could be sacrificed. Arguably, the unions had accepted what they might very well have fought and negotiated. Nowhere, either in the minutes of the MLC or in any negotiating position, did the unions submit a plan by which New York City's major corporations could be taxed directly on their "surplus" profits in exchange for a continuing level of city services. Nor were there plans suggesting a renegotiation of city debt held by major institutional lenders, such as these lenders arranged for Third World debtor nations (e.g., Zaire). The unions began their crisis strategy by accepting the one argument that would render them powerless: that the fiscal crisis necessitated their eventually sacrificing some of their membership. Already the notion of alternative solutions was being dismissed.

At this early stage there was some talk among the union leaders of job actions and strikes to halt the development of austerity budgeting. However, the crisis presented a situation heretofore not encountered by the unions; hence, a strike was deemed a radical action with unpredictable results. A strike would necessitate united action based on mutual trust and cooperation. Yet, the coalition was characterized by disunity, and the union leaders were left suspicious of one another. The labor movement in the city was less a unified social movement than it was a group splintered into factions, each vying for the remaining city revenues. Disunity, and sometimes conflict, among the unions was therefore a consequence of the structure of labor relations in the city. Indeed, it was a consequence of a complex division of labor within the public service sector itself, as well as between the public and private sector workforces. So it should not be surprising that a general strike and job actions—slow-downs and sick-outs—were, in Ed Handman's words,

> talked about but nobody wanted to do it. You would hear it but nobody really wanted to do it. For one, you always had the problem that you didn't know if everyone would go out on a general strike, particularly the uniformed people. They are averse to striking. And nobody wanted it because that's chaos and much of what was going on, you have to remember, **everything that was going on had never happened before. There was no experience** [Interview, December 1978; emphasis mine].

While the union leaders in the MLC were ruling out any militant opposition to the mayor's layoff plan and to the outcries for further austerity, their union members began to threaten resistance.

Some union leaders, particularly those in the police, transit, and fire-fighters' unions, were not in a position to passively accept the layoffs; they lacked that kind of control over their rank-and-file membership. They were all too ready to defer, as much as possible, to the leadership of Victor Gotbaum of District Council 37. From then on, Gotbaum, as president of the union with the largest membership, would take a prominent role in formulating union strategy. Ed Handman explained the situation at that time in the following manner:

Fortunately, and I'm the public relations person at D.C. 37, Vic [Gotbaum] was on the scene. He was the guy who clearly had the most and clearest vision of the problems that existed, of the extent of the problem and what it would take to rectify it and save it. The mayor never had it and was never conscious of it. He was conscious of a tremendous problem and he was ready to throw in the towel. The banks were doing business all the time. They were at that time getting 9¼ percent interest for their bonds and they were cracking the whip. And nobody had the sense that you got to get all these pieces together or the whole city is going to go down—except for Victor Gotbaum. He was the one. He, on the other hand, had the sense that the unions had to work together, which also meant not only getting one voice in terms of understanding the problem and trying to defend our position, but also getting the responsibility on the union side. It would have been easy for anybody to become a demagogic hero and call for strikes and such. And he had to keep that in mind and it was very difficult, extremely difficult because you had dozens of union presidents and each one had his own members to perform for. It meant that they had to, on the one hand, have Victor as their spokesperson, which meant that they had to look in their own eyes perhaps like lesser figures to their own membership. Some of them were inexperienced and were reluctant to take that kind of role and lose their manhood, so to speak, to their members. Most of them were, I think, delighted that Victor was there because they clearly were over their heads and they were delighted to leave it with him. Which is what happened. So our position was to maintain collective bargaining and to limit the firings. The first time, in November 1974, the ultimate solution was that we gave back to the city proportionately to the number of people in their respective unions fired and we saved their jobs [Handman interview, December 1978].

But only temporarily. Throughout the early months of 1975 investor confidence in the city continued to erode. In January Mayor Beame announced the layoff of 4050 city workers. However, union concessions saved the jobs of most of the workers newly threatened with the loss of their jobs. At this point, union strategy seemed to have stalled the austerity cutbacks designed to lower the cost of labor; indeed, actual dismissals totalled 1941 and not the 12,700 supposedly dismissed after months of public posturing, threatening, and cajoling. But during this time the Financial Community Liaison Group, representing the city's banking interests, was formed and began to exert severe pressure on the city to adopt a stringent austerity policy. The fiscal pressures mounted, and Mayor Beame found the city in a "cash-flow crisis," as New York had difficulty borrowing $260 million to pay its March bills. Later that month, in response to the bankers' suggestions, the mayor reduced the amount of projected borrowing for the remainder of the fiscal year from $3 billion to $1 billion. It was thought that this reduction would decrease the pressure on an otherwise glutted municipal securities market. The mayor then blasted critics who suggested that he had lost control of the city to the banks. " 'Nobody is going to tell me how to run the city'," said the Mayor.[9]

This brings us to an important point. Throughout the early stage of the fiscal crisis, Mayor Beame maintained that it was not a long-term problem. He suggested then that only short-term remedies were required, and he therefore resisted any major realignment in the city's institutional arrangements. The only exception to this was the acceptance of the informal connection between the Financial Community Liaison Group and the city administration. The mayor's denial of the severity of the fiscal crisis and his conflict with the comptroller was seen by many as a contributing factor in its acceleration.[10] I interviewed William Scott, then the third deputy comptroller of the City of New York, who revealed the conflicting points of view between the mayor and the comptroller.

> There were long periods of time when the comptroller and the mayor did not see eye to eye. There was a political difference between the two men. I believe that Beame honestly did not believe that the notes and the bonds of the city were no longer saleable. I think he honestly thought that this was— a conspiracy is too harsh a word—done by design by the banks and the financial institutions against the city, and even the federal government. I don't think that he really ever early on felt that there was no market for the securities. He felt this was a false premise. And he was encouraged in this by his Deputy Mayor Jimmy Cavanaugh who felt very strongly, in the choicest of languages, that the banks were anti-city. Jay Goldin, on the other hand, felt that the banks were getting a very high rate of interest for the bonds that they happened to be buying just before the point in time when they wouldn't be buying any more. But I think he even failed to realize that the market was drying up for city bonds [Scott interview, December 1978].

This assessment of the Beame administration's refusal to accept the depth of the fiscal crisis, and the exacerbating function it had on the crisis, was also Donna Shalala's analysis. Dr. Shalala, former treasurer of the Municipal Assistance Corporation, conveyed this point in the following way.

> There wasn't much we [members of the Municipal Assistance Corporation] could do while the mayor was running around acting like there wasn't a real crisis. I remember sitting in Dallas when someone stood up and said, "Hey, the mayor of your city says in the New York Times he doesn't know how many

*employees you have," or the mayor says that the crisis will be over shortly.
It was very difficult because the city wasn't acting as if there was a crisis and
taking serious steps during the summer of 1975 for us to convince anyone that
that was happening [Shalala interview, October 1978].*

This confusion then, must be seen as critical to the remainder of the crisis.
The strategies adopted here by the unions, banks, and city administration
were to be repeated often with similar effect—the institutionalization of
austerity. By this time finance capital had mobilized and unified as a class
and demanded austerity as the solution. Meanwhile, the city administration
floundered without direction and lacked a concrete awareness of the growing
depth of the crisis and was therefore unable to find alternative budgetary
or taxing strategies to counter demands by capital for a planned and exter-
nally imposed austerity program. And in this void the city's unions lacked
the unity and the class ideology, as well as the knowledge of the depth of
the crisis and the peculiar characteristics of the city's finances, to successfully
oppose the oncoming crisis resolution being developed, planned, and imposed by capital's representatives. It is within this context that we will
analyze the lack of power of the city's public employee unions.

The Limitations of Public Sector Unionism during Crisis

We must be careful not to abstract these municipal unions from the structural
and historical context within which they were operant and developed their
crisis strategies. Public employee unions do not control, nor have they direct
influence over, the municipal securities markets that so powerfully affect
city finances and from which the city desperately needed to borrow operating
capital. The unions' only influence over these markets was an inverse one:
these markets might have responded more favorably toward the city's notes
and bonds had the unions voluntarily undertaken sacrifices in wages, benefits, and work-productivity regulations. However, this action would have
been highly unfavorable to both the union leadership and the city's rank-
and-file workforce. The paradox here is that the unions seemed caught
between, on the one hand, a crisis not yet so deep as to necessitate such
stringent austerity, and, on the other, the city's need to institute drastic
worker sacrifices and restore investor confidence before the city was completely shut out from market accessibility. But in either case—voluntary
sacrifice or imposed—the city's workers would be victimized in the process.
The power of finance capital seemed to lie in its control over much-needed
operating capital; to counter this power an alternative funding source had
to be found.
To develop such a counter-strategy would have required the arousing of

public consciousness against the actions of New York City's financial and corporate class. The actions of New York's major banking institutions, denying much-needed credit to the city, provided a key to mobilizing class consciousness against capital's interests. The crisis resolution itself, that is, austerity, has been experienced by New York's working and poor classes as a real threat to the quality of everyday life. Yet the public was brought to believe that austerity was absolutely necessary in the form that it took. Furthermore, public consciousness came to view the unions' actions as self-serving and against the interests of the community at large. Labor was presented as the possessor of threatening greed, while capital was largely ignored.[11] The news media daily published and aired stories claiming that the city's workers were overpaid, overpensioned, and underworked. Ravaged by recession, inflation, and high taxes, the city's residents were easily convinced that the city's fiscal crisis was the direct result of profligate city workers. *Nowhere was a connection made between struggles for a better work life and a higher-quality community life.* The unions were unable to capitalize on the direct connection between worker layoffs and the declining services that threatened the city's neighborhoods. This combination of media effectiveness and union ineffectiveness contributed to an anti-worker, anti-union consciousness and played directly into the hands of capital. Meanwhile, New York's major commercial banks were "dumping" approximately $2.3 billion in city securities and flooding the municipal securities market, thereby making it improbable that the city could market any more debt obligations. Yet this news was not made available to the city's residents. Ed Handman described the situation at that time in this way:

> *There was not a necessity for the kind of panic and hysteria that we had. The media, of course, played a tremendous role in that. And the fact that attacking the city and attacking the public servants was such a handy thing for everybody that it just kept escalating and skyrocketing.*
>
> *We have a news media that is ecstatic about this kind of thing . . . This is the most sensational, the most salable item you have in New York City—a scandal that is anti-worker and anti-city. To suggest that civil servants are overpaid is tremendous copy, not just suggest but to say it is tremendous copy. Politicians could get hearings any day in the week . . . just by saying we got to lay off civil servants—we're paying them too much—that the bus driver retires with more money than he ever made. And you'll tell them that 12,000 city workers retired last year and that only 40 of them were bus drivers and what about the other 11,960; the others who went out with four thousand dollars a year, or three thousand dollars, or whatever. They don't even listen to you. And that kind of attitude presents a problem—there's no question about it. It's a question of what they're saying in the Times about welfare reform—about the need to get federal help. . .We were saying that in 1974 and 1975, and they wouldn't even print it. The only time they would print it is they would say, "Victor Gotbaum is raising a red herring about welfare*

reform, or something like that to take the pressure off " [Handman interview, December 1978].

Without control over the major disseminators of public information it was indeed extremely difficult for the city's working class to mobilize effective and informed mass opposition to austerity; or indeed, to even recognize such a need and possibility. Alternatives were not discussed or presented as within the realm of the politically realistic. There was, I think, a *language of limitations* that solidified and concretized the fiscal crisis and the absolute, nonnegotiable necessity for drastic austerity. One might say that the *language of crisis*—"There is no money"; "What else can we do but make severe budget cuts"; "These city workers don't work but have great salaries and pensions"; "We can't afford teachers"—came from the ideology of capital. The lack of alternative consciousness reflected, in part, this lack of control over the forum and the parameters of debate. The language of this fiscal crisis was *capital's* language, consciousness, and needs. Bankers' logic defined the parameters of discourse and served to restrict the possibility of the development of a consciousness that would view city government and city services in terms of human needs. Indeed, human needs were sacrificed to the rigid god of capital; that is, the almighty bottom line.

In this context, the unions were left institutionally isolated within the city's power structure and determined that they must devise a strategy to ensure their organizational survival along with the viability of collective bargaining—even at the expense of many city workers. It should not come as a surprise that collective bargaining, even during a crisis where wages and benefits were unilaterally reduced, was seen as the focal point of union strategy. Collective bargaining is, after all, the basis for union acceptance and legitimation within corporate capitalism. The bargaining process legitimates both capital-management and the union within the status quo of class exploitation. Indeed, collective bargaining masks the existence of class exploitation and establishes the notion that all the worker deserves and gets is a "fair day's wage for a fair day's work." Therefore, the maintenance of the bargaining process, even if this process was more illusion than reality during the crisis, was deemed by the union leaders to be absolutely necessary. Later, after the further institutionalization of austerity had weakened the unions and made the bargaining process an empty formality, Albert Shanker, president of the United Federation of Teachers and one of the most powerful of the union leaders, suggested the temporary suspension of collective bargaining. In a statement that angered the other major labor leaders in the city, Shanker said: "When there's nothing to be bargained for it is a form of torture to send people in to bargain. Maintaining bargaining as usual in a period of the combination of want and bankruptcy is ridiculous."[12] Shanker went on to suggest, not opposition to austerity, or mass resistance to the deterioration of the quality of city services caused by budget cutting, but rather, the institutionalization of a labor-management control board similar to the War Labor Board in operation during World War II. This type of board would establish a set of wage controls to monitor and regulate working-class wages, benefits, and productivity. William Scott, now assistant to Mr. Shanker, explained this proposal, which was made in November 1976.

> Much to the dismay of all the other labor leaders in this city—they didn't think it was right—[Shanker made this proposal]. But he worked on a little different level. He is more international than most of the other labor leaders in this city since he's the national president and since he represents the government and the AFL in many conventions around the world. And he had more exposure to a war board. I don't really think he meant what he said. I think what he meant was that to go in under the guise of collective bargaining and to merely bargain as to how you are going to reduce your contract is not bargaining at all. It might be better . . . to have a uniform limitation on all of labor in a particular solution, for a particular period of time, rather than to go in and let this fellow bargain away this and that fellow bargain away that. . . . Basically, I guess when Shanker said, "I don't want to bargain a contract down. Impose it on me," that he was really saying, "Don't give me the option of telling my members I'm going to take ten dollars away from them or ten days away from them. You impose it on me. Don't let me bargain for that." That's what he was saying. It was taken up generally by the press as meaning that he didn't want to collective bargain during the fiscal crisis. He didn't mean that at all. He meant . . . "You impose your conditions during the time when you can prove you can't do anything else and when I decide that you now have come to the point when you can do something else, then I will bargain with you."

Shanker was recognizing that the basic strategy of the MLC—to maintain collective bargaining—was an empty one since there was no real collective bargaining during the fiscal crisis. Still his solution, the imposition of restrictive and austere contracts through a superordinate labor-management board, also abdicated any opposition role that unions might play. Shanker was calling for more union collaboration, not less. He was willing to cooperate with a preconceived and predefined reality conforming to capital's best interests. This strategy accepted without question the legitimacy of austerity. Still, the other labor leaders, however enraged they were by Shanker's proposal, were more in agreement with him than they would care to admit. After all, they had adopted the diplomatic approach, which was also based on a perceived responsibility to a community larger than their membership or the city's working class. Before we continue to describe and analyze union strategy throughout the remaining early years of the fiscal crisis it seems necessary to understand the origin of this type of labor strategy.

The municipal union leadership adopted strategies which, no doubt, accepted sacrifice without militant opposition. They eschewed any collective, mass resistance as a threat to the security of the community at large. American labor unions, in the private as well as the public sectors of the economy, have similarly adopted a reformist ideology, which views the class interests of workers and capital as basically contiguous and not structurally contradictory. Collective bargaining allegedly functions to mediate the class interests and resolve potentially disruptive working-class activism; indeed, working-class activism is thereby channeled into constructing labor relations that ensure productivity. In this ideology, capitalism provides room for workers' economic freedom. As a result, when workers take positive, concrete actions to gain more collective control of their labor and/or community they are presented as a threat to the community at large and must do so without union support. Here, stability is defined as manageable class relations within a general status quo that legitimates and helps preserve capitalist social relations of production: equilibrium is control; fiscal health is a deteriorating wage and service network; a healthy economy is a high rate of profit and management firmly in control. Simply put, the interests of capital are viewed as sustenance for the community at large, whereas the interests of workers, when expressed independent of union hierarchy, are viewed as disruptive and chaotic. The interests of unions become identified with stability even when the consequences of this stability cause suffering for the working class. Yet this interest is not expressed in equal partnership with capital. Indeed, the basis for this partnership is the unions' acquiescence to capital's power to organize and control production in the private sector and, in the public sector, to organize and reorganize the mediating functions of local government.

As this ideology takes shape it makes sense that the cause of the fiscal crisis is not viewed as contained within the contradictory social relations of the labor process but rather as the self-serving and community-threatening activity of labor. The unions, then, must serve the community by denying workers. Yet, by doing so the unions deny the autonomy of the working class, thereby relegating the community to capital. Cooperation within such a "community" works against a potentially autonomous workers' "community."

The unions' reformist ideology of change *within* capitalism, so socially and politically conservative in its repercussions, finds further expression and influence when the workers labor and struggle in the public sector. Actions in opposition to management by public sector workers are seen as threatening to the public, the "community." Capital seems not to enter into the conflict except as victim: the flow of labor to business may be disrupted, or the circulation of capital may be stalled. Then, capital may move out of the community to find labor peace, leading a public cry of, "If only workers were less disruptive and more cooperative and sympathetic to business needs," or, "If only government paid attention to the needs of business." In such a labor dispute in the public sector, management is presented as representing the public interest—after all, government is class-neutral and protects the needs of the unity of the community, itself class-neutral. An independent and autonomous working-class consciousness seems less critical since capital's exploitativeness is denied. This absence of working-class unity, as indicated by the ideological separation of public and private, isolates the public sector worker. The public employee union then finds its interests best served in collaboration with city management and corporate capital. But in this case, the fiscal crisis of New York City, this collaboration enabled capital to deny the city the necessary operating funds to resist budgetary cutbacks and led to austerity.

> In failing to develop an independent ideological stance of its own, organized labor in America has remained a reactive movement, always more or less captive but certainly never an equal partner of private capital.
>
> The same pattern holds true in the relationship between private capital and governing institutions. Again it is private capital that makes the important decisions regarding economic growth, planning, and allocation of resources and jobs. Like organized labor, local and state governments have also become captive partners, accepting the notion that what's good for business is good for the community. Moriarty of the Congressional Coalition put his finger right on the problem when he remarked that "given the nature of the capitalist system, you have to count on them all the time to carry the major load." The role of local and state governments in this partnership has always been to accommodate to the needs of private capital, and on occasion to act as a mediator between its abuses and excesses and the reactions of an angry public.[13]

In this crisis, however, there was no effective voice representing an angry public against the excesses and abuses of finance capital. Without such active opposition, capital was able to press its demands for austerity. The public employee unions meanwhile continued to act reactively and defensively, thereby abdicating the state to those who demanded worker sacrifice. When I interviewed him in August 1978, Al Viani, then the director of research and negotiation of District Council 37, asserted that the unions were willing to make what they deemed to be necessary sacrifices:

> *because those sacrifices had to be made. There was no getting away from it. The crisis was real, the billion-dollar gap was there, everybody knew it and we had to deal with that. Now one could say that if the unions were strong there would have been no sacrifices and no cutbacks. But that was impossible. I mean it would have either been made up with layoffs or, if there were no sacrifices on the wages, or no deferral of wages, or anything of that sort, then*

it would have been made up in layoffs or dismantling of various agencies or whatever. That had to be dealt with, and, from the unions' point of view, in the most pragmatic kind of way. And that was to get out of what was admittedly a very severe crisis the best way we possibly could without any long-term erosion of either the basic salary structure or the basic fringe structure [Viani interview, August 1978].

In this regard, it is interesting to note that "pragmatism" had already been defined as cooperation with any antilabor austerity. As Viani and other labor leaders asserted, there was a crisis that inhibited labor's strategic choices. Yet it is also true that, in their strategy-making process, the unions hastily set aside alternatives to cooperation with austerity—such as more militancy, demanding more labor input into public-policy decion making, demanding labor influence over managing services—in order to demonstrate labor's responsibility to the public.

As the crisis progressed, labor's "pragmatic," "cooperative," and "responsible" strategy was used against the city's workers to develop a formal mechanism of institutional control in the form of the Emergency Financial Control Board. This control board, isolated from electoral, minority, and union influence, was authorized by the New York State Legislature to review and vote on all major city contracts. Its chief function was to adopt and maintain an austerity program that could not be effectively opposed. Serving on the Control Board were representatives of the financial and corporate sector; there were no union representatives.

Once again, Al Viani put this into perspective.

*There were people who were arguing internally that this union, D.C. 37, should, when the threat of bankruptcy came in the late spring and early June of 1975, say to the mayor, to the federal government and the state, and to the business community, "Fuck you—let the city go bankrupt. You don't want to open up the bond markets, sorry—I am going to let the whole thing go down." This would have been such a horrible threat that nobody would have allowed it to happen and they would have come up with some cash right away to prevent it from happening. We, the unions, didn't do that. The mayor—he didn't do that and first there was the Municipal Assistance Corporation, to finance the city, and then the Emergency Financial Control Board. **And all the power was openly taken away** [Viani interview, August 1978; emphasis mine].*

The unions remained uncertain throughout the early years of the crisis. Regardless of militant actions taken by its rank and file, the unions kept to their strategy of cooperation guided by their notions of what was indeed pragmatic and responsible. These notions, amidst a deepening crisis, led to their policy of investing union pension funds in city and MAC debt obligations. With this union investment, which by December 1977 totaled nearly three billion dollars in city and MAC securities and 21 percent of the total securities outstanding, the city had found its source of funding.

The ultimate irony emerging from these investments was that they were made from a position of union powerlessness, not union power. Rather than adding power, these investments restricted the unions' future options. The choice to invest was made with only two options perceived as politically viable and realistic: pension-fund investment or city bankruptcy. In their choice, we can see the decline of the unions' political influence. Public policy, in the form of austerity, could now be instituted with the unions' full cooperation; indeed, with their financial support. Union opposition to austerity might endanger city finances, which would then threaten pension investments. A new class politic had been formed to the disadvantage of the city's unions and workers. As Al Viani stated, "All the power was openly taken away."

NOTES

1. See Eric Lichten, "The Development of Austerity: Fiscal Crisis in New York City," in G. William Domhoff (ed.), *Power Structure Research* (Beverly Hills, Cal.: Sage, 1980), pp. 139–171.
2. "Fitch Update," quoted in Securities and Exchange Commission, *Report on Transactions in Securities of the City of New York* (Washington, D.C., 1977), pp. 9–11.
3. Ibid., pp. 44–46.
4. Seymour Z. Mann and Edward Handman, "Perspectives on New York City's Fiscal Crisis: The Role of the Municipal Unions," *City Almanac*, 12 (June 1977): 9.
5. Ibid.
6. Ibid.
7. Ibid.
8. Minutes of the Municipal Labor Coalition, 9 Dec. 1974, pp. 1–2.
9. Evelyn Seinfeld, "Chronology of the New York City Fiscal Crisis: July 18, 1974 to April 4, 1977," Department of Research and Negotiations, District Council 37 of the American Federation of State, County and Municipal Employees, p. 4.
10. See S.E.C., *Report*, esp. ch. 3.
11. See, for example, Wyndham Robertson, "Going Broke the New York Way," *Fortune Magazine* (Aug. 1975): 144–214; also see relevant articles in *Business Week*, 13, 20, Oct. and 10, 17 Nov. 1975. For a brief but insightful discussion of the press and the fiscal crisis, see Jack Newfield and Paul DuBrul, *The Abuse of Power* (New York: Viking, 1977), pp. 14–18.

12. Interview with William Scott, assistant to the president, United Federation of Teachers. This statement was made by Albert Shanker, president of the UFT, in November 1976. The statement was confirmed by Scott during our interview of December 1978.

13. Jeremy Rifkin and Randy Barber, *The North Will Rise Again* (Boston: Beacon Press, 1978), p. 79.

13

The Daily Apple: Medicine and Media

FRED H. GOLDNER

METHODOLOGICAL NOTE • This paper is based on the content of newspaper articles and on the experiences of the author. The data consist of files of New York newspaper articles concerned with the New York City Health and Hospitals Corporation and of notes kept while I was working at HHC. The corporation maintained a newspaper clipping service of all New York City newspapers and provided me with daily copies of those clippings. After leaving HHC I continued to maintain my personal file by clipping all relevant articles from the *New York Times*.

My position at HHC was that of a management official and not that of a sociologist or researcher. And, unlike most participant observers, I did not take the position to secure data. However, I did believe that a time would come when I might want to reflect on my participation in the organization, and I, accordingly, tried to make notes about daily activities. This proved difficult to do given the commitment to the job as such and the eleven- to fourteen-hour workdays. The task was made easier when I started dictating into a tape machine while commuting to and from work by automobile. These notes have subsequently been arranged and typed in a chronological file.

Once I decided to write an article on press coverage of HHC, I went back through my notes, searching out any that dealt with the press. I also searched through the press clippings for coverage of issues and events with which I was especially familiar and then referred to my notes for those periods to see if I had made observations at that time about those issues and events. I could, therefore, compare the press coverage to the facts of the case and my observations about them.

Scholars have long made the point that the press serves to define a community. Others have presented study after study of the way the media covers the news or creates it. They have done this mostly by studying, observing, and commenting on those who do the reporting, editing, and publishing (e.g., Gans 1979; Tuchman 1978). I would like to show, from the different perspective of a participant in an organization that was "covered" by the media, some of the reasons why the press is a significant factor in managing a public bureaucracy. The organization was the Health and Hospitals Corporation of New York City (HHC), a semiautonomous corporation that ran the seventeen municipal hospitals and ambulance service of New York City under a 1.2 billion dollar budget.

During 1977–78 New York City had over eighty private general care hospitals, each individually run by its own board of trustees. The seventeen HHC hospitals were jointly governed by a sixteen-person board, including a president chosen by the other fifteen members. They, in turn, were appointed in large measure by the mayor. Five were chosen from the heads of selected city agencies. The other ten were picked from among the general public, five named directly by the mayor and five appointed through the city council.

HHC received the bulk of its money, as did all hospitals, from Medicaid, Medicare, and Blue Cross as reimbursement for services rendered to specific patients covered by those plans. In addition, HHC received a substantial direct-payment subsidy from the city's tax levy funds. For example, during 1977 the general tax levy monies budgeted for HHC exceeded 213 million dollars, with the expectation that this subsidy would have to increase in subsequent years in the face of declining patient load and the consequent reduction in reimbursement from the major sources listed above. Although all hospitals faced financial problems in the 1970s, HHC was especially vulnerable because of the severe fiscal crisis of the city itself.

The HHC was subject to close scrutiny by the communications media and had been since its inception in 1970. During an eighteen-month period of 1977–78, as chief of staff and executive deputy to the president of the HHC, I was able to witness first hand some of the effects of that coverage. And because the HHC, unlike most other city services, had a counterpart in the private nonprofit voluntary hospitals of New York, that vantage point provided a comparative framework of the differential coverage of private and public organizations. This, then, is a participant observer's report, from one vantage point, of how press coverage of the HHC and of private nonprofit hospitals affected the administration of health care under city auspices.

Unlike the voluntary hospital sector, we were part of the political community of the city as well as of the health care sector. We were the target of a number of elected participants in that system who attempted to "succeed" through proclamations of mismanagement about those who were employed to manage public agencies. And as with most public organizations, in contrast to private ones, our internal affairs were subject to press scrutiny, resulting in the phenomenon of organizational members trying to use the press for internal battles. I will use this vantage point to make some observations about the effects of the media, the attempts by us and others to use the media with those effects in mind, and the relations between the media and the larger social system of health care in which we were involved.

The first thing I did when I got to the office every morning at eight was to open the *New York Times* to the first three pages of the second, or "Metropolitan," section. Others came in later with the *Daily News*. We looked at the *Times* not out of idle curiosity but as preparation for the day's events.[1] If there was news about us or any of our hospitals or ambulance service, we knew we would have to prepare answers to the questions that would soon flow in from the mayor's office, from other parts of the media, from union leaders, or from others with whom we had to deal. We also found out things that we had to take into consideration, such as a new action by the state or an event that would indicate changes in the relative power of those with whom we dealt.

The Press as a Community Mechanism

There are so many persons involved in any major issue who are unable to talk to each other on a face-to-face or timely basis that the only mechanism that can provide common enough experiences and rapid dissemination of information is the daily press. With some exceptions, television does not generally serve this purpose because it cannot be Xeroxed, passed around, or picked up to be read on someone's recommendation. The exception is when an event is so momentous that regular television scheduling is interrupted and the national networks devote hour after hour to continuous coverage of the event: for example, the nation becomes a community after an assassination.

Felix Rohatyn, chairman of the Municipal Assistance Corporation for New York, has claimed that the New York newspapers were a key mechanism in saving New York City during the fiscal crisis by providing common financial knowledge and a common frame of reference for the influential residents of the city (CBS, "Face the Nation," 14 December 1980). He went on to make a crucial distinction between the press and television by claiming that the latter was not able to explain, or have officials explain, what was needed in the complex economic issues facing the city. He further claimed that it is one of the disadvantages for the national economy that we have a national television media but no national newspaper and hence little opportunity to recreate that kind of community for national economic problems.

For every public issue there is a community of interest and an inner circle of people with "inside" information, and one of the ways of judging someone's placement within any series of concentric circles of influence is whether they knew of an issue before it became public and the amount they can add to the story. Others gauge one's influence by the extent to which one is or is not already familiar with what is reported on in the media and by one's ability to comment on the accuracy of those reports. To find something out in the press only at the same time as everyone else is a threat to one's perceived influence. To have others know of that fact is a form of stigma if it disturbs their image of one's influence. Accordingly, Mayor Koch is irritated when he finds out about Governor Carey's designation of Mario Cuomo as his running mate for lieutenant governor on the nightly TV news before the governor informs the mayor by phone. Similarly, the leader of the union representing the workers in voluntary hospitals complained to us that he had to find out in the press about an action of ours that threatened the jobs of a few of his members (Notes, 5 Dec. 1977).[2]

In any community or hierarchical organization, authority is legitimated in part by one's access to information not held by those below. Members expect a leader to have more information than they and, hence, all authority figures resent it when those below them find out things at the same time or even before they do. The press is also, then, a potential weapon of insult. For example, the *New York Times* chastized the newly arrived Reagan administration for the contempt it displayed when a delegate to the Sea Treaty learned that he had been removed from office only by reading about it in the *Times* while on a subway taking him to a meeting of the delegates (13 March 1981, Editorial, p. A30).

Using the Press

We worked for a mayor who was a master at controlling his press image and of substituting that image for substance. At the very start of the mayor's tenure a highly placed official who had turned down a top job in his administration warned us that the mayor was more symbol than substance (Notes, 11 Jan. 1978). Mayor Edward Koch has come to be known as "good press"— someone who says interesting things and constantly takes the initiative as a source of political entertainment. As William Honan has described him in the *New York Times Magazine:* "Koch is invariably fun. Good fun and good copy. . . . even if Koch isn't enthusiastic about attending the theatre, he certainly enjoys creating it" (1 Feb. 1981, p. 19).[3]

At a later point the president of HHC became an object of the mayor's apparent concern for symbols and images. In one of the attempts to replace our president a reason offered was that the mayor felt the president was not flashy enough to get to the public on explaining health policy (Notes, 26 Feb. 1978). The most interesting aspect of this was not the legitimate concern with image but that it really meant image over substance, because there was no policy from city hall to articulate. Neither the mayor nor his deputy mayors ever informed us that they had any kind of health policy. The mayor never even met with our president to discuss health policy except on a chance occasion shortly before his inauguration, when the president and I spent ten minutes with him.[4] In the few meetings held in early 1978 with the deputy mayor who served as chairman of our board and his aide, the only mention of health policy aside from the ambulance service was a request for us to prepare a one-page plan to close six of the municipal hospitals (Notes, 8 Feb. 1978). Our management team had in November 1977 already provided the mayor with a 56-page "transition paper" containing our ideas for health policy, to which we had never received any reply besides a comment from one of his aides that it was the best such paper received from any of the city agencies (Notes, 2 Dec. 1977).

We could only surmise from the above that the mayor equated image with policy. In this case, the image was not even symbolic phrases but his evident desire to find someone whom the press would identify as one who *looked* capable of doing the job. This experience raised the possibility that all that counts in the short-run political process is symbol, and that symbol is not just a means of controlling substance, but that it is the only substance that matters to a majority of the electorate in some political situations (see Edelman 1964). The press played a role in this process by repeating without comment or analysis in their news and editorials the mayor's assertion that his policy was to provide the "highest quality health care at the least possible cost" (*Daily News*, 10 Nov. 1978, Editorial; *New York Post*, 24 Nov. 1978). The press never questioned the deliberate vagueness of such rhetoric.

But, as the press itself noted, we too tried to use the press. An article in the *New York Times* (28 April 1977, p. B3) reported that when we entered the corporation we had drawn up an "agenda for action" with a number of specific proposals (to create neighborhood clinics; to obtain more qualified executive directors for the hospitals, and to provide them with more autonomy through performance incentives; to create an office of inspector general; and to strengthen the municipal hospitals so they could become part of a regionalized single-standard-of-care health system) and a warning that political support was necessary for the proposals to succeed. The article then noted that our document was "replete with recommendations that the new leadership become highly visible, backed up by what is called 'a steady flow of press releases.' " We also got another set of proposals on the front page of the *Times* in January 1978, dealing with a reorganization of physician care in our outpatient clinics and our relations with Blue Cross (10 Jan. 1978, p. 1; 12 Jan. 1978, p. 1). But despite the belief that our motivations were to use image in the furtherance of substance, I am not sure that the end result was any different from what we perceived as the substance-free symbols of the mayor. I have come to that conjecture because no paper ever followed up on any of our proposals to see if we had accomplished them.[5] (This ahistorical aspect of the daily press will be further discussed later in this chapter.)

The press is a way to get to people not otherwise accessible, a way to mobilize others, and a way to put an idea on the public agenda so that others will have to deal with it. Even after the president and I had left the corporation we used the press to advance an idea to deal with one of the problems faced by the corporation. The city administration had been concentrating its efforts on attempting to close hospitals in order to contain hospital costs. We used the letters to the editor forum of the *New York Times* to encourage a shift of energies from those efforts to the creation of new mechanisms of hospital reimbursement (26 April 1979, p. A22). We pointed out that the then-current structure of the Medicaid and Medicare payment system meant that any real savings realized from hospital closings would redound primarily to the federal government rather than to the city. But if the federal government were willing to share in potential savings, then plans could be set up to provide more economical alternative forms of care.

Prosecutorial Politics

Another use of the press created some interesting managerial problems that further distinguished us from the voluntary hospital sector. Persons holding such public offices as district attorney, special prosecutor, and controller all compete with one another for newspaper space and headlines. This phenomenon, which might be labeled "prosecutorial politics," is their attempt to use headlines about bureaucratic waste to gain political success. Another important category of office holder has joined the group—legislators. A number of them have turned their attention to public organizations and to public employees as safe targets who cannot effectively answer back.

Some ambitious legislators pay more attention to securing these kinds of headlines than in representing their constituencies within the legislature, because these headlines give them a wider audience for higher public office. It was the way Ed Koch prepared to move from the House of Representatives to become mayor. What is unusual in his case is that he has continued to attack his own governmental units as though he were still a legislator and not the executive responsible for running those very same units. Politicians and the press itself have noted that "he disassociates himself from all the problems he is supposed to be responsible for" (*New York Times*, 4 Sept. 1980, p. B4): "Koch himself has denounced one failed government service or another, as though the ultimate responsibility lay with someone else" (*New York Times*, 17 May 1981, p. E7).

HHC was the direct target of a series of press releases from one of the New York State legislators during the last three months of 1977. The headlines he sought and got about HHC mismanagement culminated in charges that the corporation's management was wasting 28 million dollars a year. Although the papers also printed our subsequent denials and the accusations that he was "headline hunting," the damage was done (*New York Post*, 19 Dec. 1977, p. 7; 20 Dec. 1977, p. 13). Indeed, the *New York Post* printed an editorial attacking the corporation on the basis of the 28 million dollar charge, totally ignoring our denials and the legislator's lack of substantiation of his charges (21 Dec. 1977, p. 30).

A few weeks later, the assemblyman's chief investigator visited our offices in an attempt to substantiate the 28 million dollar figure. Seven million of that was his restatement of an accusation made against HHC's previous management team that it had failed to bill the voluntary nonprofit hospitals, who supplied HHC hospitals with physicians, for research supposedly conducted by such physicians on corporation hospital premises. His attempt to document the occurrence of these research efforts consisted of his assertion that friends of his, who were interns, had told him, "Thank goodness for the heroin addicts," because they could experiment on them. However, he not only refused to identify those friends or even the hospital involved but also admitted that he had not reported the information to anyone else at the time. More importantly, he admitted that it had never occurred to him to chastize his friends for the immorality or illegality of their acts (Notes, 5 Jan. 1978). This choice of use of prosecutorial politics seemed especially cynical.

The same assemblyman had become irritated with us two months before, when we had not followed his advice in the handling of another matter. He had obtained a copy of our audit dealing with a detoxification unit located in one of the hospitals. The unit had originally been created under sponsorship of city and state addiction units. HHC had subsequently assumed financial support, but, as our audit determined, our local hospital management had not maintained administrative control. The audit identified high absenteeism among the staff of the unit and an indication that one employee was a no-show. The assemblyman threatened to issue a press release unless we forcibly removed the unit from the hospital (Notes, 10 Oct. 1977). This was, however, a complex and delicate matter, involving suspicions of radical political activism on the part of members of the unit, who had, in fact, implied threats to the safety of the hospital if an attempt at removal was made. A number of fires of suspicious origin had also occurred in the hospital. We chose to defuse the situation by getting their agreement to move from the seventh floor to the ground floor of the hospital—a step that much later allowed the successful and peaceful eviction of the group. We then issued our own press release about the audit and, as we had promised him, cited the assemblyman for his aid. None of the papers printed that release, how-ever, and two weeks later he issued his own charging us with "outrageous waste and mismanagement" and now attaching the figure of a one million dollar payroll gap to his account of the audit (*New York Post,* 14 Nov. 1977, p. 16; *Daily News,* 15 Nov. 1977, p. 8). He succeeded in getting his headlines despite the fact that it was our own audit, our solution, and a gross distortion of the amount of money involved.[6]

This use of the press did not go unnoticed in the press itself. Over two years after these events, the *Village Voice* ran an article about this assem-blyman's "investigation by press release." The *Voice* claimed he built a career out of "one slick press release a week with just enough spice to get cameras, a thin cover on the top of a problem, then on to the next headline" (28 Aug. 1978, p. 5). In the paper's words, the subcommittee he headed "existed to give him the backup he needed to get himself on camera" (28 Aug. 1978, p. 5). The *Voice* then went on to claim that in not using one of his subcommittees to attack powerful interests as had his predecessor, the assemblyman "has apparently converted an independent and fearless in-vestigative body into a political ambulance chaser" (28 Aug. 1978, p. 6).

Urban Machismo

This particular article by the *Village Voice* notwithstanding, such attacks on programs in the public sector have highlighted the interesting phenomenon of "urban machismo." This is a new form of toughness by resistance to urban "mobs." In this instance the mobs are those who are the recipients of city services, those who receive various public financial benefits, and those who are employed by governmental units. Officials show their mettle by hard-headed budget cutting, such as cutting monies to municipal hospitals on the basis that the latter must be wasteful or involved in providing charity for the undeserving. Wastefulness is assumed rather than documented because of prevailing beliefs about fat in bureaucracies. Newspaper editorials have been specifically responsible for creating such images. Thus, a *Daily News* editorial described one public figure as a "tough cookie" who was "eagle-eyed at spotting waste, give-aways and gimmicks," and, most importantly, "he never hesitated to blow the whistle regardless of what powerful interest was offended" (29 Nov. 1977, p. 35). "Powerful interests" is a term usually used to describe the opposition, no matter how weak they might be.

Our management got our biggest plaudits from the *Daily News*, not for any innovative program, not for any steps to rationalize the health system, not for any long-range or complex moves to economize, but when fifty-five headquarters workers—or bureaucrats as it called them—were laid off:

> Joseph Lynaugh has begun a long-overdue attack on bureaucratic fat at the Health and Hospitals Corporation and waste and inefficiency in the municipal hospitals. . . . We hope that Lynaugh sticks to his plan, whatever the complaints from professional staff and unions [10 Nov. 1978].

A few months prior to our entry into HHC the board chairman of the corporation, speaking about a replacement for the departing president, was quoted as stating that what was needed was a manager "with 95 percent administrative ability and 5 percent heart." The article went on to describe another example of urban machismo:

> As for his own managerial capacities, Dr. Imperato said with evident satisfaction that he was regarded in the Health Department as the "ax man" because he had succeeded in cutting its budget by 18 percent and its personnel by 25 percent. . . . as for hospital reductions, "What the community perceives as needs often are simply wants" [*New York Times*, 26 Jan. 1977, p. B2].

Urban machismo, then, is a posture of standing firm in the name of some necessary economic morality and in the face of the many who would then suffer.

The Public/Private Context

My account of both the public attacks made on HHC and of the attackers cannot avoid seeming to be self-serving and might even be labeled as "whining." I do not intend them to be so and will try to put them into a larger context.

A few months before our entry into HHC, the *New York Times* ran a story leading off with this paragraph:

> The battle over whether New York City's deficit-ridden government has enough money to run its North Central Bronx Hospital has raised a much larger question of whether municipalities should be in the hospital business at all [14 Oct. 1976, p. 24].

Five days later, one of its editorials, after making a statement about management failures in the Health and Hospitals Corporation, went on to question the role of the municipal hospital "in light of developments in health care financing which raise questions about the original case for public hospitals" (19 Oct. 1976, p. 38). While we were in office, in our effort to get our story told, we visited the editor of the *Daily News*. One of his first questions to us was, "Why should there be municipal hospitals?" (Notes, Jan. 1978).

Thus, from the time of my entrance into HHC its very existence and that of municipal hospitals in general were under attack. The recommendations that the voluntary hospitals should take over HHC's role and its hospitals usually centered on reports of mismanagement and inefficiency in the public sector, though no documentation was offered comparing the performance of municipal and voluntary hospitals.

Our management was especially sensitive to negative publicity because of HHC's vulnerability and even more importantly because it diverted our priorities, decision making, and attention away from what we considered to be the major problems of the corporation toward whatever happened to be publicized by the media.

Our executives spent countless days trying to answer each and any of the charges printed in the press. For example, the incidents with the assemblyman cited above required the time of at least five of the top executives of the corporation with little or no final benefit to the corporation, its hospital patients, or the taxpayers. And we had to spend further time in anticipation of such charges. For example, we knew early on that we could have received higher federal reimbursement for kidney-machine treatments if we could change our cost accounting methods and our reimbursement paperwork. But we made a calculated choice not to do so because the costs in time and money involved in making the changes would not benefit us as much as alternative deployment of our limited number of financial experts. In this case we took a chance with the potential negative publicity, knowing that the press would only highlight the monies lost and not the difficult alternatives created by our limited workforce. Unfortunately for our successors, the press did just that when in 1979 the *New York Times* carried a story headlined "Paperwork Gap in City Hospitals Cutting U.S. Aid." The officials at that time did not try to explain the situation but simply attributed it to the "sins of the past" (12 March 1979, p. B1).

The recruiting of a management team was one of the most important and underrated tasks that we had, as well as an important distinguishing characteristic between public and private organizations. It was one of the most difficult tasks, given the usually bad press about HHC and other public corporations. In addition, unlike most other public organizations, most of HHC's management and hospital workforce did the very same tasks that were done in the private sector. And the voluntary hospitals had no press to worry about.

The relative lack of press coverage of voluntary hospitals leaves their management freer to manage on the basis of substance and not image. Our "competition" did not have to deal with the same issues that we did. The press acts on the basis that whatever happens in public institutions is fair game, while private organizations, including voluntary hospitals, are generally off limits—and all of this despite the fact that voluntary hospitals receive over 86 percent of their funds from public sources and regulated insurance carriers such as Blue Cross (Health Systems Agency, Table IIIB).

Because of all of these events of publicity, even apparently silly claims by politicians for accomplishments became an irritant. For example, the height of absurdity was reached in prosecutorial politics by two events occurring on one day in May. On the one hand, the office of the special state prosecutor for hospitals wanted information that we had found about a drug problem in one of our hospitals so that they could take credit for the case. They needed something because they were upset that we had been turning cases over to the local district attorney instead of to them. At the same time, our own HHC inspector general was having problems with the city's department of investigation, because our hospital management had discovered someone stealing checks. When our management informed the city department of investigation, they wanted to let it continue so that they could later arrest him as someone who had been stealing hundreds of checks rather than just a few. They were told to either do something now or we would fire the person and turn it over to the local district attorney (Notes, 17 May 1978). They then arrested him and issued a press release taking all credit for uncovering the theft although mentioning, in passing, that they had done so with HHC's cooperation. By itself, the taking of credit for work done by our staff was not so disturbing. The major point is this: in the context of HHC's vulnerability, we were not concerned with credit, but their taking of credit made it look as if this was just another instance of public mismanagement, whereas it was actually just the opposite.

But even when the department of investigation did cooperate, we were still liable to get a bad press from the newspapers themselves. For example, the *New York Times* ran a story about the city's investigation commissioner breakup of a racket being conducted in one of our hospitals (21 July 1978, p. B3). The story featured a picture of the investigation commissioner but failed to mention any role played by the hospital management, again giving the impression of lax management. On the other hand, the story was printed fairly correctly by the *Daily News* with a quote from the executive director of the hospital and a third-paragraph mention that it was the hospital authorities who had initiated the probe (21 July 1978, p. 5).

Public Service and Personal Abuse

One of the more undesirable aspects of moving from the private sector to the public sector in a leadership role is the personal abuse one may have to take at the hands of the media. It is also one of the least understood phenomena. And there is an inherent contradiction in the process. Those who go into public institutions at a high level do so in part because of the excitement and visibility, but then complain about the public exposure when it is unfair—as it probably will be. A good deal of the excitement of public life comes about because of the opportunity to deal with what appear to be important and challenging issues, but their importance is frequently directly proportional to their exposure. The public is always interested in backstage gossip and explanations, but backstage can only exist if there is a front stage and an audience.

I, myself, was the recipient of such personal attention. In August 1978 I left HHC to return to City University. However, I did go two weeks earlier than planned because I was fired by the board chairman at the time— the third successor to the one quoted earlier in the section on urban machismo. A month after I left, one of the newspapers started during the New York newspaper strike of 1978 carried a story about me claiming that, although I had been fired and had returned to the university, I was doing consulting for the Health and Hospitals Corporation. The story went on:

> Highly placed sources at the corporation . . . said that the official, Fred Goldner, has also been given an office, an executive secretary and a chauffer-driven city car. . . . Sources said that Schupf fired Goldner because of Goldner's close friendship with Joseph Lynaugh, president of the corporation [*New York Daily Press*, 21 Sept. 1978, p. 5].

The next day the same paper printed an editorial decrying my consultancy as an example "that the political grip has tightened" on the Health and Hospitals Corporation" (22 Sept., p. 19). Although the paper printed a denial from the HHC director of communications and public affairs, it stated that it stood by its reporter's account of my connection "as a consultant with the Health and Hospitals Corporation" (23–24 Sept. 1978, p. 23). There was little I could do despite the fact that their story was a complete fabrication and was printed without any checking.[7]

Note that the story about me cited sources from inside the corporation. The immediate context for the story about me was as follows: two weeks before it appeared, the board chairman resigned after a series of newspaper stories reporting that he was using his personal lawyer for corporate business and had bought opulent office furniture with public funds, and after an appearance on television where the chairman shoved a TV reporter on camera who was asking him about the questionable use of company cars by executives during the beach-club party he was then throwing during working hours (*Village Voice*, 28 August 1978, p. 3; WCBS-TV Nightly News, 18 August 1978).[8]

Inside Out

Outsiders are not the only ones to try to take advantage of the existing media coverage. Insiders take advantage of possible media coverage for "whistle blowing"—public denunciation of internal waste and corruption. Along with this use of the press by insiders to legitimately blow the whistle on illegal or questionable actions of their organizations, others use it for personal aims. Still others do so to force an agenda by getting an issue into the open; to get gratification from becoming a steady source of information to a particular reporter; to win a disputed internal issue, program, or policy; or to feed the press distorted information to get even with someone or to protect one's own incompetence.

For example, the *Amsterdam News* presented an account of internal dissention at HHC. Its major source was a board member who approached the media about the terrible things happening at the corporation, namely, the elimination of some board committees. More than any of the other board members, he used his time in trying to run the day-to-day affairs of the corporation rather than on what most considered to be more appropriate concerns with policy issues. The potential loss of his committee chairmanship led him to claim in the article that the administrators were "running the corporation in secrecy" and "running things like storm troopers" (*Amsterdam News*, 20 May 1978, pp. A1, A4).

In the account cited earlier of the state representative's stories to the press about our own audit of the detox unit, the representative secured that audit simply because someone in our organization leaked it to him the same day it was prepared. We were never sure of the source or the motivation behind the leak, but did little to find it, reluctantly accepting such problems as inherent in the public sector.

The 1981 strike by interns and residents at a number of HHC hospitals was also an attempt to use the media. In this case they tried to mobilize support to get the city to change some of its policies toward, and support of, its hospitals. Although it involved some professional-organizational issues, the strike was primarily a form of whistle blowing (see Perrucci et al., 1980). Perhaps its lack of success indicates that whistle blowing is relatively ineffective when it merely documents the need for more money.

Loyalty

As I have tried to make clear, leaks were prompted by varying motivations. But even on those matters that society would consider necessary or legitimate whistle blowing, there is a thin line or, rather, a wide overlapping grey area between those things that are owed to the public and those things that are so harmful to the running of the organization that they end up harming the public.[9] This is an area where the issue of loyalty arises.

Questions of loyalty occur much less frequently in the private sector than in the public sector. The culture within the private organization—lacking ongoing press coverage—encourages neither leaks nor attempts to use the press to wage internal battles. In the public sector trust becomes an important element in recruitment and retention. But there are different forms of trust. Loyalty to one or another of the contending forces within an organization, although most common in public organizations, is also present in some private ones, such as in a struggle between medical and administrative staffs in a voluntary hospital. Another type of loyalty is loyalty in the vertical direction: protection of one's subordinates or superordinates from those at even higher levels of the organization. In the public sector, the most problematic loyalty issue involves leaks to the media or to elected politicians.

Loyalty was one of the reasons we dismissed a number of the managers of the organization when we came into office, and also one of the reasons we were criticized by some for not firing enough of them. It was the reason why there was almost a complete turnover of key personnel with every change in the top leadership of the corporation and the subsequent, almost-fatal weakening of the organization.

Demoralization in the Public Sector

One clear disadvantage for the public system is the nature of political turnover. Because of press coverage, the turnover that occurs with a change in political administration within the city and even within HHC takes an even more political bent, in that administrators insist on continuing to run for office by running against past administrations. They are ever busy showing how things have improved under their leadership. This is seldom true in private industry, nonprofit or otherwise, because leadership there is largely self-perpetuating.

The denunciation of the past frequently gets carried over into a negative image of all employees who were part of the past, regardless of how low-level those employees might be. This, combined with the tendency of politicians to run against bureaucracies, leads to a key disadvantage for the public sector. As Interior Secretary James Watt was quoted as saying soon after taking office, "[W]e fired every person in the Department of the Interior that was a Presidential appointee. I mean we cleared every one of them out and then we started appointing good people" (*New Yorker*, 4 May 1981, p. 107).

Generally, the public workforce is characterized pejoratively as different from the private one. This certainly extended to hospital workers. The head of the union representing the workers at the voluntary hospitals was not satisfied to attack the union that represented the public workers. He informed us that our workers were inferior in skill and effort to those in voluntary hospitals (Notes, 5 Dec. 1977). I had heard union leaders attack leaders of other unions in the past but never their members.

Whatever the truth of the matter, our workforce was certainly subject to the pressures of demoralization because they, like all public employees, were frequently attacked in the press and because their organization was subject to ongoing public scrutiny, as was not true of workers in voluntary hospitals. Worse than direct attacks by the press were attacks by their very own employer, duly reported in the press. This has been especially apparent in New York recently, with a mayor who continues to run by attacking city workers as if they were in some other branch of government, rather than in the executive branch, for which he is responsible.

A vicious cycle is created that is bound to lead to reduced productivity by municipal workers. Because the collective bargaining process pits them against each other, the mayor naturally takes advantage of press coverage to fight his wage battles in the press; one technique is to attack city workers so as to gain a bargaining advantage through public support. But this is done at the cost of demoralization of a workforce and certainly at the cost of worker commitment in those very municipal services that are the most sensitive to the effects of commitment on productivity. So much of what public service workers do is not subject to easy scrutiny or to measurement of a product that such attitudes cannot help but reduce productivity. If the managers of any private organization attacked its workers the way that public officials attack governmental workers, those private organizations would be bound to fail.

On Why the Press's Failure To Comprehend and Convey Complexity Both Fails To Simplify and Even Increases That Very Complexity

The press, by reporting on the municipal and not the voluntary hospitals, creates a perceptual boundary between the two. Such disparate reporting helps prevent the systemic nature of health care in New York from becoming visible, measurable, and hence subject to attention. The health care system of the city is without systemic controls and even without systemic recognition. Despite the crucial nature of the interchanges and dependencies among parts, only the parts are visible. And the press contributes to this situation.

There is no vantage point of responsibility for the system as such. For a brief period during 1976–77, the Health Systems Agency tried to assume that role but failed because its federally mandated governance structure contained too many offsetting interests. There was a concurrent attempt to create a kind of health czar for New York City, to be jointly appointed by the governor and the mayor; but the two were unable to agree on anyone and the attempt was abandoned.

The newspapers could have provided such a vantage point, and I still do not understand why they have not. For all of the natural impediments of the newspaper game, they could have done so because the major papers each had a specialized reporter who covered the hospital system over a number of years. Both the *Daily News* and the *New York Times* have had one person full time in that specialty for over four years. The *New York Post* has also had a specialized reporter but not steadily for that long a period.

The separate reporting on voluntary and municipal hospitals—or, rather, the disparity in reporting—not only creates an artificial boundary or barrier but also leaves the municipals in the position of being scapegoats. This is convenient for the voluntary hospitals, who find themselves in a position to "dump" not only patients but also criticism of rising health costs, thus diverting some attention from themselves.[10] Consistent standards of reporting would result in comparisons and comparative data, especially on productivity and quality control.

By missing the complexity, the press makes it more difficult for all to deal with the system: it encourages simplistic rather than realistic analyses, and short-range and easy rather than long-term and difficult solutions. The press's focus also prevents the evaluation of partial moves in the context of larger issues and hinders participants in the political process from focusing on the whole complex process and framing innovative, responsive solutions to problems in that process.

Complex finances, which are at the heart of the hospital system, present an immediate problem for the press. Newspapers have a good deal of difficulty handling and conveying sophisticated budget and financial information. Despite the claims by Rohatyn about the role of the press in New York's rescue, the press has not spent much time and effort improving business, organizational, or financial reporting.[11] There has seldom been an attempt to understand or convey the HHC budget or the implications of the reimbursement structure, except when the press tried to explain why ambulances competed for bodies to fill empty hospital beds (e.g., *New York Times*, 30 Nov. 1977, p. D16).

The media also oversimplify because they are generally ahistorical. Only infrequently do they build on or analyze previous actions. When discussing HHC they simply refer to it as the "traditionally mismanaged corporation."

Even when they try to report on the number of presidents HHC has had since its inception in 1970, they are liable to get it mixed up—as did the *Daily News* when it listed one president's year of departure as 1974 instead of 1977, listed someone who had been a chairman of the board as having been a president, and listed the president who predated and served with that chairman as having been his successor (26 Nov. 1978, p. 53). When they do report on a program they hardly ever bother to check back on it later, although there is a feeble attempt to do so on the first page of Sunday's second section of the *New York Times*.

Even when the media do use the past, they are likely to do so in an ahistorical manner. For example, the *New York Times* had an article in July 1978 on continuing delays in the opening of HHC's new Woodhull Hospital. The article contains the following paragraph:

> Mr. Lynaugh, the agency's former president, describes the hospital's construction as a "classic mismanagement problem from the past" [21 June 1981, p. 24].

It would appear from the quote that Mr. Lynaugh had just made that statement. Actually it was a statement made and reported over three years previously. The reporter never checked with the source to see if it was his current view. Aside from questions of ethics, such use of material implies a static image of history, in contradistinction to the nature of historical process.

The lack of history means a lack of comparative data over time, and this lack of comparative data helps prevent reasoned judgment; further, lack of history combines with the already-mentioned lack of current comparative framework in the press.

Even an exception to the disparity of reporting between voluntary and municipal hospitals lacked any comparative focus. The *New York Times* covered the threatened demise of Brooklyn Jewish Hospital in 1979 to an equal or greater degree than the concurrent threats to close HHC's Metropolitan Hospital in 1979–80. The articles never confronted the two directly or even tried to make a comparison. They treated each one as a separate issue rather than as two parts of the same health care system. More startling was the fact that the *New York Times* had stories about the difficulties of opening Woodhull Hospital but—with only one exception—did not connect that to the possible closing of nearby Brooklyn Jewish Hospital. It was unlikely that both hospitals could succeed, so that plans for either one had to take into account what was to happen to the other. The one exception occurred in May 1979 when a *Times* story about Woodhull Hospital mentioned that the closing of Brooklyn Jewish Hospital would help Woodhull

Hospital (6 May 1979, p. 20). Nevertheless, until the end of 1979, when Brooklyn Jewish Hospital was rescued, and even in subsequent articles on Woodhull, the same reporter never again made the connection.[12]

Everyone has commented on the press's concentration on "hard" news rather than on what is termed "soft" or long-term news. It certainly holds here. And the reporting of hard rather than soft news, combined with the press's ahistorical nature, encourages easy rather than hard solutions. No one looks backward, forward, or across. The press has recently found a "breaking story" in the advance of Japanese management past American management—because the United States is said to focus on the short-run rather than the long-run solution, and that, in turn, is attributed to the way American management is measured in the short run. But the press does exactly the same thing. Worse, the press's short-run focus is one of the main reasons for that kind of measurement system in the public sector.

Conclusions

I have tried in this chapter to provide examples of how the press affects the running of a public organization and how the disparity of reporting on public and private hospitals both exacerbates the management problems of municipal hospitals and prevents us all from seeing and understanding the problems associated with the health care system as a whole.

The examination of public institutions by the press will not stop, nor should it. And there is likely to be increased press coverage of private institutions, especially those receiving benefits from the public sector and those not subject to the checks of the market system. However, while the press fulfills the function of pointing out the inadequacies of these institutions, there is increasing publicity about the inadequacies of the press itself. The problem lies not in its imperfections, which are inherent in all institutions, but in the mechanisms for controlling those imperfections.

The defensiveness of those attacked by the press is now mirrored in the defensiveness expressed by the press when it too is attacked, just as the defensiveness of the public servant is now replicated by those in private nonprofit and business organizations as they are examined by the press. As I have tried to illustrate in this chapter, such scrutiny of organizations has an effect on those who run them and on their effectiveness. We still do not understand the ramifications of an organization's guts being spilled in public, but we know it is more likely to occur in the future. Both that problem, and the problem of what sort of forum can be created for discussions of the imperfections of the press itself, need further discussion and answers.

NOTES

1. The extent of this practice is illustrated by the following. In both the lead paragraph of a story about a forthcoming book by Senator Javits and in the review of that book almost five months later, the *New York Times* reported that then-Representative Javits on his wedding night "bought the newspapers as he did every night, and took them into the stateroom of his train to read before traveling down to Washington with his new bride." Javits said, "Marriage or no marriage, I had to know what was going on" (6 Dec. 1980: 28; 17 May 1981: *Books,* pp. 12–13). Throughout his career there were other things that Senator Javits obviously knew before they reached the press just as we had had inside information about this or that event before they became public, some because we were instrumental in getting them into the press.

2. Much of the material in this paper comes from notes I kept during and after my stay in office.

3. Andy Logan (1978, p. 179) noted that despite Koch's insistence during his campaign that he would not be a ribbon-cutting mayor, ". . . it has been a rare day in his nine and a half months in office that he has not taken part in some media event."

4. Whether this is unusual or not may be judged in part by the fact that the president of HHC was the highest paid official in any New York City or city-related agency.

5. HHC had a newspaper clipping service of all New York newspapers for mention of the corporation or its hospitals. I received daily copies of those clippings while I was with the corporation and have thus been able to search those files for any of the assertions made in this article. After leaving the corporation I kept my own clippings from all issues of the *New York Times* up to the present time. Unfortunately, I was not able to do so for the other major newspapers.

6. It may be amusing to note that the *Daily News* (15 Nov. 1977: 8) did quote one protest of ours, without comment: "The corporation said the audit was made public October 30 by its acting president, Joseph Lynaugh, but did not gain any attention until Schumer charged mismanagement."

7. For a detailed account of the damage that can be done by inaccurate press attacks on individuals in the public sector, see Byrne (1980) and Hersh (1981).

8. The incident of shoving the reporter on camera could only have occurred on television, illustrating the difficulties of having a live mike thrust in the face. Unlike newspapers, TV cameras frequently show reporters being rebuffed by interviewees, thus making the coverage of the story on TV part of the story itself.

9. See the *New York Times* (16 Apr. 1981: A22) for a report of a study finding apathy among federal "whistle blowers."

10. For evidence of "dumping" at Brooklyn Jewish Hospital and Roosevelt-St. Lukes Hospitals, see the *New York Times* (9 Feb. 1979: B1; 19 Jan. 1981: B3).

11. For a negative account of the recent attempt by the *New York Times* to increase its business coverage, see Morris (1981). For an interesting account of the sen-

sitivity of businessmen when they do get covered as the public sector does, see
MacDougall (1980).
12. That reporter had at least seven articles on Brooklyn Jewish Hospital from June
to December 1979.

REFERENCES

Byrne, Jeb, "The Persecution and Assassination of Robert Griffin as Performed by
Members of the Washington Press Corps," *Washington Monthly*, 12 (Sept.
1980): 33–40.

Edelman, Murray, *The Symbolic Uses of Politics* (Urbana: Univ. of Illinois Press,
1964; repr. 1977).

Gans, Herbert J., *Deciding What's News* (New York: Pantheon, 1979).

Health Systems Agency of New York, *The Regionalization of the Health Care Delivery System in New York City* (New York, Oct. 1976).

Hersh, Seymour M., "New Evidence Backs Ex-Envoy in His Role in Chile," *New
York Times* (9 Feb. 1981): A1, A12.

Logan, Andy, "Around City Hall," *New Yorker* (23 Oct. 1978).

MacDougall, A. Kent, "Flaws in Press Coverage Plus Business Sensitivity Stir Bitter
Debate," *Los Angeles Times* (3 Feb. 1980); repr. *New York Times* (27 Feb.
1980): A28.

Morris, Roger, "A Bullish Pulpit: The *NYT*'s Business Desk," *Columbia Journalism
Review* (May–June 1981): 31–37.

Perrucci, Robert, Robert M. Anderson, Dan E. Schendel, and Leon E. Trachtman,
"Whistle-Blowing: Professionals' Resistance to Organizational Authority," *Social
Problems* 28 (1980): 149–64.

Tuchman, Gaye, *Making News* (New York: Free Press, 1978).

ACKNOWLEDGMENTS

This material is based on work supported by the National Science Foundation under
Grant N. SES 800893, the Yale University Program on Non-profit Organizations,
and the Biomedical Faculty Research Grant program at Queens College. Any opinions, findings, and conclusions expressed in this publication are those of the author
and do not necessarily reflect the views of these sponsors. For help on various drafts
I would like to thank June Riess Goldner and the editors of this book, Vernon Boggs,
Sylvia Fava, and especially Gerald Handel.

PART 5

TWO FACETS OF EDUCATION

The two chapters in Part V deal with the extremes of educational experience in New York City. William Kornblum presents the life history of Alain Cooper, a young man from Harlem who has attained a positive self-image, has completed high school successfully, and is entering college despite the "odds" of family breakup, severe poverty, and ghetto life. Patricia Kendall, who interviewed teaching faculty at six nationally known medical schools in New York City, examines the influence of this faculty in orienting medical students toward a "primary care" practice rather than a medical specialization. Primary care physicians treat the "whole patient" within the family and community setting, organizing medical treatment and directing the patient to specialists as needed.

Both chapters are about the relationships between individuals and the community and city in which they live. These chapters underscore that the city is not a way of life but many ways of life.[1] The contrast between Alain and his brother Byron indicates the variation even in one family. Among other things, this contrast should caution against simplistic explanations such as the significance of the "culture of poverty."[2]

In examining the experiences presented by Kornblum and Kendall we are directed to the socialization process in the city. Both chapters focus on one aspect of socialization: formal classroom learning. In Kornblum's case we hear the voice of an elementary and high-school student, and in Kendall's, the voices of teachers at medical school. Socialization—learning of any kind—is always an individual experience, moving a person away from or toward choices and life-styles. For Alain there were, among others, the "white lady" teacher who paid students to do homework and the assistant principal in high school who devoted special time and attention to Alain; for the medical-school teachers there were varied approaches directing their students to primary-care practice, ranging from exhortation to serving as a role model.

Socialization in the city always takes place in tandem with or at least against the backdrop of the city as an opportunity structure. (The opportunities may be positive or negative.) In Alain's case this meant not only the crime and disorganization of his neighborhood, but also the cultural resources of Harlem and Manhattan to which the assistant principal directed him, and the social welfare institutions and community organizations that provided welfare, jobs, and guidance at critical junctures. Kornblum notes that it is precisely these support systems which are now threatened with extinction or cutbacks. In the case of the medical students, the voices of the medical faculty counseling primary care practice are heard against the siren song of the attractions of specialty practice in a very large city, a preeminent medical capital. The career of a specialist in such a setting includes individual fame and fortune, the opportunity to treat "rare cases," access to technologically advanced equipment and facilities, and interaction with other specialists.

Finally, the Kornblum and Kendall chapters bear on the relationship between the Big Apple and its smaller constituent communities, both spatial and nonspatial. These communities mediate between the individual and the larger urban, and national, societies. For Alain there is the physical, spatial community in which he lives and the community of achievers which he has succeeded in entering, the latter taking him away from the former. For the medical students, choosing primary care practice means joining both the nonspatial community of primary care practitioners and, to some extent, the nonspatial (and perhaps spatial) communities of their patients.

NOTES

1. For a presentation of the main arguments, see Louis Wirth, "Urbanism as a Way of Life," *American Journal of Sociology*, 44 (July 1938):3–24; Herbert J. Gans, "Urbanism and Suburbanism as Ways of Life," in A. M. Rose (ed.), *Human Behavior and Social Processes* (Boston: Houghton Mifflin, 1962); Claude Fischer, *The Urban Experience* (New York: Harcourt-Brace-Jovanovich, 1976).
2. See Oscar Lewis, "The Culture of Poverty," in Oscar Lewis, *La Vida: A Puerto Rican Family in the Culture of Poverty* (New York: Random House, 1966), pp. xlii–lii. Among the many critiques, useful collections are: Charles A. Valentine, *Culture and Poverty: Critique and Counter-Proposals* (Chicago: Univ. of Chicago Press, 1968), and Eleanor Burke Leacock (ed.), *The Culture of Poverty: A Critique* (New York: Simon & Schuster, 1971). Social scientists have devoted little effort

to understanding how and why children in the same family may pursue vastly different paths. For some beginning efforts on this problem, see Robert D. Hess and Gerald Handel, *Family Worlds* (Chicago: Univ. of Chicago Press, 1959; Phoenix ed., 1974); Gerald Handel (ed.), *The Psychosocial Interior of the Family*, 2d ed. (Chicago: Aldine, 1972). Oscar Lewis's studies of the Sanchez family are also suggestive: *The Children of Sanchez* (New York: Random House, 1961) and *A Death in the Sanchez Family* (New York: Random House, 1969). The problem still awaits adequate conceptualization.

14
Achieving against All Odds
WILLIAM KORNBLUM

METHODOLOGICAL NOTE • The material on which this chapter is based is taken from a larger comparative community study conducted at the City University of New York Graduate School during 1979 and 1980. This study, funded by the U.S. Department of Labor, enabled a team of CUNY ethnographic researchers to spend over a year of field research in seven low-income communities in four American cities (New York City, Cleveland, Louisville, and Meridian, Miss.).[1] In addition to participant observation with a wide range of youth groups in each of the communities, the study team collected life histories and interviews with about nine hundred teenagers. These histories were written by the young people themselves with the assistance of the CUNY research team. The life history material presented here deals primarily with the experiences of one young man from Harlem, Alain Cooper, whose story is rather typical of the young person who has had to overcome severe obstacles to achieve well in school. It should be noted that the larger study from which this material is drawn deals with the full range of young people's experiences in the social and economic institutions of the seven communities.

There is no typical life history in this or any other aspect of life. Every biography evinces unique experiences and conditions, which may be drawn from the common experience of struggles to survive, but which mark each person as an individual character. Study of a large number of life histories, each of them unique in their specific details, does allow the social scientist to discuss commonalities of experience and similarities in response to turns of fate. In the case of life histories such as that of Alain Cooper, it becomes evident when one compares many similar biographies that youth who achieve against all odds must not be regarded as "self-made" suc- 239 cesses. There is a tendency in American culture to attribute individual success to superior innate ability or to superior moral strength. But a careful reading of even one life history by a young man who seemingly raised himself by his bootstraps reveals much about the enduring influence of adult helpers and social institutions.

Despite all the disadvantages of poverty and faltering social institutions, a significant proportion of America's low-income youth manage to achieve well in school and in civic life. Too often the litany of disadvantages characteristic of urban slum communities neglects the tenacity with which young people cling to the belief that achievement in school will enable them to escape into the economic and social mainstream. This chapter addresses the question of how it is that some young people do manage to overcome all the odds of low social status and grim life chances. Highlighting the experiences of one such young person illustrates the kind of social processes that enable many similar adolescents to make equally unusual gains.

When one examines the biographies of achieving youth from low-income communities, it becomes clear that there is no single and sovereign explanation for how achievement out of poverty occurs. Innate ability, family influences, helpful schoolteachers, community leaders, and spiritual teachers may all play a role to varying degrees and at different stages in any given biography. In this chapter the concern is for young people who succeed in developmental paths leading toward higher education. But for every young achiever in inner-city schools there are others whose clear talents are not developed, or who are diverted from schooling into more self-destructive roles in the underground economy. And among those who do succeed well in school the majority are youth whose parents shelter them from the influences of the "fast life." Often this is accomplished in much the same way more affluent families protect their adolescents: children of the achieving poor are enrolled in church groups and special after-school classes, thus creating for them a social life relatively insulated from the negative influences of adolescent street life. In this chapter the inquiry is narrowed somewhat to exclude children whose parents have been able to give them the advantages of special attention and programs. The emphasis here is on young people who encounter the full brunt of poverty and severe social stress but who nevertheless manage to achieve well in school and in the community.

Alain Cooper's World

When he participated in the CUNY youth study, Alain Cooper was attending Benjamin Franklin High School in East Harlem. This senior high school of some 2700 students had the dubious reputation of being one of the five most problematic high schools in New York City. For at least the previous decade, junior high school teachers had been steering their more promising students away from Benjamin Franklin. By the late 1970s the school was struggling to educate an extremely troubled population of low achievers. Over 70 percent of the students were reading at least two years below grade level, and daily attendance rarely exceeded 60 percent of enrolment. To further complicate the situation, about 40 percent of the students were native Spanish speakers for whom bilingual education programs were severely underfunded. In consequence, the Spanish-speaking students were often placed in classes with native English speakers even though the former could frequently not follow substantive instruction in English. The school's student population was almost entirely Black and Puerto Rican. Despite the best efforts of an extremely dedicated and enlightened teaching and administrative staff, conditions in the school's hallways and restrooms often bordered on chaos. Young people whose abysmal school attendance records made them de facto school dropouts often disrupted the work of more dedicated students.

In this educational milieu of frustration and failure, Alain Cooper and his friends managed to succeed far beyond the norms of the troubled school. Their achievements made it possible for the school's dedicated teaching staff to face each difficult day with renewed dedication to the teaching profession. Indeed, when the CUNY team asked teachers to recommend a few young people who were achieving well in school despite the obstacles of severe disadvantage, Alain Cooper was a unanimous choice.

As Alain became involved in our field research and came to trust the adult researchers with some of the more troublesome aspects of his upbringing, he began to produce this life history. In addition to the story that follows, Alain and all the other young people who participated in the research kept daily diaries, which provided a wealth of details about daily life among disadvantaged children. All the young people who appear in this account of Alain's experiences growing up through poverty also figure in one or another aspect of the larger CUNY youth study. At this point, however, let us allow Alain himself to continue the narrative.

My name is Alain Cooper. I was born on November 26, 1962 in Harlem Hospital on 135th Street in Harlem. I come from a large family. I have eight brothers and one sister. Their ages range from 23 years of age to 9 months. I have lived most of my life with my mother. I first lived on 138th Street between Lenox and Seventh Avenue. I lived there for nearly a year and a half. My family then moved to 115th Street between Lenox and St. Nicholas Avenues. From that time my recollection of my early childhood begins. At the age of three, if I am correct, my mother was pregnant with my 3rd from youngest brother, Leonard. The event that took place at that time is one I can't seem to forget. My mother was in labor and the ambulance seemed to take forever to get there. My father had called the police who were already there. There was only one weird thing about their presence there, though. Instead of helping my mother they began watching the **baseball** game on television. A year later another weird mishap occurred. In the Spring of 1967 I was hit by a car, which is how I acquired the scar over my right eyebrow. I was still living with my mother and father then. My mother came to see me every day in the hospital but my father never came. At the age of 6 my parents then moved to 112th Street between 7th and 8th Avenues. I attended school regularly for the first time. I attended Public School 113 which was next door to my building. I missed very little school that year which was also for the first time. At that time in my life I seemed to live the life of an everyday little kid. I didn't know it was soon to end.

At the age of six I moved to 1700 Harrison Avenue in the Bronx. I attended P.S. 26 for one year. The next year I was transferred to P.S. 86 near Kingsbridge Road in the Bronx. My memory from those times is one I cannot forget. It was the starting of a great downfall. My mother and father fought very often in the past and they still continued to do so. My mother had packed our clothes and left with us many times. One day my mother and father called me in the room and my father asked me a simple, concise, and to-the-point question. He asked me what I disliked about him and my mother. I was always the one known to tell the truth but this time maybe I should have lied. I told him I didn't like him beating up my mother. He then asked, well what about my mother didn't I like and I said there wasn't anything I disliked about her. Although my mother was far from being a saint, it made no difference to me. As I remember, from that day on I received very few things from my father. Many Saturdays he would take my brothers and sister to the park and leave me home. The beatings and fights between my mother and father continued for quite some time. I didn't have a very nice time in school either. P.S. 86 was predominantly white and they did not like the color of my skin. Although nothing serious ever happened, the discrimination and disliking still existed. During the month of June 1972 my mother finally decided she was fed up with my father. This time when she packed our clothes it was for good. There was no more coming back to be done.

We moved to 35 West 110th Street in Manhattan. Everything seemed to go well for about a year. My mother provided for us everything she could. We were not wealthy by far but we didn't have any financial worries. In August 1973 my mother was arrested for illegal possession of narcotics. She was busted for a kilo of cocaine. She was sentenced for 13 years in prison. She only did three years though and . . . [went] on to serve parole. Within the three years she was gone I received an education that you cannot get from any book. I learned everything the hard way. We did not go to live with our father and none of our family stepped forward to take us. Many of my mother's friends were willing to take us. At one time it seemed as if they were auctioning us off. Everything was in a shambles.

Conny G. then stepped into the picture. She was only 20 years of age at the time but she was willing to take us. It was a shaky situation. There were *six of us at the time in the U.S.—five boys and one pregnant girl. Conny moved in with her boyfriend, Junior. The two at first made a noble gesture. Junior worked two jobs to support us while Conny worked one. Things seemed to return back to somewhat normal for awhile. My mother knew many of the dope pushers in the neighborhood. She gave many of them good deals on products and was good to them. Conny had a friend whose name was Jan. She was the street-girl type. She was 26 years old at the time. I don't know if it was because of her influence or not but Conny was soon to become a street girl also. Things were really starting to get bad. Conny and Junior began to argue almost like clockwork.*

Junior then turned Muslim and that was the final straw. Conny simply refused to turn Muslim and give up her new street life she had found. In turn, Conny asked Junior to leave. I had problems at home as well as in school. It seemed as though whenever someone wanted to get their kicks off they said, "your mother's a jailbird."

Junior left the house and it was just us and Conny. She began to slack up and eventually stopped buying food. Then she stopped paying rent. There was no reason for this to have happened. She was getting a welfare check, money from our father, as well as money from dope pushers my mother knew. I do not know to this day what she did with all that money but we surely didn't see it. Conny was seldom ever home; at times she would leave for 3 or 4 days at a time. We were virtually on our own. The oldest at that time was fifteen— my sister. She moved out to a friend's house where she stayed until my mother came home. Some of my brothers in turn resorted to stealing while the others stayed home. I went to work in a restaurant in the back of a bar. I was eleven years old at the time. My schedule was one that most grown people would never have survived. I woke each morning, went to school, and when school was out I went directly to work. I worked in what was once called the Royal Flush located on Lenox Avenue between 114th and 115th Streets. Surprisingly enough, Conny was who I worked for. To be paid was something I never experienced. I got off work at 1:00 A.M. each night, no earlier, but sometimes later. I went home, did whatever I had to do, went to sleep and to school in the morning. There were many nights on which I would get no sleep.

Conny then made one dreadful mistake. She trusted me for some unknown reason. She would leave me to take care of the restaurant. I would cook and serve the food. It was getting good for her on the street and she would leave me alone at all times. I began to tire of not being paid so I started to put the money in my pocket instead of the cash register. I had begun to learn that in this world you cannot wait for someone to give you something, you have to take it. I saw many things in that little restaurant, especially in the back. It was not unusual to see crap games with $5,000 dollars on the floor at a time. It was not unusual to see someone get shot anywhere in the body. I've seen someone get shot in the face more than once. I learned that you trust no one at all, under no circumstances. You believe only part of what you hear and accept nothing as the total truth. One thing I learned stood out amongst everything else: grown people are carbon copies of little kids; they just take everything on a higher level. Within the course of 3 years I found out you have no one in this world but yourself. I became separated from my entire family and closed myself. I became a total loner. I stayed with no one my age. It was if I was an old man enclosed in a kid's body. We lost everything we had.

Conny then had no alternative but to move us because we were being evicted. We moved into what I called a natural dust bowl. The apartment was one-quarter finished from being renovated. The little furniture we had was put into a room that had the least amount of dust. Things were the hardest ever there. I still worked in the bar and my schedule was the same. Things continued to be—that was until my mother came home.

In September 1975 my mother was released from prison on a special parole. When she returned home I was 13 years old. We had nothing left from the time before she went in. She had to start all over again. In December 1975 we moved to Baltimore, Maryland. We lived on Reisterstown Road. It was a one-family house with two floors. The first month we spent there was the hardest. We did not know anyone. Everything was totally different and new to us. The little money we had was never really enough. My mother at first could not find work. We had to go on welfare.

I attended Greenspring Junior High School that January. The people were different than anything I had ever seen. They would look at me as if I was from another planet. The students would ask questions that were very far out. Once a girl asked me, "Do the people in New York look like us?" I was faced with a problem that I had never had before. The girls liked me but the boys couldn't stand the sight of me. They would always call me a dumb New Yorker.

I soon met a few people who were involved with the Moorish Science Temple of America. I became interested and attended a few meetings. I soon joined the temple. The Moors were giving back all the names that the white man had given us. They no longer called themselves, black, Negro, or colored. They were descendants of Moroccans. They professed their nationality to be Moorish American and their race to be Asiatic. They followed the teachings of the Prophet Noble Drew Ali. He stepped forward in the year 1913 to claim his people. He died in the year 1929. When he died he left R. German-Bey as his successor. R. German-Bey was known as the Prince of Peace. I learned many things from him. The first summer I spent in Baltimore I had a summer job. The temple was allowed one worker from the Youth Corps and I was their choice. For the entire summer of 1976 I lived at the temple. The temple was located at 762 W. Baltimore Street. During the time I stayed there he taught me how to control myself. He taught me how to remain calm in almost any situation. He also taught me control of my body. I was on a schedule that most people in perfect physical shape could not keep up. I would run 4 miles every morning and 7 on Sunday. I ate only natural foods, no junk food whatsoever. My head was clean shaven, which kept me from sweating so much. At night all I ever did was read and study. In the daytime I practiced controlling my body. I was once able to hold my arms straight out for over 10 minutes and never move a muscle. R. German-Bey was into many things himself and one was the practice of Telekinesis. He was able to move special objects without ever touching them. He decided he wanted to teach me. One *day he sent me to buy some cork stoppers and some needles. When I returned he took some paper, folded it in a pyramid shape, and sat it on top of a cork with a needle sticking up. He told me to place my hands at each side and concentrate on moving the paper. I told him I couldn't move it without touching it. He told me to just concentrate and think of making the paper spin. I sat there for over a half hour and finally it actually began to move. I became so excited when it moved I stopped concentrating and it stopped moving. I thought to myself maybe it was some wind that made it move or maybe my breathing. There was no wind in the room and I wasn't breathing that hard. I then followed the same procedure and this time it moved in about 20 minutes. That night when I went to bed I really thought about what had actually happened and accepted it as real.*

In the month of August my family moved to Stricker Street, which was closer to the temple. My brothers joined but stayed only briefly. That September I changed schools and attended another Junior High School. When I went there I was faced with the same problem of being asked silly questions and disliked as a stranger. I was looked upon as something out of a comic book whenever I said I wasn't black, negro, or colored. Neither the students nor the teachers accepted me for that. In February 1977 my mother returned to New York. She decided she could no longer take on Baltimore. She took the baby with her and left the rest of us to take care of ourselves until she could find an apartment. My sister was the oldest at that time; she was 17 years old.

Everything went quite smoothly considering it wasn't the first time we were left by ourselves. My mother would come down at the end of the month to cash the welfare check and return to New York. The money from the check was left with my sister, who took care of all bills and food.

In March 1977 I found my first girlfriend. I was 14 at the time. I didn't know the girl at first. She came to my house one night and asked for me. She came in and introduced herself. She did all the talking that night. After about 2 weeks I asked her out. She was the beginning of a line of girls who approached me. I never had to approach a girl first from that time on. In April of that year my mother had found an apartment in Metro North Projects where we currently live. She found an apartment in a new development on 101st Street and 1st Avenue. She came down, got the furniture and took it to the new apartment. I was in the ninth grade and had only two months before graduation. My brothers and my sister all went to New York. My mother rented a room for me in the house next door. I was no longer affiliated with the temple. Between the temple, schoolwork and home there wasn't enough time. From April 12 to June 15 was two months I'll never forget. I had more fights in those 2 months than I had in all my life. I never started a fight but I had so many you would think I did. I didn't really know anyone and I didn't expect any girls to back me up so I was on my own. It seemed as though I always heard the same line. Someone would always say, "I'm getting you for what your brother did." I was chased home from school at least 3 times a week. It was not unusual for me to come outside and 10 guys were waiting on me. I was caught only once. I was running down an alley and tripped. The guys never punched me. They just kicked and stomped me for what seemed like 5 minutes. They didn't do any real damage. I only had a cut on my arm. I made it my personal business to get each and every one of them back one by one. I succeeded in doing this. I didn't lose any fights one on one. On June 14, 1977, I graduated from Harlem Park Junior High School. I was lucky to graduate. For two months I almost lived in the principal's office. Within 24 hours of graduation I had my clothes packed and I was on my way back to New York by myself.

During the summer of 1977 I went practically nowhere. I went as far as the basketball and back upstairs. I attended Benjamin Franklin High School that September. My first few months at Ben Franklin were quiet. I didn't know anyone and didn't try to meet anyone. The first person I met in Ben Franklin was a girl named Christine Brown. I met her through my brother. I talked to no other people except her. I met Darryl Gilliard in May 1978. I played basketball with him in gym every day. I generally kept to myself at all times but I made exceptions when it came to Darryl and Christine. My first year in Ben Franklin was one of almost complete solitude. During the summer of 1978 I worked in the Benjamin Franklin summer school. The job did not pay much but it was a good experience. It was also a good learning experience. In all my life I never had a hard time with my school work. I had adopted the habit of calling people stupid when they did not comprehend fast enough for me. It was the first time I realized the patience that a teacher must have in order to function well. I saw where I had to look at the person for what he was and not what I wanted him or her to be. They were all different in every way. I could not become mad at them. I had to be patient with them as they learned on their own pace. In my 11th year at Ben Franklin things were different. I began to communicate and associate with more people. It was not a large number of people but it was enough. I did very well that year in school. I made Arista and the Honor Roll.

In my senior year at Franklin I was the complete opposite of what I was in my 10th year there. I knew almost the entire school. Everything went just fine. I applied and was accepted to the Bridge-to-Medicine Program at City College. I did well in all my courses there except Physics. I did well in all my classes at Benjamin Franklin. I graduated #6 in my senior class and I'm going to attend the University of Bridgeport in September.

Alain's story is missing many of the details that he supplies in group discussions and longer talks. And some of the influences mentioned are ones he has not had time to fully evaluate or study, such as his experiences with R. German-Bey, his spiritual and intellectual mentor in Baltimore. Alain credits German-Bey for teaching him self-control and methods of self-discipline that proved to be of immediate and immeasurable value in his education and work experiences. But the young man is less interested at this point in his life in the great Afro-American quest for a homeland, which his spiritual master represented. This may change in the future. As Alain continues to mature and begins to assume the positions of leadership for which he is so well equipped, he will have to come to personal terms with racism and separatism. He will have to decide where to live, what attitudes toward the dominant white society to teach his children, and how to understand the bloody history of Afro-Americanism. For the moment he can dwell on being a young student.

The psychological influence of his spiritual master is evident in Alain's bearing and the way he deals with stress. A young man with a ready smile and a creative sense of humor, Alain is indeed self-controlled. To those who do not know him he may at first appear handsomely aloof, but this initial coolness must be as much a product of early experiences with trust betrayed as it is the result of German-Bey's teachings. At one point during the course of our meetings and group discussions, Alain reported on his reading of Claude Brown's Harlem biography, *Manchild in the Promised Land.* Alain was extremely moved by the similarities in Brown's violent Harlem youth and his own. He was especially struck by Brown's description of the loss of childhood in the streets. Both men had been forced to grow up quickly or very possibly die, and like the more mature Harlem author, Alain knew exactly the feeling of being a man in a child's body. Fortunately, many other adults lent helping hands to Alain and showed him how to translate his relative emotional maturity into scholastic success.

Along the way there were many teachers who took the time to devote special attention to this obviously bright and teachable boy. "In primary school," Alain remembers, "There was this teacher. She was a white lady and she would pay some of us to do our homework." The desperation of Alain's preadolescent years, and his own ability to achieve in school despite his fatigue, created powerful motivations to pursue this only way out of his violent milieu. In high school Alain gravitated toward quieter, more studious boys and girls. They were streetwise peers who knew how to stay out of trouble and still have fun in the city. Here again a teacher was an extremely important influence. Benjamin Franklin's assistant principal for supervision and English, Ronald Searcy, saw Alain's potential immediately, and as he has done for so many young Harlem men and women, he patiently brought Alain along. He challenged the boy to do better work at every stage of the high school years, and he encouraged Alain and his friends to explore the immense cultural resources of Harlem and Manhattan.

Alain Cooper is one example in our study of what researchers in the field of youth careers call "super kids."[2] They are children of the ghettoes who manage to hold down responsible jobs at the same time that they are doing well in school. In general, these are young men and women who have embraced the values of hard work and responsibility. They begin seeking work experiences and income at an early age and often think very clearly about their early experiences with work and education in relation to their futures. Alain Cooper's best friend, Darryl Gilliard, writes about these values and their origins in this portion of his life history:

> In my 17 years of living, my experiences with money, jobs and my family are something I'll always remember as lessons. The money I earned as a young kid was by hard earning because everyone else was out there trying to get money also. I had to pack bags, wash cars, carry bags, sell newspapers, run errands and do other odds and ends so I could have money. I remember when I used to get up at 6:00 A.M. every Saturday and Sunday so I could make some money for the week. After a while I became a regular with the girls on the cash registers; it was just like having a regular job. Helping people was sometimes fun because I got to make money and see how people can react to someone trying to help them. Some people are grateful and really glad to see you, but others try to do it all by themselves and end up dropping, breaking, forgetting or hurting themselves in the process. My early job experiences helped me later on when Summer Youth Corps jobs came around. Getting to talk to people when I was young helped me talk to people for jobs and helped to get jobs. Some people say these jobs are worthless, but every one of these jobs have hidden values. You relate to people, meet new friends, work in a new surrounding, work with new machines and office materials or just learn how to keep our city clean. Even some kids say these jobs are worthless because when they get these jobs they don't know anything about working. They still think that if they quit, their parents are going to give them money or if they don't they will try to get it honestly or dishonestly. By working early in life, I avoided all these problems and found it easier to get jobs. Now I'm trying to preach what I practice. The young people around my way are trying to make money, the honest way first. I tell them just be yourself, don't act like if you don't get the job, you can find another one because jobs are hard to come by.
>
> My family is great. They praise me when I do something right and let me hear it when I do something wrong. My father always expects the best from me and if I didn't do that, don't come home. My father, who was ready to graduate when he had to drop out to take care of this family, tells me, "The only way to make it is to get a good education." Everyone in this house listens to what he says because he's right. My father always says, "Don't come home if you get left back." I never knew and nobody else knew what was going to happen if they got left back because nobody in this house ever got left back. He demands respect and gets it from all of us. He always told me, "Education first, basketball second," and still says that today. My father is one in a million because he treats me the same way I treat him, with respect and pride.

Darryl Gilliard comes from an intact family of modest means. The large family lives in Harlem's Lincoln Projects, where life for parents is a daily struggle to keep the children safe and in school. Darryl's siblings are high achievers in school because, like Darryl, they know that anything less than their best efforts will not be tolerated at home. But Darryl and his friends are surrounded by young people who are not as fortunate. As recorded in one of the daily diaries kept by this group of achieving youth, one of the boys was given a new portable radio as a gift (purchased in part with his own money). As he was about to take the radio into the streets, he writes, "My mother hit me with all kinds of jive like, 'Don't let no one take that radio from y'all.' So I said, 'Will it make you feel better if I take a weapon?' She said, 'Yeah, take your father's knife with you!' "

Darryl and Alain Cooper and all their Harlem friends who seek to achieve in school and at work also take pride in their racial history. They pay attention to cultural events in Harlem; they find jobs in Harlem sports and cultural institutions when they can; and they are relative experts on local current events that pertain to racial issues. In their bearing and speech there is generally a distinct pride in being young and gifted and Black. But this does not mean that they do not experience the full impact of negative racial images and economic deprivation in the personalities of other peers and siblings. The following episode from Alain's diary demonstrates how close to home these experiences are. Alain's siblings have not all done nearly as well over the years of tumultuous upbringing as he has.

It is a hot humid Thursday afternoon. I am sitting at the dining room table when the doorbell rings. I don't get up to answer it and it rings again. I don't get up because I am reading a book. The bell rings again and I hear keys in the cylinder. I guess that whoever it is must live here. My brother Byron walks through the door. He isn't alone though. He has 3 girls with him. They all come in and stand near the door. Byron tells them to remove their shoes and go sit in the livingroom. Byron in turn goes down the hallway to his room. The girls are all black. They all seem to be between the ages of 16–18. When Byron comes from his room into the livingroom he has with him an album cover and a pack of bambu (cigarette paper). The girls in turn come out with 3 bags of marijuana. He opens the bags and begins to roll up. He rolls about 15 joints and stops. Each of the girls picks up a joint and lights it. In the meantime I'm watching what is going on. The doorbell rings again; Chris and Tank are at the door. They both come in, take off their shoes and sit down in the livingroom. Chris and Tank sit down and take out joints of their own. They light up and everyone is smoking. I'm looking at Byron as if he is crazy. He knows my mother doesn't allow any smoking of any kind in the livingroom. Chris and Tank finish their joints and leave. The surprising thing that is going on is that no one is talking. The silence was soon to end.

The youngest looking of the girls starts off by saying, "What are we going to do when we leave here?" No one answered her at first. Then one of the other girls says, "Don't worry about it, you'll see when we leave." The other girl who was with them also said the same thing. I didn't pay attention to the next few things that they said. I picked up on the conversation when they got to the kind of guys they liked. I don't know what started the conversation but they all sounded typical of the way some girls think today. The conversation as I remember it went like this:

First girl:	*I don't talk to any dudes who don't have money.*
Second girl:	*If a dude can't take me out wherever I want to go, then I don't want him.*
Third girl:	*I make sure that all my boyfriends have money at all times.*
Second girl:	*If a dude can't support me then I can't deal with him.*
First girl:	*I can't wait to see Rodger. I'm going to ask him for some money for some shoes.*
Byron:	*Y'all bitches is crazy.*
First, second, and third girls:	*What do you mean?*
Byron:	*Y'all only want a nigger for what he has and not what he is.*
First girl:	*I can't buy nothing with a nigger's personality.*
Second girl:	*I don't care what he's like, I only want the money.*
Third girl:	*I done had too many niggers use me, so now it's my turn to use them.*
Byron:	*Y'all bitches is still crazy.*
Second girl:	*Don't call me no bitch.*
Byron:	*I'll call you what you are. All that y'all think about is using a nigger for his money. I don't like that shit.*
First girl:	*If a nigger is gonna be a sucker, I'll take him.*
Second and third girls:	*That's right, if he's stupid he needs to be had.*
Byron:	*The nigger may just be trying to be kind and y'all are going to use him because of his kindness. Don't be surprised if one of them niggers seriously hurts you.*
Third girl:	*There ain't no nigger out there bad enough to do that. I've got too much pull in this town.*
Second girl:	*If a nigger hits me I'll tell my uncles and cousins. They don't tolerate anybody hitting me. They'll kick his ass.*
First girl:	*I'll just take my chances and if it happens it just happens.*
Byron:	*I don't give a fuck who you get, the nigger will still bust your ass. All the back-up in the world can't save you when a nigger wants you. You don't have that much pull.*

Second girl:	*Still, if he's an asshole I'm going to take him as a sucker.*
Byron:	*I can understand that shit if the nigger was just the flashy type but not if he is just trying to be nice.*
Third girl:	*If the nigger is that nice that he becomes blind he's stupid.*
Byron:	*Don't sleep on a nigger because he doesn't say anything.*
First girl:	*Like I said, if a nigger is a sucker I'll take him.*
Byron:	*Suppose some silly bitch was using one of y'all brothers.*
Third girl:	*If he ain't got no more sense than to be used then so what.*
First girl:	*I wouldn't like it and I'd tell him that the girl is using him but it wouldn't change my ways.*
Bryon:	*Get the fuck out of here. That bitch Sophia was using the shit out of your brother and you ain't said shit. You hang with the bitch so you can't say you didn't know about it.*
First girl:	*How do you know I didn't say anything?*
Byron:	*Because I asked your brother.*
Second girl:	*I don't have any brothers so I don't have to worry about that shit.*
Byron:	*Fuck you.*
Second girl:	*Don't say that to me.*
Byron:	*If you don't like what I say then get the fuck out.*
Second girl:	*Come on y'all let's go.*
Byron:	*When you come back with some sense in your head I'll talk to you.*
Second girl:	*You ain't never got to speak to me again.*
Byron:	*That's alright with me ya ugly freak. That's why I smoked your cheba and ain't spent a dime. How do you feel now sucker?*

The girls walk out the door and Byron slams it behind them. He then walks over to where I'm sitting and says, "Man them bitches is crazy to be popping that old dumb shit to me." Meanwhile I've been laughing on the inside and can't hold back any longer. I begin to laugh and continue to do so for about 5 minutes. When I do finish laughing I say to him, "I thought you were going to smack one of them." Byron replied by saying, "I was ready to smack that one I called an ugly freak." I said, "It's a good thing that you didn't though because it would have started alot of unnecessary shit." Byron said, "Yeah you're right," and got up and left. I went back to reading my book and committed the whole thing to memory.

At this time in his life, Alain can relax about this irritating yet amusing scene. He does not have to get involved; he can just "chill out" and observe.

Nor must he let himself feel too deeply about the lack of self-pride in his brother and friends. That they refer to themselves as niggers and bitches instead of Afro-Americans, or Moors or Asiatics or young men and women, is terribly upsetting to him. Alain's thoughts are on getting away. Soon, in a matter of weeks only, he will be meeting the challenge of the university.

Conclusion: Individual Achievement and Social Welfare

Histories of the United States in the late twentieth century will no doubt view the 1980s as a period when the more affluent segments of this uniquely rich civilization rebelled against taxation for welfare-state social programs. Ideologies of personal achievement drawn from classic economic liberalism are resurgent. The poor, it is said, can best be helped by withdrawing "handouts" in favor of exhortations to individual initiative and community development through market competition. As this chapter is written no one can predict the final outcome of this rebellion of the affluent. It is clear, however, that children from circumstances such as Alain Cooper experienced will bear more than their share of the hardships attendant to these attacks on social welfare. And in the long run the secure affluence so vigorously defended on the right must be threatened by all the Alain Coopers who do not make it into America's mainstream.

The facts that support this gloomy prediction emerge quite distinctly from the many biographies which we have gathered, including most of those of poor but high-achieving youth. Alain and the others like him in our study had the requisite innate ability to achieve well in school. But so did the majority of boys and girls in our study who today are counted as school dropouts. Alain's success, and the success of most of the young men and women in our study who had similar stories, appear to be as much the result of helping adults in social welfare institutions and community organizations, which receive state funds, as it is of individual effort. Welfare payments allowed Alain's mother to hold her family together—at immense costs in energy and emotional stress—after she was released from prison. Teachers in the public schools made extra efforts at critical stages in Alain's education. Programs sponsored by community organizations made additional educational and job experiences available during the critical years of early and middle adolescence. Analogous opportunities at critical periods in their development mark the biographies of all the high achievers who worked with us in this study of youth careers through poverty.

In the absence of opportunities provided by special social welfare programs, youths like Alain Cooper are at the mercy of the opportunities for economic survival available in the open market. Unfortunately, it tends to be true in all low-income communities that where capital is extremely scarce and economic planning absent, the most thriving markets are those that exact the greatest toll on youth. In each of the seven communities (three in New York City itself) where our work was conducted, the rates of youth unemployment were over 40 percent. Job opportunities for adults with limited education and skills were steadily decreasing. In consequence, the availability of similar low-skill, entry-level jobs for youth were in ever-scarcer supply. In the fourteen months of our field research these extremely limited job opportunities for dropouts decreased even further. The unemployment rates for youth in the labor force between the ages of 16 and 19 increased between 1980 and 1981 from over 40 percent to over 50 percent. As employment opportunities decrease, and as funding for college tuition and other educational opportunities diminish, the likelihood increases that talented young people who have been exposed to the "fast life" will remain in the world of petty hustles and criminality. The prognosis, therefore, for talented young people from troubled backgrounds becomes even bleaker than it was for Alain and his generation of low-income youth.

NOTES

1. The material in this project was prepared under Grant No. 28-36-79-04 from the Employment and Training Administration, U.S. Department of Labor, under the authority of Title III, Part B, of the Comprehensive Employment and Training Act of 1973. Researchers undertaking such projects under government sponsorship are encouraged to express freely their professional judgment. Therefore, points of view or opinions stated in this chapter do not necessarily represent the official position or policy of the Department of Labor.
2. Luis Miranda, Herman Keith, Jonathan Hughes, and Dale Mann, *Chasing the American Dream: Jobs, Schools, and Employment Training Programs in New York State* (New York: Community Service Society and NAACP, 1980).

15

Medical Faculty Influences on Trainees

PATRICIA KENDALL

METHODOLOGICAL NOTE • Field work for the study began in the summer of 1978 and continued for more than a year. Initially it was hoped that about a hundred interviews with faculty members at the six medical schools could be obtained. Despite diligent efforts, however, only fifty-three were finally interviewed. Many individuals whose names had been obtained said that they could not afford the time or made similar excuses. In some instances it was impossible to get past the faculty member's secretary, despite repeated telephone calls.

The men and women who were interviewed form what is called a "snowball sample." That is, the field workers started with the names of one or two faculty members in each medical school. At the conclusion of the interviews with these persons, each was asked to suggest other colleagues who might be interviewed. The largest number of subjects, twenty-five, were in internal medicine (four were chairmen of their respective departments of medicine). In addition, eleven pediatricians were interviewed. The remaining seventeen were scattered among other departments: preventive medicine, surgery, gynecology, psychiatry, family medicine, community medicine, and so on. Only three women faculty members found their way into the sample.

The interviews were carried out by the project director and an assistant. Although an interview guide was used to make sure that the same areas were covered in all interviews, the questioning was not confined to the guide. In fact, the interviews were quite unstructured and conversational. On the average they lasted an hour. 254

All of the interviews were tape-recorded and then transcribed. This made it unnecessary for the interviewer to take notes, which, in turn, made it possible to establish a high degree of rapport with most subjects. (In only one instance did the tape recorder seem to interfere with the frankness of replies. In this case, the faculty member, who had talked quite guardedly during the interview proper, became more voluble once the recorder was turned off.)

In the following pages, we shall consider the amount of contact the different faculty members had with medical trainees, how they defined primary care, and how they assessed their influence on the career plans of their students.

Introduction

New York City, with its six medical schools[1] and its dozens of teaching hospitals, is undoubtedly the most prominent center of medical education in the United States. Moreover, this prominence lies not only in the amount of teaching that takes place within the city, but also in its quality. At present, as well as in the past, all rankings of the top ten or twelve medical schools in the United States have included the College of Physicians and Surgeons of Columbia University and Cornell University Medical College; and the other medical centers in the city have received ratings that place them not far from the top.

The study on which this chapter is based was designed to assess the extent to which these six medical schools—as represented by some of their full-time and part-time faculty members—have kept pace with recent developments in the medical profession. It is concerned specifically with whether or not these faculty members perceive their influence on the trainees under their guidance to be in line with trends in the profession as a whole. To place this evaluation in its proper perspective, some historical notes are in order.

Over the last fifteen years there has been continuing debate as to whether *enough* physicians were being trained to take care of the health needs of the American people, and whether the appropriate *kinds* of physicians were being produced.

Regarding the first point of debate, there was considerable consensus in the earlier part of this period that the growing population, the enlarged access to medical care made possible by Medicare, Medicaid, and insurance programs, and the increased sophistication of the American people regarding medical matters called for an increase in physicians. This was explicitly recommended in such documents as the Coggeshall Report[2] and in books such as those written by the medical economist Rashi Fein.[3]

As a result of these and other studies, new medical schools were created in the 1960s and 1970s—in California, Ohio, Connecticut, New Jersey, and Rhode Island. Those that already existed were expanded to accommodate more students.

Most recent projections, however, have come to diametrically opposed conclusions. According to the Graduate Medical Education National Advisory Committee, set up in 1976 to assess trends in the medical profession, there will be a surplus of doctors in 1990 and an even larger surplus in the year 2000.[4]

Regarding the second point of debate, namely, that concerned with different kinds of physicians, there is general agreement that, however large the surplus of physicians, there will be continuing need for *primary care physicians.*

The term "primary physician" was first used in the Millis Report.[5] According to the commission of which Millis was chairman, this physician was to perform the following functions:

> He should usually be primary in the first-contact sense. He will serve as the primary medical resource and counselor to an individual or family. When a patient needs hospitalization, the services of other specialists, or other medical or paramedical assistance, the primary physician will see that the necessary arrangements are made, giving such responsibility to others as is appropriate, and retaining his own continuing and comprehensive responsibility.

The "primary physician," more recently designated the "primary care physician," is viewed by many as the cornerstone of all medical care.[6]

Most primary care physicians in New York City and other metropolitan areas are specialists in that they are eligible for certification by one or more specialty boards, usually in internal medicine or pediatrics.[7] But it has become common practice in the medical profession to distinguish these primary care specialists from those who practice on secondary or tertiary levels of specialization.

The "secondary care physician" is highly specialized in a subspecialty, such as cardiology, oncology, or pediatric psychiatry. He may not be equipped, or inclined, to give primary care to patients whose complaints fall outside his subspecialty. He, too, therefore serves as an agent of referral, generally to physicians who provide other kinds of secondary care, or to those who practice on the tertiary level of care.

"Tertiary level physicians" are usually thought of as the "super-specialists." They usually confine themselves to limited parts of the body, to limited techniques, and to limited medical problems. Thus, there are surgeons who restrict their activities to open-heart surgery; there are neurologists who limit themselves to the diagnosis and treatment of patients with multiple sclerosis; and there are hematologists who confine their professional work to patients with leukemia.

If we can accept as accurate the forecasts of the Graduate Medical Education National Advisory Committee that there will be increasingly large surpluses of physicians for the remainder of the twentieth century, but that during this same period there will be continuing need for primary care physicians, it follows that the surpluses will be made up of secondary and tertiary level physicians. (There has been some criticism of the specific predictions made by the GMENAC.[8] While one may accept such disagreements, the general trend toward specialization is indisputable.)

This oversupply of specialists has not come about suddenly; rather, it is the result of a trend that started in the 1930s and continues up to this day.[9] There are two main reasons for this trend. First, the fund of medical knowledge is ever increasing. As new diagnostic tests are developed, as disease processes are better understood, and as new drugs are synthesized, it is no longer possible for a single individual to encompass all of this new knowledge in any complete way. There are therefore pressures to carve out a particular area on which to concentrate. This generally involves a prolonged period of training, at the end of which one is certified as a specialist in a designated field of medicine.

Second, but also very important, those who qualify as specialists enjoy greater prestige and can command higher fees than those who are "mere" generalists.[10]

These two factors, the growth of medical knowledge and the greater prestige and material rewards of specialism, have been cited most often to account for the continuing trend toward specialization.

There is another factor of potentially great importance, which has not been subjected to adequate study. This is the socialization process to which medical students are subject. Sociologists have described in general the way in which prospective professionals acquire the knowledge and values of the careers to which they aspire.[11] But, in the case of medical students, one influence that has not been studied sufficiently is, paradoxically, that which is almost the most obvious—namely, the faculties of the medical schools.

Almost without exception, teachers in the medical schools of New York City are specialists of one kind or another. One might expect, therefore, that, to the extent to which they do exert influence, it would be in the direction of specialization. There was some fragmentary evidence of this in a study of medical students carried out at Cornell Medical College in the 1950s.[12] A more recent collection of papers, *Medical Education and Primary Health Care*, provides some confirmation for these earlier findings.[13]

As noted earlier, the study reported here was undertaken to see how faculty members in the six medical schools of New York City evaluated their influence on medical students and house officers, especially regarding careers as primary care physicians. Since many of these faculty members are themselves secondary or tertiary level specialists, one might expect them to encourage trainees to pursue similar paths. As medical educators, aware of the need for primary care physicians, however, they might be expected to try to steer students in that direction.

Teaching Activities

It is obvious that, if faculty members are to influence students or house officers, they must have some contact with them. And presumably, the greater the amount of contact, the greater the potential for influence.

Although the men and women who were interviewed differed in many respects—in the prestige of the medical schools from which they had graduated, in the prestige of the medical schools with which they were affiliated, in their positions, and so on—they had one thing in common: they were all teachers, some of medical students only, some of house officers only, some of both.

Within this common experience, however, there were wide variations in the extent of their teaching. Some taught a lot and were very precise about their activities. For example, one man, chairman of the department of pediatrics in his medical school, told the interviewer that he taught "at least seventeen and a half hours a week"; he then catalogued the rounds, conferences, and lectures for which he is responsible.

In other cases the teaching load appeared to be equally heavy, although, as one part-time teacher in internal medicine put it, he has "never bothered to total up" the exact number of hours he teaches each week.

Others commented, "It is difficult to separate some of the clinical care activities from teaching." Thus, the chairman of a department of medicine conducts rounds with students and house officers six days a week, and in addition, runs conferences, lectures, and so on.

Clinicians like these appear to have heavy and regular teaching duties. Of course, not all faculty members spend so much time teaching. For example, those engaged primarily in research may do very little teaching. One man who spends most of his time in research in genetics said, when asked about his teaching load, "It would be a couple of hours a month."

Because they have extensive and intensive contact with medical students and house staff, many of the men and women who were interviewed are in a good position to influence their juniors' attitudes for or against careers in primary care. Before examining how they said they behaved in this regard, it seems relevant to ascertain what they mean by primary care.

Definitions of Primary Care

The term "primary care" has many meanings, depending on such factors as the stage of development of an area or country. In many Third World countries, for example, primary care is rendered by nurse practitioners or physicians' assistants.[14]

There is general agreement, however, that in New York City and other metropolitan communities, primary care involves first or early contact with a physician, continuous contact, and coordination of contacts with other specialists or subspecialists.[15] One particularly articulate man, a professor of medicine, put it this way:

> *I think there are three important elements that characterize the practice of primary care. One is the accessibility of the physician to the patient, whether it's for the first contact or for an unscheduled contact, or a telephone contact. There is an accessible, identified physician to whom the patient turns. And the first contact is usually listed as one of the major functions of primary care. But that simply means you're getting a patient into your practice. The second element is that the physician assumes responsibility over time for managing the patient; that's called "continuity." And the third is that the physician assumes responsibility for doing what needs to be done in various organ systems and problems up to the limits of his expertise, and then orchestrates all the other consultations, and so on. So we have these three aspects that I think are fundamental.*

Most faculty members mentioned one, two, or all three of the "elements" in this definition of primary care. The only disagreement, and this did not occur frequently, was whether or not care obtained in an emergency room could qualify as primary care. One surgeon, who maintained that it could, went one step further and said that the first aid given by a mother could be considered primary care in the sense that it was the first care provided. Another faculty member, a professor of pediatrics, said that the emergency room did not render primary care because of the episodic nature of the treatment that it provides.

As mentioned, however, such disagreements were rare. There was a general consensus on the meaning of primary care.

The Influence of Faculty Members

According to their own reports, most faculty members have considerable contact with medical students and house officers. And, although they may disagree on some details, they generally have the same thing in mind when they talk of primary care.

To what extent do they convey their notions of primary care to the medical trainees with whom they come in contact? To ascertain this, several questions in each interview were devoted to details of discussions that had previously taken place. There are a variety of findings.

First of all, there is the question of the degree of explicitness with which primary care was described and encouraged or discouraged. For example, one professor of medicine said that he tries to bring students "to an understanding of internal medicine as primary care." But "in all these discussions primary care is implicit"; he does not talk with his students about primary care as a career, and he does not make any kind of "pitch."

Other faculty members who also equated internal medicine with primary care did so more explicitly. A professor of preventive medicine said, for example, that, in his discussions with students, he emphasized the fact that most internists are primary care physicians, and that "the greater area of expansion is going to be in primary care." He said, further, that he made these points "with intent" because he wanted to persuade students that "primary care is something to seriously think about in the future." He went on to say that he felt his efforts were "fairly successful."

Not all faculty members stressed pragmatic considerations, either implicitly or explicitly, in their discussions of primary care with medical trainees. Some emphasized the "enormous satisfactions" of getting to know people as friends as well as patients. Others stressed that it is "very satisfying" to follow patients over time; this was especially true of pediatricians, who spoke of the "pleasure" in seeing a young child develop.

Nor did all faculty members promote primary care either implicitly or explicitly. Some maintained a conscious neutrality, saying that it is up to the student to decide for himself, without undue influence. As one associate professor of medicine put it:

> I think it is inappropriate for a faculty member to exert influence on a student one way or the other. There is no reason to push someone against his will.

Still another man, a part-time teacher of pediatrics, said that his decision to encourage or discourage a career in primary care depends on "where the students want to live." If a trainee says that he wants to live in an urban area, then "he'd better think pretty heavily in terms of a specialty" if he wants to "survive economically and academically." But if he wants to live in "Bismarck, North Dakota, or Butte, Montana," then he can think in terms of a career in primary care.

Some faculty members went beyond neutrality, and actively discouraged students from going into primary care. One man, research oriented, said:

> I'm a specialist and I'm a snob, so fortunately I'm not in a position to influence too many students, I guess. I would want our students to be professors of this and professors of that, and researchers in this and researchers in that. So the ones I want to attract to primary care are those people who would take on leadership or research roles in primary care, which is something very different from being a primary care practitioner.

A professor of family medicine, although he personally found primary care "exciting," detailed the way in which medical trainees might be discouraged from considering primary care as a career:

> *[Faculty members] can influence a student away from primary care. [How would they do this?] Oh, simply by brainwashing a student to the effect that primary care doctors do not have the satisfaction of specialists . . . They work too hard; they are not well regarded; they have trouble getting hospital privileges; only the people who are not too bright go into primary care. There are all kinds of polite ways that students are led away from primary care.*

Finally, some faculty members said that their encouragement or discouragement of careers in primary care depended on the attitudes of the students. One pediatrician reported, "There are some people who are absolutely not interested in primary care"; when he encountered such trainees, he made no effort to convert them. But when he came in contact with "people who are interested at all," he stressed "the satisfaction one can attain" and the fact that he has been "very happy" as a primary care practitioner.

Along similar lines, a professor of pediatrics reported that

> *there are still the small percentage of students who, even by the third year, know that they are going to be ophthalmologists or orthopedic surgeons for a variety of reasons.*

He added, "One doesn't win converts among people of that type, because their convictions are well set even by then."

A question of considerable interest is the stage in their development at which trainees are most susceptible to the arguments pro and con primary care which they hear from their teachers. One might suppose that the less advanced the students, the less committed they are to particular career plans, and therefore the more likely it is that they will listen to advice and persuasion. Thus, for example, one might suppose that a resident has already made up his mind about the field of medicine he wants to enter; he is therefore unlikely to be influenced by new arguments. Several faculty members reported that this had been their experience. One chairman of a department of medicine said that he sees interns and residents in a variety of contexts, among them conferences in which they discuss their career plans; he has found that by that time "most of them really know what they want to do."

Along similar lines, an obstetrician-gynecologist has found that the "relative opportunity for career influence is far greater for students than for house staff"; by the time they arrive at the institution in which he teaches, "most interns and residents have more or less decided what they want to do."

But this appraisal was not universal. Other faculty members have found indecision, and therefore possible responsiveness to teaching efforts, as late as the residency. As one part-time teacher of internal medicine put it, "Most of them who come through for residency training are still very unsure at that point of what they want to do."

And a professor of medicine believed that faculty members exert influence whenever they come in contact with trainees:

> Well, I think that every time a faculty member interacts with a student or a medical intern or resident, he's going to have a . . . he's going to be slanting it, just by the fact that he delivers his viewpoint.

Further research specifically with trainees is needed in order to tell when trainees are most susceptible to influence, and at what point in their training they make crucial career decisions.

The Influence of Role Models

Not all influence was exerted in discussions of primary care. Some faculty members felt that they swayed their students by the example that they presented, that they were role models.

Some accomplished this by inviting students to work with and observe them in their private practices. One part-time teacher of medicine reported that the "best student" he had was going to work with him for a month. Another practitioner, a part-time teacher in the department of pediatrics, indicated that such demonstrations of what it means to provide primary care are fairly standard practice in his department:

> We've had for a long time medical students and residents at our office observing firsthand the way I take care of patients and the way my partners take care . . . It has become a recognized part of their out-patient experience in pediatrics . . . [When you speak about primary care, what kinds of things do you emphasize?] Well, it's not so much speaking but showing them. You know, in our instance it's been actually direct observation of what a primary care provider does in a private practice setting.

Here the faculty member actually corrected the interviewer to indicate that he does not so much talk to medical students and residents as *show* them what it means to be a primary care practitioner.

Other teachers talked spontaneously about being role models. For example, one part-time teacher in a Department of Medicine said that he is "fairly unusual as far as [being] a role model for students," because he is a primary care practitioner in a setting in which specialists abound. Another part-time teacher of medicine said that he is a role model for his students in showing them "the satisfactions of providing primary care for patients;" he added, "I don't proselytize; I set an example."

Some faculty members spoke rather immodestly about their influence as role models. For example, the chairman of a department of medicine said that, because he is director of the medical clinic in his teaching hospital, because he is an active preceptor, and because he has many occasions to talk with medical students and house officers, "I would consider myself one of the strong role models . . . My being a role model has an impact on the [trainees]."

Others felt that it is somewhat "arrogant" to talk about being a role model; even so, they had to admit that they served as such for their students. In the words of a professor of family medicine:

I think one of the reasons people like me are valued in these positions is that I actually . . . I practiced for seven years before I came into the academic racket, and in that way I can actually talk about what I did and what it was like. And in this way I serve as a role model.

But the faculty members of these medical schools were not always positive role models for primary care. Sometimes, especially among surgeons or research-minded physicians, they were *negative* role models. For example, a surgeon had this to say:

I think the nature of surgery and the nature of the people who go into surgery set up a situation. So that people either turn on to the kind of role model presented by a surgeon or they're turned off by it. With regard to primary care specifically, the person who is turned off by the surgeon's approach to care might turn on to primary care, because they're very different approaches.

A woman professor of pediatrics, who is herself committed to providing primary care, said that because many faculty members in the school where she teaches are interested in research, they serve as negative role models for primary care:

Interestingly enough, there are quite a few students who start out being interested in family medicine, with family medicine in thought. And quite a few students who come here interested in family medicine, by the time they leave here the institution has had its imprint on them. Because they have no role models here in family medicine, and because they perceive the pecking order is such here that academic medicine is what's high drive, by the time they leave here . . . I would think that the respected people here are probably people who are actively involved in either basic or clinical research.

Her views are seconded by two other faculty members. One, a professor of medicine, said that he found it "amazing" that so many students were interested in primary care, "because the prejudice of the faculty is so much against it"; when asked who served as positive role models for primary care, he said, "Oh, I don't think we have any here."

Finally, a professor of medicine said that the influence of the medical school in which he teaches was likely to turn students away from primary care:

I think, because their education in medical school is largely from full-time faculty who are scientists or scientifically oriented, and they see that in their formative years as a role model, and not the primary care physician. Often the only contact they have had with primary care physicians are people who are not very competent, who mismanage problems, and whose patients end up here in the teaching hospital. And so they get a very skewed picture of it.

Summary and Conclusion

A qualitative study, even when based on a relatively small number of cases, can lead to important findings. In the present instance, interviews with fifty-three faculty members in the six medical schools of New York City have uncovered the wide *range* of activities, experiences, and attitudes that are current in those institutions.

To begin with, there is considerable variation in the amount of teaching done by faculty members holding different kinds of positions. As might be expected, the full-time faculty, and especially those who are chairmen of their respective departments, have heavy teaching loads, although some find it difficult to differentiate between straight teaching and the clinical care which they supervise. Less obvious perhaps, a number of part-time faculty members spend many hours each week teaching medical students and house officers. On the other hand, members of clinical departments who are engaged primarily in research appear to do little teaching.

Second, it was found that the men and women who were interviewed for this study are generally agreed on what is involved in primary care. The only disagreement, and this did not occur frequently, was whether or not medical treatment provided in emergency rooms could be considered primary care.

The findings discussed so far can be thought of as preliminary to the main purpose of the study. This was to ascertain the extent to which faculty members in the six medical schools of New York City, virtually all of them specialists and many of them secondary or tertiary specialists, believe they influence the career plans of the trainees under their guidance, especially with regard to careers in primary care. Some engage in discussions with medical students and house officers in which they either explicitly or implicitly advocate that the trainees become primary care physicians. Several others believe that they should maintain neutrality, not trying to influence their juniors in their plans for the future. Still another segment of the faculty indicate ways in which they, or others, discourage trainees from contemplating careers as primary care providers.

Finally, according to those interviewed, faculty members can influence students not only directly in the discussions they hold with the trainees, but also indirectly by serving as positive or negative role models.

The chief merit of a qualitative study such as this is that it can point out quite graphically the range of experiences and opinions that are held by those interviewed. Such studies can also identify nuances that are not easily captured in a quantitative survey. It should be recognized, however, that because qualitative studies are not usually based on representative samples and because they do not usually obtain exactly the same information from all subjects, precise statements about the distribution of activities and attitudes are impossible. Such quantitative conclusions about how the full-time and part-time members of the six medical schools in New York City believe they affect the career plans of the trainees they teach await more systematic study.

NOTES

1. The six schools are the Albert Einstein School of Medicine, the College of Physicians and Surgeons of Columbia University, Cornell University Medical College, Downstate Medical School, the Mount Sinai School of Medicine, and the New York University School of Medicine. A seventh medical school, the New York College of Medicine, recently moved to Westchester County.
2. Lowell T. Coggeshall, *Planning for Medical Progress through Education* (Evanston, Ill.: Association of American Medical Colleges, 1965).
3. Rashi Fein, *The Doctor Shortage* (Washington, D.C.: The Brookings Institution, 1967).
4. U.S. Department of Health and Human Services, *Report of the Graduate Medical Education National Advisory Committee to the Secretary*, vol. 1, September 1980 (Hyattsville, Md.: DHHS Pub. No. 81-651, 1981).
5. The Citizens Commission on Graduate Medical Education, *The Graduate Education of Physicians* (Chicago: American Medical Association, 1966).

6. Charles E. Lewis, Rashi Fein, and David Mechanic, *A Right to Health: The Problem of Access to Primary Medical Care* (New York: John Wiley & Sons, 1976).
7. Linda Aiken, Charles E. Lewis, John Craig, Robert C. Mendenhall, Robert J. Blendon, and David E. Rogers, "The Contribution of Specialists to the Delivery of Primary Care," *New England Journal of Medicine*, 300 (1979): 1363–70.
8. Uwe E. Reinhardt, "The GMENAC Forecast: An Alternative View," *American Journal of Public Health*, 71 (1981): 1149–57.
9. Citizens Commission on Graduate Medical Education, *Graduate Education of Physicians;* Rosemary Stevens, *American Medicine and the Public Interest* (New Haven, Conn.: Yale University Press, 1971); Patricia Kendall, "Medical Socialization: Trends and Contributing Factors," in *Psychological Aspects of Medical Training*, ed. Robert M. Coombs and Clark E. Vincent (Springfield, Ill: Charles E. Thomas, 1971).
10. Stevens, *American Medicine;* Patricia Kendall, *The Relationship between Medical Educators and Medical Practitioners* (Evanston, Ill: Association of Medical Colleges, 1965).
11. Dan Lortie, "Professional Socialization," in *Professionalization*, ed. H. M. Vollmer and Donald L. Mills (Englewood Cliffs, N.J.: Prentice-Hall, Inc., 1970); Wilbert Moore, "The Formation of a Professional," in *The Professions: Roles and Rules* (New York: Russell Sage Foundation, 1970); Ronald Pavalko, "Occupational Choice," in *Sociology of Occupations* (Itasca, Ill.: F. E. Peacock Publishers, 1971).
12. Patricia Kendall and Hanan Selvin, "Tendencies toward Specialization in Medical Training," in *The Student-Physician*, ed. R. K. Merton, G. G. Reader, and P. L. Kendall (Cambridge, Mass.: Harvard University Press, 1957).
13. Horst Noack (ed.), *Medical Education and Primary Health Care* (Baltimore: University Park Press, 1980).
14. Craig Burrell and Cecil G. Sheps (eds.), *Primary Health Care in Industrialized Nations* (New York: New York Academy of Sciences, 1978); Institute of Medicine, *A Manpower Policy for Primary Health Care* (Washington, D.C.: National Academy of Sciences, 1978).
15. Joel J. Alpert and Evan Charney, *The Education of Physicians for Primary Care* (Washington, D.C.: U.S. Department of Health, Education and Welfare, 1973).

ACKNOWLEDGMENT

This research was supported by grant number RF-12237 from the PSC-CUNY Research Award Program of the City University of New York.

PART **6**

IN AND OUT
OF THE CITY

This concluding part of the volume focuses on New York City as the center of a metropolitan region. Contemporary New York City, like large cities in general, extends in a functional sense far beyond its legal municipal borders. The everyday activities of New York City residents and the surrounding suburban area are locked in a vast array of interdependencies. This urban conglomerate—technically called a metropolis—consists of a large central city together with smaller cities, towns, and villages in the adjacent suburban rings. According to the United States Census, in 1980 the New York metropolitan area (Standard Metropolitan Statistical Area) was made up of the city itself plus four counties (Putnam, Rockland, and Westchester in New York State and Bergen County in New Jersey) for a total metropolitan population of 9.1 million. A more inclusive definition of metropolitan area (Standard Consolidated Area) contains additional counties in New Jersey, Connecticut, and Long Island and has a total population of 17 million.

Donald Delano's presentation of the Port Authority bus terminal deals with one of the mechanisms for integrating the various parts of the metropolis, namely, transportation systems that funnel people in and out of the central city. The annual volume of traffic at the Port Authority bus terminal is staggering—two million buses and 57 million passengers in 1980. Most of this traffic—80 percent, according to Delano—is commuter bus traffic, indicating in part the density of the linkages among the constituent parts of the metropolis.

The Port Authority Bus Terminal is also a transportation hub for visitors from far beyond the metropolis: some of the tourists described by Gerald Handel come by bus, although plane and railroad are also important for long-distance travelers. The sociology of the bus terminal is not limited to transportation, however. Delano describes the relationship between the terminal and the local Manhattan community in which it is located. Except for airports, large public transportation facilities in American cities are typically located in old, inner-city, low-income areas, so the uneasy relationship between the terminal and residents in the local neighborhood is of broad interest. Finally, the terminal is in some ways a community of its own, and

Delano describes the modes of interaction that have developed between "mopes," "skells," and the Port Authority police.

The changing relationship between central New York City and its surrounding suburbs is explored by Sylvia Fava and Judith DeSena. The building up of residential areas beyond the city limits has been going on for decades, introducing the term "commuter" into general use. Among the old immigrant groups such as the Norwegians described in Part II by Hoover, suburbanization has left the original Brooklyn settlement area with only a sparse Norwegian population. Suburbanization increased dramatically among almost all economic and ethnic groups after World War II. As jobs, shopping, and services of all kinds became more available in suburbs, suburbanites did not need the central city as much on a daily basis.

What has been the impact of the city on young people who have been raised in post-World-War-II suburbs? Fava and DeSena found that this "suburban generation" in surrounding counties had very little direct contact with New York City through their high school years, except for entertainment attractions to which they had been brought as children or to which they traveled on their own as teenagers. For most of the "suburban generation" New York City is "a nice place to visit but not to live." Only a small proportion of the young people raised in suburbs regard New York City as a desirable place to live; few move there as adults. Fava and DeSena's chapter deals with this small segment. These people report their experiences as New York City residents in highly positive terms, allowing them self-development and fulfillment they did not believe they could have attained in the suburbs.

New York City—the central city of the metropolis—is not only a spatial location, but a symbol. "Big Apple" means the big time, the pinnacle of success, the top of the heap, images with which the song "New York, New York" is filled. The suburban migrants Fava and DeSena studied felt challenged to do well in New York City; the visitors studied by Handel had some preconceived views of what to expect in New York City: scale, pace, excitement, diversity, and liberality, qualities that they did find and enjoy.

The image of New York City and the visible symbols embodying it—the Empire State Building, 42nd Street, the theater district, the World Trade Center, the Radio City Music Hall, museums, and art galleries—are confined to the "downtown" area of Manhattan. These aspects of the Big Apple attracted the visitors Handel described, as well as the suburbanites described by Fava and DeSena. Although Winick and Boggs and Jaquez did not study the residential origins of the patrons of the licit and illicit sex industry, many patrons undoubtedly were suburbanites or out-of-towners. The downtown area provides sex services and prostitution for the whole metropolitan area as well as for a transient population. It is not accidental that 42nd Street, which is anchored at one end by the Port Authority Bus Terminal and on the other by Grand Central Station, with Pennsylvania Station and all the subway routes also nearby, is the main location of the commercial sex business. Winick in Part III notes the resistance to sex establishments in residential areas and the difficulties in decentralizing sex services.

Americans are ambivalent about cities, especially large cities such as New York. The city is a magnet but it is also good to get away from. Rolf Meyersohn and Donal Malone's discussion of the reasons why some New Yorkers maintain second homes in Vermont indicates that these New Yorkers want to get away from dirt and noise and the pressures of work, and "back to basics" such as nature and family life. These characteristics of urban life also figured in the views of the visitors studied by Handel and the suburbanites studied by Fava and DeSena. The excitement, stimulation, specialization, and diversity that make urban life so attractive may also require a respite; second homes in the country may be a protection, for those who can afford them, against the negative effects of urban living. Herbert Gans's typology of urban life-styles as varying by socioeconomic status, stage of the family cycle, and ethnicity reminds us that the impact of urban life is not uniform.[1] Meyersohn and Malone's second-home owners, middle class and upper middle class in background, have the ability to pick and choose among the elements of urban and rural living, combining them into an alternating life-style in the enlarged orbit of the metropolis.

NOTE

1. Herbert J. Gans, "Urbanism and Suburbanism as Ways of Life," in A. M. Rose (ed.), *Human Behavior and Social Processes* (Boston: Houghton Mifflin, 1962).

16

The Bus Terminal: Cops, Mopes, & Skells on the Deuce

DONALD F. DELANO

METHODOLOGICAL NOTE • This chapter is based upon the author's Ph.D. dissertation, entitled, "The Port Authority Bus Terminal in Its Community Setting: An Ethnographic Study,"[1] a qualitative case study of an urban institution that is demonstrably more than just a transportation facility. The section of New York City known as Times Square and Clinton is a neighborhood rich in urban history, and its public institutions, such as the bus terminal, have become integral factors in the functions and dysfunctions of community there.

The author serves as a police officer for The Port Authority of New York and New Jersey, and thus has been afforded a truly unique opportunity to witness the social control mechanisms and behavior in the diverse population of the community. By working varying hours and days during all seasons of the year, he has observed the temporal flow and situational encounters that contribute to the fascinating atmosphere and pace of 42nd Street.

In terms of data collection, observations and incidents during a tour of duty could be summarized at its completion, although relevant conversations (so important to understanding the "language of community") were immediately written down so their content could be preserved verbatim. As an aid to readers unfamiliar with that language, a Glossary of street language is presented at the end of the text of this chapter.

This data collection continued for most of 1978 and 1979, while the author was assigned to the Central Police Pool, a roving unit that worked all Port Authority facilities.

In 1980, the author was the recipient of the Port Authority's Howard S. Cullman Fellowship, an award providing full salary for up to one year while the employee pursues a project of benefit to the Port Authority, the community, and the individual. Therefore, for nine months, the author worked under the joint supervision of the Port Authority's Tunnels, Bridges & Terminals Department; the Port Authority police; and the Sociology Department of the City University of New York Graduate Center in conducting additional, in-depth observations of the bus terminal and surrounding community. This time, however, street attire, rather than a police uniform, could be worn in order to observe street interactions. In addition, various governmental and private agencies whose activities focused on the Times Square area were visited, thereby obtaining an "official perspective" on the situation.

Consequently, the participant-observation program and continuous reference to the literature provided information leading to the dissertation, an extensive probe of a truly diverse and sociologically intriguing community in the heart of midtown Manhattan.[2]

The Port Authority Bus Terminal

The Port Authority Bus Terminal was opened to the public on 15 December 1950. It is operated by The Port Authority of New York and New Jersey, an agency established in 1921 by compact between the states. The bus terminal provides a central location for the arrival and departure of intercity bus traffic and permits direct and connecting bus travel between virtually any two locations in the continental United States, Canada, and Mexico. Situated in the heart of Times Square, it entirely occupies 1½ city blocks between Eighth and Ninth avenues and 40th and 42nd streets. Passengers are afforded direct connections with the 42nd Street stations of the three divisions of the subway system, as well as the city buses.[3] The combined traffic volume of the terminal is enormous; approximately two million buses and fifty-seven million customers were accommodated during 1980. Commuter bus traffic comprises over 80 percent of the terminal's activity; on a typical weekday approximately 6200 buses, carrying almost 170,000 passengers, utilize it. According to Port Authority statistics, since the opening of the facility, nearly 1.7 billion passengers have been accommodated on approximately 60 million buses.

The bus terminal has four concourses, each guiding passengers to various bus platforms. The concourses have service provisions including restaurants, shops, and lavatories. Operating in conjunction with the Lincoln Tunnel, a huge vehicular artery connecting New York with New Jersey beneath the Hudson River, the bus terminal functions in a manner similar to a huge heart in an urban circulatory system. Its expansions and contractions produce the morning and evening rush periods, midday shoppers, theater and matinee crowds, and ever-present commuters. There is an information booth on the main concourse, at street level, with an endless stream of persons seeking answers to questions concerning bus schedules, locations of stores, points of interest, and so forth. Two million calls a year are handled by the telephone information center, and the public phones in the various levels are among the busiest in the world, with more than 239 in service at any given time.

Over 275 employees of the Port Authority serve as the operating force of the terminal in such categories as operations, maintenance, administration, and engineering. Law enforcement is provided by the more than 100 officers (police officers, supervisory officers, detectives) of the Port Authority police force assigned there. With approximately 1200 sworn personnel, the Port Authority police are police officers in the states of both New York and New Jersey, and are responsible for law enforcement at the Authority's twenty-five facilities in the two states.[4] They also serve as the firefighting crews for aircraft emergencies at Newark, LaGuardia, and John F. Kennedy international airports. Although the Port Authority police have jurisdiction in both states, their scope of patrol is concentrated in the individual facilities. Consequently, in the case of the bus terminal, the Port Authority police are responsible for law enforcement within and immediately surrounding it, while patrols of the surrounding neighborhood and subways are handled by the New York City police and the New York City transit police.

Policing Styles

Any town or city will be distinct in terms of both geography and the ethnic compositions and political beliefs of its residents. Within both suburban and urban areas are communities and neighborhoods, those distinctive sections that may be called "special" or "unique." For example, there is Chinatown (around Mott Street in lower Manhattan), Greenwich Village (West 4th Street and the area around Washington Square, also in lower Manhattan), and the Steeltowns of South Chicago. The bus terminal is located in the heart of one such noteworthy neighborhood: Times Square, a much publicized haven of deviance, pornography, and street crime. Marquees of formerly legitimate theaters in the area now call out erotic films to passersby, and one finds there a wide variety of pedestrians mingling with many street-corner loungers. However, this community (formerly called Hell's Kitchen; now part of Clinton) is fighting back with a resurgence of residentialism and a wide array of governmental redevelopment programs geared toward eliminating undesirable conditions.

Since 42nd Street is a transportation locus, a variety of social actors passes through the system and the population is consequently diverse. The bus terminal assists in bringing a transient (i.e., mobile) population to the midst of a distinct street-corner community, resulting in the existence of several subsystems. Further, some of the diversified actors in the terminal population may also use the facility in ways for which it was not intended. Hence, the "positive user" may be identified as one who utilizes the terminal for transportation, shopping, or other socially legitimate purposes, whereas the "negative" user (who many times is a member of the street-corner subcommunity) enters in order to sleep, commit a crime, or simply hang out. These latter individuals are seen as deviant by other segments of the population, and the police are faced with the task of controlling this diversity, providing a semblance of order to it. To accomplish this, three distinct policing styles may be identified:[5]

1. Watchman Style: The individual officer is permitted a great deal of discretion by the administrator.
2. Legalistic Style: No discretion is permitted. The enacted law is the prescription for conduct and action.
3. Service Style: A middle-of-the-road approach. A working rapport with the community is established.

One does not simply assign a random amount of police to a community and expect crime to be eliminated and order maintained. In addition to departmental administrative planning and supervision, the police themselves must be permitted to adapt to the community, becoming an integral part of the ecology and establishing themselves as the control segment of the population. For the police to be effective, they must not be seen as "outsiders."

Application of Policing Style

A policing style may be defined as the techniques employed by a police department or an individual officer in maintaining order within a community or specified sector. These styles may change because of legal stipulations, interest-group articulation, and so on. For example, in the streets, the New York City police adapted to a changing environment by eliminating the "sweep" approach, whereby officers were dispatched to a particular area in order to clear it of loiterers, prostitutes, and drunks. Paddy wagons would take the catch to the nearest precinct for processing. However, due to legal revisions, there is now a diminished emphasis on the strict enforcement of the law, and this is coupled with a heightened awareness of meeting the needs of the community. In the case of the bus terminal, there exists the uniqueness of containment: that is, the levels, passageways, and platforms are one distinct environment physically separated from the surrounding streets. Consequently, a similarly distinct method of policing is called for.

The horizontal patrol involves assigning an officer to each level of the facility. It is not a fixed post, where the officer is confined to a particular location, but a roving area of jurisdiction. The officer is responsible for monitoring criminal activity and responding to the law enforcement and service calls during the course of his eight-hour tour. He gathers facts and reports, which may lead to a subsequent investigation by Port Authority detectives; responds to radio calls of personal injuries to passengers or employees; handles disorderly persons; answers alarms; issues summonses; arrests violators, and performs first aid.

There are also vertical patrols, called roving teams, which are more mobile in that they provide backup requirements for officers responding to potentially dangerous calls or may cover the post of an officer who is issuing a summons or returning to the police desk to complete a report. A major benefit of the roving team is the elimination of patrol anticipation by members of the population who are intent on criminal activity. A mope[6] may desire to steal some candy from the newsstand counter, so he watches the officer on post for some time in order to gauge the approximate moment of his reappearance at a certain point. He notes that after passing the counter on a routine patrol, the officer does not return for fifteen minutes. This is the period in which he is most likely to commit a crime. Now, most officers realize that they must break this routine to eliminate the predictability of the patrol, yet over time everyone will establish a personal behavioral pattern within a territory. Since the mope is aware of this fifteen-minute time frame, he may walk toward the candy counter or even commit the crime, only to be surprised by the arrival of the roving team as they ride down the escalator from the suburban concourse. He did not anticipate the additional police coverage, and this will either deter him from the crime or result in his arrest should he commit it.

One case in which I was involved illustrates the situation perfectly, although it did not concern a crime. While assigned to patrol the main concourse, I would saunter from the Ninth Avenue end of the facility down to the Eighth Avenue entrance, looking in doors and walking through the waiting room on the way. However, on the return route, I would look into the drug store, the bakery, perhaps stroll into the bookstore or some other shop, and stand along the wall and observe the passersby. I did not enter the waiting room on that return trip. Since I always enjoyed watching the different types of people comprising the facility population of the moment, one individual caught my attention. He was a Black male, perhaps fifty-five or sixty years of age; his clothes told a story of harsh wear, but they were not skell-filthy.[7] I sized him up and realized that he had been around the streets for a while, but was not creating a problem for anyone, so I decided to speak to him on the way back to Eighth Avenue. (I was on my way to Ninth.) When I returned to the steps leading to the waiting room, he was neither there nor inside the room. Thinking he had left, I continued my patrol to Eighth Avenue in the "normal" manner. On the way back to Ninth again, I decided to look in the waiting room, since it seemed to have more persons in it than before. When I walked in, I saw the man reading a newspaper while lounging in a chair. He looked surprised when he noticed me staring his way, and shuffled out of the waiting room into the street. I didn't realize that he had previously been watching my patrol technique, figuring out that he could sit in the waiting room for about twenty minutes until I returned. Since my pattern was not to go inside until the Ninth-to-Eighth portion of the patrol, he could watch me pass by and get out before I came in. All he wanted was somewhere to sit and read a paper, but his use of a waiting-room seat was preventing a legitimate bus user from such use. He knew that he would be asked to leave, so he used his "street smarts" to outwit a rookie officer (who now varies his patrol).

Because of the diversity of people and events in the bus terminal and surrounding community, all three policing styles may be used in varying combinations. There is a continued temporal flow among all segments of the population and these subcommunities perceive diverse uses for the immediate environment.[8]

The Watchman Style

The watchman policing style has been described as follows:

> not simply . . . emphasizing order over law enforcement but also . . . judging the seriousness of infractions less by what the law says about them than by their immediate and personal consequences, which will differ in importance depending on the standards of the group—teenagers, Negroes, prostitutes, motorists, families, and so forth. In all cases, circumstances of person and condition are taken seriously into account.[9]

In and around the bus terminal and on nearby 42nd Street, the watchman style is the least utilized of the three styles, having been relegated to rare use in favor of more professional techniques. One elderly person interviewed in the terminal spoke of the "old days" of the police in this community.

> *Now, you know, son, you're a bit young to know this, but they didn't take any shit back then. I'll tell ya that when the good officer came down these streets, all he had to do was tap the stick on that curb and the fellas from other beats came runnin'. If ya was playin' ball and busted a window and ya gave the cop lip, ya got a kick in the seat of the pants and taken home to your mother. She would listen to the officer's story and hand over some of your father's hard-earned money to the property owner. The officer would take his*

*leave and your mother would swat the living hell out of you. And by God,
you didn't do it again. . . . Ya know, you're young. We just didn't put up with
that shit that they do now. The cop was looked up at. It was a good solid job.
And I'll tell ya, a good kick in the ass or a swat in the puss did more good
than all ya judges and courts do now.*

This was the street justice of Hell's Kitchen, the bus terminal, and countless other neighborhoods, and it lives on whenever an officer tells a petty
offender, "Get the hell out of here," or settles an argument between two
residents rather than make an arrest.

The Legalistic Style

"A legalistic department will issue traffic tickets at a high rate, detain and
arrest a high proportion of juvenile offenders, act vigorously against illicit
enterprises, and make a large number of misdemeanor arrests even when,
as with petty larceny, the public order has not been breached."[10] The main
operation of the legalistic style is typically ticketing; but within the bus-
terminal community we focus on various enforcement campaigns designed
to clear the streets of the "marginal" subcommunity. For example, the use
of the city police Tactical Patrol Unit in Times Square exemplifies the mode
of total police presence and saturation as a response to street violence. The
law may state that it is illegal to drink an alcoholic beverage on the street.
If the police wish to get rid of a bottle gang or a few drunks, they can enforce
the law by selecting such individuals from among the population of the
moment and dealing with them accordingly. If a community group complains
about a sanitary condition in the neighborhood, a police detail may be
assigned to issue summonses for uncovered garbage receptacles. If a concern
is voiced as to violent crimes, such as muggings, special plainclothes and
uniformed units may be assigned to the community for a specific length of
time in order to provide short-term results. Consequently, the mopes will
refer to the area as "hot," becoming extrawary in their dealings on the street.

I have observed some individuals, both males and females, stand around
for the entire length of my eight-hour tour, and I presume that they were
there before I came and remained after I left. Sometimes the police receive
a complaint concerning conditions on the street. When this occurs, they
may "claim the corner" by posting a uniformed officer nearby or directing
a sector car to concentrate its patrol there, issuing summonses and warnings
or making arrests. The group may disperse or relocate; in any case, the
police are seen as effective, in that the corner is now "clean" and they have
temporary claim to it. When the heat is off and "the man" has stopped
watching, the displaced group, or a new one, may return.

The legalistic style reduces the officer's discretion in dealing with events in the community. Rather than coping with situations as they arise, recognizing the uniqueness of each, the officer is required to use the law as a rigid behavioral guideline.

The Service Style

The service style is the middle-of-the-road approach in social control and policing.

> In some communities, the police take seriously all requests for either law enforcement or order maintenance (unlike police utilizing a watchman style) but are less likely to respond by making an arrest or otherwise imposing formal sanctions (unlike police with a legalistic style). The police intervene frequently but not formally.[11]

They are expected to act as professionals, that is, to be prompt to respond to calls, neat in appearance, efficient in administration and operation, and, above all, responsive to the needs of the surrounding community. By comparison, the watchman department is responsive to its own needs, whereas the legalistic is responsive to the needs of the law. The service style is most often used in residential communities, but is becoming prevalent in the bus terminal and on 42nd Street. One major reason for this is the "normalization" of the street population. As the police, utilizing both enforcement and ancillary agencies, withdraw undesirable persons from the street, the remaining segment of the population is of a more legitimate, although mostly transient, nature. The decline of a deviant population in and around the terminal signals a rise of residential and "passing-through" types, with a correlated revision of policing style. Since the environment of the terminal has been changed, the police within it are able to emphasize a service approach: they can respond to articulation from tenants and positive users as to their needs, and they can focus on prevention rather than enforcement. The "derelicts' haven"[12] is no more.

This operational environment of the police is constantly changing, indicating the change in clientele. However, legalistic efforts, though still employed in some cases, produce only short-term gains. The service style will go beyond pure arrest or displacement in an attempt to work with the community rather than to control it. Specialization is one way in which this is accomplished. At meetings of the community planning boards, merchants and community residents suggested to the police their desire for increased foot patrols. The police were receptive to these needs and promised to implement them.

Community Ecology and the Police

One of the unique factors of this community, namely diversity, contributes to conflict within it. Were the police to assume an unwavering approach in dealing with the population, some segments would receive unfair advantages and others would be penalized. At a community meeting where several merchants gathered along with board members, police commanders, and participants from some other agencies, including the Port Authority, the merchants congregated in one group, discussing the goings-on among themselves. They wore rumpled sweaters, open-collared shirts, or neat dresses; one wore sneakers; another, work boots. The hall in which we sat had peeling green paint swaying from the walls, while chipped folding chairs were scattered about. A flag dropped from a tarnished pole behind the "dais," as one of the speakers paged through a pile of papers, his eyes darting across the figures before him. The meeting began with the introduction of principal speakers and the identification of community personalities seated in the audience. The speaker, wearing a neat gray suit, rambled along with brief news items concerning fire hydrants, parking problems, and the like, finally arriving at the topic of litter. At this point, a member of the audience raised his hand and said, "Listen, what can we do about some guys throwing out garbage when there's no pickup? This stuff piles up and draws bums." The man wore a tattered brown sweater, pierced by the pointed collars of a blue shirt. He looked as if he knew his way around the neighborhood in ways that the man in the gray suit would never understand. (I later found out that the man in the sweater owned a local tavern.)

Gray Suit countered with, "Well, we've spoken to Sanitation about this sort of thing. . . ."

"They don't have enough guys to patrol our streets," said the Sweater; "I've seen bums rummaging through piles of junk on the street corners." The audience nodded approval on this point. (The problem was that private sanitation carters picked up commercial refuse on a prearranged schedule, and some merchants were ignoring this, putting litter out on days or hours other than those marked for pickup. The refuse would stand by the curb, piling up during the day or night, and was a magnet for skells seeking returnable bottles or other items of "value.")

Representatives from the New York City police were present, and Gray Suit looked to one: "Perhaps we can get some assistance from the police here." The member of the force, an inspector, described the issues of concentrating on serious offenses within the community, but promised to have roving officers issue summonses to violators.

The Sweater interjected, "Listen, I know I have problems with this sort of thing, and I know she does (pointing to a female merchant on his left), so maybe we can get together and work something out."

A young merchant with a Hispanic accent looked at the Sweater and the female. "You see, you open later than me. If we going to get time to put out garbage, maybe we should put it in one place on the block. Everybody can go to this spot and put it out for the dumper."

"Johnny," said the Sweater, "I don't want a pile of junk in front of my place, and neither do you."

As Johnny shook his head in agreement, the audience began speaking among themselves. Gray Suit quickly regained order with, "Okay, we have to move along. I'll check with Sanitation on this and we can get together to see about some sort of schedule."

The audience seemed pacified, when the sound of a latecomer turned their heads toward the rear of the hall. A N.Y.C. mounted police captain strode in, boots shining and brass gleaming, and, recognizing the sitting inspector, said, "Hello, Inspector, how ya doing?" The inspector smiled and nodded as the captain took a seat behind him.

"Now that we have an authority on the matter here," said Gray Suit with a smile, "maybe we can touch on the mounted police in the area." The heads turned to the captain, who hadn't expected to speak so soon, if at all. He proceeded to describe the role of the mounted police in the community, stressing their high visibility as a deterrent against crime. When he finished, Gray Suit thanked him and asked if anyone had questions.

The woman raised her hand: "Maybe you can tell us if the mounted police have the same power as the regular police. Can they make the same arrests . . .?"

The captain looked shocked, and the inspector's lips tightened into a sneer. "The mounted police," he announced, "are a branch of the regular police. We have the same power. We're the same job."

Gray Suit called attention to some "last items of business before we call it a night." Soon afterward, everyone promised to be in touch with one another, and left the hall. The Sweater was seen walking uptown on Eighth Avenue; the captain got into a blue-and-white police car with "MTD" on the side; the inspector eased into a four-door sedan with the telltale two antennas on it; and Gray Suit, holding a portfolio, stood by the doorway, talking with the woman.

Discretion in Policing the Community

In a community like the bus terminal and 42nd Street, the existence of a wide variety of norms is concomitant with the diversity of the population.

Various neighborhoods and subcultures have their own levels of tolerable disorder; what may appear to be weaker norms are only different norms. Nor are the members of such subcultures a threat to persons in other neighbor-hoods—police statistics show that almost all disorder, tolerable or intolerable, occurs among persons who are likely to share common norms because they are acquainted or related. Justice is not an absolute; it can be rationed, pro-viding more or less of one kind rather than another to different neighbor-hoods.[13]

The commuter, himself well versed in codes of behavior and acceptable conduct in public places, may see the values of a bottle gang as weaker than his own, and a police officer may view the gang's norms of public behavior as weak simply because they are different. The bottle gang (a temporary street group whose basic social tie is formed by the bottle of liquor they pass among themselves) maintains strong codes of behavior and affiliation, in the same manner as passing commuters, merchants, residents, and other segments of the population. The norm that the first sip goes to the bottle-gang participant who brings the liquor is as honored by the bottle gang as the norm of the queue procedure is honored by commuters—and not really that different. Consequently, although justice must be administered to the entire population in the process of social control, particular attention is paid to the segment with whom the officer is dealing.

The police officer possesses a wide latitude of discretion in dealing with this, or any, population. Unless he is assigned to a legalistic function such as an enforcement detail, his day-to-day activities bring him into contact with a wide variety of situations, all requiring immediate and equitable resolution. Three examples illustrate this clearly.

Example 1

It is a cold windy day in February, the kind where the wind seems like a finely honed knife slicing against defenseless skin. A gray sky hovers over the formless tops of skyscrapers whose gray walls form an icy canyon for people walking up 42nd Street. Near an old newsstand presided over by a huddled old woman, whose dull eyes peer from within a shawl, stands the speaker of the day. Looking about thirty-five years of age, she wears a filthy once-green parka coat, blue pants, and black boots whose plastic shine betrays their cost. "Repent, you sinners, for the Lord is coming. Jesus loves you. He is the Messiah, the Savior, the lover of all." Her blue eyes widen as she screams to unhearing ears, "Obey the Lord—your Lord—or you'll burn forever in the fiery abyss. He says so." Few passersby take note of her performance, walking turtlelike as they concentrate on avoiding the wind by lowering heads into coats. A police officer walks by, glancing at the speaker but focusing his attention on the occupants of theater lobbies and storefronts along the way.

Example 2

The cold has found its way into the recesses of the 42nd Street subway station, keeping the stench of urine at bay. A train pulls into the station, the sound of its whistle filling the air. A transit police officer comes down the stairs and walks to the middle of the train, where the conductor points out a dispute between two passengers. As the train pulls out, the trio—two passengers and the officer—stand on the platform, discussing the situation. After about ten minutes, the two passengers go their separate ways and the officer goes back up the stairs.

Example 3

The Port Authority police officer stands outside the Ninth Avenue entrance to the bus terminal, watching traffic flow downtown as pedestrians ignore the light in an attempt to get across the street and out of the wind. He carries a portable radio on his belt and now there is a message for him. "BT to Post 100." "Post 100 go," he replies. "Post 100, respond to the vicinity of Platform 35, report of a sleeper." The door closing behind him, the officer is well on his way as he returns the call. "Roger, BT. En route." Upon arriving at the scene, he is met by a maintenance man who informs him that someone is sleeping in one of the lavatory stalls. The officer walks into the room and looks at the green stall doors. All are closed; crouching down, he sees a pair of feet in the second stall. He notices that although the person is sitting, the pants are not around the ankles. Knocking on the door, he hears a stirring from within and realizes that the sleeper has locked the stall. A louder knock produces a "Yeah?" from within, and this is met by a "Police, let's go." The door opens to reveal a middle-aged man who looks warily at the blue-clad intruder, who now says, "Come on, move along. Get the hell out of here." The skell shuffles out of the lavatory, past the seated long-distance bus passengers whose eyes drift downward as he goes by. Some of them turn their heads for a last look as he disappears through the doorway to Ninth Avenue.

Each police officer was presented with the opportunity for making a legitimate arrest, yet chose to remain on post and continue patrol. Each used discretionary powers to maintain order by either enforcing the law or normalizing the situation without an arrest.[14] The police are sworn to uphold the law, but they may do so in a variety of ways. In the first place, the officer's mere presence in uniform may act as a control mechanism, since a potential criminal may wait until he leaves before committing an act, or may not commit it at all. In this case, order is maintained within the surrounding segment of the population through no overt action of the officer. This situation may be observed in the waiting room of the terminal where, while working in uniform, I have walked in to see a commuter or OTB (Off-

Track Betting) customer standing with one foot propped up on a nearby seat. The former would usually be waiting for the lavatory to clear out before going in, and the latter would be perusing the racing section of the *Daily News*. At first sight of the police, the foot would immediately drop to the floor, the man meanwhile avoiding eye contact with me. The commuter would realize that he was "out of line" in placing his foot where someone might have desired to sit, so he would defer to the authority of the police in relinquishing the territory. The OTB customer behaves in the same way, as he realizes that he may be asked by the officer to step inside the store while sizing up the program, rather than obstruct passage to those seeking a seat. None of this is criminal behavior, yet those performing the activity are instinctively aware of its "out-of-the-ordinary"—and specifically anti-social—nature for the terminal, and anticipate police intervention of a peace-keeping nature. By requesting that they move, the officer enhances both the order and population flow of the facility.

The Mopes' View of Deviance and Crime in the Community

To understand the perspective of the community, it is imperative to focus on the issue of territoriality. Each segment of the temporal community of the bus terminal has a claim to some part of it at any particular moment. Commuters see the facility as "serving them" for the time that they use it in getting to and from work. During the morning rush, they and their buses are drawn to the city, processed through the terminal, and dispatched to the urban core. The process is reversed in the evening.

To police officers, the bus terminal is their "turf," the territory dependent upon their protection. They are responsible for conditions on their posts and important decisions must be made concerning temporal activity in and around them. Similarly, the merchants' shops are their livelihoods; they make their money by attracting the population into their establishments. Skells and mopes, however, also have vested interests in the community. These needs may be served by the bus terminal in a variety of ways, such as by sleeping in the waiting room or obtaining protection from the elements. Some elderly persons view the terminal as their "turf," since their homes were once located on the site. Some skells think the terminal was built specifically for them, as they become indignant when disturbed. More important, these individuals, like the merchants, may use the bus terminal for generating income. They may pickpocket passersby, steal luggage, panhandle, or search for discarded bus or OTB tickets.

The skell in the street harbors similar perceptions of the community as prostitutes, three-card-monte dealers, con men, pornography-shop owners, transvestites, and bottle gangs, who all use the territory for their own purposes. Many of these mopes and skells will not hesitate to inform the police or others that they feel at home in this community. During one evening rush period, a disheveled female skell had set up an enterprising panhandling operation outside the Eighth Avenue entrance to the terminal. Sitting on a wooden milkbox, she would look with mournful eyes at the rushing passersby and implore, "Wouldn't you help a lady in need?" Her stillness as she sat there was in stark contrast to the hurry of those who stopped their routine long enough to drop a dime or quarter into the coffee can resting on her lap. A blue housedress, filthy from the grime of the streets, hung sacklike from her thin frame; torn white tennis sneakers graced her feet. Her hair had once been black, but now the gray had all but obliterated the last defenders. The police officer on duty observed that her presence on the sidewalk was forcing the crowd to veer around the "business," so he walked over and asked her to leave. "Ma'am, you can't sit here, because someone might trip over you and get hurt. Why don't you move away from the building?"

The mournful eyes suddenly burst forth with fire. "Why don't you go fuck yourself, you scummy motherfucker. I'll do whatever I damn please and you won't touch my fuckin' money."

"I asked nice once," said the officer, "and I don't want to see you here when I come back in five minutes. Now pick up your things and go." The woman said nothing as she watched the officer disappear inside the Eighth Avenue entrance. It seemed like no time before he was beside her again. "Okay, you'll have to leave." This time, some passersby stopped to hear her discourse.

"You fuckin' pig, you lousy motherfucker. Who the fuck do you think you are? I live here, and this is my job." The officer picked up her can and placed her milkbox inside the terminal, away from where someone might trip on it. As the pair walked to the police desk, where the woman would be given a summons, she continued her verbal barrage, stressing that it was her spot.

Obviously, the skell felt that she was entitled to panhandle whenever and wherever she pleased, viewing the police as intruders in her business. Again, had the woman conducted herself in a "normal" manner, the officer would most likely have acted as a peace-keeper, chasing her from the area. However, she chose to claim the territory, forcing the officer to act as a law enforcer and issue the summons. In a similar display, a man who was wanted for shooting a police officer was arrested on 39th Street and Eighth Avenue. When asked why he did it, he replied, "Fuck it, I'd do the same to you."

These individuals see the police as interfering with their community activity. Deviance does not enter into the case; they use the terminal or streets for reasons seen as legitimate to them, and the remaining segments of the population depend upon the police to maintain order according to their own standards. Deviance does come into play when legitimate users see the mopes, skells, and "characters" as interfering with their participation in the community. The commuter sees the bottle gang as a bunch of mopes, whereas one or more of them may see him as an easy mark for a wallet lift.

Controlling the Police

Although in theory the police are the formal social control agents in this community, responsible for maintaining order among the population, there are occasions to the contrary, when mopes attempt to control the police.

The mope, unseen by the nearby police officer, stands near the Ninth Avenue entrance of the bus terminal. His eyes scanning the passersby and passing cars, the officer does not realize that he too is the object of the same intensive scanning method, which takes in his appearance, gait, and demeanor. The mope has now reached a decision, and, approaching the officer from behind, asks in a deep voice, "Can you tell me how to get the bus to Short Hills?"

Before he even turns completely around, the officer is replying, "Sure, sir, just go inside and upstairs to Platform 220. You can get it there."

The mope nods and walks away, but not in the direction indicated by his benefactor. "That stupid motherfucker is new, man. I told ya," says the mope to his colleagues on the corner of Eighth Avenue and 40th Street. The reason? Even though the mope wore dirty clothing and unshined shoes, had not shaved in days, and carried a wine bottle, wrapped in a paper bag, in his rear pocket, he wasn't recognized as a street mope by the rookie cop. The mope had used him as a "mark," testing him by asking directions to one of the more affluent communities in New Jersey. The new officer, whose street smarts were not yet finely honed, did not recognize this obvious incongruence. The successful jive job had marked him as new. Had he replied, "Why?" or "Get the hell out of here," the mope would have realized that he was dealing with a seasoned man who could deal with the streets as well as he.

Mopes are conscious of the demeanor of the police assigned within their territory. Conflict arises when these divergent subcommunities interfere with one another, that is, in the situations where members of the particular population deviate from tolerable norms. The men at the shoeshine stand on 42nd Street and Eighth Avenue will probably not be bothered by the police unless they become rowdy, blatantly drink in front of a passing patrol car, and so forth. On the other hand, they will not pass comments at or harass a beat officer unless he should take what they deem to be intolerable action (such as issuing a littering summons to one of them). The subcommunities exist within the parameters of tolerable deviance, and once a segment oversteps its boundaries, the other segments will mobilize to restore order to the community at large.

The community skells maintain their own peer groups, similar to those maintained by the police, bus drivers, maintenance men, merchants, and commuters. Within these groups, there is also pressure to "do the right thing," that is, show that you are "one of the boys." For the skells, this may mean taking chances and showing that one is not afraid of the police. A story is told about the vagrant who told his "partner" that a passing police officer was a particularly easy mark, so he should go up and test him. The officer, known to the first skell as a very streetwise cop, proceeded to humiliate the second skell, causing the latter to lose face in front of his friend.[15] The attempt to mark the cop and control him in this situation had failed, though the first skell had certainly marked his "friend," the second skell. The result of this encounter was an upgrading of the cop's reputation and a downgrading of the marked skell's.

Consequently, besides being true users of the bus terminal and integral segments of the community population, the deviant (mopes, skells, street loiterers, etc.) may be seen as coexisting with the police only insofar as they remain within tolerable norms. This would not be the case with a legalistic enforcement campaign, as the police would concentrate on all violations, thereby diminishing their discretion. However, as long as the normal peace-keeping/service style is maintained by the police and all segments of the population observe tolerable norms, the tendency is for the subcommunities to coexist amicably.

Summary

Considering its role as a true social institution in the diverse ecology of the 42nd Street community, the Port Authority bus terminal is more than just a transportation facility. Although it is a most comprehensive terminal, providing a valuable service to the region, its location in a true "natural area"[16] results in the existence of a diverse population composed of many subcommunities, which perceive the facility and the environment in various ways. Consequently, to study the bus terminal is to evaluate the coexistence of a disparate population and its relationships to both residential and transient communities.

Glossary

Bag   Police term for the uniform. In street parlance, it may mean a quantity of narcotics, as in a "nickel bag."

Bag lady   A female derelict identified by her belongings carried in a shopping bag. They can be any age; however, most seem to be from the forties upward. There can also be "Shopping-Bag Men," but they are less common.

Blow   Port Authority police term for a meal period. City and transit police usually use the term "meal." However, in street parlance, "blow" may also refer to a sexual act.

Bompie   New Jersey police term for a mope or skell. It is rarely heard in New York except by those Port Authority police who may be accustomed to working in New Jersey.

Boss   A police supervisor of any rank.

B.T.   Police abbreviation for the bus terminal. Also used by civilians within the Port Authority.

Busted   Arrested. Primarily used by mopes.

Caper   Police term for a complicated incident.

Catch a case   Detective term for being assigned to a case.

Chicken   A young male prostitute.

Chicken hawk   Man who preys on the chickens.

Civilian   Anyone not a police officer.

Collar   Arrest. Primarily used by police.

Cop   Slang for police officer. Street term for purchasing narcotics, as in, "I'm gonna cop some shit."

CPCS   Abbreviation for "Criminal Possession of a Controlled Substance." "I have a CPCS collar" is a police officer's way of saying that he has made a narcotics arrest.

Deuce, the   42nd Street.

Dick   Detective.

D.O.A.   Abbreviation for "Dead on Arrival."

Down   Police term for shortage of manpower. "The tour is down two."

Eyeball   To watch intently.

Felony flyers   Police term for sneakers.

Fixer   Police term for a stationary post.

Heavy hitter   Police term for an officer who makes many arrests.

Hole, the   Police term for the Lincoln Tunnel.

Hot   Street term for an area that is being watched by the police. "This place is too hot." It can also refer to stolen merchandise, as in the phrase, "hot cameras."

House   City police term for their precincts.

Jive job   Street term for one person making a fool out of another.

John   Prostitute's customer.

Jostler   Police term for a person who places his hand in the proximity of another's wallet, etc.

Jump   Attack.

Lady　Prostitute. Commonly used by street persons.

Looking　Police term for an officer who wants to make an arrest.

Mark　A person who looks like an easy victim.

Mope　Police term for a criminal. Not all mopes are skells. A well-dressed man who is arrested for grand larceny (pickpocket) would be a mope, as would a suspicious character seen hanging around the terminal. A mope is usually a clean skell. Cf. the phrase, "moping around."

M.T.D.　City police term for the mounted unit.

Mutt　Police term for a criminal.

O.J.T.　"On-the-Job Training." Required of a new officer in order to indoctrinate him to facility or precinct operation.

One Under　Police term for a person under arrest.

On the Job　Police term for being a police officer. The most common way a police officer introduces himself to an unknown colleague is to say, "I'm on the job."

O.T.　Police term for overtime.

Poolie　Port Authority police term for a member of the Central Police Pool, a unit in which officers are not permanently assigned to a facility. An officer may work at the bus terminal one day and Kennedy Airport the next.

Police desk　Port Authority police term for their precincts. Also called "the Desk."

Port　New Jersey police term for a Port Authority officer.

Pross　Police term for a prostitute.

Psycho　Police term for a deranged person.

Reserve room　Port Authority police term for the police rest and report area.

Rip　Police term for an administrative penalty. A five-day rip constitutes five working days without pay.

Ripoff　To rob, a robbery.

Skell　Police term for an unkempt mope. A drunk who has urinated in his pants is a skell; so too is a Bag Lady.

Sleeper　Police term for an individual sleeping in a train or in the Bus Terminal, or any other public place.

South, the　Police term for the NYPD Midtown South precinct.

T.C.　Police term for the tour commander.

Time served　The interval between the time of arrest and subsequent disposition by the court. If this period is six months and the sentence is one year with time served, a person may actually do only six months in jail.

Tip　Street term for "I have to leave."

Trick　A working period for a prostitute.

Write　Police term for issuing a summons ("I wrote him") or for a supervisor issuing a disciplinary report on an officer ("He was written up").

NOTES

1. Donald F. Delano, "The Port Authority Bus Terminal in Its Community Setting: An Ethnographic Study," Ph.D. diss., City Univ. of New York, 1981.
2. This was of course in addition to the public documents available, i.e., Port Authority of New York and New Jersey, *Bus and Bus Passenger Surveys: 1980* and *Bus Terminal Fact Sheets* for 1979–1981.
3. The IND (Independent), BMT (Brooklyn-Manhattan Transit) and IRT (Interborough Rapid Transit) constitute the three divisions of the New York City Subway System, while MABSTOA (Manhattan and Bronx Surface Transit Operating Authority) is responsible for operating street buses in the boroughs indicated in its name. All are under the auspices of the Metropolitan Transportation Authority.
4. These facilities include (in addition to the airports and the bus terminal) the World Trade Center; the Lincoln and Holland tunnels; the George Washington Bridge; the Staten Island bridges—Goethals, Bayonne, and Outerbridge Crossing; PATH commuter railroad; New York and New Jersey marine terminals; Journal Square (N.J.) Transportation Center; passenger ship terminal.
5. James Q. Wilson, *Varieties of Police Behavior* (Cambridge, Mass.: Harvard Univ. Press, 1970).
6. Refer to Glossary at the end of the chapter.
7. Refer to Glossary at the end of the chapter.
8. This situation is distinct in its contradiction to a rural or suburban community such as Crestwood Heights. In such a location the police are able to assume a distinct and consistent patrol style rather than a fluctuating one. This is a result of the "mechanical solidarity" in the rural area and the "organic solidarity" in the diversified city. See John R. Seeley, *Crestwood Heights* (New York: John Wiley & Sons, 1965).
9. Wilson, *Varieties of Police Behavior*, p. 141.
10. Ibid., p. 172.
11. Ibid., p. 200.
12. McCandlish Phillips, "Bus Terminal at Night: A Derelict's Haven," *New York Times*, 8 Jan. 1967, 1:1.
13. Charles P. McDowell, *Police in the Community* (Cincinnati: Anderson, 1975), p. 153.
14. Egon Bittner distinguishes between the concept of "peace keeping" and "law enforcing" by the police when dealing with derelicts. Bittner, "The Police on Skid Row: A Study of Peace Keeping," *American Sociological Review*, 32 (Oct. 1967): 699–715.
15. Suttles observed the identical situation in Chicago's Addams section. "A man who has a reputation as a petty thief may be made fun of if he gets caught or admired if he gets away with his ventures. Another in the same group who is perfectly 'straight' would be thought foolhardy or stupid if he took similar risks. At first sight each group seems to include a number of utterly incompatible individuals. But the members of these street groups have been compromised together and assurances of personal trust exempt them from the fears and ap-

prehensions that might otherwise develop. Even the best known prude or thief is assumed to put his friends above his principles." Gerald Suttles, *The Social Order of the Slum* (Chicago: Univ. of Chicago Press, 1968), p. 79.

16. "A territorial area with some common, unifying characteristic. The term has been used primarily in human ecology, and usually refers to an area that emerges without planning from the operation of ecological processes. It is frequently contrasted with an administrative area having arbitrarily delimited boundaries, and has been most often applied to specialized areas of a city—areas characterized by distinctive land use or population type, such as a central business district, slum, wholesale district, rooming house area, financial district, Negro district, Italian district, etc." George and Achilles G. Theodorson, *Modern Dictionary of Sociology* (New York: Crowell, 1969), p. 271.

ACKNOWLEDGMENT

The author wishes to extend gratitude to the Port Authority for technical assistance received; all observations and conclusions are strictly his own.

17

Visiting New York

GERALD HANDEL

METHODOLOGICAL NOTE • This chapter is based on interviews with 114 visitors to New York City, conducted by the author's undergraduate class in Qualitative Research Methods at the City College. The interview guide, prepared by the author, consisted entirely of open-ended questions, except for a few face-sheet items. The guide was designed to encourage interviewees to talk about their visit to New York in their own terms. Although any question asked—even the most general—sets some kind of limit to an interviewee's potential response, the open-ended question is far less constraining than the structured question used in the survey interview. Interviewees are encouraged to express ideas, feelings, and experiences in their own words. When the researcher examines many individual responses, he usually finds some patterns, trends, or themes, as well as some surprising or distinctive responses. A number of idiosyncratic responses sometimes reveals a theme, as happened in this study.

Almost any community anywhere may be visited sometime by someone who does not reside there. Kinship and commerce are perhaps universal in creating rationales for someone's visits to any human settlement, no matter how small, remote, or unprepossessing. Certain human settlements, however, have gained preeminence as attractions for visitors who have no commercial or kinship reasons for visiting them. Such places embody, or are 291 believed to embody, distinctive values not to be found in most residential communities. They attract travelers who have no established social ties to the place. They are worth a visit for themselves.

Places to visit are of various kinds and can be categorized on the basis of the qualities that define them and the activities that may be pursued in them. Resorts offer tranquility, rusticity, a low ratio of factory-made artifacts to natural objects, and facilities for recreational activities of an athietic kind. Mountain, ocean, and lake resorts, different as they are, have these features in common. The Rocky Mountain ski resorts, Cape Cod, and the small-lake vacation communities of Wisconsin and Michigan offer general "nature values" of the kinds mentioned, as well as values distinctive to each place.

Historic places offer their own distinctive values—a sense of continuity with the stream of human events beyond one's own life-span, a sense of contrast between old-fashioned hardship and modern convenience, a contact with the awesome magnitude of fateful efforts. These are some of the values offered to and presumably sought by visitors to Sturbridge Village, in Massachusetts, the restorations at Colonial Williamsburg, in Virginia, or the Gettysburg battlefield, in Pennsylvania.

Certain cities have gained distinction as tourist attractions, cities to which one goes even if one knows no one there and has no business to conduct. New York is one of those cities that attract visitors from all over the world. In this chapter I want to sketch, in a very preliminary way, how visitors experience New York—the qualities that define the city as they experience it, that endow it with its touristic values.

Interviewees can be grouped into three categories, from the perspective adopted at the outset of this chapter: those who came to New York for the sole purpose of visiting the city; those who came for business and then utilized the occasion to visit the city, and those who combined visits to relatives with visits to the city. For the purposes of this chapter, the differences among these categories are of little consequence. Those who combined tourism with a visit to relatives usually say that their relatives planned much of the sightseeing for them. Some of those who were combining business with pleasure found themselves in New York at the direction of their employers. If these circumstances distinguish these two categories in other ways from those who came to the city purely for tourism, the present study is not sufficiently refined to capture the differences. The responses of all three categories of visitors to their experiencing of New York appear to be substantially similar.

New York Is a Focus of Expectations

One of the first things to be said about New York City is that it is an object of people's expectations. It seems probable that if one presented people with a list of cities that they had never been to, one would find that they have expectations about some cities but not about others. Certain cities gain a reputation or acquire an aura as social objects of a particular kind. The reputation may be limited to a special segment of the population outside the city. For example, art lovers all over the country may know that Worcester, Massachusetts, has a superb art museum, but few others outside a radius of a couple hundred miles of Worcester are likely to have any expectations at all about that city. Mass media attention may help to generate expectations. People all over the country may expect that Cleveland is a fairly dull place, because it has been defined as such by comedians and other media, whereas they may have no expectations of any kind about Omaha or Des Moines, Syracuse or Spokane, because these cities receive little nationwide public attention for any reason.[1]

New York is a city about which people have expectations. It is an object in their minds, in their imaginations. When visitors are asked. "Before you ever came to New York, what ideas did you have about what it would be like? What had you heard about it? What did you expect?" responses are variable but certain topics and dimensions emerge as salient.

People

I heard that the people were not very friendly. I heard that the people were very cold. I thought that the people would be cold, but I was wrong. They are very nice people. (Woman, 40–49, schoolteacher, Seattle.)

Crime

Before my first time I thought I'd have to watch out for crooks, people trying to get your money. I heard the people were unfriendly and I was ready for this. Now I know if you got money, everybody's friendly. (Man, 40–49, farmer, upstate New York.)

Stimulation

I figured it would be fast paced, with different cultures. It had the best night life in the U.S. I expected exactly what I've seen. Nothing surprises me. (Man, 20–29, margin clerk, Dallas.)

Energy

I expect a big city that never sleeps, that the persons live in constant fear, and fighting for power and fame. (Man, 30–39, writer, Taxco, Mexico.)

Crowds and Dirt

> *I expected it to be crowded and dirty, and it was. Usually, the Pittsburgh newspapers only have the bad side of New York City. (Woman, 40–49, secretary at iron works, Pittsburgh.)*

Beauty

> *I was told and also read that New York boasted some of the most beautiful sights in the world. (Man, 30–39, civil clerk, Belize City, Belize, Central America.)*

One of the less typical responses dealt with economic hardship:

> *I knew it is a very big city. I saw a lot about New York on TV in Russia. They showed people on strike and unemployed. (Woman, 30–39, chemist, Russia.)*

Virtually none of the respondents said that they did not know what to expect, that they had no ideas at all about New York before they got here.

Deciding To Come

For some, a trip to New York is the fulfillment of a long-term goal, planned for a year or more or even a lifetime:

> *I had planned to come here for about a year, and I finally saved the money to come, so I came on my vacation. (Man, 30–39, photographer, France.)*

> *Well, I started planning for this trip a year ago. Ever since I was a young child I wanted to visit New York. My older relatives would visit New York and come back and tell me how nice a place it was. Getting up in age—I'm 49—I said that before I die I wanted to visit the place everyone talks about. (Woman, 40–49, telephone company worker, Darien, Georgia.)*

> *It's a group tour club. Every year we visit someplace. This year everyone voted on New York, so we visit places together, and we have free time to visit different things and places. (Woman, 50–59, housewife, Gadsden, Alabama.)*

For others, the decision to come is taken casually:

> *I told my partner I was coming, made reservations on the plane and came, just a spur-of-the-moment thing. I decided I'd play it by ear as to what I'll do when I get here. (Man, 50–59, liquor store owner, Chicago.)*

We figured we'd take a bus up to New York and get a brochure on the highlights. We made reservations at the Hilton. (Man, 40–49, clerk, Myrtle Beach, South Carolina.)

Some visitors, of course, come for business or professional reasons. Some of these visits have a routine quality, but some have a suggestion of particular stimulation.

Well, I'm here for a Fire Department seminar. We're looking for ways to improve our department. So I guess it's a business trip. (Man, 60–69, Fire Chief, Belfast, Northern Ireland.)

New York is, clearly, for some an object of longing, a place that must be visited for rounding out one's life. For others, it is a place for a lark, a quick change of scene, a place to come without much thought because there is enough going on that one is bound to find diversion without much planning for it. Visitors on business often want to use the occasion to sample the sights.

Experiencing the City

Why do people visit New York? In addition to visiting relatives and conducting business, they come to see the sights and to do things. They come to see buildings, plays, museums. They come to dance, to hear music, to shop, to tour around. But these activities only partially answer the question as to why they come and only partially account for their experiencing of the city. Visitors tend to find an added dimension to their touristic activities. Going to a play in New York is not merely going to a play in New York; it is going to "a Broadway play." There is a sense of participating in something outstanding, of having an experience larger or more intense or more distinctive than can be described by the activity itself. Responses to various questions reveal a number of qualities that define visitors' experiences of New York.

Scale

Largeness of scale is perhaps the quality that first strikes the visitor to New York, especially the visitor to Manhattan, where most of the interviewing was done. The buildings are very tall, the crowds in the streets are very large. But it is not merely these most visible manifestations of bigness that define the sense of large scale. One visitor from another metropolis says that the aspect of New York City that interests her the most is:

The major department stores. There is a bigger range of fashion here. (Woman, 30–39, keypunch operator, Los Angeles.)

And another visitor says:

I won't miss to visit Radio City Music Hall. I think it is a very exciting place. I believe it is the largest of the world, and I love the Rockettes. (Woman, 20–29, accountant, Dominican Republic.)

The scale of the city is perceived from another angle by a young man who says:

Anything which I couldn't find in New York is not in the world. (Man, under 20, soldier, Iowa, stationed at Fort Dix, N.J.)

New York is believed to "have everything."

First Rank

Visitors tend to see New York not only as "the biggest" but, in several respects, as "the best." The most widely shared perception among the visitors interviewed is that New York is the leading entertainment center. The combination of best night life, Broadway theaters, pace-setting discotheques, fine restaurants, and apparent nonstop activity leads many visitors to judge that there is no equal place for entertainment.

The city has a number of sites that are considered symbols of one or another kind of excellence. The Statue of Liberty as a symbol of freedom, Wall Street as a symbol of top financial power, Yankee Stadium, the Metropolitan Museum of Art, the Museum of Modern Art, American Museum of Natural History, Central Park, Radio City Music Hall—all are locales that some visitors feel they must see because, in a particular way, the place symbolizes and displays some standard of excellence not found elsewhere. Nor are these well-known places the only symbols of excellence. Idiosyncratic needs can find shrines that embody the kinds of excellence they crave. Thus, a North Carolina discotheque owner visits a leading New York disco and finds just the new idea—a machine blowing bubbles—that he can take back to liven up his own establishment. A young woman, a self-described "rock music freak" from Mexico City, spends her entire first afternoon in New York at the Sam Goody record store, overcome with the breadth of choice. There are many kinds of excellence in New York.

Energy and Excitement

Experiencing New York is experiencing energy and excitement. The visible pace of New Yorkers often impresses visitors:

> *I find people here very energetic and in a rush. In Shaker Heights people are geared to a slower pace. (Man, 20–29, fashion model, Shaker Heights, Ohio.)*

> *Where I come from, we don't move this fast. Everything here is rush, rush, rush. (Man, 40–49, clerk, Myrtle Beach, South Carolina.)*

The visible fast pace is undoubtedly one key ingredient in generating the sense of excitement reported by some visitors:

> *[What aspects of New York City interest you the most? Why those?]*
> *The way the city seems to breed excitement. People turn me on here. (Man, 50–59, liquor store owner, Chicago.)*

> *I like the city at night. People seem to be in a better mood. I always enjoy myself when I come here. I like the excitement. (Man, 40–49, farmer, upstate New York.)*

> *I expected to have a good time here but instead I'm having the time of a lifetime. (Man, 50–59, doctor, Spain.)*

Pace alone is probably insufficient to generate excitement. Surely the largeness of the city, the wide range of its visible endeavors, and its perceived excellence also play a part.

> *What I like is the diversity you have in this city. For example, the Broadway shows, the very fine restaurants, and a lot of tall buildings. (Woman, 30–39, store employee, Beaufort, South Carolina.)*

> *I like the variety of things here. I like the stores and its clothes and the beautiful places to see and things to do. In New York City you never get tired of seeing things. (Man, 30–39, hotel manager, San Juan, Puerto Rico.)*

At least three other factors also probably contribute to the sense of excitement: diversity of population and culture; liberality; and exoticism.

Diversity of Population and Cultures

For many visitors, New York offers diversity of population and culture that are significantly greater than what they are accustomed to in their own home towns, and they seem to find the diversity attractive, at least for vacation purposes. In response to the question, "Suppose someone who has never been to New York asks about it when you get back, what would you tell them?" one young woman replies:

> If you are looking for a fun place, different, with unique people of different nationalities, then go to New York. (Woman, under 20, student, South Dakota.)

Asked to say what aspects of New York interest her the most, another young woman responds:

> The variety of different people. I come from a monolithic society where everyone has the same ethnicity. For example, here there's a large number of homosexuals. (Woman, under 20, student, Jamaica.)

For a South American man, one of the main differences between New York and his home town is:

> The different ethnic backgrounds of the people. The only place I've seen where people do not blend in together in uniformity, which is what makes this city a great city. (Man, 30–39, engineer, Cuzco, Peru.)

The diversity of the city's cultures can sometimes be savored in a direct, personal way:

> Walking through Greenwich Village was the best because it is unusual. I had a slice of pizza, a taco, a falafel, and a cappucino. (Woman, 20–29, radio station assistant program director, Nebraska.)

The varied and unfamiliar foods available at small shops and street stands, the diverse skin colorings and dress of the people, the great variety of personal styles, the bits of foreign speech overheard—all these combine to create streams of sensory stimulation that lead many visitors to feel that they are in a different kind of place from what they are accustomed to.

Liberality

For some visitors, an important quality in their experiencing of New York is its freedom from some of the restraints and restrictions found elsewhere. New Yorkers are believed to have a mental freedom that distinguishes them from others:

> People here are more open-minded about almost everything. (Man, 30–39, store manager, Puerto Rico.)

This open-mindedness leads, in turn, to lesser social control over what people do:

> *It's been a good experience because I can do things here that I can't do in Philly. I can stay out late without being bothered by the police. (Woman, under 20, student, Philadelphia.)*

> *Where I come from is a very restrictive kind of life. You cannot do things that you people do here. (Woman, 30–39, military employee, Camp LeJeune, North Carolina.)*

> *I went out on 42nd Street to buy souvenirs for my family and everyone was trying to sell me drugs, with the police right in the area. (Man, 50–59, salesman, Wichita Heights, Kansas.)*

> *Probably the most interesting experience was when I walked down through 42nd Street, because I never imagined that I will find that kind of variety in sex show. Also, when I saw the people selling drugs on the street freely. (Man, 30–39, computer programmer, Venezuela.)*

For some visitors, the degree of liberality they find is unexpected, and by no means do they uniformly find it welcome. The pornography and drug selling are decidedly unwelcome to many; the loose social controls over these activities are unpleasant surprises. But others clearly welcome the liberality of mind, spirit, attitude, and conduct that they find. The apparently freer outlook of New Yorkers and the social ambience it creates is part of what gives a sense of adventure to a visit here. New York is a city of many wonders, and some visitors, at least, are drawn to its wonders of liberality along with its wonders of achievement.

Exoticism

One of the wonders of New York is its street life. The diversity of culture and population and the liberality in the exercise of social control contribute to a continuing stream of experience that comes to be taken as characteristic of a visit to New York and that distinguishes it from what many feel is the more mundane stream of experience in their home towns. But every once in a while a visitor has an experience that seems especially exotic.

> *The most interesting experience that I had happen was when I was walking down 45th Street there was this young man doing pantomime with his face painted up like a clown and in black-and-white striped pants and black shirt. I never saw anything like that in my life. I stood there for about a half hour watching him. (Man, 30–39, building contractor, Macomb, Illinois.)*

> *I went to Central Park. It is full of life and surprises behind every bush. I*

was sitting on a bench and a man dressed in a fire suit asked me for money. I was astonished. (Man, 30–39, executive, Seattle.)

The most interesting experience that I had happened on Jamaica Avenue in Queens. This preacher was giving the Word of the Lord right out in the middle of the shopping area. Nothing like that has ever happened where I live. (Woman, 40–49, housewife, Charlotte, North Carolina.)

Well, I've had so many interesting experiences, but I guess the most interesting was seeing 42nd Street and being propositioned by a Black transvestite in a blond wig. (Man, 30–39, health care investigator, Minneapolis.)

The astonishments of the street range from the sacred to the profane, but some are not readily classifiable:

I went to the Village two days ago and I saw a guy on roller skates wearing a wedding gown and a helmet skating down Seventh Avenue. I was amazed but I was told this is not strange in New York City, especially in the Village. (Woman, 20–29, accountant, Dominican Republic.)

The exotic is not strange in New York. It happens all the time, or so the amazed visitor is told. Even law enforcement can be exotic:

I seen a little old lady fighting off a mugger. It was fascinating because the old lady turned out to be a cop. (Woman, 30–39, housewife, Quebec.)

When the professional model from Shaker Heights told his interviewer that New York is the fashion capital of the world, he was thinking of the official garment world that gives him his modeling assignments and that decrees what large numbers of people will wear. The New York observer, however, sees that costume inventiveness does not reside entirely with officially recognized designers. The streets disclose a number of independent costume strategies, each directed at shaping a social relationship in a particular way. The young man dressed as a clown converts the street into a theater and passersby into an audience. The cop dressed as a little old lady converts a mugger into a potential convict. The man dressed in helmet, wedding gown, and roller skates—does he realize that he gives his viewers a transcendent experience?

The Negative Side

If experience can be said to have a positive side and a negative side, then up to now we have been discussing the positive side of the New York visitors' experience. There seems little doubt that, so far as the visitors interviewed are concerned, their visit has given each of them an enlargement of life. Enjoyment, elation, excitement are widely reported, and most visitors seem to come away with some new appreciation of New York, whether they are first-time or repeat visitors. Appreciation of the city among the latter is particularly indicated by their return visits purely as tourists. A woman who has been to New York five times says:

> *My job requires me to do a lot of traveling, and I travel almost all over the world, but this particular trip was planned as a leisure vacation, and it does not have anything to do with my occupation. I already knew ahead of time what places I was going to visit, and I decided to expend most of my time going to discos and see a couple of Broadway shows. (Woman, 20–29, airline stewardess, Galicia, Spain.)*

Even the most enjoyable visit to New York, however, is likely to have a low side. That is, there are aspects of the city that prove to be unpleasant and disagreeable, sometimes sufficiently so to mar the visit.

Dirt and Noise

One widely stated complaint is the dirtiness of the city. Many of the visitors find it much dirtier than they expected. The streets and the subway system are found to be surprisingly dirty.

> *I hate the subway system. I'm talking about the filth and graffiti. In Canada, if anyone is caught vandalizing the trains, you are arrested and fined. (Woman, 40–49, secretary, Ontario.)*

> *I expected the place to be cleaner and the streets in better condition. (Man, 40–49, construction worker, Birmingham, England.)*

Noise is often mentioned in tandem with dirt as objectionable. The streets are noisy as well as dirty, and the same is true of the subways.

> *I get turned off by the noise of so many cars and the noise done by the trains; I hate the filth on the subway station and [in] the streets. The people seem not to care about it. (Woman, 20–29, accountant, Dominican Republic.)*

Pornography and Vice

Forty-second street is one of the major arteries of New York. Both Grand Central Terminal, one of the two major train stations, and the Port Authority bus terminal are located on this street. The Broadway theater district begins on it. Many major subway lines have stations on the street, and the shuttle train between Times Square and Grand Central is a major way to transfer from West-Side to East-Side subway trains. Finally, the street is the location of numerous movie houses and bookstores purveying sexually explicit materials, as well as persons purveying commercial sex services. The street attracts visitors who want to look at or buy what is offered for sale, but, because of its transportation importance, it is also traveled by people who must use the street and do not like what they see.

> *[What aspects interest you the least?]*
> *The area of 42nd Street. I walk by and I see a lot of prostitution, drugs. The people seem to be of a very low class. (Man, 20–29, student, Ecuador.)*
>
> *I do not like the pornography that is being exposed in the streets. (Man, 30–39, plant engineer, Greece.)*

Incivility

New York has a legendary reputation for incivility, somewhat counterbalanced by a reputation for garrulous friendliness. Consequently, expectations are somewhat mixed, and experiences are also somewhat mixed because they are evaluated in relation to expectations.

> *In my home I have been taught to address older people as "Sir." These people should be treated with respect, but the people of New York is lacking in manners for their elders. And the obscene language is appalling. (Man, 30–39, carpenter, Trinidad.)*

Experiences on the subway seem to be particularly unpleasant:

> *The pushing on the subways is really disgusting. (Woman, 30–39, keypunch operator, Los Angeles.)*
>
> *"Well, first this lady stepped on my foot in the train and didn't say she was sorry, and on the same train all these men were sitting down and this pregnant woman came in and not one got up and gave her a seat, so I did. People here are just insensitive and impolite." (Woman, 20–29, student, Danville, Virginia.)*

Those who encounter particularly glaring incivilities are joined by others who find New Yorkers cold, unfriendly, unwilling to respond to requests for directions. On the other hand, visitors quite often find New Yorkers friendlier than they expected, often—surprisingly—no different from the people they know at home. And a rare visitor finds New Yorkers friendlier than the people at home:

> *Most here will help you out if they can. Back home, with all the fighting, no one talks to anyone. (Man, 60–69, fire chief, Belfast, Northern Ireland.)*

About the only specific category of New Yorker that emerges from these interviews in a negative light is the taxi driver, mentioned by a small number of interviewees, but invariably critically.

> *The taxi drivers do not treat you with respect. (Man, 30–39, plant engineer, Greece.)*

> *[What aspects interest you the least?]*
> *The way cab drivers try to run you over if you get in their way. (Man, 30–39, engineer, Cuzco, Peru.)*

> *People are different here. They don't seem to trust you. I told the cab driver to stop so I could get some cigars. He got out of the cab and stood by the store door until I came out like he thought I was going to run away. In the north country we know each other, don't even lock our doors when we go out. (Man, 40–49, farmer, upstate New York.)*

Crime

Expectations of crime are prominent in the image that visitors had of New York prior to visiting. When asked how New York is different from what they expected, they often reply that there is less crime than they expected, or "I haven't got mugged yet." Two of the interviewees were victims of crimes: a young woman had her gold chain snatched from around her neck, and a young man was mugged. The strong expectation of crime leads the young man to refer to his experience in a minimizing way:

> *I only got mugged one time. I thought it would have happened more often. On the media there's always talk about a policeman or some innocent victim being killed. (Man, 20–29, student, Jamaica.)*

He limited his loss, however, because he had been forewarned of New York's dangers, so carried most of his money in his socks.

Conclusion

Visitors to New York are diverse in background, and their visits are varied in purpose. The city is complex, offering a wide range of experiences and satisfactions, catering to multifarious tastes. Yet, as varied as the visitors are, as diverse the objects that engage their attention, they nonetheless seem to participate in a shared definition of New York as a social object. There is an essential visitors' New York displayed in discos, art museums, Wall Street, 42nd Street, Broadway, the Statue of Liberty, the twin towers of the World Trade Center, and numerous other places and activities. This essential New York is by no means necessarily the residents' New York. But for visitors, New York is an unmatched concentration of energy, audacity, enterprise, and monumentality—tinged with incivility, menace, and squalor.

NOTE

1. As part of an effort to restore Cleveland's once-positive image, the *Cleveland Plain Dealer* distributes poster ads and bumper stickers that proclaim, "New York Is the Big Apple but Cleveland's a Plum." This delicious competition does not seem to have gained much national attention.

ACKNOWLEDGMENTS

The interviews were conducted by Carmen Alicea, Thomas N. Atwell, Leon Baxton, Jean E. Brown, Elaine Constantine, Richard Cormier, Milagros Espinosa, Irma Guzman, Dwayne Johnson, Elvis Lockward, Isola Miller, Forooza Parvin, José A. Rivera, Theresa Ross, Stanley Simpson, Ron Snyder, Peter Taras, Gabriel Velez, and Benjamin Williams. I would like to thank Vernon Boggs, Sylvia Fava, and Ruth D. Handel for helpful comments on the manuscript.

18

The Chosen Apple:
Young Suburban Migrants

SYLVIA F. FAVA
& JUDITH DESENA

METHODOLOGICAL NOTE • Why is New York a magnet for some young adults—migrants from suburbs—who have never lived in cities? How do they adjust to living in the city? What are the consequences for their personal development? These questions have not been dealt with systematically before this. In order to generate preliminary findings and to develop guidelines for large-scale future research, our study used lengthy, open-ended interviews with a small number of young adults who now live in New York City but who grew up in suburbs.

The interview instrument was a long questionnaire that we used to introduce topics for discussion, rather than a preset list of response categories. We chose this relatively unstructured method because we wanted as broad a range of responses as possible, expressed in the migrants' own words. We wanted their own views of what they regarded as significant experiences in suburban and New York City living. In an exploratory study, where little is known beforehand about the possible factors influencing behavior, it is especially important to have the data-gathering process flexible enough for new ideas to emerge. Our major finding—that suburban-reared migrants underwent "urban conditioning," typically related to special college experience—developed from this process. In the course of describing their residential histories, one respondent after another noted spontaneously the central importance of college location or aspects of the college experience in influencing their evaluation of urban (and suburban) life. We had asked no direct questions about this. 305

Our study of suburban migrants to the city is part of a larger study of the "suburban generation"—the group whose childhood and adolescence were spent after World War II in the suburban America that became a major residential environment during that period. The preliminary findings on those who moved to New York City as adults led, in turn, to hypotheses that will be tested in further study of the larger group. The research on migrants reported on here is, in effect, part of an effort to formulate a valid research design to study a new phenomenon.

Urban study in the United States has dealt with successive types of city residents; first, the city dwellers of the small, preindustrial cities, a tiny minority in an agricultural nation; second, the rapidly expanding urban populations of the industrializing cities of the nineteenth century. The development of urban sociology as an academic discipline paralleled this explosion of urban growth, and its concerns reflect the salient questions of the period: the absorption into the city of rural migrants, many of them immigrants from European farms and villages; the maintenance of "moral order" and consensus in cities of transients and newcomers; the interactive process in ethnic enclaves, ghettos, and class-stratified communities, as large urban populations were sorted into smaller constituent communities. The theoretical framework and field studies of the Chicago School are, of course, the prime example.

The era of "peopling and building" the city was followed, however, by a third period, namely, the emergence of very large cities that spilled over their municipal boundaries into the surrounding area. In this period urban sociologists shifted their focus to the study of decentralization from city to suburb. Herbert Gans's *The Levittowners* and Bennett Berger's *Working Class Suburb* are examples of this genre.[1] The research questions focus on the impact of suburban residence on former city dwellers; how and why their attitudes, social participation, political behavior, and family life changed as they moved from city to surrounding suburbs.

The Suburbanization of America

A fourth type of urbanite is now emerging as the dominant type in American society: those who are suburban born and suburban bred. The "suburban generation" has spent its whole life in the suburban rings of the metropolis, with little direct experience of dense urban living and related life-styles: high-rise housing, public transportation, and pedestrian access, the concentration of multiple activities and diverse peoples, and racial and ethnic ghettos so large they have an extensive institutional infrastructure. Relatively few suburbanites now commute to the city for their jobs; a survey of a national representative sample conducted in 1977–78 by Louis Harris and Associates for the Department of Housing and Urban Development found that less than one-third of working suburbanites had jobs in the city.[2] In 1978 the *New York Times* suburban poll found an even lower percentage— only one in five New York suburbanites worked in New York City.[3] Despite the paucity of daily and direct contact with the city, suburbanites are, in fact, linked to the city where the policy-making and cultural institutions of our society are still very much concentrated. Suburbs are not "islands unto themselves"; the economic engine supporting their life-styles is run from the central cities.

In 1950, according to the U.S. Census, only about a quarter of all Americans were suburban (that is, lived in metropolitan areas but outside the central cities); by 1960 suburbanites still accounted for less than 33 percent; by 1970 it had risen to 38 percent, and suburban residents were the most numerous residential category, outnumbering central-city residents (31 percent). The United States is well on its way to becoming a suburban nation: while suburban residents rose to 45 percent in the 1980 census, central-city residents declined to 30 percent and nonmetropolitan residents to 25 percent. During the postwar period suburbs also became increasingly self-sufficient and independent of the central cities on a daily basis. It became possible to live an almost totally suburban life, making lateral moves within the suburban ring for jobs, housing, and a wide range of shopping and services. The *New York Times* suburban poll of the New York metropolitan region found that in 1978 less than one-third of the suburbanites had ever lived in New York City.[4]

Studying the Suburban Generation

This chapter presents one portion of an exploratory study of the suburban generation.[5] We conducted lengthy (1¼ to 2½ hours) semistructured interviews with thirty-four current residents of the New York metropolitan area.[6] Our interviewees were the result of purposive sampling.[7] We sought people between the ages of eighteen and thirty-five, those who had been born after World War II, when the relationship between central cities and suburbs changed both quantitatively and qualitatively. In addition, our interviewees has been deliberately selected to provide us with four different combinations of suburban/urban experience in community of origin/community of destination: (1) the "pure" suburbanites—those born in suburbs after World War II and still living and working in New York suburbs; (2) the suburban-born and bred, who moved to the city at some point after graduating from high school and now live and work in New York City; (3)

the urbanites, who were born in large cities and live and work in New York City; and (4) the urban-born, who moved to suburbs at some point after high-school graduation and now live and work in New York area suburbs.

Among our interviewees there were eleven who had migrated as young adults from suburbs to New York City; that is, they represented the second cell of the four-part division just described. The suburban migrants we interviewed were upwardly mobile and upper-middle class both in their own reported class identification and in their objective characteristics: occupationally they were all in professional, managerial, or sales positions; all had college educations and most had postgraduate study or degrees; five were single and had 1980 incomes before taxes ranging from $10,000 to almost $75,000, and the six married respondents had 1980 gross family incomes of $25,000 to almost $100,000; all were white;[8] four were male and seven female; their ages ranged from twenty-two to thirty-four. Their childhood and youth—none had moved to New York City until some time after graduating from high school—were spent mainly on suburban Long Island (six respondents); three others were raised in New Jersey suburbs, and two were from the suburbs of Philadelphia and Los Angeles.

Young adult migrants from suburb to city shed light on the nature of both urban and suburban experience. Their migration is rare and goes against the mainstream of current American residential movement in which city populations are declining rapidly. Presented with a range of residential alternatives only 13 percent of white Americans would choose the large city (over 250,000) as their very first choice of a place to live, according to the Louis Harris study for HUD, a cross-section survey of 7074 Americans in cities, suburbs, towns and rural areas.[9] The Harris survey indicates that the American's image of the large city as a place to live is overwhelmingly negative—poor public schools and housing, high taxes and crime rates; yet Americans view the large city very positively as an economic, cultural-intellectual, and recreational "service-center." Apparently what is said of the Big Apple applies to large American cities in general: "New York is a nice place to visit, but I wouldn't want to live there."

The Harris survey also examined the destinations of those who said they were actually planning to move within the next two to three years: among white suburbanites only 3 percent said they planned to relocate to the central city in their metropolitan area; the leading destinations chosen by suburbanites were other suburbs (43 percent) or small towns, villages, or rural areas (38 percent).[10] For the New York metropolitan area, Reynolds Farley's analysis of 1965–70 data shows that among whites there were five or more movers from the city to the suburban ring for every mover from the suburbs to the city.[11] Similar ratios continued to prevail even in the mid-1970s, when the costs of the "energy crisis" had become facts of life, according to data for the New York metropolitan area gathered in the 1976 Annual Housing

Survey.[12] Clearly, Americans in general, and suburbanites specifically, reject large cities as desirable places to live.

Learning To Be a City Person

Why then have suburban migrants to New York City bucked the statistical trend? Our interviews, which were intended to generate hypotheses, reveal one striking focus for future research: before migrating, the respondents had all had temporary, but prolonged, daily exposure to life in large cities, which enabled them to define cities as acceptable, even preferred, places to live. College looms large in this regard: of our eleven respondents three spent a junior year aboard in a large European city (Paris, Florence, Pisa): seven attended private colleges in New York City or in another large city (Baltimore, Boston, Dallas, Pittsburgh) or in a large college town (Evanston, Ann Arbor): one went to San Francisco on vacation, liked it so much she stayed for four months and then moved to Honolulu for five months. Undoubtedly these experiences are to some extent artifacts of upper-middle-class life-styles. However, the fact remains that for each individual there was some form of "urban conditioning" followed, not necessarily immediately, by city jobs and city residences.

Did their temporary stays in urban colleges or in large cities abroad teach them not just how to be upper-middle class but how to be *urban* and upper-middle class? Did their temporary stays provide them with an image of an urban residential option to counteract the prevailing negative views of American cities as places to live? Several of our respondents noted that when they were growing up in the suburbs they didn't think "people like us" lived in the city. One commented:

> When I graduated from high school it didn't occur to me that I would ever live anywhere but in a suburban sort of place . . . I grew up thinking the only people who lived in apartments were grandmothers and unmarried because they were the only people I knew [in cities] and the only people who lived in the cities were people who couldn't get out. You know, who were either grandmothers who lived there because their friends lived there or Black people or middle-class people who were just waiting for the chance to get to the suburbs. I just thought that was the way to live. [Mark.][13]

These questions are of particular interest in view of the lack of childhood urban exposure among both suburbanites who later moved to the city and the "sedentary suburbanites" who as adults still live and work in a suburban setting. Our interviews suggest a much lower level of urban use than is reported in either the Harris national survey or in the *New York Times* poll conducted among New York suburbanites. The *New York Times* poll, conducted by telephone among 3496 residents of fourteen counties surrounding New York City in New York State, New Jersey, and Connecticut and an additional 1192 residents of the exurban belt surrounding those counties, found that the largest proportion of respondents—25 percent—said that they had not gone into New York City in the previous year; another 16 percent had visited New York City only once or twice during the year.[14] Half the suburbanites polled said they went into the city fewer than five times a year for nonbusiness purposes. Our interviews with the "suburban generation"— both those who later migrated to the city and those who stayed in the suburbs—indicate that as children they were taken to the city only for "a special treat" on "a real occasion" (Christmas tree in Rockefeller Center, theater, museums, birthday dinner in a special restaurant, Radio City Music Hall); almost the only urban residential areas they saw were on visits to relatives, typically grandparents. As teenagers and young adults the "sedentary suburbanites," who remain in the suburbs as adults, appear to increase their use of New York City, but not by visits to residential areas. For these suburbanites New York City often appears as "another world" about which they obtain information through newspapers, television, and magazines, and by word of mouth from any remaining relatives. Direct contact with the city is minimal and restricted to a few stellar attractions.

In reviewing the interviews of the suburban migrants to New York City we can generate some preliminary findings on the nature and importance of "urban conditioning" for suburban migrants to large cities. The process of urban conditioning may be viewed as anticipatory socialization for city life: being exposed to the city in the supportive group setting of the urban college or in the structured junior year abroad at any urban university; seeing a variety of cities as a tangential component of extracurricular activity; taking a course in urban geography. In these activities, reported on in the following interviews, the student is introduced to the city gradually as part of the ongoing organization of the college, rather than facing the city as an isolated individual.

> [W]hen I was in Boston in college, just being exposed to new ideas and different kinds of people. And I lived away from home. And I think that's when I started to examine what I had come from and where I wanted to go . . . growing up in . . . a suburb with a small-town atmosphere . . . and my family was probably a very typical Irish-Catholic bigoted family—and the effect on me has been more, afterwards, moving around . . . I don't think I'd want my kids to grow up in the same atmosphere. I went to [elementary and high] school with lily-white upper-middle-class kids and I just don't feel I got a lot of variety . . . I think people who have grown up closer to the city are probably a little bit more open-minded, a little more flexible in what they think about other people, maybe a little more tolerant . . . I don't find that [bigotry against Blacks or Jews among supposedly educated people] with my friends who grew up in Queens or Manhattan. [Marianne.]

Marianne noted how her husband, who was not interviewed, grew up in the rural Midwest ("middle of the cornfields, thirteen miles to the nearest grocery store") and later learned about cities:

> *It's funny, my husband is from . . . and I thought that he would not adapt well to the city and if anything he's even more adamant about it . . .*

Q: *When did he first get in contact with large cities?*

A: *When he was at . . . University he was in the university glee club and twice a year at Thanksgiving and Eastertime they would go on tours, concert tours, and he saw thirty-eight states in four years and he sang at the San Francisco Opera House and went to—you name a city and he was in it. He really loved the East Coast—New York and Boston especially. It was probably when he was with the glee club that he developed his liking for places other than [his home area].*

In the next excerpt, Mark's description of how his fortuitous enrolment in a college course changed his career choice and life pattern amounts almost to a conversion experience.

> *[M]y first semester in [a large university town], I was planning on being an experimental educational psychologist and a journalist, and focusing on that, I took a human geography course to fulfill a science requirement and immediately wanted to be an urban planner . . . And I started taking lots of geography courses . . . and they have an urban studies major so I started taking lots of urban studies courses, became fascinated with cities, and found that when I went back to [my suburban home] what I did was explore all types and parts of [the central city] that I never did before, started giving tours to all my friends who came to visit me, and started doing things in [a very large city near the university] more.*
>
> *I started realizing that cities were what I really enjoyed . . . as soon as I got out of college I knew I couldn't live in the suburban areas; they held no interest for me any more. There was no street life; it would be boring. So I moved to [a large Eastern city] because I figured I could handle it. After walking the entire city in one afternoon I realized it was too small for me, so I moved to New York. So yes, New York has in that way lived up to my expectations, there's constantly new things to explore, new things to learn. Now I can't stand to go back to the suburbs at all any more. My in-laws live in the suburbs so we go up there fairly often; my parents still live where I grew up so I go back there and after about fifteen minutes I'm itching to get back into the city. . . . [T]here's one part of me that always wonders why it is I turned out to be the type of person who can only live in the city when I was brought up to live in the suburb and would have been in so many ways so much more comfortable.*

Rejection of Suburbs

For some of our suburban migrants the choice of an urban college or a junior year abroad in a European city was deliberate and associated with a positive view of the city and a negative view of suburbs. These views had already formed at high-school age before they left the suburbs. Why did they react this way to urban and suburban life in contrast to their peers?[15] Brian O'Connell's follow-up study in 1978 of 1968 Nassau County high-school graduates suggested that there is a "brain drain," as judged by higher grades and the superior socioeconomic status of those who left Nassau County (however, the extent to which the brain drain migrated to the cities or further out to exurban and rural locations is not pinpointed in the research design).[16] Joseph Zelan's much earlier study of a national sample of college graduates found that the more "intellectually-oriented" and "creative" preferred urban life.[17] David Popenoe's study of Levittown found that many of the teenagers there were "bored" and had "nothing to do."[18] John Goodman's recent examination of the reasons for suburban migrants to the city indicates that dissatisfaction with commuting, the high cost of suburban housing, and desire for independence from one's family are the main motivations, with the alleged sterility of suburban life not a major factor.[19] These studies, and our own interviews, are provocative rather than definitive, and to some extent contradictory, indicating a specific aspect for "suburban-generation" research. Why do some young suburbanites form an early distaste for suburban life? Paula, who attended college in a large East Coast city, says:

> I couldn't wait to get out of the suburbs. I had figured out when I was about twelve how many more days I had left before I would leave for college. I hated it [the suburbs] the whole time I was there. . . . I hated that feeling of depending on someone else to take me somewhere . . . I just felt stranded all the time. I couldn't wait to have the freedom to move around. [What I didn't like about the suburbs was] . . . the isolation, the needing a car, and the boredom. There wasn't the cultural stimulation that you get walking the city streets and seeing what there is to do without looking for something to do. It's thrown at you. You're bombarded. You can't escape the posters, the announcements. What's happening is more easily accessible to you. In the suburbs you have to read the paper to find out what to do whereas in the city it's all over the place. You open your eyes, you can't help but notice something to do.

Richard says that when he was a junior in high school he had already decided to attend a college (which was not located in a city) because it had a program that enabled him to spend a college year abroad in a large Italian city. By the time he was nineteen or twenty he reports that he had decided to spend some time in New York City.

> *[I didn't like suburbs because] I dislike the fact that everything looked the same. I'm talking about the housing . . . the fact that all the schools looked the same—they had so much land they put the school wherever it was needed—they would just paint it a different color.*

> *I didn't like suburbs because everything was so spread out. The distances were incredible; I mean, you grew up with a car. The day you could drive your parents gave you a car just to get you out of their hair . . . age sixteen. When I was six or seven I could bike to school—it was such a relief.*

> *My first experience in big cities was with Los Angeles. I realized there was a much greater diversity outside the suburbs. The more diversity I found outside the suburbs the more I found I didn't like where I was growing up [this occurred when I was a junior and senior in high school].*

> *When I was growing up there weren't any Blacks—no, there was one—in my high school. There was one Black family and it was a status symbol to have one of them as your friend. That was the mix we had. It wasn't until later that I found a couple of miles [away] there was a large Chicano community but they were outside the realm of where I traveled, I had no reason to get in that direction and so I didn't know it existed, I found out about the Chicano community in the first two years of junior college where I had friends then who pulled in from a much greater area and then I also had full access to the car.*

> *There's very little mix in . . . County where I grew up—white and middle class—it's now becoming upper-middle class. [contrast this with] . . . two international cities in Italy—wide spectrum of other people. Easy to pick up French, German, American newspapers or magazines; same thing in Manhattan; nice selection of [specialized] bookstores.*

> *I like a nice density with four- or five-story walkups or elevator buildings, not highrises. Some parts of Manhattan and Florence.*

Judy, who went to college in a large university town and accepted a job in a "rough setting" in the Bronx shortly after graduation, presents her views of suburban and urban life.

> *It was a very small community in [suburban New Jersey] and I really got to know most of the people that I grew up with, which I think has both positive and negative effects. It became a little claustrophobic as I got older, but I think especially as I was growing up in my preteen years . . . By the time I got to high school I realized there was very little stimulation and that everyone looked alike, thought alike, and did the same things. There were very few new and open experiences to be found there, and what I did was to start going to*

New York to look for new experiences. . . . I was about fifteen and there's a bus that goes from the town to the city and I started going in with friends to go to Central Park, or go to the theater or shopping, or just somehow to go somewhere where there was something to do. . . . When I was in high school I really had a sense of wanting—when I started to come to New York on those weekend excursions—I had a sense of, "I want to live there at some point." . . . In high school I really didn't have that much in common except with a few people and those people just scattered—those were the people who went farthest to college, mostly up to Chicago, Boston.

The city definitely lived up to my expectations [when I moved to the Bronx after college]. I think I was looking for a lot of stimulation and a lot of different kinds of experiences and a sense of excitement that I never got in the suburbs. . . . I took this job and there was a concrete reason for moving into New York City. But I think I wanted a sense of being in a large bustling place, and a sense of challenge.

I know about six months after I lived here I kept getting this sense of being outside of myself, saying, "My God, she's really living in the city"; I talked to a lot of people who had moved to the city from smaller places and who all had that same kind of sense of looking at themselves adapting to life in the city.

[Adaptations] included putting up with crowds, putting up with time delays, putting up with the craziness that's legend in New York City in terms of transportation and just moving around. Any other place I've ever lived, traveling for an hour would be unheard of, a major trip, and in New York City you just don't think twice about traveling for an hour. You just get on the subway and travel . . . learning your way around, learning how to do things successfully in the city, which require some kind of negotiation—where to walk, who to talk to, when to talk to someone, when to respond to someone . . . All of those kinds of things are adaptations that are probably very different in New York and probably any large city than they were in the suburbs.

Geraldine chose a college in a large Eastern city because she thought "all cities were like New York." She describes the role of her high-school experience in prompting her move to the urban college and to later settlement in New York City.

I graduated in '69 . . . the end of '68–'69 there were racial things happening and the way they hit my school was very different than I think they hit other schools. We were involved in doing things. I had kids in my class who were associated with the Black Panthers. But it was so few. . . . It was a whole different reaction. You know in suburbs there's more of an opportunity to stay away from all that—just to read about it. It did affect me. I was aware of it and my reaction to all that was going on and then seeing other people not really aware of it really sort of affected me. Really it had something to do with what I did, five or seven years after that—after eighteen. It was part of the reason I moved to the city.

[C]ompared to my peers who stayed in suburbs I feel I'm more tolerant than they are. I've taken on more of the characteristics I would attribute to someone who grew up or was affected by the urban environment. . . . I feel I can see two different kinds of people and say, "There's a difference," as opposed to, "This one is different to me"—as opposed to judging it. I think my point of reference can move around easier than other people's.

Q: *Have you discussed this with any of your suburban friends?*

A: *Recently, sometimes. Some of them can't even discuss it—think I'm judging them. . . . If I had a lot of money I'd like to move to Manhattan. [She now lives in Brooklyn.] If I didn't have a lot of money I wouldn't want to be there.*

Q: *What sort of life-style did you find that you were able to have in Manhattan? [She had lived there before moving to Brooklyn.]*

A: *There was more different kinds of people; you could feel less conspicuous in Manhattan. Sometimes you could blend into the crowd. You're more anonymous—I wanted that at the time. Things are very accessible. Everything's always open. There's always something to do.*

Alice spent a junior year abroad and had also traveled before then in Europe and the United States with her parents. She lived in San Francisco before moving to Manhattan. She does not couple her plan to live in New York City with a critique of suburban life and, as we shall note later, is much more likely to return to the suburbs.

[Moving to Manhattan was] something I always knew I'd do anyway . . . [I]t was a job. I just always knew I'd live in Manhattan . . . I always knew I would come into the city and try that for a while. I wanted the independence and so I only looked for a job in Manhattan.

Looked at as a group, the preceding interviews suggest that former suburbanites view the city, especially New York City, as having characteristics of density, diversity, stimulation, and anonymity, which they did not perceive as suburban characteristics. They regard themselves as having been changed for the better by these urban characteristics. They believe that living in the city has enhanced their personal development, specifically in making them more humane, more competent, more broad-minded and tolerant, more sophisticated, more autonomous, and more complex. Put another way, our interviewees regard these as desirable outcomes of their socialization in the city.

Several of our respondents described aspects of the actual socialization process they experienced in adjusting to New York City, including the reluctance and fear they sometimes felt as well as some of the negative features of urban density, diversity, stimulation, and anonymity. Thus, Martha, who spent a junior year in Paris but whose move to New York City from the Long Island suburbs was triggered by her job as a social worker ("My boss suggested that I move") answers the question.

Q: *Was there culture shock for you when you moved to Brooklyn?*

A: *Definitely. The dirt, the number of people, I would say the many different areas—y'know, in Brooklyn . . . segregated areas as opposed to . . . on Long Island it's much more [homogeneous], and I'm really amazed to see an Italian section and a Black section and a Puerto Rican section. I've never really seen that as much . . .*

Q: *Do you ever see the people you grew up with in the suburbs?*

A: *Yeah. . . . They all think I'm crazy moving to Brooklyn. They are definitely frightened of the city.*

Louis, who grew up on surburban Long Island, attended a private college in New York City but moved from the suburbs to Manhattan only under the duress of losing his job, although he now says he has a "negative stereotype" of the suburbs.

I used to work in Nassau County for this company and they transferred me into the city. They did that—it kind of gave me the incentive to move into the city.

Q: *Do you think you would have done it without that?*

A: *No, I was scared of the city. It was intimidating to think about moving in.*

Q: *What scared you?*

A: *It was just that coming from the suburbs where I lived—a small city— it just seemed to be overwhelming. I didn't know the city at all and had never spent any time in the city . . .*

Q: *How long did it take you to get used to it?*

A: *I think I'm used to it—the three months I spent here before I moved broke me into the city. I worked here three months before I moved in . . . It just broke me into the commuting situation, geographics of where places are located. It gave me a reason to be here. I spent my time here, I ate here, I started to socialize here a little bit, and then it became an attractive place for me, . . . my whole attitude toward the suburbs is very negative. I think I place a stereotype on it. I think a lot of people growing up in the suburbs are victims of that stereotype . . . they develop a routine, you know the organization, the groupings of homes, and every-thing like that. The Joneses are next door, and the Smiths are next door to them. That's something I think of when I think of the suburbs.*

I've lived in an environment all my life which is pretty well settled. The suburbs where I've lived were settled, and the city is settled and yet it never is settled. And I'm addicted to that type of excitement, I think it's great.

Bertha, who had lived in San Francisco and Honolulu, gave a revealing explanation for her relative ease in adjusting to Manhattan.

Q: *Was there any adjustment for you when you moved to Manhattan?*

A: *Well, by that time—no, not really. Growing up in New Rochelle . . . is only a half-hour from New York City, I suppose if I had grown up further from New York, New York would have been an awakening of sorts.*

Joseph, who attended a private college in the Bronx and had a job transfer to Boston before he was able to transfer with that company to New York City, reminisces about the personal consequences of the perceived contrasts in racial and class composition in cities and suburbs in a way that is typical of our interviews:

I think I was exposed to a different type of life-style than, say, if my parents hadn't left the Bronx [and moved to suburban Nassau County when I was a child]; I think I would be a different person. [Of the Nassau suburb he lived in.] It's middle, middle, middle class, 90 percent Catholic, it's just your sort of middle-class New York suburb, it's not too big. . . . I think people are too segregated in suburbs. There's economic barriers, like racial barriers. People [who] grew up in a place like [my Nassau suburb] tend to get this idea that the whole world is white and middle class, because they're surrounded by white and middle class, but it's not like that at all.

Q: *Were you aware of any nonwhite, non-middle-class areas in suburbs?*

A: *Yeah, but I never really had any reason to go there, maybe to drive through going to someplace else.*

Q: *Were there any Blacks in your [private] elementary school?*

A: *I can't say for sure. But I think there was one Black family and a few kids.*

Unanswered Questions

An important research question arises from Joseph's statement and similar statements from other interviewees. What is the nature of the racial diversity that former suburbanites seek and value in the Big Apple? With only one exception, they live in New York City neighborhoods that they characterize as "all white" or "mostly white" and state that this is the neighborhood racial mix they prefer. Perhaps significantly, the one exception is Judy, who lives in and prefers a neighborhood that is "half white and half minority." Judy's initial job placement in New York City was at a drug rehabilitation center in the Bronx, a "rough tough area" with "many minorities."

A second major question for research is, How do suburbanites who move to the city search for jobs in the city? Does their initial urban conditioning set a framework in which they actively search for or at least reluctantly accept jobs in or transfers to New York City? Most of our protocols illustrate the active search, but several, such as those of Martha, Louis, and Joseph, indicate reluctant acceptance, sometimes followed by enthusiasm for the city. Do suburban migrants differ in their job search from suburbanites who remain in suburbia as adults to live and work? A discussion with a subject in another phase of our research is most suggestive. Professor O'Reilly (not her real name) had moved from the Bronx to suburban Rockland County, where she currently teaches.

Q: *Where are the graduates from your college going to look for jobs?*

A: *[They are] frightened of going to the city. . . . I have a classic story. This kid came—he was graduating and he went to the chairman of the department. He's an accounting major, and the chairman is an accounting professor. This fellow said, "I'm looking for a job. Do you know of anything?" The chairman said, "Yeah, a buddy of mine who runs an accounting firm in the city." "No, no," he [the student] said, "I couldn't go in the city." The chairman said, "How about Westchester?" . . . "No, no" [said the student], "I couldn't go over the bridge—too much, too much!" So at this point the chairman was getting a little exasperated, and said, "I think there's a firm in [a neighboring suburban town]." The student said, "That's kinda far."*

Q: *Where did he ultimately get a job?*

A: *I haven't the foggiest. . . . There was a fellow . . . in an MBA program here, and I said to the woman who runs the program, "What happened to Ray?" . . . well, he's finished, he graduated, so I said, "What's he doing? Is he working?" She says, "No, no, he's probably going to get a job at a gas station around the block from his house." Local jobs they get: girls waitresses, hotels, construction for boys—with college degrees. I **nudge** [Yiddish for "pressure"] them madly. I start out with them as freshmen—tell them, "You better look in the city." It's funny, some of them come back to me after a year and say, "I think I'll consider it now." . . . I personally think my **nudging** them may change their minds— a year of talking about this at every opportunity. . . . A student came to my door the other day and she was talking about she wants to do design—*

*layout and design—so she wants to work for an advertising agency. So
I said, "Well, you'll probably have to go in the city; that's where most of
the large agencies are. They have some training programs and they'll hire
you." She looked rather perplexed. "Do they have parking?" I said, "No,"
and she said, "Well, you mean you park in front of the building?" I said,
"No, you don't drive. You have to take the subway, the bus, or the train
and the subway." "You do!" she said. Oh, I want to scream sometimes—
I can't believe it.*

On Becoming a Permanent New Yorker

Finally we may ask whether our suburban migrants to New York City are
likely to become permanent residents of the Big Apple. Most do not intend
to live in New York City or any large city for the rest of their lives. The
Harris survey indicated clearly that very few Americans are willing to raise
their children in large cities. Our young migrants to New York City are by
and large using it as a "staging area"[20] for upward job mobility and for social,
recreational, and cultural pursuits in their single years or when married,
before raising children.

*Right now the large city is my very first choice. Right now that's how I feel
but I know when I raise a family things will change, because I already know
that my priorities for children and that sort of stuff will change. To raise a
family I would want a more rural neighborhood, definitely, under fifty thousand or rural . . . way out where I grew up. Deep down I identify with where
I grew up.* [Alice.]

*We're both [my husband and I] in agreement we wouldn't want to have
children in the city, or have them go to schools in the city.* [Martha.]

*I would have always said I wouldn't move back to the suburbs until recently
because I don't know how I would feel about raising a child in the city.*
[Geraldine.]

*I spent seven very happy years in New York City. I did everything that I
wanted to do. I don't want to be here any more. I want to be close enough
to New York. I never want to live in the Midwest or the South—God forbid!—
or even go back out West, because I love New York, but I don't want to live
in it. I want to have trees and grass around me and squirrels.*

Q: *What did you accomplish in those seven years?*

A: *Wonderful. Well, I went to the theater all the time, walking distance to everything that people have to take trains to and stay in hotels to do.* [Bertha.]

One of the main reasons I moved to the city was the entertainment, the social type thing, being single . . . [I]f I was settled, I might move back to suburbs. [Joseph.]

Q: *Do you ever consider going back to the suburbs?*

A: *I don't want to. Truthfully, I don't want to right now. I think I'm very comfortable. I can stay this way for at least another ten years. . . . If I had my choice, I'd probably want to stay in the city, get married in the city, live in the city, and then get out, go away someplace else. Change is always permanent.* [Louis.]

It's hard to make a lifelong New Yorker. Only two or three of our migrants are likely candidates. One has already borne a child in the city and, with her husband, has purchased a home in Brooklyn. She believes, as does a young married male migrant in our study, that "the large city is the best place to raise children."[21] There is some suggestion that those who are likely to remain permanently in New York City are also more likely to move out of Manhattan into one of the outer boroughs where housing is more afford-able and where families can participate in local neighborhood life. In this they resemble our "real New Yorkers," our interviewees who were born in New York City and still live and work there: many of them think of "the city" as Manhattan and identify strongly with small communities in one of the four outer boroughs.

Conclusions

Our findings in this explanatory study suggest that a small proportion of the "suburban generation" experience a form of "urban conditioning," typically in their college years, which enables them to define the large city as a desirable residential setting. When they actually move to the city their experience is, on the whole, positive. They find self-development and per-sonal fulfillment in the city, relating these directly to the diversity, variety, rapid change, and unpredictability of the city. Their experience contradicts the widespread negative stereotype about the quality of urban life. One senses, however, in the fact that few of them plan to live out their lives in

New York City, the continued competition between the values of suburban tranquility and homogeneity and urban disorder and enrichment.

NOTES

1. Herbert J. Gans, *The Levittowners* (New York: Pantheon, 1967); Bennett M. Berger, *Working-Class Suburb* (Berkeley: Univ. of California Press, 1960).
2. Louis Harris & Associates, Inc., *A Survey of Citizen Views and Concerns about Urban Life*, Part 1 (Washington, D.C.: U.S. Government Printing Office, May 1978), p. 8; similar results were obtained in the 1975 Annual Housing Survey, conducted by the Census Bureau, which found that 32.4 percent of employed household heads who reported a fixed place of work commuted into central cities. See U.S. Bureau of the Census, "The Journey to Work in the United States: 1975," *Current Population Reports*, Series P-23, no. 99 (Washington, D.C.: U.S. Government Printing Office, 1979), p. 2.
3. Richard L. Madden, "The New York Times Suburban Poll," *New York Times*, 14 Nov. 1978, B4.
4. Ibid.
5. For earlier statements on the need to study the "suburban generation," see Sylvia F. Fava, "Beyond Suburbia," *Annals*, 422 (1975):10-24; and Sylvia F. Fava, "Women's Place in the New Suburbia," in Gerda Wekerle, Rebecca Peterson, and David Morley (eds.), *New Space for Women* (Boulder, Colo.: Westview Press, 1980), pp. 129-51.
6. For our purposes the New York metropolis is the census-defined New York Standard Consolidated Area. The SCA definition was developed in 1960 for the very largest metropolitan areas, with each SCA composed of a number of census-defined Standard Metropolitan Statistical Areas. The 1970 Census showed a New York SCA population of over 17 million, distributed in nine SMSAs over three states—New York, New Jersey, and southern Connecticut. An important indication of the increased self-sufficiency and independence of suburbs was the designation by President Nixon in November 1972 of Nassau and Suffolk counties on Long Island as an SMSA of their own, the first wholly suburban SMSA to be designated. The Nassau-Suffolk SMSA is included within the New York SCA.
7. We express our thanks to June Mosca, Linda Seubert, and Susan Sutherland, who helped us find individuals with suitable residential histories and age characteristics.
8. Our interviews were only with whites because Blacks have very different migration patterns within metropolitan areas.
9. Harris, *Survey of Citizen Views*, pp. 17, 4-6.
10. Ibid, p. 84. The remaining 7 percent of the suburbanites were not sure of their destination or planned to move outside the United States.

11. Reynolds Farley, "Components of Suburban Population Growth," in Barry Schwartz (ed.), *The Changing Face of the Suburbs* (Chicago: Univ. of Chicago Press, 1976).

12. See U.S. Bureau of the Census, *Current Housing Reports* (H-170-76-53), New York, N.Y. SMSA, Housing Characteristics for Selected Metropolitan Areas, Annual Housing Survey: 1976 (Washington, D.C.: U.S. Government Printing Office, 1978), p. D-05.

13. All names are pseudonyms: other identifying information has also been deleted or disguised.

14. Madden, *Times Poll.*

15. This chapter had already been completed when a most provocative study was published, indicating that "child density" and land-use patterns in the immediate neighborhood may be influential factors in differentiating children's experience in suburbs and cities. See Willem van Vliet, "Neighborhood Evaluations by City and Suburban Children," *Journal of the American Planning Association*, 47 (Oct. 1981): 458–67.

16. Brian O'Connell, "Where Have All the Children Gone?" *New York Affairs*, 5 (1979):84–87; Brian O'Connell, *The Residential Mobility of Young Adults from Suburbia: A Case Study of Nassau County, New York* (available in pamphlet form from the Department of Sociology, Human Ecology Laboratory, Ohio State University, September 1980).

17. Joseph Zelan, "Does Suburbia Make a Difference?" in Sylvia F. Fava (ed.), *Urbanism in World Perspective* (New York: Crowell, 1968).

18. David Popenoe, *The Suburban Environment* (Chicago: Univ. of Chicago Press, 1977).

19. John L. Goodman, Jr., "Reasons for Moves out of and into Large Cities," *Journal of the American Planning Association*, 45 (1979):407–17.

20. The use of cities as "staging areas" is indicated as a general trend in the United States in Long and Glick's analysis of migration data 1960–1975. Larry Long and Paul Glick, "Family Patterns in Suburban Areas: Recent Trends," in Schwartz (ed.), *Changing Face.*

21. We have since learned that the young woman and her husband sold their home in Brooklyn and moved with their child to a *suburb* of another Eastern city.

ACKNOWLEDGMENTS

This research was supported by grant number RF13512 from the PSC-CUNY Research Award Program of the City University of New York. The material in this chapter was first presented at the meetings of the American Sociological Association, Toronto, 28 August 1981.

We are grateful to Vernon Boggs, Gerald Handel, Larry Long, and Brian O'Connell for their helpful comments. Special thanks go to our anonymous interviewees, each of whom became a very vivid person to us in the course of the interviews.

19

Social Meanings of Second Homes for Urban Dwellers

ROLF MEYERSOHN & DONAL MALONE

METHODOLOGICAL NOTE • How do second homes connect the hinterlands with the metropolis? What does owning a second home mean to city dwellers? To what extent does owning a second home help stabilize the metropolitan area by keeping middle-class people from becoming suburbanites? Does it provide a safety valve for releasing pressures built up by city life? How does the alternation between city and countryside affect second-home owners' outlook on both living in the city and living in the country?

With such questions in mind we carried out a mail survey of 110 owners of second homes whose primary residence is in the urban areas of the Northeast, including New York City. A random sample was selected of second-home owners in Vermont whose primary residence is in a standard metropolitan statistical area (SMSA). Their names were obtained through tax records from various counties in the state. The mailing resulted in 111 usable returns (including 14 from New York City). The research instrument consisted of a self-administered questionnaire. We limited the study to one locus of second homes, Vermont. The study was restricted to this one area so that we could limit the variations of distance from primary residence, the nature of the kinds of recreational activities available, and general scenic values.

It must be recognized that the sample is a small one; the study was carried out by mail only; the site was restricted; and the time of the survey coincided with the fuel shortage of 1979. What is reported here is therefore exploratory.

There has been an exodus from the countryside to the city ever since the industrial revolution. The hinterlands provided a steady supply of labor; the cities, jobs. But in the past few years one could detect a reverse flow—there is now a migration back to the countryside.

The original migration was based on a search for greater opportunities for work, but this new migration is based on a different kind of search—not for a better job, but for a better life. The Urban Land Institute report *Growth and Change in Rural America* discusses the migration turnaround and notes that

> economic incentives are playing a much smaller role than had been the case previously. The influence of individual economic motivation, the cornerstone of human capital migration theory, has . . . been reduced in recent years. No longer are job-related factors the dominant influences on migration behavior.[1]

Confirmation of this new trend has come with the 1980 census. An analysis made by computer maps at the University of South Carolina showed large population increases from 1970 to 1980 "along seashores, inlets, lakes, rivers, mountainsides, ski resorts, hunting preserves and other such places, as well as in picturesque towns and villages."[2] According to this report, the most rapid growth areas in the United States have been those "providing outdoor recreation, a pleasant climate or natural beauty."[3] This reverse migration from the urban areas has flowed not only from the Sunbelt to the Snowbelt—a phenomenon well known and much discussed—but also (and especially) to what David Cowen of the University of South Carolina has called "amenity-rich areas,"[4] amenities apparently consisting of rural and not urban pleasures.

One such amenity-rich area lies in the hinterlands of New York City and the northeastern Megalopolis. ("Megalopolis" is a term coined in 1962 by Jean Gottmann for the area between Boston and Washington, which he saw as one vast urban corridor. Although most inhabitants of this region never considered themselves a part of Megalopolis, they do indeed share the rural areas lying on its fringes.) Even while the Northeast sustained population losses between 1970 and 1980, there were substantial gains in the mountain regions of upper New York State, Vermont, New Hampshire, and Maine.[5] These areas represent the shared playground, the common backyard, the rural life space of the Northeast.

The rediscovery and resettlement of the hinterlands by new migrants is only part of the story. Other, more frequent if less permanent, visits to the hinterlands consist of day trips, of vacations, and of second-home ownership, our particular concern.

Second-Home Ownership and Ties to the City

Second-home owners are, not surprisingly, largely middle class. Middle-class people "enrich" life in any community by their presence, by the exercise of their civic responsibility, by their expenditure of money for cultural and recreational activities, by their participation in the social and intellectual life of their community—in short, by their public life. How much does a community suffer when such people become "part-time residents" and alternate between the city and the country? To what extent do second-home owners withdraw their affect and their financial support from municipal life? Do the hinterlands drain off the resources of the metropolitan area by taking in the second-home owners along with the permanent migrants?

Our study provides few clues. On the one hand, for some, second-home ownership is a functional alternative to a move to the suburbs. In our sample, approximately 20 percent of the respondents said that they would have moved to the suburbs had they not bought a second home. Hence "draining off" is a relative term.

Yet no one reported an increase in their community and civic activities since acquiring a second home, and 10 percent of the respondents said that they are now engaging in fewer community activities.[6] At least to some degree, then, the middle-class support that nourishes cities is slighted by the people who spend their weekend time and money in their second homes.

The public life of second-home owners is less altered than their social life. Sociability and social life are affected once people go away weekends. One-fifth of the respondents reported that they were seeing their city friends less frequently than in the past, and only a few (7 percent) reported seeing them more frequently. For the majority, however, acquisition of a second home did not affect social life in the city.

Other activities that declined for some of our respondents since they acquired their second home include dining out (a 9 percent decrease), watching TV (a 10 percent decrease), and moviegoing (a 9 percent decrease). In other words, there is a slight indication of a decline in community life and social life in the city. But there is no indication of a comparative increase in these activities in the second-home community. Public life is virtually nonexistent. Not a single respondent reports being registered to vote in Vermont; no one is involved in local politics, although 14 percent did state that they attend some local meetings. Where the interest shows itself is in such more passive community involvement as reading the local newspaper and expressing concern with local environmental issues. Such concerns can be easily understood as reflecting the second-home owners' interest in issues that have direct bearing on their investment in the second-home community and in their interest as consumers of leisure, rather than as a reflection of more abstract concern with the second-home community for its own sake.

The second home is not a base for public and community life in another setting. Second-home ownership, while loosening some of the ties that may have existed to the urban community, has not led to the creation of fresh ties to the second-home community. The house in the country, as we see now, is a place for private and personal use.

Second-Home Ownership and Ties to the Self

The second home is a source of great pleasure for our respondents. This pleasure is evoked in several themes, some of which are connected with life in the city, others more universal as expressions of life itself.

First Theme: Back to Basics

Second-home owners alternate between the city and the countryside. This alternation is itself deep within the American grain. It helps us to understand this phenomenon if we consider a description of it by American writers.

In an essay entitled "Pastoral Ideals and City Troubles," Leo Marx identifies alternation between the city and the countryside as a quintessential motif in American writing. Using what he calls the "symbolic landscape" of well-known American writings—Thoreau's *Walden*, Melville's *Moby Dick*, and Mark Twain's *Huckleberry Finn*—Marx charts a three-part movement: (1) the retreat from civilization; (2) the exploration of nature; and (3) the return.[7]

The retreat constitutes a refuge from

> an oppressively mechanistic system of value, a preoccupation with the routine means of existence and an obliviousness of its meaning or purpose. Here, Thoreau says, men have become the tools of their tools. Unable to relate his inward experience to his environment, the narrator retreats in the direction of nature.[8]

But the exploration of nature has its own hazards. After the first idyllic interlude:

> [W]hen the beauty of the visible world inspires him with a sense of relatedness to the invisible order of the universe, . . . [when] he enjoys an unusual feeling of peace and harmony, free of anxiety, guilt and conflict, [there comes the recognition that] an unchecked recoil from civilization . . . may extinguish his uniquely human traits.[9]

Going native, becoming too enraptured with nature means becoming uncivilized. This leads inevitably to the third phase, the return. "Having discovered the limited possibilities of withdrawal, above all its transience, the narrator now returns, or seems to be on the point of returning, to society.[10]

When our respondents leave the "civilized" world for Vermont, they see the passage in terms of change and note the contrast between the city and the country. Some even talk about nature. One respondent from Queens says, "I like to get away from the hustle and bustle of the city to enjoy nature, and a life with few frills." Another says that going to the second home is "a chance to get back to basics," where stars and planets that in New York are visible only in the Hayden Planetarium can really be seen. The city is unnatural, the country is natural.

"The second home," says one respondent, "provides for a variety of surroundings." One particular change that impresses second-home owners about the country is the change of seasons. "It turns winter into pleasure," according to one respondent. Another way of getting back to basics comes from the solitude "to be surrounded by beauty and quiet," and to experience the "feeling of tranquility that comes from being amidst trees and lakes."

These are the reactions to moving from the metropolis (or Megalopolis) to the hinterlands. They are part of the same American voice that Leo Marx, along with many other writers, has noted. It represents what Marx calls the idyllic interlude. Completely missing from our respondents' perception of their second homes is any notion or sense of wilderness. There is never an abandonment of civilization. The second home is not a place in which to experience the awesome, to get lost, to challenge nature, to attempt mastery over the wilderness.[11] Instead, nature and the hinterlands are seen as tranquil, peaceful, orderly, regular, seasonal, pure, and uncontaminated. The second home is not a place for risk taking, adventure, challenge or struggle, but, indeed, a place to get away from all these elements.

Second Theme: A Place for Family Life

Judging from our sample, most second-home owners are married. Increasingly, singlehood is a stage that reaches deep into adulthood, and singles of various kinds are also a likely group to participate in the second-home phenomenon. It may be that the fixed nature of the destination that the second home implies deters a number of singles who prefer to spend weekends and vacations at different locations and locales. (They might constitute a significant target for acquiring shares in vacation condominiums.)

In any event, singles do not constitute a significant part of our sample. The ideal second-home owners, or at least the most enthusiastic, are those with children living at home. One respondent writes, "The second home provides good family activity." Another identifies the second home as "a family vacation spot." A third talks about the second home as a place for "family gatherings." Similarly, another says that his place is "a retreat for the family."

For these respondents, alternation between city and country is movement between weekday work and weekend family life. The city is the place for work; the Vermont second home is the place for the family. The *temporal* division of weekdays and weekend is complemented by the *spatial* division of city and countryside.

Implicit in these responses is the absence, during the week, of an opportunity to play out family roles. The breadwinner (often breadwinners) of the family sustain certain losses during the week, which they attempt to recapture on the weekend. The second home, writes one respondent, is "ideal for children." Included in that response is the sense that it is "ideal to be with the children."

Here is the place to play out family dramas, to permit the more uninterrupted assumption of family roles. However, for most families, such a stage is not available right away. The middle-class pattern of capital accumulation is usually not geared to the family's life cycle in such a way that there is sufficient surplus or credit for the acquisition of a second home when the children are very young. More commonly, second homes are acquired at a later stage, when the children's early years are past. One respondent looks back to say, "We enjoyed the second home very much when . . . [the children] were younger." When children become adolescents they are less likely to be willing to travel to the country with their parents, and to give up the weekends as prime time for peer relationships. Sometimes they make the concession and accompany their parents, provided they can bring their friends.

As children grow up and leave home, the uses of the second home change; escape into the country and return to the city may not have the same urgent quality, and attention begins to be paid to the possibility of converting the second home into a retirement home, or of giving it up to make some other move that provides a single rather than double residential life. Retirement migration will be discussed in a later section.

Third Theme: Getting Away from Work

The world of the city is inextricably connected with work. The second home to our respondents represents a place permitting a respite, even an escape, from work. Their images of city life are reminiscent of Leo Marx's theme of retreat. No respondent said that men have become the tools of their tools, but they came close.

One second-home owner, from Brooklyn, writes, "The city is too hot, noisy. One wants a change and one wants to be out of doors and closer to nature, I guess." Another, who lives in midtown Manhattan, writes, "New York is dirty, stressful and cold; people are rude, indifferent, callous, and there are too many people who are taking advantage of others." The second home, says one man from Queens, provides "a release from the usual problems and obligations of the workaday world." The second home also acts as a kind of safety valve for those who find it difficult to stop working, a place of sobriety for workaholics. One respondent describes it as follows: "It forces me to take off from work . . . a place to be far away from the office so I won't be called."

Work, of course, is an ambiguous term. The second home is also for many a place in which to get away from work in order to work at something else. A man from Brooklyn describes the "working at" process as a desirable change. "Here in the city, life tends not to be very physical. There [in the country] one tends to be involved with more arduous work." This includes household maintenance, which for some is a great source of satisfaction. A Bronx respondent writes: "Learning to make repairs, working with my hands, has been exciting and rewarding. Things I thought I couldn't possibly do, like repairing a pane of glass, are now commonplace for me." The work that is one's vocation is replaced by an avocation that becomes work that is at least as enjoyable.

The alternation between the city and the country, then, is not only to breathe fresh air or to enjoy nature or to play out a family drama. It also means getting into another kind of work. The paradoxical phenomenon that people are often at least as busy during their leisure time as at work can be nowhere better seen than among second-home owners.

The second home is indeed a place for the tranquil enjoyment of nature, the active enjoyment of one's family, the more or less enthusiastic pursuit of various leisure activities for which Vermont is famous (such as cross-country and downhill skiing); but to realize such goals second-home owners must carry on a lot of household maintenance, repairs, chores. These constitute a part of every homeowner's life, whether for the first home or the second home, whether they are delegated to hired help or done personally.

Those who live in apartments are more likely to find such activities interesting and enjoyable: puttering around, fixing things, having a place of one's own can be satisfying. But many second-home owners are also first-home owners, and repairing the roof or fixing a broken window in two residences can be a taxing challenge. Similarly, maintaining two kitchens, filling two refrigerators (and remembering which one is lacking mustard) can be harrassing.

For these reasons, and others, some respondents would like to move to Vermont permanently. The most eligible group are those who are near retirement, when alternation between the city and the country would no longer serve the same functions. Research into retirement migration in France has found that a substantial portion of the Parisian population departs from Paris once they are no longer working.[12] Where do they go? Those who do not return "home" (the place from whence they came to Paris at the start of their working life, perhaps forty years ago), often retire in resort areas. Settlement in the resort areas of the United States, which has expanded so greatly in the past decade, is also attributed to retirement migration.

Since our study is one of second-home owners and not of those who have converted their second home into a retirement home, we do not have primary data on this phenomenon. Some of our older respondents do confirm the trend; they indicate that they have considered or are considering moving to Vermont altogether. Such a move would constitute one possible end stage, for both the life cycle and the urban-rural alternation.

The Second Home as Investment

Fred Hirsch pointed out in 1976, in his *Social Limits to Growth*,[13] that it is only recently that the hill lands in Wales and West Virginia "have acquired a value above their relatively low worth in agriculture. The value of scenic land, and of houses situated on it and protected in their access and views, has risen relative to other prices on average."[14] This trend has, if anything, accelerated since the time of Hirsch's book. Who is prepared to pay the "leisure premium" for land acquired for its leisure value is not clear from our study. Other studies have shown, not surprisingly, that second-home ownership is consistently biased toward upper income groups, although the bias grows smaller in those countries—such as Sweden and France—where second-home ownership has become widespread.[15]

Concern about real estate values did crop up in our survey. Two-thirds of the respondents mentioned "investment potential" as one reason for owning a second home; one-third included monetary reasons as one of the main benefits of owning a second home. Throughout the 1970s, the value of land kept rising. But the energy crisis of 1979 created a note of worry.

A New Problem: The Energy Crisis

The second home is a luxury. So long as abundance prevails, it constitutes a feasible part of middle-class life. But what happens in times of scarcity?* Shortly before our survey came the gasoline shortage of 1979, and a sense of crisis overtook the whole nation. Naturally we asked our respondents about the extent of their own concern with energy.

We asked the question, "How has the energy crisis affected you as a second-home owner?" Respondents addressed the question in two ways:

*For a general discussion of changes in attitude toward abundance and scarcity, see Rolf Meyersohn (1979).

first, in terms of availability of gasoline to reach their second home, and second (less often), in terms of the rising cost of heating their second home.

In Europe, where gasoline has traditionally been expensive, though availability not normally in doubt, travel time to second homes is normally shorter. In Sweden, for instance, 80 to 90 percent of second-home owners live within forty miles of the second home. (See Bieluck 1977; Coppock 1977.)

In our study, concern with gasoline was expressed in terms of availability rather than cost, and the price of gasoline, in 1979 at least, constituted a negligible part of the total second-home-expense budget. The uncertainty about the availability of gasoline, on the other hand, was seen as a more severe problem, and shared equally.

What are the consequences of a permanent energy crisis? Some respondents reported that they will use their second home less frequently and will stay there longer when they go, possibly eliminating trips on normal weekends (rather than three- or four-day weekends). Others are considering renting out their place if they don't use it for long periods of time. (Areas in the Snowbelt are subject to extremely cold weather in the winter, and many second-home owners keep their house heated even when they are not occupying it; this could become very expensive.)[16]

The greater the distance to the second home, the greater the concern about gasoline. This relationship is set forth in Table 19.1. Two-thirds of the respondents whose second home is more than four hours away from their first expressed concern with the energy crisis. Although that constitutes a minority of all the respondents (nearly three-quarters of the respondents live less than four hours away from their second home), the concern is symptomatic. Travel time in other parts of America is at least as long (see Clout 1972), and uncertainty about the availability of gasoline, were it to become a chronic condition, would no doubt affect the willingness of American second-home owners to endure this problem on a permanent basis—especially since second homes are supposed to be for pleasure.

The New Yorkers in our sample are not unlike other second-home owners in their concern over increased energy costs. One respondent from Manhattan writes about the cost of fuel and its effect on the frequency with which he could visit his second home. "We make slightly less [frequent] trips to it."

The higher maintenance costs are also mentioned. One Manhattan respondent laments, "It's becoming more expensive to operate and travel to our house." Concern with property values is triggered by the energy crisis. A place in the country that costs more to reach and more to operate may also be more difficult to sell. One Manhattan respondent put it succinctly when discussing the cost of energy: "It's kept the value of the house from appreciating."

Table 19.1 Travel Time and Energy Concerns

Second Home	Respondents Expressing Concern	
	Percentage	Number
Up to 3 Hours	41	42
3–4 Hours	47	32
More Than 4 Hours	66	32

Table 19.2 Reasons for Second Homes

	Attractions of Countryside (Positive)	Detractions of City (Negative)	(Neutral)
Human Concerns	Sense of community		
	Reunion of family		
Nonhuman Concerns	Escape into nature	Dirt, noise, pollution	Equity appreciation
	Desire to participate in the outdoors		Retirement possibilities
	Frontier fantasy*		

*"Frontier fantasy" is a theme that appears in Richard Ragatz (1974) as a reason for acquiring a second home.

Summing Up: An Accounting Scheme

The various themes mentioned by our respondents can be grouped into larger dimensions, particularly (1) those that involve other people (human concerns) as against those that involve the land itself (nonhuman concerns), and (2) themes referring to the attractions of the countryside as against those referring to the detractions of the city. We can organize these two dimensions into an "accounting scheme"[17] to help us summarize the responses, see where they are "located," and identify areas that seem to be left out of consideration.

Table 19.2 makes clear that the nonhuman concerns of equity appreciation and retirement possibilities are on different levels of conceptualization from the other reasons and themes. They address the issue of investment without particular regard to the specific attributes or gratifications that might be derived from the second home. Investment possibilities here must presumably be compared with other forms of investment; retirement possibilities involve speculations about conditions at some future time.

Leaving these considerations aside, the responses center around positive aspects of the countryside and negative aspects of the city. They evoke echoes from the American past: the desire to enjoy nature and the distrust of the city. The migration turnaround phenomenon can be better understood in the light of what second-home owners say. These people are, after all, temporary migrants into the hinterlands, some of them trying out, on a part-time basis, what it is like to live "out there." Others—the majority—continue to remain essentially urbanites whose commitment to the city is likely to be preserved rather than undercut by their alternation with the hinterlands.

NOTES

1. Fuguitt and Voss, "Population Trends," p. 17.
2. This quotation is taken from a front-page story, "Resorts Are Found a Lure in Population Shifts," *New York Times*, 28 July 1981.
3. Ibid., p. 1.
4. Ibid., p. 7. David Cowen is identified as director of the Social and Behavioral Science Lab at the University of South Carolina. Also mentioned in the story is Ronald Briggs, who is preparing an article with Mr. Cowen for *American Demographics*.
5. Ibid.

6. This information comes from a question that asked respondents to indicate how their lives in the city have changed since they acquired a second home. Such retrospective questions are of course hazardous. People's interpretation of the past is altered by current circumstance; some people acquired second homes very recently, others a long time ago; changes in the life cycle lead to changes in life patterns regardless of second-home ownership, and so forth.
7. Marx, "Pastoral Ideals."
8. Ibid., p. 95.
9. Ibid.
10. Ibid., p. 96.
11. Such transcendent feelings may of course be missed in our kind of study. On the other hand, they may also be played down by the nature of second-home life, which is rather more regular and frequent than, for example, a back-packing trip or a mountain climb. "Flow experiences" in which individuals pursue activities which challenge them and where they are neither bored or overly anxious are probably more likely to occur in such situations. Csikszentmihalyi, who has identified such feelings and labeled them "flow experiences," observed them among rock climbers, for example. (*Beyond Boredom.*)
12. Cribier, *Une Generation.*
13. Hirsch, *Social Limits.*
14. Ibid., p. 34.
15. Ibid. Also see Downing and Dower, *Second Homes,* p. 20.
16. Some respondents mentioned installing cheaper forms of fuel, such as wood-burning stoves and solar heating. The two are hardly comparable, however. Wood stoves can be purchased relatively inexpensively, and since wood is abundant in Vermont, they constitute a good investment even when used only occasionally. Solar heating requires a large capital investment, which is probably practical only if the house is to be kept fully heated year-round.
17. See Kadushin, "Reason Analysis," for a discussion of reason analysis and accounting schemes.

REFERENCES

Bielcuck, C. L., "Second Homes in Scandinavia," in Coppock (ed.), *Second Homes.*

Clout, H.D., "Second Homes in the United States," cited in Coppock (ed.), *Second Homes.*

Coppock, J. T. (ed.), *Second Homes: Curse or Blessing?* (New York: Pergamon Press, 1977).

Cribier, Francoise, *Une Generation de Parisiens Arrive a la Retraite* (Paris: Cordes-CNRS, 1974).

Csikszentmihalyi, M., *Beyond Boredom and Anxiety: The Experience of Play in Work and Games* (San Francisco: Jossey-Bass, 1975).

Downing, P., and M. Dower, *Second Homes in England and Wales* (London: Countryside Commission, 1973).

Fuguitt, G. V., and P. R. Voss, "Recent Nonmetropolitan Population Trends," in *Growth and Change in Rural America* (Washington, D.C.: Urban Land Institute, 1979).

Gottmann, J., *Megalopolis: The Urbanized Northeastern Seaboard of the United States* (New York: Twentieth Century Fund, 1961).

Herbers, J., "Resorts Are Found a Lure in Population Shifts," *New York Times* (28 July 1981).

Hirsch, Fred, *Social Limits to Growth* (Cambridge, Mass.: Harvard University Press, 1976).

Kadushin, Charles, "Reason Analysis," in D. Sills (ed.), *International Encyclopedia of the Social Sciences*, vol. 13 (New York: Macmillan and Free Press, 1968), pp. 338–42.

Marx, Leo, "Pastoral Ideals and City Troubles," in I. Barbour (ed.), *Western Man and Environmental Ethics* (Reading, Mass.: Addison-Wesley, 1973; orig. ed. 1968).

Meyersohn, Rolf, "Abundance Reconsidered," in Herbert Gans et al. (eds.), *On the Making of Americans: Essays in Honor of David Riesman* (Philadelphia: University of Pennsylvania Press, 1979).

Ragatz, Richard, *Recreational Properties: An Analysis of the Markets for Privately Owned Recreational Lots and Leisure Homes* (Eugene, Ore.: Ragatz Associates, 1974.)

ACKNOWLEDGMENTS

Research underlying this chapter was supported by a grant from the City University Faculty Research Award Program (PSC-BHE Grant #11817). This support is gratefully acknowledged. The material in this chapter was first presented at the Symposium on Leisure Research of the National Recreation and Park Association, New Orleans, October 1979.

Epilogue: The Apple Tree

JOSEPH BENSMAN

The separate studies that comprise the chapters of this book, as noted in the Preface, are not part of a single, preplanned study of the various communities and cultures of New York City and of the elements that bond together or separate these various communities and cultures. Rather, they represent the work of individual (or conjoint) scholars and students, each studying one or more facets of the city from the standpoint of a particular perspective or problem. Yet the studies, when considered as a totality, come remarkably close to an overall profile of what might emerge from such a planned study of New York City.

In the pages that follow, I will attempt to draw out from the separate studies their common themes and interrelations in order to present a hypothetical profile of New York City as a metropolis, a supercity. In doing so, I will have to note the communities and cultures in New York City that are not represented in this volume and concepts suggested by individual studies which are not the central focus of those studies. In doing so, I will suggest the interrelationship between communities and cultures and the concepts that connect them. Thus this volume deals with the Big Apple sliced, but not with all of the slices. By studying some of the slices, we may be able to imagine the shape and composition of the entire apple, and of the tree from which it grew.

336   Georg Simmel, Max Weber, and Louis Wirth were classical sociologists

who provided us with powerful images of the city, the metropolis, and the urban way of life. These images are not radically different from those held by visitors and tourists, as indicated in Handel's second chapter in this volume, or those articulated by respondents to Fava and DeSena. Even city dwellers buying second homes, as Meyersohn and Malone report, have similar images of the city. The city has extremely wide ranges of economic, cultural, ethnic, and national diversity, including—at one extreme—dirt, noise, crime, and poverty. It provides economic and cultural opportunity to many, but is a source of commercial calculation—a cash nexus—and isolation and coldness. But it is also the site of a wide variety of communities and cultures to which individuals may attach themselves to achieve symbolic or social identities. Individuals not attached to or isolated from stable communities may become part of transient and, sometimes, "deviant" communities, which, while not being residential in character, have a special locus, as does Jacob Riis Park for homosexuals and the Times Square area for prostitutes and pimps, pornographers, and the purveyors and customers of licit sex as well as for "mopes" and "skells."

But New York City is unique, different from the ideal-typical metropolis of classical social theory and from the composite of characteristics of all other great cities. New York was a seaport and the entry point for an empty continent that drew millions of immigrants to its shores. The immigrants sought economic opportunities and escape from overcrowded agrarian societies and, later, from overcrowded and "overdeveloped" third-world cities. Some sought to escape political oppression, a phenomenon that has encouraged emigration from the colonial era to the present. A substantial proportion of these immigrants entered the United States through New York Harbor, and a substantial proportion of these settled in and around what is now New York City and formed communities with cultures of their own. Unlike old-world cities, New York and other American cities had no ethnic base population of their own. Even the original Dutch and English settlers were strangers to a new land. They became "Americans" only because they arrived first and defined all later arrivals as strangers. This process of "Americanization" was repeated by each new group of immigrants. The process of immigration and settlement in New York City has virtually been a continuous one throughout the city's history. Thus new communities are continuously being formed and their cultures become part of the ever-changing culture of the city.

In this volume, Koreans, Dominicans, and West Indians are examples of relatively new immigrants, communities, and cultures. They stand for Puerto Ricans, Blacks, Colombians, Israelis, Russians, and the many other new communities that a planned, systematic study would focus upon. Most, but not all, of these immigrants settled in territorial clusters, ghettoes, and enclaves, and, in them, strove to maintain their homeland cultures. A characteristic of the newer immigrations (as Bahn, Kim, Bonnett, and Hoover report) is that they vary this pattern by the frequent use of air travel to their homeland. Bahn and Jaquez illustrate the attempt of Dominican women to maintain some of their homeland and Hispanic culture even when that culture is undergoing rapid change in the homeland. Bonnett suggests that new institutions, such as rotating credit associations, are created bulwarks against the isolation and impersonality of the city, which enable their members to gain a foothold and legitimacy in the city. Kim suggests how Korean green-grocers use highly formal associations to ensure both personal and cultural survival in the city.

In the age-old process of immigration and settlement, some settlers and their descendants disperse to other parts of the city, the suburbs and exurbs, and the nation as a whole, as many chapters in this volume indicate. Some lose their original language; and their culture becomes attenuated as it is diluted by the incorporation of the language and cultures of the outside society. Hoover documents this process with regard to the Norwegian community and, especially, its press. The same processes could be studied in every ethnic community that has ever been formed in the city. Most of the historical studies in this volume (especially Handel's and Aronson's) suggest the process of attenuation of old cultures and the acquisition of the new, while Fava and DeSena, among others, refer to the suburban dispersion (and return) of former residents.

Members of old ethnic communities and their descendants may, as in the case of the Anglo-Saxons (e.g., Cornelius Vanderbilt, Jr.), become part of a nonethnic—"American"—class, status or occupational community based upon nonethnic values. Their ethnic identity with a community may be symbolic, a sense of pride in their ethnic roots that requires little support through frequent social interaction within their ethnic community. Their identification with an old ethnic culture or community may be reinvoked when other new, lower-class ethnics threaten their space, property, or political prerogatives (as in the case of Cornelius Vanderbuilt, Jr.). Older immigrants may also attempt to "socialize," civilize, or control the behavior of their newly arrived compatriots and ethnic peers.

As a result of these combined processes, the various communities and cultures in New York are continuously changing in composition and balance; and each is in a continuously changing "stage" of assimilation, acculturation, and autonomy from its homeland culture. Thus, New York City as a whole is ever changing in its communities and cultures, even as it changes as a result of other economic and political processes that affect the various communities and cultures of the city.

The almost unlimited number of immigrant groups who continuously settle in given neighborhoods, ghettoes, and enclaves and who later abandon them as they move upward, onward, and outward, leads to continuously emerging patterns of ethnic succession and conflict. Many of the studies in this volume report mixed neighborhoods in which two or more ethnic groups occupy and struggle over the same space. Conflicts between Blacks and Italians, between Jews and Irish and Italians, and between Blacks and Jews are only some of those reported, while hundreds of others could be reported if our hypothetical, planned historical study were done.

The studies, in addition, report on multiple conflicts between older, more "assimilated," middle-class, more Americanized groups and newer, more "backward" immigrant groups. These conflicts, from the perspectives of the older middle- and upper-class groups, are seen as battles against noise, dirt, odors, crime, deviancy, and prostitution, all of which attend the processes of immigration and first settlement and the ultimate transition of demoralized immigrants to membership in solid ethnic or American communities.

It is quite clear in all the reports of such conflicts that the struggles over turf and jobs (in the case of the dock workers) and in the political process are intrinsic aspects of community construction in the city. But no matter what the state of their culture, ethnic communities are only one form of community in the metropolis; and residential communities are also only one form. Other varieties include "deviant" communities, "mopes" and "skells," homosexuals, prostitutes and pimps, and the purveyors of licit sex (pornography) and their customers. As demonstrated in this volume, these non-residential, nonethnic-based communities have spatial bases; that is, particular locales where adherence to the activity or values upon which their community is based is openly expressed or acted out. The communities may be avocational (Jacob Riis Park) or commercial (prostitution, pornography, and licit sex); but each has a distinct culture of its own. Moreover, frequently each community is divided into subcultures. The cultures, and subcultures, as Boggs and Jaquez illustrate, include highly developed, specialized languages, norms, customs, codes, expectations, and patterns of ambience. The latter include bars, hangouts, parks, and home bases where adherence to the culture is most openly expressed and accepted. Even mixed ethnic communities, in their own time and place, have developed street cultures of their own. These are quite separate from the cultures of the ethnic communities to which their members respectively belong. The street cultures include patterns of ambience, favored trips, tours, and excursions outside the neighborhood or "the street"; these travel patterns may be the attempt of youth to bridge the gap between their own home-based world and the larger city, as Handel has suggested.

Other bases of community and culture are occupational in origin. Thus the dock workers exhibit one variety of working-class culture whose particular form is, in part, based on the work history of Italians in Brooklyn, including their residential dispersal from the docks, and, in part, on changes in the organization of their work. Their pattern of ambience is, to a large

340 Epilogue: The Apple Tree

degree, determined by their union contract and its mandated hiring practices. Their occupational interest is a significant ingredient of that culture; but their response to the mass media, news and TV sports broadcasts and the wire services, along with practical jokes and ethnic commentary, all constitute the material of a culture that has a relatively transient occupational and no residential community. Kim's study of Korean green-grocers is also a study of a segment of an ethnic, i.e. racial, community that has an occupational center. Virtually every ethnic community in New York at one time had one or more occupational bases. The Jews once had the garment and needle trades, the Italians construction, the Irish the police, school teaching, and municipal services. But occupational succession supplements residential succession in the historical "career" of ethnic groups and communities in the city.

The communities and cultures of mopes and skells, pimps and prostitutes, are also, of course, based in part upon occupation. Kendall's study is of one attempt to create an occupational subculture, focusing upon primary care within one profession, medicine, if not one occupational community. Medical students can identify with role models who are either specialists or exponents of primary care. Socialization to occupational cultures and community standards is, of course, an intrinsic part of the creation of communities and the maintenance of their cultures, as numerous essays in this volume indicate. Yet if occupational communities and cultures are an intrinsic part of metropolitan society as a whole, then the study of New York City would include an almost infinite number of occupational communities based upon their residence or operations in the city. These would include dancers and musicians, stockbrokers and bankers, professors, diamond dealers and flower merchants, and virtually all occupations and professions whose members are self-conscious of their occupational identity and who associate with one another more than required by their work alone.

In following up the study of professional communities and cultures, we would undoubtedly be led to "class" communities, in which members of similar incomes, education, and occupations select common residential sites for their lives and for a class or status-based culture. Such cultures are usually more than just ethnically based, though a class-based community may consist primarily of members of one ethnic group, for example, a gilded ghetto.

Social and economic classes at all economic levels thus can become the basis for community. Middle- and upper-class communities, based upon occupations in the city, exist within the city, suburbs, and exurbs and extend even as far as Vermont. Thus, the communities and cultures of New York extend far beyond its city limits, and these—in some attenuated form—are part of the city. At times, as Fava and DeSena, Meyersohn and Malone indicate, they may become weak autonomous communities, having almost no base in their residential site outside the city and only weak connections to the city.

The focus on prostitution, deviancy, and licit sex, the libertarian permissiveness of the city, attracts visitors and tourists, as do the arts and other leisure-time and recreational facilities. These attractions are based upon not only a libertarian tradition but on the actual existence of cultural and leisure-oriented communities. Again, our hypothetical master study would focus upon a myriad of other such communities, including those centered around chess clubs, bridge playing, the opera, dancing, and perhaps conventional and unconventional modes of sexual play and exploration.

Any examination of all the types of communities, whether based on race, ethnicity, deviancy; profession, occupation, or class; or leisure, the arts or avocation; or whether based on residence, spatial concentration, or ambience would suggest an almost uncountable number of specific communities in New York City and in the outlying areas into which these communities extend. Given these myriad of often unknown, unrelated, and conflicting communities, a central problem for the study of the city and for all urban sociology is the means by which these separate communities coexist and are integrated, at least to the extent that such integration exists. To state it differently, the basic question is, Why do all these separate communities and cultures not fly off in all directions or erupt in a war of all against all? These are problems raised by some of the studies and answered directly and indirectly by many other studies in *The Apple Sliced*. Thus, the police mediate in the struggles over turf between ethnic groups, and have been the means by which the upper and middle classes preserve their prerogatives, property, purity, and safety. But the police are continuously subject to community pressures, which, as Delano notes, have caused them to change the very basis of their techniques and the profession of police work.

Social-work agencies, settlement houses, and neighborhood improvement associations all have been, among other things, pressure groups for their community; but they have also striven to create an urban civility that makes civic life possible despite ethnic, race, and class differences and conflicts. They have also served to socialize their clientele to the wider cultures of the city. Teachers in parochial and public schools, and even in colleges and universities, Kornblum and Fava and DeSena report, also serve these functions.

The mass communications, especially TV and the newspapers, broadcast a wider, mass culture that tends to weaken particular, traditional cultures, and their audiences enter the wide, wide world of mass culture.

The coordination of cultures and their integration is so great a task that it is, necessarily, not fully covered in this volume. This is true, in addition, because the volume reflects the individual interests of its contributors. Thus the volume contains no studies focused directly on party politics, party machines, or political bosses as coordinators of community and other interests and as promoters, channelers, and compromisers of and between interest groups. In older and more traditional studies of social policy formation in great cities, these topics would have been central. In the present and in this volume, the focus is on higher-level integration of the city, through the municipal services, i.e. the welfare state, and upon very large-scale organizations, banks, real estate interests, trade unions, and the press. These deal with major policy issues that affect all communities. The issues, however, are often resolved at levels above that of local communities.

Goldner's study is of one municipal agency, the Health and Hospital Corporation of New York City, that has major, city-wide responsibility for the health care of the city's poor. In so doing, it becomes enmeshed in the political processes of the city. State legislators, candidates for city office, the mayor, and officials of voluntary hospitals (who are competitors for public support) make the administration of HHC a political football, as do some militant community groups. The complex issues regulating Medicare and Medicaid payment and record keeping, hospital budgets and financing, as well as the complexity of the entire health system, make it virtually impossible for the public to understand the system as a whole or even its specific problems in relation to the wider health care system. The press has the classic problem of reporting these issues and providing the information necessary for voters to evaluate charges against and defenses of government agencies so that they can make informed decisions. Goldner charges the press with being irresponsible, of both oversimplifying complex issues and of producing a greater complexity and confusion than necessary. This occurs when reporters accept propagandistic news releases without checking and when the media themselves indulge in sensationalism. Goldner indicates that the integrating function of the press is badly performed, resulting in policies that deprive the poor of needed medical services, in the demoralization of hospital services, and in competitive advantages for voluntary hospitals. Goldner implies or, rather, takes for granted what is explicit in other chapters in this volume, that community conflict becomes increasingly expressed in higher realms of policy and in complex administrative and budgetary issues that are far removed from the immediate neighborhood or community.

Struggles over turf and even jobs are, in the welfare society, replaced by struggles over budgets, administrative codes, and entitlements, i.e., access to services and funds. The abstract nature of these issues makes it necessary for community leaders to become legalists and policy experts.

Robison deals with a similar macroscopic and technical issue, that of the attempt of the Lower Manhattan Development Association, under the guidance of David Rockefeller, to redevelop lower Manhattan in order to create Battery Park City, a new upper-income residential community. In accomplishing this, the Chase Manhattan Bank, headed by Rockefeller, would buttress its plans for the corporate redevelopment of the area. Rockefeller's plans were not initially inconsistent with those of Mayor John V. Lindsay, who wanted to make New York City a headquarters center for national corporations. An increase in the number of corporate center employees would replace the blue-collar employees being lost due to other changes in the city's economy.

Rockefeller's "private redevelopment" of a major area of New York City was, however, dependent upon the powers of the government, as revealed in struggles over building codes, tax abatements, loan guarantees, subsidies, and government quotas for subsidized rentals and the income levels permitted for tenancy. Private banking and real estate operators wanted to redevelop the city to fit their own corporate, financial, and housing needs; but they wanted government to bear the risk and part of the costs. The struggle to gain business and government support for the Battery Park plan split the business community and government agencies, delayed the entire process for more than a decade, and resulted in a project that was miniscule in comparison with the original plans.

Robison's study, like Goldner's, reveals the operation of modes of centralized decision making that place policy formation in public and private hands far removed from the community. Both studies reveal the complex, legalistic, administrative bases for issues that are vital to local communities. They also reveal that conflict is sublimated, that is, hidden in the very complexity of the issues.

Some of the same actors and interests are present in Lichten's study of the New York fiscal crisis. These include the bankers and financial interests, the trade unions and the press. In all three "integration" studies, government and political leaders and candidates, primarily but not exclusively in municipal government, make the final, official decisions; but they are not necessarily the decisive actors in formulating the policies so announced. Lichten reports that the banks and other financial institutions (finance capital in his terms) who underwrite and hold municipal bonds also hold the fate of municipal services in their thrall. Like Goldner, he reports that candidates for political office exacerbate and attempt to profit from the ill fortunes of the city. The press, whose responsibility is to inform its citizens is, at best, an unwitting ally or propaganda conduit of these interests. Leaders of trade unions who represent municipal employees are by necessity cast in the role of representing all the recipients and beneficiaries of municipal services. Earlier, DeFazio had suggested that the International Longshoreman's Association mediated (to the dissatisfaction of Italian longshoremen) between Blacks and Italians. In Goldner's and Lichten's studies, union leaders, driven by the necessities of representing their members, are reported as being forced to intervene at the highest levels of policy formation. They become, even if ineffective, policy makers on broad, citywide issues. Goldner, DiFazio, and Lichten all report that union leaders are ineffective in this function, though each author has a different criterion for effectiveness. The bankers, special interests, and the press (they and Robison suggest) are much more effective, even though their effectiveness is achieved at the expense of citizens, i.e., members of local, nonelite communities. Union members are ultimately left holding the bag because of the incompetence of political leaders and the press, the lack of militancy of union leaders, and the greed of finance capitalism. That bag includes the necessity of underwriting Big Mac bonds,* loss of jobs, blame for low productivity, and—in the case of union leaders—blame for not being militant enough.

In all three studies of the integration of the city, it is clear that the unions, the press, financial institutions, and municipal agencies are important parts of the political and legislative structure of New York City, even though they have no such functions in the New York State constitution or city charter. Their struggles are of men at the top, bypassing grass-roots communities though profoundly affecting them.

All three power-struggle studies take place in the context of the fiscal crisis of New York. That crisis is the central issue in Lichten's study and the backdrop to Goldner's and Robison's. The fiscal crisis not only created financial problems for the municipal government but also caused the curtailment of municipal services and support for private projects. In part the fiscal crisis was caused by the flight of industries and their employees from New York to the suburbs, the Sunbelt, and other nonunionized, low-cost, and low-service areas of the country and the world. This has left the city under the strain of supporting services to a large unemployed population with a decreasing tax base. The same problems face all major cities in the Northeast and Midwest.

In similar ways, earlier changes in the national economy and in federal and state policies have affected the character and composition of the city, its communities, and their problems. We have noted—and many studies in this volume can be cited in support—that throughout the city's history, federal immigration policies and national expansion were the bases of the city's growth and composition. The welfare state that emerged after World War II, along with earlier philanthropic social services, were important elements in the processes of the socialization and acculturation of immigrants to the city. Conversely, the federal highway legislation of the 1950s, it has been charged, led to a flight of millions of city residents to the suburbs, especially its middle-class taxpayers. Federally financed superhighways in

---

*Bonds issued by the Municipal Assistance Corporation, an agency of New York State, established in 1975 to provide financial assistance and fiscal oversight for New York City. The corporation has no taxing powers, but repays the bonds it issues on behalf of the city by drawing on sales tax and other revenues of the city.

the cities made suburban commutation and residence possible; and the destruction of homes and businesses to make way for these highways also destroyed and divided viable territorial communities within the city.

In the present, the fiscal crisis of the city is exacerbated by inflation, high interest rates, and the budgetary austerity imposed by the Reagan administration. Federal support for remedial services in education, for social services, and for health care are declining, as costs continue to rise and unemployment rates are high. Kornblum has noted that schools and social services provide models and opportunities by which talented and ambitious ghetto residents can rise above and surmount the poverty and degradation of the ghetto. The current fiscal and economic crises at both national and municipal levels thus become a crisis for lower-income communities, their residents and youth. In the present political, economic, and social climate, the prospects facing all but the affluent in New York City are grim, at least when compared with the "Golden Age" of 1945 to 1965. Yet it is in this grim situation that all urban communities (and urban sociology) will have to operate, at least in the near future.

Conclusions

The studies in this volume suggest an almost infinite number of communities and problems that sociologists study. These include "microscopic research"; the study of a specific community or cultural milieu, or even an aspect of each. Sociologists can also study the macroscopic integration and conflict of communities, as well as the specific agencies and complex mechanisms that articulate and express the conflict and integration of communities and cultures and that produce the city as a whole. Sociologists can attempt to do all these things with reference to either the past or the present. It is in this sense that they can describe and analyze slices of the Big Apple, its tree, root, and branches and can evaluate the species itself.

These studies also illustrate not only various ways sociologists perform these tasks, but also the methods by which the tasks are accomplished. All but one of these studies are based on methods other than that of the standardized quantitative survey. They include the use of participant observation, semistructured and focused interviews, and interviews uniquely tailored to gain access to the special knowledge and testimony of decision makers. The methods also include the interviewing of senior citizens to reconstruct, through the analysis of their reported memories, images of the city as it once existed. Published autobiographies, selected on the basis of time of birth and upon the author's participation in the city and its cultural life, also can provide the basis of quantitative and qualitative images of the city; and the life histories of living residents provide images of contemporary urban realities. Analyses of historical documents, government reports, minutes of meetings, newspaper accounts, and other primary and secondary sources supplement the direct and indirect analysis of eyewitness accounts.

Sociologists, in analyzing slices of the Big Apple and in creating images of historical and current realities, can use one or a combination of these various methods. In doing so they evaluate the data drawn from one source or method against those drawn from another. The criteria for the adequacy of their data and methods are the extent to which their use helps them to solve the problems they pose at the outset of their research.

This volume and this essay, in particular, point to the problems posed by one group of investigators of the city, who operate with a variety of theoretical approaches. But all approaches are related to the ever-moving history and change in the complex collectivity of communities and cultures and in the integrating and coordinating institutions that we call the Big Apple.

The range of problems, theories, and methods and the almost infinite variety of communities and cultures in the Big Apple, especially as these change over time, constitute an inexhaustible opportunity, challenge, and source of excitement to those who seek to understand their immediate social environment, the way it was, the way it is, and the way it is becoming.

Index